Safeguarding Against Statelessness at Birth

Rodziana Mohamed Razali

Safeguarding Against Statelessness at Birth

International Law and Domestic Legal Frameworks of ASEAN Member States

Springer

Rodziana Mohamed Razali
Faculty of Syariah and Law
Universiti Sains Islam Malaysia
Nilai, Malaysia

ISBN 978-981-19-5373-6 ISBN 978-981-19-5371-2 (eBook)
https://doi.org/10.1007/978-981-19-5371-2

This Springer imprint is published by the registered company Springer Nature Singapore Pte Ltd.
The registered company address is: 152 Beach Road, #21-01/04 Gateway East, Singapore 189721, Singapore

For my parents, husband and children in love and gratitude.

For the stateless children who are caught in no man's land and are facing endless hurdles in life as a result.

Foreword by François Crépeau

Statelessness is a scourge of the modern world. Being stateless means being considered a foreigner anywhere on this planet and facing considerable difficulties when requesting a state to respect and protect one's rights and freedoms.

States have committed to protecting the rights and freedoms of all persons who are on their territory or subject to their jurisdiction. However, many states have interpreted this obligation as meaning that it applies essentially to their citizens, and that they retain considerable administrative discretion in how they treat non-citizens.

The situation of two population groups is a particular preoccupation: low-wage migrant workers and shunned minority populations.

Some non-citizens will be favoured, for example, permanent residents and highly skilled or rich foreigners, such as expats or executives. However, states often restrict to a minimum, if any, the extent of the protection offered to low-wage temporary migrant workers and to undocumented migrant workers. These migrant workers often have access to very limited services and are offered very limited protection when exploited at work, discriminated against or otherwise abused.

For their part, some resident minority populations are considered foreigners, even when they have been on the territory for centuries. The case of the Rohingyas in Myanmar is now well known. Very often, there is a majoritarian political choice to marginalise a minority population, in order to stigmatise them as not being part of the body of the 'nation'. This has been seen elsewhere, for example against the Romas in Europe or against various indigenous populations on most continents.

For those denied recognition as citizens, refusing access to government services and increasing physical and psychological repression are part of a strategy aiming at physically expelling them from the territory. This was what the Nazis did to the Jews in the early days of Hitler's regime, before deciding to exterminate them. This is what is happening to the Rohingyas today. And the world offers no more comfort and support to the Rohingyas today as it did to the Jews who tried to escape from Germany in the 30s.

It was an ambition at the UN in the 50s and 60s to reduce statelessness to a minimum. Even if the number of stateless persons in the world has not considerably diminished, the ambition has not been abandoned. On the 60th anniversary of the 1954

Convention in 2014, UNHCR launched a 10-year campaign to eradicate statelessness by 2024.

Moreover, the human rights doctrine has considerably developed over the past decades, as international organisations, international courts, UN treaty bodies, UN special procedures, constitutional courts, national human rights institutions, and civil society organisations have all contributed to multiplying and refining standards and norms, exchanging good practices and lessons learned, as well as vocally denouncing human rights violations in the media. Such good work has had the effect of highlighting some particularly abhorrent situations on all continents.

However, the current nationalist populist moment, in various parts of the world, threatens this progress. It strives for identity politics, spewing hostility towards any 'other' and pitting one group of insiders (the citizens) against all those 'outsiders' who are deemed to threaten the cohesion of society and the body politic. We seem to be returning to an era in which governments can legitimately consider that certain human groups cannot 'assimilate', for whom the only solution is their disappearance, by emigration or destruction.

Among several political techniques to make them 'disappear' as a group, the most egregious will target the children. In particular, refusal of access to birth registration, to administrative documentation, to healthcare, and to schooling will make life particularly difficult for the children of shunned minorities, such as the Rohingyas. Only through the reversal of such odious practices and the adoption of more inclusive policies can one hope to reduce statelessness over the long term.

We must thank Dr. Razali whose book offers a comprehensive presentation and analysis of the strengths and shortcomings of the international and Southeast Asian legal framework governing statelessness, with a particular focus on ASEAN countries' standards and practices. With this book, among others, she shares with us the hope that international cooperation inside regional forums, especially regarding eradicating 'statelessness at birth', can reduce the hostility against certain human groups and enhance the protection afforded to their children, so that tomorrow they will be proud citizens of 'their' countries.

Prof. François Crépeau
Director of the McGill Centre for
Human Rights and Legal Pluralism,
The Hans & Tamar Oppenheimer Chair
in Public International Law
Faculty of Law of McGill University
Montreal, Canada

Prof. François Crépeau Director of the McGill Centre for Human Rights and Legal Pluralism (2015–2020) and holder of the Hans & Tamar Oppenheimer Chair in Public International Law at the Faculty of Law of McGill University, and UN Special Rapporteur on the Human Rights of Migrants between 2011 and 2017.

Preface

Statelessness was a nascent subject of research when I first embarked on my PhD studies back in 2013. In that year, an article aptly titled 'A Forgotten Human Rights Crisis' looked at statelessness as a social problem that had been slow in emerging onto the international human rights agenda. The enormity and complexity of the problem have contributed to this sluggishness in no small way.

Also in that year, I was fortunate to be able to attend a course on statelessness in Southeast Asia, which was held in Bangkok and organised by UNHCR and Tilburg University. It had a pivotal role in clarifying many of the technical and theoretical debates I found myself bogged down in, and in providing more practical insights of experienced scholars, advocates, and practitioners who were directly confronted with statelessness and its pressing challenges and profound consequences in their respective academic and non-academic capacities.

Since then, statelessness has grown and expanded significantly as a field of inquiry and subject of engagement among various actors and institutions at multiple levels across the globe. The momentum of the discourse has steadily picked up since 2014, the year UNHCR set an ambitious goal of eradicating statelessness within 10 years through its Global Campaign. At the first Global Forum on Statelessness in The Hague in 2014, I found myself infused with a sense of dynamism and optimism for the cause.

The UNHCR statistics on persons under UNHCR's statelessness mandate at the end of 2014 reported that almost 40 percent of such persons were residing in six countries in Southeast Asia. This large percentage, despite the lack of comprehensive mapping, critically points to the prevalence of statelessness in this sub-region, which means that greater attention should be focused here. Against this landscape, I found the courage to take up the study on statelessness focusing on Southeast Asia, the sub-region where I come from.

While writing this preface at the Centre for Human Rights and Legal Pluralism, Faculty of Law, McGill University, where I was undergoing my post-doctoral fellowship in 2019, I could not forget the faces of the young children and their mothers whom I had met during the course of my research. This work is especially dedicated to them, as well as to my own children.

August 2019

Rodziana Mohamed Razali
Faculty of Law of McGill University
Montreal, Canada

Acknowledgements

I would like to especially thank Associate Professor Dr. Rohaida Nordin for her supervision and guidance throughout my PhD research that eventually led to the publication of this book based on her supervised thesis.

My immense gratitude goes to Professor Gerard-René de Groot and Dr. Olivier Vonk for sharing their expertise and experiences in the field of statelessness during my stint as a guest researcher at the Faculty of Law, University of Maastricht, the Netherlands, in 2016. Thanks to my research colleagues who facilitated my research and my stay there, as well as to my Malaysian and Dutch hosts at The Hague and in Maastricht. I am most grateful to the Government of Malaysia for funding most of my research undertakings in the country and abroad.

I owe a debt of gratitude to the Institute on Statelessness and Inclusion (ISI), especially to Laura van Waas and her amazing team at ISI for their invaluable insights on my research, and for opening doors to further training and networking opportunities with wonderful people who are dedicated to addressing statelessness in Southeast Asia and across the world.

I would like to place on record my appreciation to UNHCR for its support to my research and presentations at international, regional, and local fora, and for collaborative efforts in research, agenda-setting, and other projects on statelessness. I also want to thank all my interviewees and respondents for their inputs that have informed my research and added depth to it. Let me also thank my expert reviewers who gave helpful and constructive comments on the book manuscript.

I am indeed grateful for the opportunity and space given by the Centre for Human Rights and Legal Pluralism, Faculty of Law, McGill University where I undertook my research as a Steinberg Postdoctoral Fellow between 2018–2019. The cutting-edge facilities and opportunity to participate in interesting discourses on migration and human rights have tremendously helped expand and enrich my perspectives. This would not have been possible without the vision and generosity of the late Arnold and Blema Steinberg who established this fellowship, and the dynamic leadership of Professor François Crépeau and Professor Nandini Ramanujam.

I highly value the support and advice of my esteemed supervisor, Professor François Crépeau, the Hans & Tamar Oppenheimer Chair in Public International

Law at the Faculty of Law, McGill University, and United Nations Special Rapporteur on the Human Rights of Migrants between 2011 and 2017. It was largely due to his strong encouragement that this book came to be published. Indeed, I am honoured to have Professor Crépeau write the foreword.

Last but not least, to my family and friends who are always there for me, I am forever grateful for your abundant patience, love, support, and inspiration.

List of Cases

Abdulaziz, Cabales and Balkandali v. United Kingdom (1985) 7 EHRR 471. Application no. 9214/80; 9473/81; 9474/81

Decision of the Constitutional Court of the Republic of Indonesia (17 February 2012) No. 46/PUU-VIII/2010

Dickson Car Wheel Company (U.S.A) v. United Mexican States (1931), Reports of International Arbitral Awards Vol. IV 678

Genovese v. Malta (European Court of Human Rights (ECtHR), Judgment of 11 October 2011, App. No. 53124/099)

Grace Poe v. Commission of Elections and Elampro (Promulgated 8 March 2016), G.R. Nos. 221697 & 221698-700

Expelled Dominicans and Haitians v. Dominican Republic, Preliminary Objections, Merits, Reparations and Costs, Judgment, Inter-Am. Ct. H.R. (ser.C) No. 282, p 157 (Aug. 28, 2014)

Institute for Human Rights and Development in Africa (IHRDA) and Open Society Justice Initiative on behalf of Children of Nubian Descent in Kenya v. The Government of Kenya (Decision: No 002/Com/002/2009) [22 March 2011]

Inter-American Court on Human Rights, Proposed Amendments to the Naturalization Provision of the Political Constitution of Costa Rica, Advisory Opinion OC-4/84 of 19 January 1984, Series A No. 4

Kalderas Gypsies v. the Federal Republic of Germany and the Netherlands (Judgment of 6 July 1977), Application No. 7823/77-7824/77

Mennesson v. France (Judgment of 26 June 2014), Application no. 65192/11

Marckx v. Belgium (Judgment of 13 June 1979), Application No. 6833/74

MK (A Child by her Litigation Friend CAE), R (On the Application of) v. The Secretary of State for Home Department (2017) EWHC 1365 (Admin) (14 June 2017)

Nationality Decrees in Tunis and Morocco 1923. Advisory Opinion No. 4, PCIJ Series B, No. 4

The Republic of the Philippines vs Nora Fe Sagun (G. R. No. 187567, 15 February 2012)

Yean and Bosico v. Dominican Republic (Series C, Case 130, 8 September 2005)

Table of Statutes

Brunei	Births and Deaths Registration Act 1979 (Chap. 79) (Revised Edition 2013)	Retrieved from https://www.refworld.org/pdfid/528346844.pdf
	Brunei Nationality Act, No. 4, 1961 (Revised Edition 2002)	Retrieved from http://www.refworld.org/docid/4c56c01d2.html
	Islamic Family law of Brunei (CAP 217) (Revised Edition 2012)	Retrieved https://www.ftcam.de/ft_files/Scheidung_BruneiDarussalam1.pdf
Cambodia	Cambodian Law on Nationality, Decree No. NS/RKM/1096/31, 1996	Retrieved from http://www.refworld.org/docid/3ae6b5210.html
	Law on Immigration of 1994 (Promulgated by Decree No. 05/NS/1994 on 22nd September 1994)	Retrieved from http://www.refworld.org/docid/3ae6b52f8.html
	The Kingdom of Cambodia, Sub-Decree on Civil Status (Civil Registration) No. 103 of December 2000	https://chhoridalawbrary.files.wordpress.com/2016/06/ank-103-00-civil-status-e.pdf
Indonesia	Law No. 62 of 1958, Law on the Citizenship of the Republic of Indonesia	Retrieved from https://www.refworld.org/docid/3ae6b4ec8.html
	Undang-undang Republik Indonesia Nomor 1 Tahun 1974 Tentang Perkahwinan	Retrieved from luk.staff.ugm.ac.id/atur/UU1-1974Perkahwinan.pdf
	Law on Citizenship of the Republic of Indonesia, Decree No. 12, 2006	Retrieved from https://www.refworld.org/docid/4538aae64.html
	Undang-Undang Republik Indonesia, Nomor 24 Tahun 2013 Tentang Perubahan Atas Undang-Undang Nomor 23 Tahun 2006 Tentang Administrasi Kependudukan (Law 24 of 2013 on Population Administration)	Retrieved from https://www.bpn.go.id/Publikasi/Peraturan-Perundangan/Undang-Undang/undang-undang-nomor-24-tahun-2013-4797
	Peraturan Pemerintah No. 37 Tahun 2007 Tentang Pelaksanaan Undang-Undang No. 23 Tahun 2006 Tentang Administrasi Kependudukan	Retrieved from https://www.hukumonline.com/pusatdata/detail/26783/node/758/peraturan-pemerintah-nomor-37-tahun-2007

(continued)

(continued)

	Peraturan Presiden Nomor 25 Tahun 2008 Tentang Pensyaratan dan Tata Cara Pendaftaran Penduduk dan Pencatatan Sipil	Retrieved from https://www.hukumonline.com/pusatdata/detail/27909/node/1010/peraturan-presiden-nomor-25-tahun-2008
	Peraturan Daerah Provinsi DKI Jakarta Nomor 3 Tahun 2012 Tentang Retribusi Daerah sebagaimana diubah dengan Peraturan Daerah Provinsi DKI Jakarta Nomor 1 Tahun 2015	Retrieved from https://pelayanan.jakarta.go.id/download/regulasi/peraturan-daerah-nomor-3-tahun-2012-tentang-retribusi-daerah.pdf
	Peraturan Menteri Dalam Negeri Republik Indonesia Nomor 1 Tahun 2016 Tentang Percepatan Peningkatan Cakupan Kepemilikan Akta Kelahiran	Retrieved from https://www.dukcapil.kemendagri.go.id/izCFiles/uploads/downloads/Permendagri_9_Tahun_2016_tentang_Percepatan_Kepemilikan_Akta_Kelahiran.pdf
Lao PDR	Law on Lao Nationality, No. 06/90/PSA, 1990	Retrieved from https://www.refworld.org/docid/3ae6b4f014.html
	Law on the Protection of the Rights and Interests of the Child No. 05/NA of 27 December 2006	Retrieved from https://www.ilo.org/dyn/natlex/natlex4.detail?p_lang=en&p_isn=81057&p_country=LAO&p_count=58
	Decree of the President of the Lao PDR on the Promulgation of the Family law No. 97/P, 1990	Retrieved from https://www.google.com/webhp?sourceid=chrome-instant&ion=1&espv=2&ie=UTF-8#q=Family+Law+of+the+Lao+PDR+No.+97%2FP+1990
	Decree of the President of the Lao People's Democratic Republic on the Promulgation of the Law on Family Registration No. 21, 1992	Retrieved from https://www.hitpages.com/doc/4935851209392128/1
Malaysia	Federal Constitution of Malaysia, 1957	Retrieved from http://www.refworld.org/docid/3ae6b5e40.html
	Birth and Death Registration Act 1957 (Act 299)	Retrieved from http://www.commonlii.org/my/legis/consol_act/badra19571983376/
	Sabah Birth and Death Registration Ordinance 1951 (Cap. 123)	Retrieved from http://www.sabahlaw.com/RBDO.pdf.
	Islamic Family Law Enactment of Sabah 2004 (Enactment No. 8 of 2004)	Retrieved from www.esyariah.gov.my
	Sarawak Birth and Death Registration Ordinance 1951 (Cap. 10)	Print Version
	Immigration Act 1959/1963 (Act 155)	Retrieved from http://jpt.mohe.gov.my/images/InstitusiPengajianTinggi/MengenaiJPT/AKTA/Bil11.aktaimigresen.pdf
	Passports Act 1966 (Act 150)	Retrieved from http://www.agc.gov.my/agcportal/uploads/files/Publications/LOM/EN/Act%20150.pdf
	Passport Act 1996 (Passport Order (Exemption)(No.2), Amendment 1972	Print Version

(continued)

(continued)

	Education Act 1996 (Act 550)	Retrieved from http://planipolis.iiep.unesco.org/upload/Malaysia/Malaysia_Education_Act_1996.pdf
	National Registration Regulations 1990	Print Version
	Peraturan-Peraturan Pendidikan (Penerimaan Masuk Murid ke Sekolah, Penyimpanan Daftar dan Syarat Bagi Pengekalan Murid Belajar di Sekolah) 1998 (P.U. (A) 275)	Print Version
Myanmar	Constitution of the Republic of the Union of Myanmar (2008) (The 2008 Constitution of Myanmar)	Retrieved from http://www.burmalibrary.org/docs5/Myanmar_Constitution-2008-en.pdf
	1982 Burma Citizenship Law (An unofficial translation of the Act, the Pyithu Hluttaw Law No. 4 of 1982. Published in 'Working People's Daily', 16 October 1982)	Retrieved from http://www.refworld.org/docid/3ae6b4f71b.html
The Philippines	The 1935 Commonwealth Constitution, The 1973 Constitution, The 1986 Freedom Constitution, The 1987 Constitution of the Republic of the Philippines	Retrieved from http://www.refworld.org/docid/3ae6b5470.html
	Commonwealth Act No. 473, An Act to Provide for the Acquisition of Philippine Citizenship by Naturalisation and to Repeal Acts Numbered Twenty-Nine Hundred and Twenty-Seven and Thirty-Four Hundred and Forty-Eight.	Retrieved from http://www.lawphil.net/statutes/comacts/ca_473_1939.html
	Commonwealth Act No. 63, An Act Providing for the Ways in Which Philippine Citizenship may be Lost or Reacquired (as amended), 21 October 1936	Retrieved from http://www.refworld.org/docid/3ae6b4fd1c.html
	Family Code of the Philippines, Executive Order No. 209, 1987	Retrieved from http://www.refworld.org/docid/3ae6b5470.html
	Office of the Regional Governor, Executive Order No. 21, Series of 2012, Extending the Implementation of Free Birth Registration and Its Area of Coverage and Target Beneficiaries with DSWD-ARMM as Lead Implementing Agency. (3 July 2012)	Retrieved from http://dswd.armm.gov.ph/
	Republic Act No. 8171, An Act Providing for the Repatriation of Filipino Women Who Have Lost Their Philippine Citizenship by Marriage to Aliens and of Natural- Born Filipinos	Retrieved from http://asean.org/storage/2016/08/P24_An-Act-Providing-for-the-Repatriation-of-Filipino.pdf
	Republic Act No. 9225, An Act Making the Citizenship of Philippine Citizens Who Acquire Foreign Citizenship permanent. Amending for the purpose of the Commonwealth Act. No. 63, as amended and for other purposes	Retrieved from http://www.comelec.gov.ph/?r=References/RelatedLaws/ElectionLaws/OAV/RA9225
	Republic Act No. 9255, An Act Allowing Illegitimate Children to Use the Surname of their Father, Amending for the Purpose Article 176 of Executive Order 209 and Administrative Order No. 1, Series of 2016	Retrieved from https://psa.gov.ph/civilregistration/republic-act-9255

(continued)

(continued)

	The Civil Registry Law (Act No. 3753)	Retrieved from https://psa.gov.ph/civilregistration/civil-registration-laws/act-no-3753
	Presidential Decree No. 651, January 31, 1975, (as amended by Presidential Decree No. 766, August 8, 1975) Requiring the Registration of Births and Deaths in The Philippines Which Occurred From January 1, 1974, And Thereafter	Retrieved from http://www.lawphil.net/statutes/presdecs/pd1975/pd_651_1975.html
	Republic Act No.10625, An Act Reorganizing the Philippine Statistical System, Repealing for The Purpose Executive Order Numbered One Hundred Twenty-One, entitled 'Reorganizing and Strengthening the Philippine Statistical System and For Other Purposes'	Retrieved from http://www.gov.ph/2013/09/12/republic-act-no-10625/
	Administrative Order No. 1 Series of 1993 Implementing Rules and Regulations of Act No. 3753 and Other Laws on Civil Registration (Volume 89, Number 2, Official Gazette; January 11, 1993) (Administrative Order No. 1 Series 1993)	Retrieved from www.nsor12.ph/pdf_files/ CIVIL REGISTRATION LAWS/AO1-1993 (IRR on Civil Registration Laws &Procedures).pdf
Singapore	The Constitution of the Republic of Singapore, Act 8/65, 1965	Retrieved from http://www.refworld.org/docid/3ae6b5054.html
	Registration of Births and Deaths Act (Chap. 267) (Revised Edition) (1985)	Retrieved from http://statutes.agc.gov.sg/aol/search/display/view.w3p;page=0;query=DocId%3Ad148dedc-a872-45e4-87af-1aa9ed362c76%20%20Status%3Ainforce%20Depth%3A0;rec=0
Thailand	Thai Civil Registration Act (No.2), B.E. 2551 (2008)	Retrieved from http://www.refworld.org/docid/4a5464942.htm
	Thai Nationality Act, B.E. 2508 (1965) as amended by Acts No. 2 and No. 3, B.E. 2535 (1992) and Act No. 4, B.E. 2551 (2008)	Retrieved from http://thailaws.com/law/t_laws/tlaw0474.pdf
	Thai Nationality Act 1972	Retrieved from http://www.ilo.org/dyn/natlex/docs/ELECTRONIC/82873/109378/F2029485846/TH
	Thai Immigration Act, B.E. 2522 (1979)	Retrieved from http://www.refworld.org/docid/46b2f9f42.html
	Thai Nationality Act (No. 4) B.E. 2551 (2008)	Retrieved from http://www.refworld.org/docid/4a54695f2.html
Viet Nam	Decree No. 158/2005/ ND-CP of December 27, 2005, on Civil Status Registration and Management (Decree No. 158/2005)	Retrieved from http://moj.gov.vn/vbpq/en/lists/vn%20bn%20php%20lut/view_detail.aspx?itemid=6374
	Decree No. 60/2014/ QH13 of 20 November 2014 on Law on Civil Status (Decree No. 60/2014)	Retrieved from https://vanbanphapluat.co/law-no-60-2014-qh13-on-civil-status

(continued)

(continued)

	Law on Vietnamese Nationality, Order No. 22/2008/L-CTN, 2008	Retrieved from http://www.refworld.org/docid/4ac49b132.html

Contents

Abbreviations

AALCO	The Asian-African Legal Consultative Organisation
ACERWC	African Committee of Experts on the Rights and Welfare of the Child
ACRWC	African Charter on the Rights and Welfare of the Child
ACWC	ASEAN Commission on the Promotion and the Protection of the Rights of Women and Children
ACMW	ASEAN Committee on the Protection and Promotion on the Rights of Migrant Workers
ACTIP	ASEAN Convention against Trafficking in Persons (adopted 22 November 2015, in force 8 March 2016)
AICHR	ASEAN Intergovernmental Commission on Human Rights
AmCHR	American Convention on Human Rights (adopted 22 November 1969, in force 18 July 1978, OAS Treaty Series No. 36)
ASEAN	Association of Southeast Asian Nations
ASEAN Member States	The 10 member countries of ASEAN
CEDAW	Convention on the Elimination of All Forms of Discrimination against Women (adopted 18 December 1979, in force 3 September 1981, 1249 UNTS 13)

CERD	International Convention on the Elimination of All Forms of Racial Discrimination (adopted 21 December 1965, in force 4 January 1969, 660 UNTS 195)
CMW	Committee on Migrant Workers
CNMW	Convention on Nationality of Married Women Convention on the Right of the Child (adopted 20 November 1989, in force 2 September 1990, 1577 UNTS 3)
CRC	Committee of the Rights of the Child
CRCI	Covenant on the Rights of the Child in Islam (adopted 2005)
CRPD	Convention on the Rights of Persons with Disabilities (adopted 13 December 2006, in force 13 May 2008, 2515 UNTS 3)
CRVS	Civil Registration and Vital Statistics
Dakar Conclusions	UNHCR Expert Meeting: Interpreting the 1961 Statelessness Convention and Preventing Statelessness among Children
DHRRA	Development of Human Resources for Rural Areas (A Malaysian voluntary non-profit and non-political organisation registered in 2006 under the Societies Act of Malaysia 1966)
ECHR	European Convention on Human Rights (Formally the Convention for the Protection of Human Rights and Fundamental Freedoms) (adopted 4 November 1950, in force 3 September 1953)
ECN	European Convention on Nationality (adopted 6 November 1997, in force 3 January 2000, ETS No. 166)
ECtHR	European Court of Human Rights
ENS	European Network on Statelessness
ECOSOC	United Nations Economic and Social Council
EU	European Union
HR Committee	United Nations Human Rights Committee

HR Council	United Nations Human Rights Council, the body of independent experts monitoring the implementation of the 1966 ICCPR
Guidelines No. 4	UNHCR's Guidelines on Statelessness No. 4: Ensuring Every Child's Right to Acquire a Nationality through Articles 1-4 of the 1961 Convention on the Reduction of Statelessness, 21 December 2012, HCR/GS/12/04
ICCPR	International Covenant on Civil and Political Rights (adopted 16 December 1966, in force 23 March 1976, 999 UNTS 171)
ICESCR	International Covenant on Economic, Social and Cultural Rights (adopted 19 December 1966, in force 3 January 1976, 993 UNTS 3)
ICMW	International Convention on the Protection of the Rights of All Migrant Workers and Members of their Families (adopted 18 December 1990, in force 1 July 2003, 2220 UNTS 3)
1954 Convention	Convention relating to the Status of Stateless Persons Convention (28 September 1954, in force 6 June 1960, 360 UNTS 117)
1961 Convention	Convention on the Reduction of Statelessness, (adopted 30 August 1961, in force 13 December 1975, 989 UNTS 175)
ICJ	International Court of Justice
ILC	International Law Commission
IOM	International Organisation for Migration
IIMM13	Social Visit Pass issued by the Malaysian Government under Regulation 11 (10) of the Immigration Regulation 1963
1951 Refugee Convention	Convention Relating to the Status of Refugees (28 July 1951, in force 22 April 1954, 189 UNTS 137)
MKN	*Majlis Keselamatan Negara* or the Malaysian National Security Council

MKN Sabah	National Security Council at the state level of Sabah, headed by the State Security Secretary
MYKAS	Temporary identification card issued by the NRD under Regulation 5(3)(c) of the National Registration Regulations 1990
NRD	National Registration Department of Malaysia
Pas Lepa	Informal letter of identification of an individual of the Bajau Laut ethnicity issued administratively by the relevant Bajau Native Chief in Sabah
PLKS	A social visit (temporary employment) pass, i.e. a temporary employment pass for semi- skilled and unskilled workers in designated sectors issued by the Malaysian Immigration Department under the purview of the Malaysian Ministry of Home Affairs
PR	Permanent residency
Recommendation 2009/13	Recommendation CM/Rec (2009) 13 of the Committee of Ministers of the Council of Europe on the nationality of children, 9 December 2009 (Adopted by the Committee of Ministers on 9 December 2009 at the 1073rd meeting of the Ministers' Deputies)
SEA	Southeast Asia
SDG	Sustainable Development Goals
The 1930 Hague Convention	Convention on Certain Questions Relating to the Conflict of Nationality Law (adopted 13 April 1930, in force 1 July 1937) 179 UNTS 89
The 2000 Palermo Protocol	Palermo Protocol to UN Convention against Transnational Organised Crime on the Smuggling of Migrants (adopted 15 November 2000, in force 28 January 2004) 2241 UNTS 507
The 2000 Protocol to Prevent Trafficking	Protocol to Prevent, Suppress and Punish Trafficking in Persons, especially Women and Children (adopted 15 November 2000, in force 25 December 2003) 2237 UNTS 319
UDHR	Universal Declaration of Human Rights
UN	United Nations

UNICEF	United Nations Children's Emergency Fund
UNDP	United Nations Development Programme
UNESCAP	United Nations Economic and Social Commission for Asia and the Pacific
UNHCR	United Nations High Commissioner for Refugees
UNGA	United Nations General Assembly
UNSD	United Nations Statistics Division

List of Figures

List of Tables

Chapter 1
Introduction

Despite the international legal recognition of the fundamental right to a nationality and the international legal framework introduced to find solutions to statelessness, approximately 10 million of the global population are still affected by statelessness.[1] It was estimated before that almost half of this overall size consisted of stateless children.[2] To add to the problem, according to the United Nations High Commissioner for Refugees (UNHCR), a child is born stateless every ten minutes[3] and 70,000 children are born into statelessness annually.[4]

Such global magnitude of stateless children challenges some of the central tenets of international human rights law, in particular, those that have elevated the rights of children on the international legal and political platforms. This extant scenario strongly signals the need to centralise the right to a nationality and the fundamental principle of prevention of statelessness that uniquely targets children for a durable solution to statelessness.

Statelessness as the antithesis of nationality is a complex legal anomaly that affects men, women, and children of all regions with overwhelming legal, political, and humanitarian repercussions. Traditionally, the phenomenon of statelessness has been linked to reasons such as displacement due to dissolution or succession of

[1] UNHCR, *Ending Statelessness* (2016). Retrieved from http://www.unhcr.org/pages/49c3646c15e.html [Accessed 20 December 2016]. Experts point to quoted figures as cautious estimates since the presence of stateless populations is seldom acknowledged by the host states and those who should by right be termed stateless are instead identified as 'nationality unknown' or 'aliens' in general. See B. Frelick & M. Lynch, 'Statelessness: A Forgotten Human Rights Crisis', *Forced Migration Review*, V. 24 (2005), p 66.

[2] The estimation is made by the Office of the UN High Commissioner for Refugees (UNHCR) as quoted in Plan International, *Stateless Children Deprived of Their Basic Rights* (2011). Retrieved from http://news.trust.org//item/20110824161100-1xdyc/ [Accessed 4 August 2014].

[3] UNHCR, *Ending Statelessness within 10 Years* (2014). Retrieved from http://www.unhcr.org/546217229.pdf [Accessed 22 January 2016].

[4] UNHCR, *Global Action Plan to End Statelessness: 2014–2024* (2014). Retrieved from http://www.unhcr.org/protection/statelessness/54621bf49/global-action-plan-end-statelessness-2014-2024.html [Accessed 4 June 2017].

R. M. Razali, *Safeguarding Against Statelessness at Birth*,
https://doi.org/10.1007/978-981-19-5371-2_1

states, arbitrarily drawn borders that typically cause separation between ethnic groups following de-colonisation,[5] deprivation of nationality by governmental acts on the basis of ethnic, racial or gender discrimination, conflict of laws, and loss of nationality due to technical operation and effects of nationality laws. These varied and intersecting sources of statelessness invariably leave children in legal limbo often through no fault of their own.

The late twentieth and twenty-first centuries have witnessed the transnational movement of migrants and lack of birth registration among children as the new sources of statelessness.[6] In countries without the necessary legal frameworks addressing prevention and protection of stateless persons such as those found across many states in Southeast Asia (SEA), the affected populations at risk of falling into statelessness are commonly not identified. Not only that, such populations are very less likely to be eligible to apply for citizenship later in life through naturalisation procedures of the countries in which they reside. This is often the case so long as their 'irregular' status quo remains, regardless of the reality that the populations consist of individuals having parents and grandparents who were in fact born and have lived out their entire lives in such countries. These new sources of statelessness may easily be the root of inheritance of statelessness by children if the states do not design measures to halt the transfer of statelessness from one generation to another.[7]

The scale and scope of statelessness and its humanitarian ramifications can be overwhelming in some regions. Around 40% of the identified stateless populations of the world live in the Asia Pacific region.[8] Southeast Asia and the Association of Southeast Asian Nations (ASEAN) are home to some of the largest stateless populations in Asia. Myanmar alone had publicly reported the figures of almost

---

[5] State succession results in nationality law having to establish questions of new membership, identity and belonging in relation to an emerging state. Historical passage proves that individuals or sometimes an entire group were excluded or overlooked in the process, creating statelessness among them. The major affected groups include the Bihari following the independence of Bangladesh and the Russians who did not obtain citizenship in Latvia and Estonia after the dissolution of the Soviet Union. See L. van Waas, *The Situation of Stateless Persons in the Middle East and North Africa* (2010). Retrieved from http://www.unhcr.org/protection/statelessness/4ce63e079/situation-stateless-persons-middle-east-north-africa-laura-van-waas.html [Accessed 20 May 2014].

[6] L. van Waas, *Nationality Matters: Statelessness under International Law* (School of Human Rights Research Series V. 29, 2008), pp 151–187; S. Nonnenmacher & R. Cholewinski, 'The Nexus Between Statelessness and Migration' in A. Edwards & L. van Waas (Eds.), *Nationality and Statelessness under International Law* (Cambridge: Cambridge University Press, 2014), pp 247–263; A. Paxton, 'Finding a Country to Call Home: A Framework for Evaluating Legislation to Reduce Statelessness in Southeast Asia', *Pacific Rim Law & Policy Journal*, V. 21 (2012), p 628–633.

[7] Institute on Statelessness and Inclusion, *Addressing the Right to a Nationality through the Convention on the Right of the Child: A Toolkit for Civil Society* (2016), p 6. Retrieved from http://www.institutesi.org/ourwork/children.php [Accessed 15 September 2016].

[8] Institute for Statelessness and Inclusion, *Stateless Persons in Asia and the Pacific* (2015). Available from http://www.worldsstateless.org/continents/asia/stateless- persons-in-asia-and-the-pacific [Accessed 17 September 2018].

1–1.5 million stateless people.[9] Apart from Africa, Asia, and the Pacific have been reported to have among the highest number of unregistered children.[10] Not only facing denial of access to public primary schools, publicly funded healthcare and essential state resources to protect their rights, the majority of stateless children, and children at risk of statelessness are forced to endure lives in extreme poverty, and are exposed to physical and legal insecurities, primarily due to risks of arrest and detention, human trafficking and child labour.[11]

Against the foregoing background, the research inquiry that this book seeks to analyse is, 'whether children are protected against statelessness at birth, and if so, to what extent are they protected?' The qualitative legal research undertaken to address this question is essentially motivated by the twin objectives of (i) optimally contributing to durable solutions to statelessness through the imperative strategy of prevention of childhood statelessness; and (ii) promoting the best interests of children through protection against statelessness at birth.

The overarching question shall be examined at the level of international and domestic laws and principles of ASEAN Member States on (i) children's rights to birth registration and nationality, both forming the right to a legal identity; and (ii) the framework of prevention and reduction of statelessness. This introductory chapter aims to outline the background of this volume, the concept of statelessness and the context of protection against statelessness at birth as its central theme, and the structure as well as boundaries of the ensuing inquiries and discussions.

1.1 Introducing Statelessness, Related Connotations, and Contexts

Statelessness denotes a situation where a person lacks any nationality, due to non-recognition by any state that the person is a national under the operation of the state's law. The determination of whether a person is stateless or otherwise is essentially a legal question that is answered based on the substance and application of the state's

---

[9] Institute on Statelessness and Inclusion, *Stateless Persons in Asia and the Pacific*. Retrieved from http://www.worldsstateless.org/continents/asia/stateless-persons-in-asia-and-the-pacific [Accessed 20 September 2018]. As of end of 2016, Myanmar recorded 925,939 stateless persons and persons of undetermined nationality whereas Thailand was reported having 487,741 stateless persons and persons of undetermined nationality under UNHCR's statelessness mandate. See UNHCR, *UNHCR Statistical Yearbook 2016* (2017), p 44. Retrieved from https://www.unhcr.org/en-us/statistics/country/5a8ee0387/unhcr-statistical-yearbook-2016-16th-edition.html [Accessed 27 January 2017].

[10] UNICEF, 'One in Three Children under Five Does Not Officially Exist' (11 December 2013). Retrieved from http://www.unicef.org/media/media_71508.html [Accessed 20 May 2014]. Out of some nearly 230 million children under the age of five who have never been officially recorded, half of them are said to reside in the Asia–Pacific region. See United Nations Economic and Social Commission for Asia and the Pacific, *Get Every One in the Picture: Civil Registration and Vital Statistiocs in Asia and the Pacific* (2019). Retrieved from https://www.getinthepicture.org/partners/unicef [Accessed 1 January 2019].

[11] B. Berkeley, 'Stateless People, Violent States', *World Policy Journal*, V. 26 (1)(2009), p 6.

nationality law. This is in itself reflected in the definition of a 'stateless person' provided in Article 1(1) of the 1954 Convention relating to the Status of Stateless Persons[12] (1954 Convention). The definition of a 'stateless person' under this provision is a legal and technical one, strictly capturing the de jure category of stateless persons. As a result, the scope of statelessness is said to be inadequate, as it excludes persons who may be in possession of a nationality, but are unable to enjoy the benefits attached to it. Such persons, labelled as 'de facto stateless', are usually outside of their countries of nationality and do not benefit from diplomatic and consular protection from their countries. De facto statelessness has also been linked to persons who are in their own countries of nationality, yet are in a disadvantaged position for not being able to provide proof of their nationality.[13]

In both situations above, the decisive factor that is commonly shared is their lack of protection from any state. In many of the situations describing de facto statelessness when such persons are in their own countries, the phrase 'at risk of statelessness' has been put forward as the more appropriate term to describe otherwise than the de jure stateless persons.[14] Simply terming individuals residing in their own countries as 'stateless' may cause adverse consequences to their protection interests. By the same token, de jure statelessness appears to come to light when denial of evidence of nationality experienced by them proves consistent and enduring across generations.[15]

In discussing the multiple contexts in which statelessness may arise, aside from the de-jure-de facto dimension of statelessness, it must be understood that statelessness can both occur in migratory and non-migratory situations.[16] In a non-migratory setting, statelessness usually affects those who have a deep-rooted attachment to their countries, yet are not recognised as nationals by such countries. Many stateless populations in the world have in fact been living in the same countries for decades and across many generations without acquiring a nationality. Such so-called *in situ* stateless populations live in a protracted statelessness situation in countries that do not grant citizenship based on place of birth ('jus soli') to their descendants.[17] For *in situ* stateless populations, experts regard the grant of nationality through recognition of nationality or naturalisation by the countries in which they live as the most

---

[12] Convention relating to the Status of Stateless Persons (28 September 1954, in force 6 June 1960) 360 UNTS 117.

[13] J. Bhabha, *Children Without a State: A Global Human Rights Challenge* (Cambridge MA: MIT Press, 2011), p 3.

[14] Institute on Statelessness and Inclusion, *The World's Stateless* (2014). Retrieved from http://www.instituesi.org/worldstateless.pdf [Accessed 10 October 2016], p 7; L. van Waas, 'The UN Statelessness Conventions in A. Edwards & L. van Waas (Eds.), *Nationality and Statelessness under International Law*, Cambridge: Cambridge University Press, 2014), p 80–81.

[15] Institute on Statelessness and Inclusion, *The World's Stateless* (2014), p 7.

[16] European Network on Statelessness, Statelessness Determination and the Protection Status of Stateless Persons (2013). Retrieved from http://www.refworld.org/pdfid/53162a2f4.pdf [Accessed 24 July 2015].

[17] Asia Pacific Refugee Rights Network, Statelessness. Retrieved from http://aprrn.info/wiki/tiki-index.php?page=Statelessness [Accessed 19 April 2015].

suitable and durable solution to their statelessness.[18] Their long-established connections to the countries through birth and long-term residence and the absence of factual and/or legal ties with any other country serve as reasonable and well-founded grounds for them to claim the nationality of such countries in which they reside.[19] In their case, conducting procedures to determine whether they are stateless for protection purposes may not be the appropriate response, as this would prolong their 'statelessness' status.[20] The examples of *in situ* stateless populations where conferment of nationality would be the best modality to resolve statelessness include stateless Rohingyas in Myanmar, stateless Kurds in Syria, and stateless Nubians in Kenya.[21]

Regionally, statelessness featured prominently in Europe where nation-states first originated, due to conflicts of laws and the subsequent mass denationalisation and displacement during and following the two devastating wars. The ensuing fragmentation of states in the former USSR and Yugoslavia brought about a lasting legacy of stateless persons falling through the cracks of nationality regimes in the new states that emerged. Latvia, Estonia, Ukraine, and Russia as the successor states of the Soviet Union are home to almost half a million stateless persons in their territories.[22] Stateless persons in these countries who historically have a migratory background, are considered to be *in situ* stateless due to their substantial ties to the countries in which they reside despite lacking a nationality.

In Africa and Asia, statelessness traces its genesis to arbitrarily drawn borders that ignored concepts such as cultural ties and ethnicities, and to the immediate task of defining who should be the citizens and comprehensively registering them in the process of post-colonial state formation. In the context of Africa, its long colonial vestige created statelessness for descendants of people who historically migrated or were forced to do so in the colonial era, who both came from outside of and especially within the region itself. The latter include farmworkers in Zimbabwe, farmers on cocoa plantations in *Côte* d'Ivoire and Nubian soldiers in Kenya.[23] According to Gyulai, both historical political context and ineffective methods to prevent statelessness at birth have a role in instigating statelessness *in situ*.[24]

---

[18] G. Gyulai, 'Statelessness in the EU Framework for International Protection', European Journal of Migration and Law, 14(3)(2012), p 165.

[19] European Network on Statelessness, Statelessness Determination and the Protection Status of Stateless Persons (2013).

[20] UNHCR, Statelessness Determination Procedures and the Status of Stateless Persons (Geneva Conclusions) (2010). Retrieved from http://www.refworld.org/docid/4d9022762.html [Accessed 13 June 2014].

[21] G. Gyulai, 'The Determination of Statelessness and the Establishment of a Statelessness-Specific Protection Regime' in A. Edwards and L. van Waas (Eds.), Nationality and Statelessness under International Law, (Cambridge: Cambridge University Press 2014), p 118.

[22] As of 2016, Latvia hosted the largest number of stateless persons in Europe (252,195), followed by Estonia (85,301), Sweden (31,062) and Germany (12,569). See UNHCR, *Global Trend* [2016]. Retrieved from https://reliefweb.int/sites/reliefweb.int/files/resources/5943e8a34.pdf [Accessed 3 July 2017].

[23] See B. Manby, *Citizenship and Statelessness in Africa: The Law and Politics of Belonging* (AH Oisterwijk: Wolf Legal Publishers, 2015).

[24] G. Gyulai, *Statelessness in the EU Framework for International Protection*, p 280.

While children may be born stateless within *in situ* or non-migratory populations, the current age of global inequality, shrinking geography, and civil wars features statelessness as a highly cross-border issue. Around the world including in SEA, transnational migration additionally gives rise to statelessness among more recent migrants whose movements are induced by multiple and usually mixed factors, mainly involving asylum seeking, labour, trafficking, and family reunification. International Organisation for Migration (IOM) estimated in 2008 that 30–40% of all migration in the region of SEA is through undocumented channels, with Malaysia and Thailand having approximately three million undocumented migrants.[25]

Statelessness in Europe currently plays out in the context of one of its recent global refugee crises that ushered in a record number of 1.2 million forcibly displaced persons in 2015 and early 2016 from major refugee-producing countries such as Syria, Afghanistan, South Sudan, Somalia, Iraq, Yemen, and Democratic Republic of the Congo. Nationality problems have been identified within such recent arrivals. The risk of statelessness has been associated with children born in Europe who are unable to acquire nationality through their mothers as a result of gender discriminatory laws in countries like Syria, loss of identity documentation and statelessness that is already experienced by certain groups such as the Palestinians and the Kurds.[26]

Within Africa, dilemmas continue to surround questions on how to integrate new migrants, including refugees and their children into the new polity and citizenry. Those highly at risk of statelessness include the descendants of former refugees returned to their countries of origin following the relevant cessation clause that was invoked under the 1951 Convention relating to the Status of Refugees (the 1951 Refugee Convention). Recognition and reacquisition of nationality are both challenging due to lack of proof of attachment to their countries of origin.[27]

In SEA where mixed population mobility is the region's hallmark, children born to undocumented migrants abroad, including children of refugees and asylum seekers particularly face a heightened risk of statelessness owing to the region's predominant *jus sanguinis* nationality regimes, civil registration systems of birth and marriage that lack universal coverage in law and/or practice, unavailable or inadequate consular services, and challenges arising from the status of the affected children or their migrant parents. Non-registration of births entails prolonged undocumented status and onerous bureaucratic procedures to establish one's proof of birth and/or nationality.

Meanwhile, the western model of citizenship regimes in the post-colonial period is up until today, inadequate to accommodate the distinctive lifestyles of the mobile and

---

[25] J. J. Larsen, 'Migration and People Trafficking in Southeast Asia', *Trends and Issues in Crime and Criminal Justice*, 401 (2010), p 1.

[26] Institute on Statelessness and Inclusion, *The World's Stateless Children* (Oisterwijk: Wolf Legal Publishers, 2017), p 80. Retrieved from http://www.institutesi.org/worldsstateless17.pdf [Accessed 5 January 2017].

[27] B. Manby et al., 'The Right to a Nationality in Africa: New Norms and New Commitments' in L. van Waas & M.J. Khanna (Eds.), *Solving Statelessness* (AH Oisterwijk: Wolf Legal Publishers, 2017), p 267.

migratory populations lacking a fixed home and belonging to an established community and polity across several continents. In SEA, this fissure affects among others, the traditionally migratory populations of Moken and *Bajau Laut*. The risk of statelessness could be aggravated further by gender discrimination and/or ethnic criteria in citizenship laws, and inadequate coverage, inapplicability, or flawed application of *jus soli* legal safeguards to prevent statelessness through nationality provisions.

While those *in situ* stateless populations with a clear and more stable connection may be targeted for citizenship campaigns, more recently-arrived migrants are habitually treated as non-citizens or foreigners.[28] The line between statelessness *in situ* and statelessness in the migratory context is not crisp and transparent.[29] Yet for such migrants who lack a clear attachment to a specific state and are unable to acquire the nationality of the country of residence including through naturalisation, a different response is necessary, namely, meaningful and rights-based protection mechanisms.[30]

Against the challenging environment of lack of binding international legal frameworks for refugees and stateless in the majority of the ASEAN Member States, the stay and status of the affected populations are substantially described as irregular by the countries hosting them. Policies and procedures for their identification and protection are extremely lacking. Local integration is often politically contested and legally inaccessible. The adverse repercussions witness the affected children being born and subsequently growing up undocumented into 'rightlessness' in numerous contexts, as a result of inheriting their parents' irregular status, including undetermined nationality, and statelessness.

In Europe, the problem of statelessness is more comprehensively mapped and studied compared to the situations in other regions. The mapping and studies resulted in numerous reports, guidelines and jurisprudence by the European Union (EU) institutions, such as the European Council, the EU Court of Human Rights, European Parliament, and other actors within academia and active networks of non-governmental bodies, including European Migration Network, Institute on Statelessness and Inclusion and European Network on Statelessness. It appears that statelessness has broadly gained a strong foothold on the agendas of the regional human rights institutions in Europe, the Americas and even Africa, as reflected in the regional consensus achieved, and vigorous undertakings along regional standard-setting.[31]

---

[28] UNHCR, Regional Expert Roundtable on Good Practices for the Identification, Prevention and Reduction of Statelessness and the Protection of Stateless Persons in South East Asia' (2011). Retrieved from http://www.refworld.org/cgi-bin/texis/vtx/rwmain?docid=4d6e09932 [Accessed 10 July 2013].

[29] G. Gyulai, *Statelessness in the EU Framework for International Protection*, p 279- 295; G. Gyulai, 'The Determination of Statelessness and the Establishment of a Statelessness-Specific Protection Regime' in A. Edwards and L. van Waas (Eds.), *Nationality and Statelessness under International Law*, Cambridge: Cambridge University Press, 2014), p 118.

[30] G. Gyulai, 'The Determination of Statelessness and the Establishment of a Statelessness-Specific Protection Regime' in A. Edwards & L. van Waas (Eds.), *Nationality and Statelessness under International Law* (Cambridge: Cambridge University Press, 2014), p 116–143.

[31] For Latin America, see for instance, the Brazil Declaration on a Framework for Cooperation and Regional Solidarity to Strengthen the International Protection of Refugees, Displaced and Stateless

In contrast, gaps in the data collection of stateless persons including stateless refugees (the so-called 'known unknown') still widely persist in Asia and the Pacific. In the sub-region of SEA, such gaps are attributable to among others, lack of interest of the host governments in protecting vulnerable populations such as the stateless and refugees, political sensitivity around extending assistance to 'others', low level of awareness on the importance of legal identity by the affected populations, and lack of effective collaborations as well as technical expertise on the part of various actors.[32]

The ASEAN human rights bodies, especially the ASEAN Intergovernmental Commission on Human Rights (AICHR) and the ASEAN Commission on the Rights of Women and Children (ACWC) have put the subject of statelessness onto their agendas. Yet the mandates of such bodies are largely advisory, and mostly limited to providing important forums for regional dialogue and collaboration on statelessness. Regional consensus through instruments such as a declaration that could herald concrete action plans on statelessness has yet to emerge. These partly speak to the slow progress and results to be achieved by such socially, politically, and economically diverse member states of ASEAN. Furthermore, the regional grouping of ASEAN continues to operate through consultation and common consensus in their decision-making process, as well as respect for the principles of sovereignty and non-interference in the domestic affairs of other member states.

1.2 Exploring the Concept of Prevention of Statelessness

While the right to a nationality can be acquired by birth or otherwise than by birth (mainly through naturalisation and marriage), for the former, prevention of childhood statelessness calls upon states to adopt the combined elements of jus sanguinis and jus soli citizenship as the mechanism to avoid and gradually reduce statelessness through conferral of citizenship.

At the international level, the 1961 Convention on the Reduction of Statelessness[33] (the 1961 Convention) constitutes the key instrument that presents the formula for the avoidance of childhood statelessness. Together with the rights of children to birth registration and to acquire a nationality under Article 7(1) of the 1989 Convention on the Rights of the Child (CRC)[34] and Article 24(3) of the 1966 International Covenant

Persons in Latin America and the Caribbean within a Framework of Cooperation and Solidarity (Brazil Plan of Action), 3 December 2014 and for West Africa, Abidjan Declaration of Ministers of ECOWAS Member States on Eradication of Statelessness, 25 February 2015.

[32] Rodziana Mohamed Razali, Summary of Day 1, Workshop on Researching Statelessness and Citizenship in the Asia Pacific, organised by UNHCR, Melbourne School of Government & Melbourne Law School, Melbourne, Australia, 29–27 January 2016.

[33] Convention on the Reduction of Statelessness, New York (30 August 1961, in force 13 December 989) (1975 UNTS 175).

[34] Convention on the Rights of the Child (adopted 20 November 1989, in force 2 September 1577) (1990 UNTS 13).

on Civil and Political Rights (ICCPR),[35] they form the main legal framework for the prevention of statelessness around which international legal standards are set and developed. This framework is further complemented by other human rights rules and norms fortifying children's rights to a legal identity and to be prevented from statelessness.

In many countries adopting *jus sanguinis* nationality regimes such as in SEA and Europe, children would otherwise be stateless if they could neither be attributed the citizenship of their parents nor benefit from nationality *jus soli* of their birth countries. The risk of statelessness predominantly confronts children who are left with no proof of birth and parentage and children who are affected by gender and racial discriminatory nationality laws.

The categories of such children may overlap, and they usually comprise: (i) children born to unknown parents including abandoned children; (ii) children who are separated from parents including unaccompanied children and victims of trafficking; (iii) children born to stateless parents; (v) children born to undocumented parents of undetermined nationality; (vi) children of refugees (or former refugees) and asylum seekers (usually undocumented); (vii) children born out of wedlock; and (viii) children of mixed marriages (born to parents of two different nationalities or to a national and another undocumented or stateless parent). These children may be born to parents of *in situ* background or of a recent migratory background.

In the crucial years of childhood, statelessness prevents children access to free and affordable public education and health services, and exposes them to immigration threats of arrest and detention, and to other forms of exploitation, such as child labour and trafficking. Owing to children's highly vulnerable nature and their dependence on the state for protection, particularly when they belong to marginalised communities, are affected by conflicts and without parental support, the book argues that statelessness affecting children deserves a separate and focused attention in the larger statelessness discourse.

Moreover, ensuring every child a nationality at birth and immediately after it, would naturally serve as a starting point for a durable solution to the global problem of statelessness, namely, by preventing children from growing up without a nationality, or from lacking an established nationality into their adulthood, and from the effect of self-perpetuating statelessness across subsequent generations. Recognising the fact that nationality acquisition may not be straightforward at birth for many different cohorts of children, placing a great concern on the prevention of statelessness at birth is, therefore, crucial. Its practical significance is pointed out in the following observation:

> At and soon after birth, evidence of relevant facts and links is most fresh, witnesses likely available and procedures relatively straightforward. Without help early on, a stateless child will readily grow up to be a stateless adult, who may live their entire life without

[35] International Covenant on Civil and Political Rights (adopted 16 December 1966, in force 23 March 1976) (999 UNTS 17)1.

> ever acquiring a nationality. This underlines the importance of taking early, ideally even preventative action, to stay ahead of statelessness and negate its impact.[36]

With the values inherent in the prevention of statelessness at birth, this volume hopes to bolster the commitment of UNHCR to a 10-year campaign to eradicate statelessness by 2024, launched in conjunction with the 60th anniversary of the 1954 Convention in 2014.[37] Specifically, on 4th November 2014, UNHCR through its #IBelong Campaign to End Statelessness in 10 years, adopted 10 Actions to be undertaken by states with the support of UNHCR, civil society, and other partners. The questions explored in this book align with Action 2 that seeks to ensure the implementation of legislative safeguards so that no children are born stateless.[38] Addressing Action 2 is significant as it will positively impact on Action 1 (Resolve existing major situations of statelessness); Action 4 (Prevent denial, loss or deprivation of nationality on discriminatory grounds); Action 7 (Ensure birth registration to prevent statelessness); and Action 8 (Issue nationality documentation to those entitled to it).[39]

At the regional level of SEA, the book responds to the calls by ASEAN human rights bodies such as AICHR and ACWC to reduce and prevent statelessness in the Member States of ASEAN. From the perspective of migration-induced statelessness, AICHR during the Joint Workshop on Statelessness and the Rights of Women and Children in 2011 made the following recommendation:

> to undertake a study to analyse nationality laws of ASEAN Member States in order to identify conflicts and gaps that could result in statelessness, particularly in the light of high levels of migration in the region, and the reality that the lives and families of migrants often span multiple countries.[40]

Significantly, the work contained in this volume is contextually relevant to the promotion of the right to a nationality for women and children, in the efforts to foster ASEAN Community building and the realisation of the rights of peoples of ASEAN.[41]

---

[36] Institute on Statelessness and Inclusion, *The World's Stateless Children* (Oisterwijk: Wolf Legal Publishers, 2017), p 126. Retrieved from http://www.institutesi.org/worldsstateless17.pdf [Accessed 5 January 2018].

[37] See generally UNHCR, *#IBelong Campaign to End Statelessness* (2014). Retrieved from http://www.unhcr.org/ibelong-campaign-to-end-statelessness.html [Accessed 10 January 2015]; See also UNHCR, *I Am Here, I belong, The Urgent Need to End Childhood Statelessness* (2015). Retrieved from http://www.unhcr.org/ibelong/wp-content/uploads/2015-10-StatelessRep ort_ENG16.pdf [Accessed 15 February 2016].

[38] UNHCR, *#IBelong Campaign to End Statelessness* (2014).

[39] UNHCR, *Good Practices Paper: Ensuring That No Child is Born Stateless'* (2015), p 3. Retrieved from https://www.refworld.org/pdfid/58cfab014.pdf [Accessed 5 January 2017].

[40] UNHCR, *Report of the Regional Workshop on Good Practices in Birth Registration* (2011), p 19. Retrieved from http://www.getinthepicture.org/docs/unhcr-birth-reg-rpt.pdf [Accessed 8 October 2014].

[41] Opening Remarks of H.E. Lily D. Purba, Chair of the ASEAN Commission on the Promotion and Protection of the Rights of Women and Children (ACWC) for the Workshop on the Rights

With a wide audience in mind, including advocates, academics, legal practitioners, policymakers, and students, the work presented in this book hopes to provide insights and stimulate wider and deeper engagement in respect of this multidimensional and complex subject in the overall literature on statelessness.

1.3 Structure

The following Chap. 2 identifies and lays down the underlying key concepts governing nationality, statelessness, and prevention of statelessness, together with the historical basis and development of the rules and norms in these areas. It commences with a series of desk reviews and analyses of primary texts of the related international conventions, UN documents, case law, and soft law instruments incorporating the relevant norms, comprising inter alia; principles and declarations, as well as interpretative guidelines, comments, and observations issued by the relevant international and regional bodies. These bodies largely hold their mandates addressing particularly the subjects of statelessness, the human rights of children, refugees and migrants, and other regional human rights law and standards.

The examination of the diverse normative instruments in Chap. 2 is performed to trace and identify a specific, constant and comprehensible segment of the broader jurisprudence forming the legal framework for the protection of children against statelessness at birth. This legal framework shall constitute the paradigm, namely, the structuring context containing rules, theories, principles, and norms within which the subsequent legal analyses on the availability and extent of protection of children against statelessness at birth are undertaken.

Prior to embarking on the domestic analysis of the laws and norms of the ASEAN Member States pertaining to safeguards against statelessness at birth, Chap. 3 presents an evaluation of the rules and norms constituting the international legal framework on the protection of children against statelessness at birth. This assessment pursues the objective of evaluating whether any perceived lack of, or, ineffective protection against statelessness at birth, flows from gaps and limitations in the normative components of the legal framework itself.

Chap. 4 illustrates the dynamics of the countries of ASEAN across ethnicity, language, religion, legal, political, and constitutional systems. The nationality principles and methods of its acquisition shall be outlined, followed by an overview of the acceptance of the main human rights treaties by the ASEAN Member States. Importantly forming the background to the analyses of the legal safeguards against statelessness at birth in Chaps. 5 and 6 are the situations of statelessness, their magnitude, and common causes that lead to a cascading effect of creating the cycles of childhood statelessness in the region. Finally, the chapter highlights some of the

---

to Nationality for Women and Children in the ASEAN Community 23–22,2020–2016 September 2016, Da Lat, Viet Nam September 2016 (on file with author).

best practices in addressing statelessness that has been implemented by the ASEAN Member States.

Chapter 5 contains an analysis of the nationality laws and to some degree, relevant practices of the ten Member States of ASEAN. This exercise is undertaken with a view to assessing the availability and extent of protection via nationality provisions that may benefit specific categories of stateless and otherwise stateless children identified. The purpose of this assessment is to test whether childhood statelessness could be prevented at birth rather than to simply measure compliance with or violation of international legal standards on the subject, which could be explained in light of the lack of binding commitments to Statelessness Conventions among the majority of the ASEAN Member States. Going on this basis, the standards on protection of children against statelessness at birth against which such assessment is conducted are abstracted from the previously examined rules and norms based on the best or ideal benchmarks that as far as possible, leave no room for children to be left stateless at birth.

The subsequent analysis in Chap. 6 entails a similar assessment of another legal safeguard against statelessness at birth, namely, birth registration. As Chap. 3 shall reveal, international standards on birth registration appear to be varied and unsystematic. The scheme of assessment of birth registration laws of the ASEAN Member States, therefore, has to be premised on a set of deduced standards on birth registration from a mixture of substantially soft law instruments containing the standards and recommendations around the norms and practices in the area of birth registration, as identified in Chap. 2, and summarised later in Chap. 3.

In Chaps. 5 and 6, the analyses conducted across the laws and norms on the safeguards in the different states embody comparative accounts of the related provisions relating to protection against childhood statelessness. Through this method, exemplary laws and best practices can be learned, and possible grounds for moving forward towards achieving common solutions can be identified at the level of the ASEAN member countries.

The conclusions of the foregoing investigations into such ultra-diverse and distinct legislation (and to some extent, practices) on nationality and birth registration systems shall be drawn using tables constructed to map the patterns of the availability and the different scales of strength of the safeguards offered.

In the final Chap. 7, reflections on the key findings will be presented alongside some brief propositions formulated to address the oversights, problems, and issues identified. It is hoped that the recommendations can be further taken up and explored by relevant actors and stakeholders through dialogues, discussions, and further research into their viability, for better progress to be made in order to achieve the reduction and elimination of statelessness.

1.4 Contours

This section sets out the parameters of this book, as in what the book shall cover and what it shall not, together with other acknowledged limitations. The contours of this book place due regard to the following five important scopes.

1. **Protection against Statelessness at Birth**

A person may become stateless at birth or later in life. In the former context, a child may be born into this world stateless due to conflicts between the nationality rules of two different jurisdictions, or for being born to stateless parents and parents of unknown nationality. The interface between cross-border migration, *jus sanguinis* nationality regime, and the lack of or ineffective safeguards against statelessness, particularly in ensuring universal birth registration and gender—neutral citizenship provisions, further intensify the risk of being born stateless for some children. On the other hand, a national may lose or be deprived of his nationality by his state and become stateless at a later stage in his life. Such could be triggered, for instance, by discriminatory practices in the area of nationality and a subsequent loss of proof of identity by child victims of trafficking and other child migrants on the move.

The scope of this book is limited to childhood statelessness that occurs at birth, namely, those involving children who are at risk of statelessness from birth, in contrast to statelessness that affects children later in life, such as through loss or deprivation of nationality. Reduction of statelessness is a natural outcome of prevention of statelessness. Nonetheless, it is not the intention of this book to delve into reduction through the naturalisation modality. Instead, the focus is placed on the pre-emptive remedy that targets prevention of statelessness before it occurs, as opposed to naturalisation remedies, and remedies in terms of protection of the rights of the stateless. It should be noted, however, that available pathways to prevent the protraction of statelessness among children may involve some discussion on the aspects of naturalisation, as well as the acquisition of nationality by registration or application.

2. **The Targeted Children**

Children of migratory and non-migratory backgrounds could be prevented from statelessness at birth through similar prevention tools, namely, birth registration and nationality legislation containing the necessary safeguards against statelessness. It is tragic that some children are born to migrant parents possessing a nationality but are unable to transmit it to their children. In that regard, gender discriminatory nationality law is often present to further amplify the risk of statelessness for children born to such parents.[42] Children born of mixed parentage between a national and a non-citizen (or to parents of mixed nationalities), and children born out of wedlock (which can overlap in many instances), are the two groups that are highly affected

[42] R.M.M. Wallace et al., *Mother to Child: How Discrimination Prevents Women Registering the Birth of Their Child* (Plan & the UHI Centre for Rural Childhood, 2012), p 11; B.L. Fisher, 'Why Non-Marital Children in the Mena Region Face a Risk of Statelessness', *Harvard Human Rights Journal Online*, 28(1)(2015), p 4–5.

by gender inequality and barriers in the form of administrative procedures required for nationality to be acquired through their citizen parents.

Within and outside of the context of migration, statelessness affects children born to unknown parents (commonly referred to as 'foundlings'), abandoned children, and children separated from parents with no proof of legal identity. Mobile or nomadic and semi-nomadic populations whose territories straddle international borders are at a particular risk of statelessness for being without birth registration and other identity documents.[43]

Such diverse and dynamic categories of children are either stateless or would otherwise be stateless in the context of the 1961 Convention. As this book is built on the premise of protection of children against statelessness at birth, as such, the foregoing categories of children are central to the analyses conducted throughout this book, including those involving the Member States of ASEAN.

3. **Safeguarding against Statelessness at Birth: The Focus on Birth Registration and Nationality Legal Frameworks for Avoidance of Statelessness at Birth**

This book places its focus on the two vital safeguards in examining the levels of protection against statelessness at birth. Aside from birth registration forming one of the safeguards against statelessness, nationality legislation in many host countries provide for legal provisions for children to acquire a nationality if they would otherwise be stateless. The widespread problem of lack of birth registration, the absence of 'nationality' safeguards, or the presence of safeguards that are narrowly interpreted and inadequate to cover the various categories of children who would otherwise be stateless, mutually form the combined sources among others, of statelessness at birth.

4. **Level of Analysis, Region, and Jurisdiction**

The assessment of the legal frameworks related to prevention of statelessness at birth is done at two main levels, namely, the international level (inclusive of the regional legal frameworks) and the domestic level of the ASEAN Member States.

SEA is a sub-region of Asia comprising eleven states of extensive diversity in religion, culture, ethnicity, and history. The countries in this sub-region are Brunei, Burma (Myanmar), Cambodia, East Timor, Indonesia, Laos, Malaysia, the Philippines, Singapore, Thailand, and Viet Nam. ASEAN was established as a regional body on 8 August 1976 in Bangkok, with the primary aims of accelerating the Member States' economic growth, promoting regional peace and stability, and promoting active collaboration and assistance in various sectors on matters of common interest to its Member States.[44] Out of these eleven countries, only East Timor is not a Member State of ASEAN.

Notwithstanding the presence of evidence of widespread statelessness in SEA, a limited access to and availability of data on the size, situation, legal resources, and practices relating to nationality, birth registration and statelessness in this region

---

[43] M. Manly, 'UNHCR's Mandate and Activities to Address Statelessness' in A. Edwards & L. van Waas (Eds.), *Nationality and Statelessness under International Law* (Cambridge: Cambridge University Press, 2014), p 108.

[44] *About ASEAN: Overview.* Retrieved from http://asean.org/asean/about-asean/overview/ [Accessed 10 February 2014].

presents a significant challenge throughout the course of research leading to this publication. UNHCR previously acknowledged the absence of reliable statistical data on stateless populations in countries such as Cambodia, Indonesia, Lao PDR, Singapore, and Timor-Leste.[45] The extent of coverage of the countries studied herein is further delimited by the availability of existing primary data and secondary literature in the English language.

Given the nature of desk review, the foregoing constraints, and the constantly-updated legislation in the areas studied herein, the evaluation of the legal frameworks and available practices on nationality and birth registration, including within the ASEAN Member States, which have for the most part been updated as of 2018–2019 (except for some recent developments able to be accommodated as of 2020–2021), some analyses may run the risk of incompleteness, inaccuracy, or bias. It is, therefore, recommended that more exhaustive research is conducted to verify particular information and original sources, which are more current and updated for purposes of dissemination and publication.

[45] N. Oakeshott & Bongkot Napaumporn, 'Statelessness in South East Asia', Presentation Slides, Regional Statelessness Course: South East Asia Focus, Bangkok, Thailand, 4–8 November 2013.

Chapter 2
Protection against Statelessness at Birth: Definitions, Key Concepts, and Legal Framework

2.1 Introduction

This chapter undertakes the preliminary tasks of distilling and overviewing the underlying key concepts, definitions, applicable legal rules, principles and soft norms underpinning statelessness, and the right to a nationality and avoidance of statelessness, both at the international and regional levels. The aim of this chapter is to systematically identify and clarify the normative standards, by examining their evolution, significance, and implications, so as to better understand their contextual relevance and application within the domain of prevention of childhood statelessness. This chapter has two parts. The first part expounds and clarifies the theoretical imperatives, namely, the definitions, concepts, and circumstances underscoring nationality, statelessness, and childhood statelessness. It importantly weaves into the analysis the initial challenge of building agreed definitions and understanding of the key concepts in working out effective strategies to solve statelessness. This prior discussion shall lead to a more intensive tracing and appraisal of an ordering development of the rights to a nationality and birth registration, both of which constitute the legal safeguards to prevent statelessness and the right to a legal identity. Meanwhile, the fundamental aim of the second part is to perform a more narrowed search for a rational, consistent, and coherent set of the legal framework, including the guiding principles that govern the core subject of the legal protection of children against statelessness at birth. Possible causes for concern, shortcomings, and anomalies in the components of the identified legal framework for the protection of children against statelessness shall also be succinctly examined, in order to grasp and appreciate the potentials and limits of the current international legal framework in curtailing statelessness at birth.

R. M. Razali, *Safeguarding Against Statelessness at Birth*,
https://doi.org/10.1007/978-981-19-5371-2_2

2.2 Definitions and Key Concepts

The debate concerning the broad subject of statelessness beginning with its emergence right up to its solution essentially revolves around the concept of the right to a nationality. The acquisition and retention of 'nationality' are essential to prevent and reduce the incidence of statelessness among the population in this centuries-old nation-state system. The right to a nationality is a fundamental human right and serves as an underlying safeguard against statelessness as provided in the international instruments, including the 1961 Convention.

1. **Nationality and Citizenship**

Nationality denotes the legal bond between an individual and a state. Nationality and citizenship are often used synonymously in literature to delineate membership of a state, with its resulting conferral of certain rights, imposition of certain obligations, and expectation of loyalty towards particular principles.[1]

In his seminal work, 'Nationality and Statelessness in International Law', Weis indicated that 'nationality' is a politico-legal term that is synonymous with 'subject' and 'citizenship'.[2] Historically in English law and its feudal context, the term 'subject' entails a person's relationship with its Sovereign that is determined by territoriality and the bond of allegiance of the subject to the King.[3] In the Roman conception, however, nationality is a matter of a genuine personal relationship established through descent. Such different approaches have traditionally formed the backbone of the *jus sanguinis* principle of nationality, mainly prevailing in Roman law countries, and *jus soli*, widely ascribed to by countries in the common law system.[4] Van Panhuys alludes to the customary international law character of these two principles of nationality attribution and acquisition, which until now remain the dominant state practice.[5]

From the international legal standpoint, the link between a person and a state, and its underlying substratum are well captured in the Nottebohm Case (Liechtenstein

[1] C.A. Batchelor, 'Stateless Persons: Some Gaps In International Protection', *International Journal of Refugee Law*, 7(2) (1995), p 234–35.

[2] P. Weis, *Nationality and Statelessness in International Law,* 2nd Ed (The Netherlands: Sijthoff & Noordhoff International, 1979), p 4.

[3] P. Weis, *Nationality and Statelessness in International Law,* 2nd Ed (The Netherlands: Sijthoff & Noordhoff International, 1979). The common law describes this inherent, permanent, and insoluble bond as the doctrine of 'nemo potest exuere patriam', i.e. 'no man may abjure his country'. In the second half of the nineteenth century, this insoluble allegiance was gradually substituted with the exclusive yet transmutable concept of allegiance. See Sir William Blackstone, *Commentaries on the Laws of England* (117) (1884), as quoted in footnote 49 in K. Rubenstein & D. Adler, 'International Citizenship: The Future of Nationality in a Globalized World', *Indiana Journal of Global Legal Studies*, 7(2) (2000), p 530–531.

[4] P. Weis, *Nationality and Statelessness in International Law,* 2nd Ed (The Netherlands: Sijthoff & Noordhoff International, 1979), p 4.

[5] H.F. v. Panhuys, 1959, *The Role of Nationality in International Law* (Leyden: A.W. Sythoff, 1959), pp 160–161 as quoted in L. van Waas, *Nationality Matters: Statelessness under International Law* (School of Human Rights Research Series, V. 29, 2008), p 17.

v Guatemala) (the Nottebohm case).[6] The International Court of Justice (ICJ) in its decision views nationality in the following sense:

> According to the practice of States, to the arbitral and judicial decisions and to the opinion of writers, nationality is a legal bond having as its basis a social and genuine connection of existence, interests and sentiments, together with the existence of rights and duties.[7]

The social and genuine link here refers to 'social fact of attachment', evidenced by a number of different 'linking points': place of birth, descent, residency, family affiliations, language, and ethnicity.[8] Based on the judgment in the Nottebohm Case, the lack of a 'genuine link' between an individual and a state disqualifies the state from exercising its diplomatic protection on behalf of that individual.

Sloane, however, observes that the 'genuine link' theory sits uneasily with the positive law on nationality that confers upon states a wide enjoyment of power to ascribe nationality.[9] Quoting critics of the genuine link theory, inter alia, the dissenting opinion of Judge Read in the Nottebohm Case, it would appear that 'thousands or even millions of Chinese, French, British and Dutch nationals were apparently excluded from diplomatic protection by the majority's new theory'.[10] In an age where cross-border migration is pervasive, many migrants could, therefore, risk losing diplomatic protection for lacking adequate genuine link with the state of origin.

Conversely, it has been argued that the technical legal approach to addressing statelessness bypasses the questions of sense of belonging and factual existence and link,[11] denying statelessness as a human problem.[12] In the context of displaced children, scepticism, however, has been expressed over whether the genuine link theory can be said to apply to a case of a refugee child born and raised abroad in her state of refuge. This uncertainty is depicted in the scenario below:

> Can we talk about social attachment or a genuine connection of existence with reciprocal rights in the case of a 12-year-old Somali refugee child living in Europe, who has never been to Somalia, and has neither a chance to be registered as a Somali national by the competent Somali authority, nor a realistic prospective to ever return there to live? This is doubtful.[13]

---

[6] The *Nottebohm Case (Liechtenstein v. Guatemala),* 1955 ICJ Reports 4.

[7] *The Nottebohm Case (Liechtenstein v. Guatemala)*, 1955 ICJ Reports 4.

[8] L. van Waas, *Nationality Matters: Statelessness under International Law* (School of Human Rights Research Series, V. 29, 2008), p 32.

[9] R.D. Sloane, 'Breaking the Genuine Link: The Contemporary International Legal Regulation of Nationality', *Harvard International Law Journal*, 50 (2009), pp 17–19.

[10] *Nottebohm (Liechtenstein v. Guatemala)*, 1955 ICJ 4, 44, as quoted in footnote 96 by R. D. Sloane, 'Breaking The Genuine Link: The Contemporary International Legal Regulation of Nationality'.

[11] *The Nottebohm Case (Liechtenstein v Guatemala),* 1955 ICJ Reports 4.

[12] C.A. Batchelor, 'Developments in International Law: The Avoidance of Statelessness through Positive Application of the Right to a Nationality' (2000), *1st European Conference on Nationality - Trends and Developments in National and International Law on Nationality*, Strasbourg, European Convention on Nationality, (1997), p 50.

[13] G. Gyulai, 'The Long-Overlooked Mystery of Refugee Children's Nationality' in Institute on Statelessness and Inclusion, *The World's Stateless Children* (2017). Retrieved from http://children.worldsstateless.org/3/migration-displacement-and-childhood-statelessness/the-long-overlooked-mystery-of-refugee-childrens-nationality.html [Accessed 5 July 2017].

Scholars like Spiro call for the significance of Nottebohm to be limited to the field of diplomatic protection, as opposed to the specific context of determination of one's membership of a sovereign nation.[14] While 'genuine connection' is still considered a factor for sustaining status as a national, it is inadequate to create the legal status of nationality.[15]A rethink of the existing approach to determining citizenship has also been suggested. Manby opines that for one to have a meaningful citizenship, he or she should be allowed to renounce the nationality of their ancestral country and instead apply for the nationality of the country of their habitual residence.

> Commonly, the right to change nationality is interpreted in a limited sense to mean that a state should not prevent a national from renouncing nationality, provided that statelessness is not a result. It has not, to date, been found by any international authority to include the duty of a state to provide access to nationality for a person who as a matter of fact has the closest connections to that state, but may have the (even theoretical) right to another nationality.[16]

For clarity purposes, although the terms 'citizenship' and 'nationality' are employed across a range of academic disciplines, this book is concerned with legal citizenship in its assessment of protection against childhood statelessness, denoting the formal status of membership in a state. Instead of the genuine link principle, the 1954 Convention adopts a concept of nationality that symbolises 'a formal link, of a political and legal character between an individual and a certain state'.[17] The definition of 'national' in Article 1(1) of the 1954 Convention, therefore, does not entail the requirement of 'genuine and effective link' with the state of one's nationality.[18] This book shall also use the terms 'nationality' and 'citizenship' interchangeably. It echoes the view that contemporary scholars, particularly those in the sphere of human rights, do not see how a strict distinction between the two terms can be practically helpful. Nowadays, nationality and citizenship are created and governed by

---

[14] See P.J. Spiro, 'Citizenship, Nationality, and Statelessness' in V. Chetail & C. Bauloz, *Research Handbook on International Law and Migration* (London: Edward Elgar Publishing, 2014), p 284. The International Law Commission (ILC) also adopts the view that the genuine link requirement is to be limited to the facts of the Nottebohm case, in particular, the fact that the ties between Mr. Nottebohm and Lichtenstein were 'extremely tenuous', precluding the latter from exercising its diplomatic protection over the former. See International Law Commission, *Articles on Diplomatic Protection with Commentaries* (2006), p 32–33. Retrieved from http://untreaty.un.org/ilc/guide/9_8.htm [Accessed 1 April 2016].

[15] E. Fripp, *Nationality and Statelessness in the International Law of Refugee Status* (Oxford and Portland: Bloomsbury, 2016), p 6.

[16] See B. Manby, *Citizenship and Statelessness in Africa: The Law and Politics of Belonging* (2015), p 456.

[17] UNHCR, *Guidelines on Statelessness No.1: The definition of 'Stateless Person' in Article 1(1) of the 1954 Convention relating to the Status of Stateless Persons* (Guidelines No. 1) (2012). Retrieved from http://www.refworld.org/docid/4f4371b82.html [Accessed 6 January 2014], para 45.

[18] On a related note, a paradigm transition effected through progressive development of international law from the previous rule denying protection to stateless persons as proclaimed in *Dickson Car Wheel Company v. United Mexican States* (1931) (Reports of International Arbitral Awards Vol. IV 678) is recognised under Articles 8 (2) and 8(3) of the ILC's Draft Articles. States now are able to exercise their diplomatic protection over refugees and stateless persons based on their ties of lawful and habitual residence with the states.

the domestic law of the state. The subjects are usually codified as part of the constitutional law considering their significance to citizens.[19] As such, for the most part, the content and scope of their meanings ultimately depend on the context of one's country's citizenship law and the limits set by international law.[20]

(a) ***Modes of Acquisition of Nationality at Birth and Later in Life***

The main two modes of nationality attribution and acquisition at birth are through birth in the territory, and parentage or familial blood ties. Other ties forming the basis of nationality attribution and acquisition include marriage and adoption, being the secondary facts of attachment that states commonly recognise.[21] A certain period of residence and additional requirements such as language proficiency and good character are the conditions for naturalisation, the main method to attribute nationality to non-citizens later in life.[22] Adoption by, or marriage to a national, may be strong reasons to allow for facilitated naturalisation on the principle of family unity.[23]

Birthright citizenship that is granted based on one's birthplace on a territory is essentially derived from *jus soli* ('law of the soil'), a tenet that arose out of the common law of England. As for *jus sanguinis* ('law of blood'), citizenship is conferred through descent, which is principally determined by the parental nationality of both or either parent or of distant ancestors.[24]

At present, one doctrine may be preferred over the other, but the mix of both has been apparent in many state policies on the grant of nationality at birth.[25] Other grounds of nationality include *jus domicile*, also known as 'the law of residence', serving as the common basis for naturalisation. This nationality doctrine flows from an attachment that a non-citizen ordinarily develops with a state after a certain period

[19] E. Fripp, *Nationality and Statelessness in the International Law of Refugee Status* (Oxford and Portland: Bloomsbury, 2016), p 9.

[20] A. Edwards & L. van Waas, *Nationality and Statelessness under International Law* (2014), p 14.

[21] L. van Waas, *Nationality Matters: Statelessness under International Law* (School of Human Rights Research Series, V. 29, 2008), p 32.

[22] L. van Waas, *Nationality Matters: Statelessness Under International Law* (School of Human Rights Research Series, V. 29, 2008).

[23] R. Bauböck et al., *Acquisition and Loss of Nationality. Policies and Trends in 15 European States. Summary and Recommendations* (Eds.) (2006), p 34. Retrieved from http://www.ft.dk/samling/20051/almdel/ifu/bilag/81/261233.pdf [Accessed 25 April 2015].

[24] S. Konsiki, 'State of Uncertainty: Citizenship, Statelessness, and Discrimination in the Dominican Republic', *Boston College International & Comparative Law Review*, 32(2) (2009), p 377–398. The former concept is dominantly practised in countries of immigration, whereas the latter prevails in 'emigration states', particularly in Europe, Asian, and Arab nations. See also S. Castles & A. Davidson, *Citizenship and Migration: Globalization and the Politics of Belonging* (London: MacMillan Press, 2000), p 85; L. van Waas, *Nationality Matters: Statelessness under International Law* (School of Human Rights Research Series, Vol. 29, 2008), p 33.

[25] L. van Waas, *Nationality Matters: Statelessness under International Law* (School of Human Rights Research Series, Vol. 29, 2008), p 33.

of migration and residence, reflecting an element of choice rather than 'an accident of birth', as in the case of *jus soli* and *jus sanguinis*.[26]

In relation to children's right to a nationality, de Groot stresses the importance of children securing their nationality at birth or as soon after birth, as clearly underlined by Article 7(1) CRC. Article 7(1) CRC provides

> The child shall be registered immediately after birth and shall have the right from birth to a name, the right to acquire a nationality and as far as possible, the right to know and be cared for by his or her parents.

The above provision expands the scope of its predecessor, Principle 3 of the UN Declaration of the Rights of the Child that reads, 'The child shall be entitled from his birth to a name and a nationality'.[27] Failure of a child to acquire or be attributed a nationality at birth sends a strong signal that the child is highly likely to be rendered stateless for a protracted period, which could outspread his or her lifetime with detrimental impacts.[28] The grant of nationality at birth to children who would otherwise be stateless is perhaps the best tool to not only eradicate statelessness, but also to prevent its intergenerational transmission.[29]

Without a nationality, a child will experience childhood statelessness, which means losing his key to access and benefit from a wide range of basic protections and assistance, from schooling and healthcare, to social assistance and adequate living standards.[30] Weis further associates the effects of a person's failure to acquire a nationality at birth ex lege or by operation of law with 'original' or 'absolute statelessness'.[31] This is contrasted with the situation of 'subsequent' or 'relative' statelessness, which is experienced by a person losing his or her nationality without

---

[26] H. Bauder, 'Jus Domicile: In Pursuit of a Citizenship of Equality and Social Justice', *Journal of International Political Theory*, V. 8(1–2) (2012), p 188.

[27] *Declaration of the Rights of the Child*, General Assembly Resolution 1386 (XIV), UN Doc. A/RES/14/1386, New York: United Nations, 1959. This document is the basis for the promulgation of CRC, adopted 30 years later by the UN General Assembly in 1990.

[28] G.R. de Groot, Children, 'Their Right to a Nationality and Child Statelessness' in A. Edwards & L. van Waas (Eds.), *Nationality and Statelessness under International Law* (Cambridge: Cambridge University Press, 2014), p 144. Nationality that a person acquires from birth as of right connotes 'nationality of origin' (*nationalité d'origine*) as opposed to naturalisation, for instance, yet this must not be confused with citizenship by birth (i.e. citizenship by birth in a country, as opposed to citizenship by descent), which is no longer in force in most countries nowadays. See B. Manby, *Nationality, Migration, and Statelessness in West Africa: A study for UNHCR and IOM* (2015), p iv. Retrieved from http://www.unhcr.org/ecowas2015/Nationality-Migration-and-Statelessness-in-West-Africa-REPORT-EN.pdf [Accessed 16 December 2015].

[29] European Network on Statelessness, *No Child Should be Stateless* (2015) http://www.statelessness.eu/sites/www.statelessness.eu/files/ENS_NoChildStateless_final.pdf [10 January 2016]. See the excerpt quoting Nils Muižnieks at p 11.

[30] G.R. de Groot, 'Children, Their Right to a Nationality and Child Statelessness' in A. Edwards & L. van Waas (Eds.), *Nationality and Statelessness under International Law* (Cambridge: Cambridge University Press, 2014), p 144.

[31] P. Weis, *Nationality and Statelessness in International Law*, 2nd Ed (The Netherlands: Sijthoff & Noordhoff International, 1979), p 162.

obtaining another. Both situations could lead to de jure statelessness, if the affected person remains without any nationality at all.[32]

(b) **Modes of Loss and Deprivation of Nationality leading to Statelessness**

The 1961 Convention regulates the rules on how nationality can be lost or deprived, causing one to experience statelessness. Nationality may be lost either automatically or through deprivation, the latter either as a result of unilateral legal or administrative acts.[33] An automatic loss of nationality usually results from a change in one's personal status following marriage, termination of marriage, legitimation, and recognition or adoption.[34] Long residence abroad and failure to renew one's passport, register with a consular or diplomatic office, or notify one's intention to keep his or her nationality may also lead to an automatic loss of nationality.[35]

Renunciation, a voluntary act to give up one's nationality in favour of another, as well as by acquisition of another nationality in countries where dual or multiple nationalities is barred, may as well trigger loss of nationality.[36] On the other hand, deprivation of nationality could occur in a number of circumstances. Such include when nationality has been obtained by fraud or misrepresentation, as well as due to disloyalty to the state, or commission of actions that are seriously prejudicial to the interest of the state.[37] In principle, loss, renunciation, and deprivation of nationality that results in statelessness are not prohibited if the person concerned could acquire another nationality.[38] However, arbitrary deprivation on racial, ethnic, religious, or political grounds is strictly prohibited, regardless of whether it leads to statelessness or not.[39]

2. **Examining Concepts around Statelessness: 'Stateless Persons', 'At Risk of Statelessness', 'Undetermined Nationality', and 'Otherwise Stateless'**

The discussion moves on to conceptually explore a number of notions underpinning statelessness. These notions have been subject to varying and often complex interpretations, the permutations of which constitute part of the initial challenges in the identification of stateless persons.

(a) ***Stateless Persons***

Article 1(1) of the 1954 Convention defines a stateless person inversely as 'a person who is not considered as a national by any State under the operation of its law'. The

[32] P. Weis, *Nationality and Statelessness in International Law,* 2nd Ed (The Netherlands: Sijthoff & Noordhoff International, 1979), p 162.

[33] P. Weis, *Nationality and Statelessness in International Law,* 2nd Ed (The Netherlands: Sijthoff & Noordhoff International, 1979), p 115.

[34] Article 5 of the 1961 Convention.

[35] Article 7(3) of the 1961 Convention.

[36] Articles 7(1) and (2) of the 1961 Convention.

[37] Article 8 of the 1961 Convention.

[38] Article 7 (2) of the 1961 Statelessness Convention.

[39] Article 9 of the 1961 Statelessness Convention.

International Law Commission (ILC) has also affirmed this definition 'as having acquired a customary nature'.[40] It constitutes the starting point at which states may decide to whom the 1954 Convention applies at the national level, and serves to be a common standard for defining statelessness and facilitating harmonisation of approaches as between states.[41] An identification of who a stateless person is relates to all the other three pillars of response to statelessness, namely, prevention of statelessness (through identification of gaps in legislation that may create stateless persons), reduction (by allowing the identified stateless persons to be targeted for solutions), and protection (by allowing stateless persons including persons born to them to receive protection of their human rights).[42]

The category of statelessness as reflected in Article 1(1) of the 1954 Convention is typically referred to as *de jure* statelessness, although it is to be noted that the term itself appears nowhere in the 1954 instrument.[43] A Study of Statelessness undertaken by the United Nations Economic and Social Council (ECOSOC) refers to *de jure* stateless as 'persons who are not nationals of any State, either because at birth or subsequently, they were not given any nationality, or because during their lifetime they lost their own nationality and did not acquire a new one'.[44]

Some scholars and practitioners criticise the above definition for being too narrow, and in total disregard of the attribute and usefulness of one's citizenship. They feel that the insufficient coverage of the definition of statelessness hints a gap in the protection of *de facto* stateless persons,[45] being an issue of 'rightlessness', or the

---

[40] International Law Commission, *Articles on Diplomatic Protection with Commentaries* (2006), p 49. Retrieved from http://untreaty.un.org/ilc/guide/9_8.htm [1 April 2016]. Fisher in her article identified a number of selected cases that to a large extent favour the practice of adjudicators establishing a 'stateless person' or otherwise, by examining no more than the codified nationality law of the individual's country of origin, i.e. the country with which the individual may have a link, either through birth, heritage, or residence. Based on the author's analysis, the phrase 'operation of law' appears to be largely omitted in defining 'statelessness', such as the practice of birth registration. See B. L. Fisher, 'The Operation of Law in Statelessness Determinations under the 1954 Statelessness Convention', *Wisconsin International Law Journal,* V. 33 (2015), p 254.

[41] UNHCR, *The 1954 Convention relating to the Status of Stateless Persons: Implementation within the European Union Member States and Recommendations for Harmonisation* (2003). Retrieved from http://www.refworld.org/docid/415c3cfb4.html [19 October 2013].

[42] UNHCR, *Stateless Actions—Identification.* Retrieved from http://www.unhcr.org/pages/49c3646c16d.html [10 December 2013].

[43] UNHCR in its Guidelines on Statelessness No.1 pertaining to its interpretive legal guidance on the definition of 'stateless person' in Article 1(1) of the 1954 Convention avoids qualifying stateless persons as defined in Article 1(1) as *de jure* stateless persons as that term is never referred to in the treaty itself. See para 8 of Section II (a), Guidelines No. 1.

[44] *A Study of Statelessness.* UN Doc. E/1112; E/1112/Add.1 (New York: United Nations, 1949). See para III.1.

[45] C. A. Batchelor, 'Stateless Persons: Some Gaps in International Protection', *International Journal of Refugee Law*, 7(2)(1995), pp 232–259; J. Bhabha, 'Arendt's Children: Do Today's Migrant Children have a Right to have Rights?', *Human Rights Quarterly*, 31(2) (2009), pp 410–451; J. Bhabha (Ed.), *Children Without a State: A Global Human Rights Challenge* (2011); A. Macklin, 'Who Is the Citizen's Other? Considering the Heft of Citizenship', *Theoretical Inquiries in Law*, V. 8(2) (2007), pp 334–366; D. Weissbrodt & C. Clay, 'The Human Rights of Stateless Persons',

violation of the rights attached to nationality, as opposed to the violation of the right to nationality itself.[46] The former is seen as a real and widespread problem in practice.[47]

While a clear definition is provided by the 1954 Convention with respect to *de jure* statelessness, unpacking the definition of '*de facto* statelessness' proves to be rather a strenuous exercise, mainly due to the absence of its legal definition, how statelessness was first perceived by the international community, and how it has gradually evolved to encapsulate a wider category of persons without a meaningful nationality. The debate over its definitions is relevant not only in the context of appreciating the scope of persons entitled to the protection as a 'stateless person' under the 1954 Convention, but also in relation to who should be targeted for prevention and reduction of statelessness.

Manley Hudson, the Special Rapporteur of ILC on the subject of nationality and statelessness, warns that official solution alone might decrease the number of stateless persons, but not the number of unprotected persons.[48] Batchelor strongly calls for the need to see the gap and treat it as an issue of protection rather than the technical question of recognition under the law.[49] Weis further contends that both the terms *de jure* and *de facto* stateless are misleading, for it is the legal status that is addressed rather than the protection. He, in turn, suggests the use of the terms '*de jure* unprotected person' and '*de facto* unprotected person'.[50]

De facto statelessness was excluded from the scope of the 1954 Convention as its drafters were working under the assumption that such denoted refugees, whose protection needs were already catered for by the 1951 Refugee Convention. Hence a strict legal definition was adopted, excluding the question of persecution from the definition of statelessness in order to avoid the overlap between the 1951 Convention and the 1954 Convention.[51]

Notwithstanding, *de facto* statelessness appears both in the Final Acts of the 1954 and 1961 Conventions. The Final Act of the 1954 Convention provides a recommendation for the Contracting States to extend protections at par with those received by (*de jure*) stateless persons. Such *de facto* stateless persons as understood by the drafters were persons who have renounced the protection of the State of which

---

Human Rights Quarterly, V. 28(1) (2006), pp 245–276; P. Weis, *Nationality and Statelessness in International Law,* 2nd Ed (The Netherlands: Sijthoff & Noordhoff International, 1979).

[46] M. Wells-Greco, *The Status of Children from Inter-Country Surrogacy Arrangements: The Past, The Present, The Future* (2016), p 443.

[47] L. van Waas, *Nationality Matters: Statelessness under International Law* (School of Human Rights Research Series, V. 29, 2008), p 22.

[48] M. O. Hudson, 'Nationality, Including Statelessness', UN Doc. A/CN 4/50. Extracted from the *Yearbook of the International Law Commission, V. II* (1952), p 49. Retrieved from http://legal.un.org/ilc/documentation/english/a_Cn4_50.pdf [1 April 2016].

[49] C.A. Batchelor, 'Stateless Persons: Some Gaps in International Protection', p 233–234.

[50] P. Weis, *Nationality and Statelessness in International Law,* 2nd Ed, p 164.

[51] D. Weissbrodt & C. Clay, 'The Human Rights of Stateless Persons', p 252; C. A. Batchelor, 'Statelessness and the Problem of Resolving Nationality Status', p 172.

they are nationals.[52] The 1961 Convention that calls for prevention and reduction of statelessness acknowledges the concept of persons with ineffective nationality by also recommending (as opposed to obligating) the Contracting States to extend to them similar treatment as is accorded to *de jure* stateless, to enable them to acquire a nationality.[53]

A broader definition of '*de facto* stateless persons' was in fact put forward in 'A Study of Statelessness' by the United Nations in 1949, capturing not only those who are refused protection by the country of their nationality as indicated in the Final Act of the 1954 Convention, but also persons who renounce such protection. In both situations, the reference to 'protection' relates only to the protection of nationals who are abroad.[54] Consequently, *de facto* statelessness correlates strongly with individuals in the context of migration, compared to persons who may have ineffective nationality in their own country of habitual residence, commonly termed the '*in situ* stateless'.

Hugh Massey concludes his 2010 study on 'UNHCR and de facto Statelessness' by further clarifying that *de facto* stateless persons must not only be outside of their country of nationality, but also must demonstrate (i) their inability to avail the diplomatic and consular protections generally by their state of nationality, including their return to the state of nationality and (ii) for valid reasons, their unwillingness to avail themselves of the protection of their country of nationality.[55]

What constitutes valid reasons may differ between countries concerned. What is certain is that, refusing one's country's protection when such is available cannot constitute a valid reason for renouncing the protection of the person's country of

---

[52] Article 1 of the Final Act of the 1954 Convention provides that the Conference of Plenipotentiaries 'Recommends that each Contracting State, when it recognises as valid the reasons for which a person has renounced the protection of the State of which he is a national, consider sympathetically the possibility of according to that person the treatment which the Convention accords to stateless persons'.

[53] Resolution I, Final Act of the 1961 Convention provides: 'The Conference recommends that persons who are stateless *de facto* should as far as possible be treated as stateless *de jure* to enable them to acquire an effective nationality'.

[54] *A Study of Statelessness,* UN Doc. E/1112; E/1112/Add.1 (New York: United Nations, 1949), see para III.2. The recommendations put forward by this Study became the basis for the ECOSOC, through resolution 248 B (IX) of 8 August 1949, to appoint and request an ad hoc committee consisting of representatives of 13 Governments to consider, among others, measures of eliminating the problem of statelessness, including the desirability of the ILC to prepare a study and make recommendations on this subject. See United Nations Audiovisual Library of International Law, *Convention on the Reduction of Statelessness* (2011). Retrieved from http://legal.un.org/avl/pdf/ha/crs/crs_ph_e.pdf [21 September 2014]. See also the background paper prepared for the Expert Meeting on the Concept of Stateless Persons under International Law by Hugh Massey in April 2010. H. Massey, *UNHCR and De Facto Statelessness* (2010), p 6.

[55] H. Massey, *UNHCR and De Facto Statelessness* (2010), p 61; K. Utsymenko, *Defining Statelessness: The Conception of the Definition and Why It Matters Today*, Thesis submitted in partial fulfilment of the requirements for bachelor degree in human rights, Columbia University in the City of New York (2013), p 17–18.

nationality.[56] Inability to avail oneself of protection, on the other hand, signifies reasons beyond a person's control, such as when the country is in a state of war or does not have diplomatic or consular ties with the country of refuge.[57]

The aforementioned explanations have been illustrated in Massey's study in the context of refugees. As for undocumented migrants, he holds the view that there must be 'a request for, and a refusal for protection before it can be established that a given nationality is ineffective'.[58] It also depends on whether the country of nationality cooperates in identifying the nationality of a particular individual and/or permits his or her return.[59] Massey's findings have been echoed and adopted by the Expert Meeting on the Concept of Stateless Persons under International Law ('Prato Conclusions' 2010). The term 'de facto' must be defined on the basis of the protection by a state to its nationals abroad, with two key points of inability and unwillingness to avail oneself of the protection of his state underpinning its concept.[60] Protracted non-cooperation including silence or lack of response to the host country's communication may also be treated as a refusal for protection in this regard.[61]

Recent debates advance the claim that arguments over the limited scope of *de jure* statelessness under Article 1(1) of the 1954 Convention are untenable. Various situations coming under 'de facto statelessness' could have in fact transmuted into those of *de jure* statelessness under the 1954 Convention. In essence, this suggests that those of undetermined nationality, for instance, might have already met the requirement of 'not considered as a national under the operation of [any state's] law'.[62] Such determination centrally takes into account the manner of how a particular state interprets and applies its domestic law on nationality.[63] For a person deemed citizen by the state, yet is deprived of the rights attached to citizenship, such as voting

---

[56] H. Massey, *UNHCR and De Facto Statelessness* (2010), p 62; S. Gruberg, 'De facto Statelessness Among Undocumented Migrants in Greece', *Georgetown Journal on Poverty & Law*, 18(3) (2011), p 536–537.

[57] H. Massey, *UNHCR and De Facto Statelessness* (2010), p 65.

[58] H. Massey, *UNHCR and De Facto Statelessness* (2010), see para 11.5 at p 65.

[59] H. Massey, *UNHCR and De Facto Statelessness* (2010), p 65. This follows the logic of state's recognition of an individual's statelessness status, which explains the coverage of stateless persons by UNHCR that prioritises de jure rather than de facto stateless. See B.K. Blitz, Protection through Revisionism? In M.K. Land, K.R. Libal & J.R Chambers (Eds), *Beyond Borders: The Human Rights of Non-Citizens at Home and Abroad*, Cambridge: Cambridge University Press, p 71–93.

[60] See para 2 of Part A at p 6 of the text of the Summary Conclusions cited as UNHCR, *Expert Meeting—The Concept of Stateless Persons under International Law* (Prato Conclusions) (2010).

[61] See part II (D) of the text of the Prato Conclusions, p 7.

[62] L. van Waas, 'The UN Statelessness Conventions' in A. Edwards & L. van Waas (Eds.), *Nationality and Statelessness under International Law* (Cambridge: Cambridge University Press, 2014), p 81; A. Harvey, 'Statelessness: The "De facto" Statelessness Debate', pp 257–258, at p 259.

[63] This is in line with UNHCR, Guidelines No.1 on the definition of 'Stateless Person' in Article 1(1) of the 1954 Convention, see para 17.

and property ownership, human rights violation is argued to be his or her plight, not *de facto* statelessness.[64]

For UNHCR, mischaracterisation is to be avoided, so that persons recognised to be stateless under the 1954 Convention would not be excluded from the protections offered by the said Convention for being labelled '*de facto* stateless'.[65] Moreover, simply classifying persons suffering from ineffective nationality as stateless would undermine their legitimacy of claims to be treated as citizens similar to other fellow citizens, when their bond of nationality in fact remains.[66] Outside of UNHCR's statelessness refugee mandate which extends to *de facto* stateless refugees, the organisation's mandate on statelessness requires it to be more accurate in identifying the category of *de facto* stateless persons not only for protection objectives, but also for prevention and reduction of statelessness.[67]

(b) ***Undetermined Nationality***

The precise connection between lacking identity documents and statelessness is delicate.[68] Following the preceding arguments, one always finds problematic the category of 'persons of undetermined nationality', normally referring to individuals having difficulties proving their nationality status or the lack of it. In the face of little implementation of statelessness determination and/or nationality verification by states, they appear largely to sit between a rock and a hard place in terms of their legal status and protection. For a person who is abroad and without national protection, at the same time not being (officially) stateless and neither a refugee, international protection will be a matter of state's discretion.[69] For a person whose tie to a country can be established as a matter of history if not of law, due to having been born there or having parents who hold its nationality, denying entitlements

---

[64] L. van Waas, 'The UN Statelessness Conventions' in A. Edwards & L. van Waas (Eds.), *Nationality and Statelessness under International Law* (Cambridge: Cambridge University Press, 2014); J. E. Tucker, 'Questioning De Facto Statelessness by Looking at De Facto Citizenship'. Retrieved from http://papers.ssrn.com/sol3/papers.cfm?abstract_id=2317141 [23 January 2014].

[65] UNHCR, *Handbook on Protection of Stateless Persons* (2014), para 7.

[66] J.E. Tucker, 'Questioning De Facto Statelessness by Looking at De Facto Citizenship', p 6. Retrieved from http://papers.ssrn.com/sol3/papers.cfm?abstract_id=2317141 [Accessed 21 January 2014].

[67] UN General Assembly, Office of the United Nations), para 7; UNHCR, *Conclusion on Identification, Prevention, and Reduction of Statelessness and* High Commissioner for Refugees, resolution adopted by the General Assembly, 9 February 1996. UN Doc. A/RES/50/152 (New York: UNGA), para 14; UN General Assembly, Office of the United Nations High Commissioner for Refugees: resolution adopted by the General Assembly, 25 January 2007. UN Doc. A/RES/61/137 (New York: UNGA, *Protection of Stateless Persons*, No. 106 (LVII). General Assembly Document. A/AC.96/1035 (Geneva: UNHCR).

[68] Institute on Statelessness and Inclusion, *The World's Stateless* (2014), p 85.

[69] L. van Waas, 'The UN Statelessness Conventions' in A. Edwards & L. van Waas (Eds.), *Nationality and Statelessness under International Law* (Cambridge: Cambridge University Press, 2014), p 81; H. Massey, *UNHCR and De Facto Statelessness* (2010), p 22.

deserved by other nationals may facilitate the acceptance that the person in question is not a national, and charges of discrimination against the state averted.[70]

Persons who are undocumented and of undetermined nationality and children born to them in countries devoid of mechanisms to identify their nationality or statelessness status are likely to remain in that default situation of uncertain nationality for a prolonged period. As Harvey points out in her analysis on the issue:

> Neither references to a person 'who formally possesses a nationality but where it is ineffective' nor the definition in UNHCR working paper (even if we subtract from it the requirement to be outside the country of one's nationality) copes with cases of persons of undetermined nationality.[71]

Although individuals may initially experience *de facto* statelessness, which is likened to a statelessness-like situation for their uncertain legal status, or inability to prove nationality, paragraph 12(f) of Part II of the Prato Conclusions adopts the position that unsettled cases of *de facto* statelessness, in particular, beyond two or more generations, may transform the *de facto* status into that of *de jure*.

For UNHCR, it internally reports persons of undetermined nationality based on the following indications:

(i) lack of possession of any nationality;
(ii) having links to more than one state on the basis of birth, descent, marriage, habitual residence; or
(iii) being perceived and treated by the authorities in the state of residence as someone having links leading to a claim of nationality of another state, on the basis of elements such as historic ties, race, ethnicity, language, or religion.[72]

Relying on the assumption that most cases of undetermined nationality could be resolved through provisions related to access to identity documentation and confirmation of nationality,[73] the mechanisms of proving and confirming one's nationality may still be fraught with 'the potential complexity of nationality issues and of the relative roles and capabilities of both applicant and the state of application'.[74] Importantly, the category of persons of undetermined nationality according to the foregoing criteria would not include those persons who 'are not cooperating with efforts to establish their identity or nationality'.[75] Despite the identification and internal reporting by UNHCR, where the determination procedure is not speedy, merely describing such persons as individuals who may turn out to be nationals/stateless would not

---

[70] A. Harvey, 'Statelessness: The "De facto" Statelessness Debate', p 257–258.

[71] A. Harvey, 'Statelessness: The "De facto" Statelessness Debate', p 261.

[72] R. Govil, 'Statelessness and Key Concepts', Presentation Slides, Workshop on Researching Statelessness and Citizenship in Asia and the Pacific, organised by UNHCR, Melbourne School of Government and Melbourne Law School, 27–29 January 2016, Melbourne.

[73] This corresponds with Action 8 of the Global Action Plan to End Statelessness: 2014–2024 that targets issuance of nationality documentation to those who are entitled to it. See UNHCR, *Global Action Plan to End Statelessness* (2014), p 4.

[74] E. Fripp, *Nationality and Statelessness in the International Law of Refugee Status* (2016), p 80.

[75] R. Govil, 'Statelessness and Key Concepts', Presentation Slides.

alleviate their statelessness-like situation and resolve their current and immediate predicament as persons who have no formal and confirmed nationality.[76] In effect, their continued invisibility and unrecorded existence pose obstacles to prevention and reduction of statelessness, contributing inter alia, to gaps and inaccuracies in the statistical information on stateless populations.[77]

(c) 'Persons at Risk of Statelessness' and 'Otherwise Stateless Children'

The semantics and concepts presented above contribute to the complexity of trying to pin down and classify those who are to be targeted for identification, prevention, reduction, and protection of stateless persons. To add to the permutations is the usage of another phrase of 'persons at risk of statelessness'. The term 'at risk of statelessness' is not defined in any legal instrument. It is often used to refer to persons, who, due to their circumstances, face diverse risks of becoming stateless. Risks that one confronts are a matter of degree. For instance, lacking a birth certificate does not always place a person to be at risk of statelessness.[78] Yet, for undocumented border populations and ethnic minorities who lack birth certificates, they could be considered to be at risk of statelessness due to their predisposition to vulnerability and marginalisation.[79]

The risk of statelessness is said to be the greatest among children born to stateless persons, and other marginalised groups unable to access civil registration systems, such as nomadic, migrant, and refugee populations.[80] Without an express obligation undertaken by states through their domestic legal frameworks to identify and determine their nationality; merely categorising them as being 'persons at risk of statelessness' is equally insufficient to fill the lacuna resulting from their unconfirmed and unproven legal identity.

In *Expelled Dominicans and Haitians versus Dominican Republic*,[81] the Inter-American Court of Human Rights had to decide on whether the Dominican-born persons of Haitian descent were not stateless as they derived Haitian nationality *jus sanguinis* under the Haitian Constitution. Instead of pronouncing the affected persons as stateless, as what the Court held in the previous *Yean and Bosico,*[82] as a result of the refusal of the Dominican Republic to register the girls, it declared the undocumented victims of mass deportation to Haiti without process in this case to be 'at risk of statelessness'. This finding, in turn, triggered the obligation to guarantee

[76] A. Harvey, 'Statelessness: The "De facto" Statelessness Debate', p 257–258 at p 261.

[77] L. van Waas, *The Situation of Stateless Persons in the Middle East and North Africa* (2010), p 17.

[78] Tilburg University, Statelessness Programme, 'Nationality: A Summary', Presentation Slides, Regional Statelessness Course: Southeast Asia Focus, 4–8 Nov 2013, Bangkok, Thailand.

[79] R. Govil, 'Statelessness and Key Concepts', Presentation Slides.

[80] UNHCR, *Conclusion on Civil Registration No. 111 (LXIV)*. Doc. A/AC.96/1035, Geneva: UNHCR (17 October 2013). Retrieved from http://www.unhcr.org/525fdfef9.pdf [16 December 2013].

[81] *Expelled Dominicans and Haitians v. Dominican Republic*, Preliminary Objections, Merits, Reparations and Costs, Judgment, Inter-Am. Ct. H.R. (ser. C) No. 282, p 157 (28 August 2014).

[82] *Yean and Bosico v. Dominican Republic* (Series C, Case 130, 8 September 2005).

Dominican nationality to such persons. It has been contended that the expansion of the scope of protection against statelessness via this case law for persons who face a 'risk of statelessness' is 'unnecessary' and the policy implications that ensue may 'cause the progressive development of norms to backfire'.[83] Such is because the approach promotes statelessness protection to *de facto* stateless (in this case, persons whose nationality was disputed), without conducting the prior statelessness status determination procedure for a finding of 'de jure statelessness' to actually trigger such protection.

The term 'otherwise stateless children' is particularly relevant to UNHCR's mandate on prevention of statelessness. The term is expressly spelled out in the 1961 Convention where the reference to it appears to be more specific in its formulation. A child would be 'an otherwise stateless' unless he or she is able to acquire either the nationality of his or her parent, or the nationality of the state in which he or she is born.[84] As shown in *Expelled Dominicans and Haitians versus Dominican Republic,* one could likewise imagine that establishing the negative, as into what degree must a child be proved to be otherwise stateless for not being able to acquire a nationality through his parent(s) or place of birth, would be no less clear and straightforward.

The various technical key concepts discussed in this section certainly create the challenging dynamics in the doctrinal and practical spheres of efforts to forge a common and coherent understanding on statelessness, and to guide states and other actors working to identify, prevent, and protect stateless persons. The extent to which these terms and concepts may influence the identification of statelessness and its risks for the purposes of protection and prevention of statelessness remains capricious at best. Predictably, statistics on stateless persons have proven to be difficult to come by and compile, among others, as a result of (i) unclear citizenship or nationality, including that which is often disputed and (ii) ambiguous concept of statelessness.[85]

One must not forget that individuals likely to be affected by statelessness are often marginalised populations who are unequipped with the knowledge, capacity, and resources to resolve their uncertain legal identity, a condition highly symptomatic of protraction of their lack of both established nationality and legal status. Countries that do not accede to the 1954 and 1961 Conventions are less likely to possess the

[83] D.C. Baluarte, 'The Risk of Statelessness: Reasserting a Rule for the Protection of the Right to a Nationality', *Yale Human Rights and Development Journal,* 19 (2017), p 78.

[84] See Articles 1 and 4 of the 1961 Convention, para 12 of Dakar Conclusions and para 18 of Guidelines No. 4.

[85] The reluctance of governments to collect and spread information, lack of desire of the stateless persons to obtain a nationality or to be identified due to fear of immigration consequences following their irregular status, and limited operational involvement of UNHCR have also been cited as the hurdles in the area of identification. See M. Lynch, *Lives on Hold: The Human Cost of Statelessness* (2005). Retrieved from http://www.refworld.org/docid/47a6eba00.html [9 August 2013], p 7. See further UNHCR, *Guidance Document on Measuring Stateless Populations* (2011), pp 4–5. Retrieved from http://www.refworld.org/docid/4f6887672.html [25 August 2014].

political will, knowledge, and capability to identify stateless persons.[86] Immigration law and policy frameworks devoid of the element of protections of stateless persons and refugees are normally the tools to deal with these individuals.[87] Poor economic condition, uneducated background, and discriminatory treatment together create intractable barriers in the steps to establish one's legal identity to avoid being stateless.

At the operational level, organisations like UNHCR may have to further cope with different conceptions of statelessness that states develop and adopt in policy and practice, which can often be heavily driven by an entitlement to a nationality under their national legal frameworks, without due and sufficient regards to human rights considerations.[88]

2.3 Childhood Statelessness: Causes and Consequences

Childhood statelessness has not been a topical issue until recently, in particular, after the visibility and momentum brought about by UNHCR's 2014 campaign on the elimination of statelessness. Prior to that, the predicament of children as a subcategory of stateless individuals did not really attract a sufficient level of attention from academics, human rights advocates, and those in policy-making positions. Regrettably, their rights to a name, identity, and nationality as underlined in the CRC constitute the least investigated facet in the overall spectrum of human rights and social scientific work pertaining to statelessness.[89]

'Childhood statelessness' somehow carries no scientific connotation in the literature, rather being a phrase that represents the various situations of children affected by statelessness, whether in their early or later stage of childhood. Maureen Lynch and Melanie Teff in their article published by the *Forced Migration Review* entitled 'Childhood Statelessness', and European Network on Statelessness in its article entitled 'Preventing Childhood Statelessness in Europe: Issues, Gaps and Good Practices', discuss the topic of 'childhood statelessness' without according any specific definition to that phrase itself.[90]

---

[86] L. van Waas, *The Situation of Stateless Persons in the Middle East and North Africa* (2010), p 18.

[87] L. van Waas, *The Situation of Stateless Persons in the Middle East and North Africa* (2010), p 18.

[88] N. Oakeshott, 'Statelessness in the Asia Pacific: Introduction and Context', Presentation Slides, Workshop on Researching Statelessness and Citizenship in the Asia Pacific, organised by UNHCR, Melbourne School of Government and Melbourne Law School, Melbourne, Australia, 27–29 January 2016.

[89] B.K. Blitz, 'Neither Seen nor Heard: Compound Deprivation among Stateless Children' in J. Bhabha (Ed.), *Children Without A State: A Global Human Rights Challenge* (Cambridge, Mass: MIT University Press, 2011), p 43.

[90] See M. Lynch & M. Teff, 'Childhood Statelessness', pp 31–33; European Network on Statelessness, *Preventing Childhood Statelessness in Europe: Issues, Gaps and Good Practices* (2014).

The following section canvasses some of the common and contemporary causes of childhood statelessness that begin at birth as well as the consequences of being in legal limbo for children.

1. **Common Causes of Childhood Statelessness**

There are many ways in which children may become stateless at birth. Children may be brought into this world stateless due to technical causes,[91] involving situations of conflict of nationality laws due to marriages between parents of different nationalities,[92] or as a consequence of migration.[93] In this regard, *jus sanguinis*, being the preferred doctrine of nationality attribution in European countries, Asia, as well as in the Middle East, has a major role in instigating statelessness. Not only it increases the chances of conflicts between two nationality laws, its notable element of heredity inevitably perpetuates statelessness among children across generations. Childhood statelessness, thus, becomes part of the vicious cycle in countries embracing the *jus sanguinis* nationality regime, as citizenship is predominantly granted to children if their either parent is a recognised citizen.[94]

Jus sanguinis also predisposes children born out of wedlock to statelessness at birth. Nationality laws based on *jus sanguinis* commonly differentiate between the ability of parents to confer nationality upon marital and non-marital children. In many countries including Denmark, Norway, Sweden, Switzerland, and Egypt, a non-marital child acquires the nationality of the mother as a natural consequence of

Retrieved from http://www.statelessness.eu/blog/prevention-statelessness-birth-%E2%80%93-adequate-nationality-law-inconsistent-implementation [Accessed 12 February 2015]. The term 'childhood' can be understood as a phase prior to the life cycle in which human beings fully assume adult roles and responsibilities. Meanwhile 'early childhood' according to the working definition proposed by the Committee on the Rights of the Child is the period below the age of 8 years, taking into account the general range of 4–7 years of age, prior to their transition to school. See para 4 of General Comment No. 7 (2005): Implementing Child Rights in Early Childhood. UN. Doc. CRC/C/GC/7/Rev.1, Geneva: CRC (2005), p 4.

[91] Technical causes are varied and can have impacts on creating statelessness at birth and later in life. Technical causes of statelessness basically refer to individual actions or the operation of domestic laws or policies that have the unintended result of creating statelessness. Refer to L. van Waas, *Nationality Matters: Statelessness under International Law,* (School of Human Rights Research Series, V 29), p 49.

[92] A straightforward illustration for this involves a person born in state A that adopts citizenship *jus sanguinis* or by descent to parents who are nationals in State B, which subscribes to the citizenship rule of *jus soli* or by place of birth. In such a situation, the child would be exposed to statelessness for not having the right to claim citizenship in state A as the parents are the nationals of state B. Neither could he or she claim to have citizenship in State B as the child was born outside the state. Incidents of statelessness resulting from conflicting nationality laws will be worsened by the highly complicated nature of nationality legislation and rules of both the first and second states. Refer to *W. Samore,* 'Statelessness as a Consequence of the Conflict of Nationality Laws', *American Journal of International Law,* 45(1951), p 476–477.

[93] UNHCR, *Under the Radar and Under Protected: The Urgent Need to Address Stateless Children's Rights*, p 7.

[94] Open Society Justice Initiative, *Children's Right to a Nationality*. Retrieved from http://www2.ohchr.org/english/issues/women/docs/OtherEntities/OSJIChildrenNationalityFactsheet.pdf [20 January 2014].

birth. If the mother is stateless, then the child would also be stateless, unless he or she could acquire the father's nationality through an establishment of paternal affiliation, either by way of recognition or judgment.[95] For another group of countries such as France and Belgium, a non-marital child acquires the nationality of the parents to whom affiliation can be established in the first place, either voluntarily or through recognition. Until such affiliation takes place, and in the event that the national law provides no safeguard for children of unknown parents to acquire a nationality, then the said child could be left stateless.[96]

In view of legal restrictions in many countries imposed on the rights of irregular migrants to marry and found a family, it is also common for informal and unregistered marriages to be contracted between irregularly staying-men and women, or between an irregular spouse and a national of a state. Consequently, children born out of such union technically become 'illegitimate' children, who would comparably be placed at risk of statelessness.

Children also face persecution on the basis of discrimination on the ground of their particular race, ethnicity, or religion. Ethnic groups that have been deprived of the right to birth registration, citizenship, and citizenship documentation include children of Roma in Central and Eastern Europe, Kurds living in Syria, Tartars in Ukraine, Russians living in Estonia and Latvia, children of Haitian descent in the Dominican Republic, and the Rohingyas in Myanmar.[97] Children born to indigenous groups including some of the hill tribes in Thailand and children born to nomads or migratory populations crossing borders who are typically conflated with foreigners and could not benefit from officially recognised avenues for registration as nationals at independence due to their inability to prove residence and strict documentation requirements are equally at risk of not being recognised as citizens of any state.[98]

Discriminatory citizenship laws based on gender, which are still widely practised in some 26 countries around the world, prohibit women from passing on nationality to their children. Laws that do not recognise the independent and equal right of women to transmit nationality to their children would have the serious effect of leaving children without any nationality in situations where the father passed away before his child is born, the father is unknown, the father is himself stateless, the father is unable to transfer his nationality, the child is born abroad or out of wedlock, and the

---

[95] International Union for Child Welfare, *Stateless Children, A Comparative Study of National Legislations and Suggested Solutions to the Problem of Statelessness of Children,* 1st Ed (Geneva: International Union for Child Welfare, 1947). For instance, see Swiss Civil Code of 10 December 1907 (Status as of 1 July 2014).

[96] International Union for Child Welfare, International Union for Child Welfare, *Stateless Children, A Comparative Study of National Legislations and Suggested Solutions to the Problem of Statelessness of Children,* 1st Ed (Geneva: International Union for Child Welfare, 1947), p 11.

[97] M. Lynch, *Lives on Hold: The Human Cost of Statelessness* (2005).

[98] UNHCR. 2012. *The State of the World's Refugees: In Search of Solidarity.* Retrieved from http://www.refworld.org/docid/5100fec32.html [Accessed 12 December 2018]; G. Acciaioli et al., 'Statelessness and Conservation: Exploring the Implications of an International Governance Agenda', (2014) *Tilburg Law Review.* For a detailed analysis of statelessness of the nomads, see H. Alexander. 2017. *The Nationality and Statelessness of Nomads.* Retrieved from https://www.academia.edu/34503088/The_Nationality_and_Statelessness_of_Nomads [Accessed 20 August 2019].

father is unable or unwilling to execute the required administrative steps to ensure that his child acquires a nationality.[99] Algeria, Egypt, Morocco, and Tunisia are among the countries that have taken the initiatives to remove gender discrimination through legal amendments that allow women the right to transfer nationality to their children.[100]

Children may also be exposed to statelessness when their registration records and citizenship documents, and those of their parents are destroyed or missing due to damage to the relevant state registration systems, typically in situations of conflict, or due to disasters. For instance, the Civil Registry in the capital city of Phnom Penh had been totally destroyed during the civil war in the 1970s. As a result, most Cambodians had no birth registration documents until 2002. The large-scale birth registration campaign conducted between 2004 and 2005 including the employment of mobile birth registration, effectively increased the rate of birth registration from less than five percent to practically close to 95 percent by 2008.[101]

Not the least, children who are born on the state's territory to unknown parents commonly termed 'foundlings' and therefore of unclear or unknown lineage and nationality are highly affected by statelessness. This is especially so if no mechanism is made available for their automatic attribution of nationality. Aside from foundlings, abandoned and separated children including orphans with unidentified parentage easily fall victim to statelessness. UNHCR, for instance, has accounted that thousands of children in orphanages are affected by statelessness.[102]

2. **Contemporary Causes of Childhood Statelessness: Birth Registration and International Migration**

(a) ***Birth Registration***

UNHCR has identified faulty administrative procedures and failure or refusal of a state to fulfil the right of children to birth registration as a cause of statelessness for the first time in its report, 'The State of the World's Refugees', published in 1997.[103]

---

[99] The Women's Refugee Commission and Tilburg University Statelessness programme, 'Briefing on Qatar, Iraq, Bahrain for Committee on the Elimination of Discrimination against Women (CEDAW), 57th Pre-session Working Group' (2013). Retrieved from http://tbinternet.ohchr.org/Treaties/CEDAW/Shared%20Documents/BHR/INT_CEDAW_NGO_BHR_14648_E.pdf [12 March 2016].

[100] Women's Refugee Commission, *Our Motherland, Our Country: Gender Discrimination and Statelessness in the Middle East and North Africa* (2013). Retrieved from https://www.womensrefugeecommission.org/images/zdocs/Our_Motherland,_Our_Country_final_for_web.pdf [20 February 2013].

[101] UNHCR and ASEAN Intergovernmental Commission on Human Rights, *Report of the Regional Workshop on Statelessness and the Rights of Women and Children* (19 November 2011), p 12. Retrieved from http://www.refworld.org/docid/50f674c42.html [Accessed 20 January 2014].

[102] C.A. Batchelor, 'The International Legal Framework Concerning Statelessness and Access for Stateless Persons', p 2–3. Contribution to the European Union Seminar on the Content and Scope of International Protection. European Union Seminar on the Content and Scope of International Protection, organised by the General Directorate of Immigration and Foreigners of the Spanish Ministry of Internal Affairs. Retrieved from http://www.unhcr.org/refworld/docid/415c3be44.html [Accessed 10 October 2013].

[103] UNHCR, *The State of the World's Refugees: In Search of Solidarity* (2012).

Defective birth registration, together with poor civil registration practices, including the non-registration of marriages, has since then been addressed as part of the geneses of statelessness.[104]

Birth registration is not only an important tool for the protection of stateless children but also prevention of statelessness. It is, nevertheless, important to differentiate between birth registration and the process of gaining a nationality. The latter is a legal method of acquisition of nationality through either *jus sanguinis* or *jus soli.* While it does not in itself confer nationality, birth registration and proof of birth certificate will serve as evidence of a person's parental connection and his or her place of birth, both of which are essential in establishing the link between an individual and a certain state for purposes of gaining a nationality.[105]

Despite the growing awareness on the importance of birth registration to realise one's legal identity, children's rights and access to state services, the high rates of children without birth registration in countries of origin are still prevalent.[106] UNICEF in conjunction with its 67th birthday on 11 December 2013 issued a report drawing attention to the reality of almost 230 million children under five whose births have never been registered. This represents roughly one in three in all children under five worldwide. The lowest rates of birth registration are reported to be in South Asia and sub-Saharan Africa. Another unfortunate setback is that despite being registered, many children have no evidence of their birth registration.[107]

Unregistered births are indicators of social inequities and disparities, as children who are not counted will be legally invisible and vulnerable to neglect and abuse. The children who are highly affected by such inequities include children of particular ethnic or religious groups, children living in remote places, children belonging to poor families, and children born to uneducated mothers.[108] Additionally, children born to refugees, asylum seekers, and irregular migrants face mounting

---

[104] L. van Waas, *Nationality Matters: Statelessness under International Law* (School of Human Rights Research Series, Vol. 29, 2008), p 151–152.

[105] UN Human Rights Council, *Birth Registration and the Right of Everyone to Recognition Everywhere as a Person before the Law* (17 June 2014), para 24. Apart from that, birth certificate contains evidence of the child's age that goes a long way in ensuring a certain level of safeguard against child exploitation, such as child labour, underage marriage, illegal adoption, sexual abuse, enlistment into armed forces, and child trafficking. The importance of birth registration also lies in its recorded data that can be relied on for family reunification purposes. See Standing Committee of the Executive Committee of the High Commissioner's Programme, *Birth Registration: A Topic Proposed for an Executive Committee Conclusion on International Protection* (9 February 2010). Retrieved from http://www.refworld.org/docid/4b97a3242.html [Accessed 10 January 2016].

[106] Committee on the Rights of the Child, *Report of the 2012 Day of General Discussion: The Rights of All Children in the Context of International Migration* (2012), p 9. Retrieved from http://www2.ohchr.org/english/bodies/crc/docs/discussion2012/DGD2012Outline.pdf [3 March 2013].

[107] UNICEF's Press Centre, 'One in Three Children Under-Five Does Not Officially Exist', UNICEF, New York. Retrieved from www.unicef.org/media/media_71508.html [Accessed 7 January 2014].

[108] UNICEF's Press Centre, 'One in Three Children Under-Five Does Not Officially Exist', UNICEF, New York. Retrieved from www.unicef.org/media/media_71508.html [Accessed 7 January 2014].

barriers in accessing birth registration, due to their irregular status, insecurity, and discriminatory governmental practices.[109]

(b) ***International Migration***

The next contemporary source of statelessness is international or cross-border migration.[110] A line is commonly drawn between two types of migrants, namely, 'voluntary' and 'forced' migrants. Taken from the definition promoted by the International Association for the Study of Forced Migration, 'forced migrants' are people who have been displaced by conflicts, environmental, chemical or nuclear disasters, famine or development policies and projects.[111] These people may comprise refugees, without prejudice to the exact definition of 'refugee' in the 1951 Refugee Convention, which excludes some of these forced migrants.[112]

Voluntary migrants frequently involve economic or labour migrants, who either belong to the low skilled or highly skilled. According to ILO, around 90% of international migration consist of migrants who are economically active and members of their families. Merely 7 to 8% of migrants actually belong to the category of refugees and asylum seekers.[113] In between these two categories are migrants whose movements are induced by socially related reasons. They usually consist of women and children crossing borders for family reunification purposes, such as to re-join husbands working abroad. These dependents comprising women and children, including individuals who move with their families from the beginning of the migration process, tend to settle in the new countries as part of the 'continuation of their life at home'.[114]

---

[109] UNICEF, *A Passport to Protection: A Guide to Birth Registration Programming* (2013), p 13.

[110] L. van Waas, *Nationality Matters: Statelessness under International Law* (School of Human Rights Research Series, V. 29, 2008), p 167–170; S. Nonnenmacher & R. Cholewinski, 'The Nexus Between Statelessness and Migration', p 247; Rodziana Mohamed Razali et al., 'Migration and Statelessness: Turning the Spotlight on Malaysia', *Pertanika Journal of Social Science and Humanities*, 23(S): 19–36.

[111] S. Castle, 'Migration and Community Formation under Conditions of Globalization, International Migration Review'. Retrieved from http://www.forcedmigration.org/about/whatisfm [Accessed 10 April 2016]; See further *Forced Migration Online (FMO),* 'What is Forced Migration?' (2012). Retrieved from www.forcedmigration.org/about/whatisfm [Accessed 12 December 2015].

[112] Article 1 A(2) of the 1951 Refugee Convention defines the term 'refugee' in the following manner: 'As a result of events occurring before 1 January 1951 and owing to well-founded fear of being persecuted for reasons of race, religion, nationality, membership of a particular social group or political opinion, is outside the country of his nationality and is unable or, owing to such fear, is unwilling to avail himself of the protection of that country; or who, not having a nationality and being outside the country of his former habitual residence as a result of such events, is unable or, owing to such fear, is unwilling to return to it'.

[113] International Labour Office, *International Labour Migration. A Rights-Based Approach* (2010), p 2. Retrieved from http://www.ilo.org/wcmsp5/groups/public/---ed_protect/---protrav/---migrant/documents/publication/wcms_208594.pdf [Accessed 23 November 2013].

[114] L. van Waas, 'The Children of Irregular Migrants: A Stateless Generation', *Netherlands Quarterly of Human Rights*, 25 (2007), p 443.

Experts have observed that illegal or irregular migration has outgrown all the other types of international migration in recent time,[115] reflecting the incapacities of states in their migration management policy and design. Irregular migration covers an irregular entry without legal documents or with faked or forged documents (undocumented migrants), a legal entry followed by an overstay after the expiry of one's visa or work permit, or breaches of any of the conditions attached to one's permit or visa, such as restrictions relating to employment, family reunification, and welfare benefits.[116]

The patterns of population movements have over the years progressed towards the complex mix of movements consisting of labour migration, family reunion, humanitarian migration, and irregular flows. Such mixed movements include voluntary undocumented movements beyond international borders, people smuggling, and human trafficking.[117] The foregoing patterns of international mobility also suggest that international migration is no longer a temporary and short-term occurrence, as migration with families including women and children, and proliferation of families abroad, rapidly grow as its common features.[118]

International migration intensifies many of the existing causes of statelessness through conflict of laws resulting from marriages between two different nationals, children born in a country to non-citizen parents and inconsistency between the laws on loss of nationality in the country one originates and on naturalisation in the country one migrates to.[119] There are several other ways in which migrants may lose their nationality as a result of cross-border migration, which include their long-term residence abroad[120] and state succession that takes place when they reside in another country. Alongside these implications are overwhelming concerns over issues of religious, cultural, linguistic, and economic implications that migrants pose to their host countries. Such pressure, whether individually or cumulatively, invites

---

[115] Migration Policy Institute, *New Concepts in Regularisation: Earned Legalisation* (2005). Retrieved from http://www.migrationpolicy.org/newconcepts.php [Accessed 30 December 2015].

[116] The International Conference on Population and Development that promoted the use of 'undocumented' excludes from the meaning of the word, migrants who gain legal entry with tourist documents who subsequently breach the entry requirements by securing a job. See International Labour Office, *Towards a Fair Deal for Migrant Workers in the Global Economy Report VI* presented at the International Labour Conference, 92nd session. Report VI, Agenda Item 6 (Geneva, 1–17 June 2014), p 11.

[117] B. Vollmer, *Irregular Migration in the UK: Definitions, Pathways and Scale* (2011). Retrieved from http://migrationobservatory.ox.ac.uk/briefings/irregular-migration-uk-definitions-pathways-and-scale [Accessed 12 December 2014].

[118] L. van Waas, 'The Children of Irregular Migrants: A Stateless Generation', *Netherlands Quarterly of Human Rights*, 25 (2007), p 441–443; Y.N. Soysal, *Limits of Citizenship: Migrants and Postnational Membership in Europe* (USA: University of Chicago Press, 1994), p 21.

[119] L. van Waas, *Nationality Matters: Statelessness under International Law* (School of Human Rights Research Series, V. 29, 2008), p 163.

[120] Some of these causes will be further illustrated in Chap. 4 of this book.

racism, xenophobia, and discrimination that usually lead to denial or deprivation of citizenship to such groups.[121]

Migration, discrimination, and lack of birth registration are known to be the major reasons that continue to heighten the varying risks of statelessness, especially among those whose presence as non-nationals, contravenes domestic immigration laws.[122] Aside from irregular and undocumented migrants, such may include the presence of migrants in need of protection such as refugees and asylum seekers, especially in countries without the legal frameworks for recognition of their status and protection needs. Although refugee status determination procedures may take place among such asylum seekers through UNHCR's presence in their host countries, such recognised persons under the UNHCR's refugee mandate have no legal status under the domestic laws of the host countries, and largely no prospect for integration.[123]

Whenever migrants, asylum seekers, and refugees cross borders without identity documents or 'irregularly', or become irregular and undocumented after gaining their entry into destination countries, access to birth registration for their children born in such countries is typically impeded as a result of their parents' unrecognised legal status. Being undocumented, the affected children are debarred from access to their fundamental rights on many fronts, including their right to acquire and preserve their identity, and consequently the enjoyment of the attendant benefits of state protection.

Forced displacement often causes refugees to flee without proof of their legal identity. Turning to the authorities of their home countries to seek assistance in acquiring identity documents may not be an option for them due to the risks and danger that it creates. These inevitable situations explain their over-reliance on the authorities of their countries of refuge, or on UNHCR, for securing some form of a valid legal identity.[124] For children born to these refugee and minority populations abroad, the host states typically display an adverse attitude towards aiding the birth registration of such children.[125]

The right to a nationality of second-generation migrants onwards born to foreigners understandably raises a particular concern. There is no denial that birthright citizenship has been adopted in major immigration countries. Even so,

---

[121] L. van Waas, *Nationality Matters: Statelessness under International Law* (School of Human Rights Research Series, V. 29, 2008), p 164.

[122] Program in Tilburg University, 'Statelessness and Nationality: No Nationality at Birth', http://www.whatisstatelessness.org/The%20Causes%20-%20No%20nationality%20at%20birth.html [Accessed 10 December 2014].

[123] J. W. Heffernan, 'Human Security Dilemma in South and Southeast Asia'. Prepared for the Commission on Human Security (2002), p 6.

[124] UNHCR, 'Identity Documents for Refugees (Ec/Scp/33)' (1984), paras 6–7. Retrieved from http://www.unhcr.org/3ae68cce4.html [Accessed 1 April 2016].

[125] This in part is driven by the host states' own deliberate policies of evading the conferment of nationality to the children of refugees. See M. Miller, *Birth Registration: Statelessness and Other Repercussions for Unregistered Children* (2004), p 11, 3rd European Conference on Nationality, Palais del'Europe, Strasbourg; European Network on Statelessness, *Preventing Childhood Statelessness in Europe: Issues, Gaps and Good Practices* (2014), p 21.

in terms of the normative value and strength of birthright citizenship, Aleinikoff and Chetail affirm that:

> [i]t has not been the product of conventional or international law norms. There are no international conventions significantly regulating the acquisition of citizenship; and under customary international law, states are generally free to decide upon whom to confer citizenship.[126]

Empowered by their broad discretion, states remain the controller that sets choices and contours of citizenship attribution and acquisition.[127] States may, for instance, choose to extend citizenship at birth to children of habitual residents, particularly children of parents who were themselves born on their territories (*double jus soli).* Many states have come to introduce some aspect of *jus soli* in the acquisition of citizenship given the discriminatory nature of citizenship regime entirely based on *jus sanguinis.*[128] The children of immigrants forming the second generation of immigrants in many European countries are generally able to acquire citizenship after fulfilling specific residency or age requirements. For instance, Germany decided to relax its traditional *jus sanguinis* laws in 1999 with a liberal *jus soli* policy. France also allows children born to both non-French parents who have reached 18 and completed 5 years of residence in France to become French citizens.[129]

The holding of more than one citizenship has become a common scenario in Europe and the United States. This may be the result of the operation of different nationality laws apart from one's own choice, vigorous human mobility, the ability of both parents to transfer citizenship to their children, and the overall growth of democratic norms and human rights standard.[130] Yet, in other parts of the world such as in Asia Pacific and the Middle East, dual nationality is rarely tolerated.

Recent trends have also seen *jus soli* citizenship being made contingent upon other additional criteria. The legal residence of a parent has been a condition imposed in the UK and Portugal since the 1980s, and in Ireland, since 2004.[131] Even in the

---

[126] T.A. Aleinikoff & V. Chetail (Eds.), *Migration and International Legal Norms* (The Hague: T.M.C. Asser Press, 2011), p 21. See also K. Hailbronner, 'Nationality' in T.A. Aleinikoff & V. Chetail (Eds.) *Migration and International Legal*, p 78.

[127] The Equal Rights Trust, *Unravelling Anomaly: Detention, Discrimination and the Protection Needs of Stateless Persons* (2010), pp 29–30. Retrieved from http://apo.org.au/resource/unravelling-anomaly-detention-discrimination-and-protection-needs-stateless-persons#block-ds-extras-publication-details [Accessed 13 July 2005].

[128] P.J. Spiro, 'A New International Law of Citizenship', *American Journal of International Law*, V. 105(4) (2011), pp 694–746.

[129] T.A. Aleinikoff & D. Klusmeyer, *Citizenship Policies for An Age of Migration.* (Carnegie Endowment for International Peace, 2011) (Carnegie Endowment for International Peace, 2011), pp 12–13 and p 19.

[130] Migration Policy Institute, 'Citizenship in a Globalised World' (2006). Retrieved from http://www.migrationpolicy.org/article/citizenship-globalized-world [Accessed 30 December 2015].

[131] P.J. Spiro, 'A New International Law of Citizenship', p 65–68. For instance, since 2004, jus *soli* has been made subject to certain restrictions, which include not less than 3 years of residence or the aggregate of periods of not less than 3 years of one parent in Ireland during the period of 4 years immediately preceding the birth of the child concerned in the country. See Section 6A of the Irish Nationality and Citizenship Act of 2004 (Act No. 38).

context of the 1997 European Convention on Nationality (ECN),[132] the possibility of naturalisation through the domestic law is to be provided for persons lawfully and habitually resident in the territory of the State Party.[133] Lawful and habitual residence has also been made a condition for facilitated naturalisation, including for stateless persons and persons reacquiring nationality that they previously lost.[134]

3. Consequences of Childhood Statelessness

The absence of a legal bond of nationality carries with it manifold consequences upon a child's rights and life opportunities. They can be felt right from birth to adulthood, with a risk of entrenched disadvantages if the problem remains unresolved.

Access to affordable and publicly supported healthcare and education is greatly hampered as such rights and facilities are frequently available subject to recognised documents and legal status of a person. In extreme cases, non-citizen and irregular statuses may result in the exclusion of the most basic rights to primary education and immunisation.[135] Post-primary education opportunities are rare owing to similar reasons whereas private education and health facilities are often not affordable due to poverty and low living standards commonly experienced by stateless populations. Other social welfare benefits are for the most part reserved for nationals of a state.

Liberty and security of person is a right that is critically at risk given the lack of predictable legal status of a person without a nationality. The following case of statelessness of the traditionally migratory population of *Bajau Laut* in Sabah, Malaysia, illustrates the climate of fear that engulfs the daily lives of stateless children.

Tasmi, who is a holder of *pas lepa* (a letter issued administratively by the *Bajau Native* Chief certifying the holder to be of the *Bajau Laut* ethnicity) with three children born at home (aged 20, 11, and 9) recounted their avoidance of hospitals. In terms of education, two of her children attended an alternative centre of education in their village. However, most of the *Bajau Laut* children are illiterate and spend their days playing in the water or assisting their parents selling seaweed (*latok*) at the night market. In terms of freedom of movement and freedom from arrest, she confessed that her *pas lepa* is of no value to the enforcement authority. As she related:

> Once police officers are spotted, we and our children scramble and run in all directions as if we've just seen a ghost. Even if we show them our *pas lepa*, they would still take us away.

---

[132] Adopted 6 November 1997, in force 3 January 2000, ETS No. 166.

[133] Article 6, para 3 of the 1997 ECN.

[134] See Article 6, paras 4(e), (f) and (g) and Article 9 of ECN. See further L. van Waas, *Nationality Matters: Statelessness under International Law* (School of Human Rights Research Series, V. 29), p 172. It is to be noted that the 2006 ExCom Conclusion on Identification, Prevention, and Reduction of Statelessness and Protection of Stateless Persons has conditioned the call for facilitated naturalisation of stateless persons in states not yet Parties to the 1954 Statelessness Convention on the basis of 'habitually and lawfully' residing stateless persons. See para (u) of Conclusion No. 106 on Identification, Prevention and Reduction of Statelessness and Protection of Stateless Persons.

[135] J. Kanics, 'Migration, Forced Displacement and Childhood Statelessness' (2017). Retrieved from http://children.worldsstateless.org/3/migration-displacement-and-childhood-statelessness/migration-forced-displacement-and-childhood-statelessness.html [Accessed 7 February 2018].

> Those caught would be taken to Kepayan, then to Kimanis (i.e. the detention centres). The children would be taken as well.[136]

The right not to be separated from one's parents as upheld in Article 9(1) CRC[137] is equally at stake for children without a legal identity including a nationality, another challenge associated with irregular migration and lack of documentation as elucidated below:

> Children who are stateless or born to families affected by statelessness are less likely to be able to challenge decisions relating to their care arrangements. Further, when families are divided, children who are stateless or lack legal identity often encounter barriers to reunification with parents and relatives. A lack of documentation combined with excessive documentary requirements can work against the best interests of stateless children and prevent or delay reunification.[138]

The right to return to one's country of origin is unavailable and indefinite detention by authorities or traffickers may haunt the life of a stateless child. The following anecdote serves to be a classic example of profound human rights violations that stateless Rohingya children have to endure.

> Criminal trafficking syndicates frequently detain the migrants in jungle camps in Thailand while attempting to extort money from the victims' relatives in order to deliver them to Malaysia. The refugees that are intercepted by Thai authorities on their way to Malaysia are held in detention camps or shelters for victims of trafficking. The Rohingya children as young as age 10 have been documented in these facilities with limited access to healthcare, physical activity, and fresh air... All Rohingyas, including children, face mandatory detention upon arrival until UNHCR is able to register them and secure their release, a process that has become increasingly difficult and can take months due to limited UNHCR capacity.[139]

The following case study further illustrates how childhood statelessness that persists until adulthood impinges on another fundamental right to family formation, creating agony, and psychological pressure, which may lead to other negative consequences.

> Hamsi is a young man of 27 residing in Germany without any identity documentation. He is the son of traveling parents who were passing through the Netherlands at the time of his birth.

---

[136] Rodziana Mohamed Razali, *Protection against Statelessness at Birth: International and Domestic Legal Frameworks of ASEAN Member States with a Special Case Study on Kota Kinabalu, Sabah,* Thesis submitted in fulfilment of the Degree of Doctor of Philosophy, Faculty of Law, National University of Malaysia (2017), p 365.

[137] Article 9(1) of CRC provides that 'States Parties shall ensure that a child shall not be separated from his or her parents against their will, except when competent authorities subject to judicial review determine, in accordance with applicable law and procedures, that such separation is necessary for the best interests of the child'.

[138] Institute on Statelessness and Inclusion, 'Submission to the Committee on the Rights of the Child for the 2021 Day of General Discussion on Children's Rights and Alternative Care' (2021). Retrieved from https://files.institutesi.org/CRC_DGD_ISI.pdf [Accessed 20 September 2021], para 2–3.

[139] F.X. Bagnoud, *The Impact of Persistent Exclusion: Rohingya Leaving Myanmar* (Centre for Health and Human Rights, 2016), pp 169–170. Retrieved from https://cdn2.sph.harvard.edu/wp-content/uploads/sites/114/2017/12/ChildOnMove_Rohingya.pdf [Accessed 20 April 2017].

His parents are undocumented but identify themselves as former Yugoslavian. Hamsi's birth was not registered in the Netherlands. He now wants to marry and start a family but this has become impossible because he lacks a birth certificate. Efforts to obtain a birth certificate in the Netherlands have proven very difficult. Proof of his place of birth cannot be produced due to the illiteracy of his parents and the time that has passed since his birth. While trying to find solutions for the many bureaucratic difficulties we lost touch with Hamsi as he became frustrated and disillusioned about the whole procedure.[140]

There are many other devastating stories around the world that depict the various levels of harm to children who are undocumented, much less stateless. As Bhabha indicates, nationality does not necessarily promise them a safe and rights-guaranteed life yet its absence or deficit is strongly associated with tragic human rights violations, as well as broad and damaging consequences on a child's healthy growth and life potentials.[141]

2.4 Conclusion

This chapter has sought to understand the key notions and concepts of nationality and statelessness. Nationality and citizenship, taken mutually as a legal concept under international law, define an individual legal connection to a state. The evolution of international law has raised its normative value by characterising it as a human right, the limits of which are not only determined by domestic laws but also international law as developed from time to time. It was observed that the multiple concepts around statelessness and variance in their meanings and contexts forewarn stakeholders working to identify, prevent, and protect stateless persons of the challenges of incoherent approaches in implementing their strategies to resolve statelessness. The lack of uniform conceptions of nationality and statelessness, as they remain largely a matter for states to determine, further compounds the apparent heterogeneity.

The nature, sources, and effects of childhood statelessness have been discussed, highlighting the main two contemporaneous causes of lack of or defective civil registration system, and international migration. A child's right to acquire a nationality is well established. Its recognition precedes the modern CRC, as documented in the 1959 UN Declaration of the Rights of the Child. The development of other international human rights law has only reinforced its authority, sending a clear and strong signal that children deserve to acquire a nationality, a legal imperative to counteract statelessness.

---

[140] L. Bosch, *Birth Registration Problems in Complex Migration Context–Case Studies from the Netherlands*. Retrieved from http://children.worldsstateless.org/3/migration-displacement-and-childhood-statelessness/birth-registration-problems-in-complex-migration-contexts-case-studies-from-the-netherlands.html [Accessed 20 January 2018].

[141] J. Bhabha, 'The Importance of Nationality for Children' in Institute on Statelessness and Inclusion, *The World's Stateless Children* (2017), p 118. Retrieved from http://www.institutesi.org/worldsstateless17.pdf [Accessed 30 January 2018].

It will be shown in the next chapter that the doctrinal position on the grant of nationality as a safeguard against statelessness for otherwise stateless children aligns with customary international law via its wide recognition by states through international treaties. From the child's rights perspective, the immediate acquisition of nationality at birth or immediately afterwards is squarely in consonance with the best interests of the child principle. Delays in its fulfilment entail profound adverse repercussions for the child. Particularly at stake are their access to social and economic rights and freedom to enjoy human security.

Chapter 3
Protection against Statelessness at Birth: Development and Evaluation of the International Legal Norms

3.1 Introduction

This chapter details the evolution and identification of the rules and norms that together formulate the legal framework for protection against statelessness at birth. It begins with an historical overview of the emergence of the right to a nationality as a response to the growing humanitarian problem of statelessness in the early twentieth century. It then moves on to uncover the gradual concretisation of this right with the emergence of other international and regional rules, norms, and related jurisprudence that uphold prevention and reduction of statelessness within and beyond the UN treaty system. While unfolding and identifying the normative development of such rules and norms, this chapter shall concurrently unveil gaps and issues of both substantive and procedural nature that could compromise the aims and effectiveness of protection against statelessness at birth. The subjects of the analysis revolve around the right to acquire a nationality, the interconnection between birth registration and nationality, and those challenges arising under the specialised legal instrument on prevention and reduction of statelessness, namely the 1961 Convention. The findings from the overview and discussions will be summarised in the concluding section at the end of the chapter.

3.2 The Development of the International Legal Framework for Avoidance of Statelessness

1. **The History of Avoidance of Statelessness**

As early as 1923, it has been affirmed by the Permanent Court of International Justice in the case of Tunis and Morocco Nationality Decrees that at the time, nationality matters were within the reserved domain of states, without particularly ruling out the possibility of international law to exert influence on the competence of states

R. M. Razali, *Safeguarding Against Statelessness at Birth*,
https://doi.org/10.1007/978-981-19-5371-2_3

to govern the subject matter.[1] The Inter-American Court of Human Rights in its Advisory Opinion Requested by the Government of Costa Rica (1984) 60 years later echoed this doctrinal development in stronger terms, as follows:

> It is generally accepted today that nationality is an inherent right of all human beings...The classical doctrinal position, which viewed nationality as an attribute granted by the State to its subjects, has gradually evolved to the point that nationality is today perceived as involving the jurisdiction of the State as well as human rights issues.[2]

When it was first envisaged, nationality was intended to regulate relationships among sovereign states.[3] It was not until the twentieth century that statelessness was perceived to be an international concern.[4] The turmoil of World War I left a great number of people stateless and in need of state protection. Conflict of laws primarily due to the presumption that another state has the obligation to grant nationality,[5] conflicts between *jus soli* and *jus sanguinis*,[6] geopolitical changes, and the rise of totalitarian regime in the 1930s, became the major drivers of *de jure* statelessness between the First and the Second World Wars.[7] States enjoyed a large amount of discretion in the conferment and withdrawal of nationality that led to nationalisation and denationalisation to the point that it was not certain what limits existed to constrain such competence.[8]

The strictly-guarded autonomy of states on determination of nationality and membership of a nation through the creation of different doctrines of nationality

---

[1] Nationality Decrees in Tunis and Morocco (1923). Advisory Opinion No. 4, PCIJ Series B, No. 4 (*Tunis & Morocco*).

[2] Inter-American Court on Human Rights, Advisory Opinion OC-4/84 of 19 January 1984, Series A No. 4 para 32–35. In this case, the Costa Rican government asked for the Court's opinion on the effects of its proposed amendments to Costa Rican nationality law. Specifically, the Government wished to know whether the suggested amendments would run counter to the right of every person to a nationality provided in Article 20(1) and Article 17(4) of the AmCHR with regard to its principle of equality between spouses.

[3] J.M.M. Chan, 'The Right to a Nationality as a Human Right', *Human Rights Law Journal*, 12 (1991), pp 1–14, at p 1.

[4] C.F. Doebbler, 'A Human Rights Approach to Statelessness in the Middle East', *Leiden Journal of International Law*, 15(3) (2002), pp 527–552, at p 530.

[5] For instance, a woman married to an alien man should receive the husband's nationality, as what was provided in the laws of the U.S. and Great Britain.

[6] For example, the conflict may occur as a result of the birth of a child to U.S. American parents in Germany, with the U.S. adopting *jus soli* and Germany *jus sanguinis*.

[7] M. Stiller, 'Statelessness in International Law: A Historic Overview', *DAJV Newsletter*, 37 (2012), p 98; F. Costamagna, 'Statelessness in the Context of State Succession: An Appraisal under International Law' in A. Annoni & S. Forlati, *The Changing Role of Nationality in International Law* (New York: Routledge, 2013), pp 38–39.

[8] M. S. McDougal et al., 'Nationality and Human Rights: The Protection of the Individual in External Arenas' in *Yale Law School Legal Scholarship Repository* (1974), p 918. Retrieved from http://digitalcommons.law.yale.edu/cgi/viewcontent.cgi?article=3663&context=fss_papers [2 November 2014].

attribution led to both deliberate and involuntary emergence of statelessness.[9] The League of Nations started assisting in spreading awareness of the growing problems of minorities and vulnerable populations. States began to work towards preventing statelessness and ensuring basic human rights protections for the stateless people.[10] This consequently called for the intervention of international law to provide the necessary guidance with the aims of managing arising conflicts, avoiding and resolving statelessness in its different scopes.[11]

The preparatory work following the 1930 Hague Conference finally culminated in the adoption by the Conference of the 1930 Convention on Certain Questions relating to the Conflict of Nationality Laws (1930 Hague Convention). This Convention became the first instrument to introduce certain constraints on the power of states over nationality matters and to ensure the right to a nationality to every person. Its Article 1 is instrumental in this respect when it provides:

> [t]his law [of nationality] shall be recognised by other States in so far as it is consistent with international conventions, international customs and the principle of law generally recognised with regard to nationality.[12]

It was through the 1930 Hague Convention and the 1930 Hague Protocol relating to Certain Case of Statelessness[13] that avoidance of statelessness was for the first time tackled.[14] The two instruments targeted prevention of *de jure* statelessness among children and women, and to some extent among men.[15] Meanwhile, the 1930 Protocol relating to a Certain Case of Statelessness adopted the formula of *jus sanguinis maternus* combined with that of *jus soli* so that a child could acquire the nationality of the state of birth if the child's mother was a national of the state of birth and her father was of unknown nationality.[16]

---

[9] The denationalisation of nationals of German and Hungarian race in Czechoslovakia and of German race in Poland and Yugoslavia are notable examples. See P. Weis, *Nationality and Statelessness in International Law,* 2nd Ed (The Netherlands: Sijthoff & Noordhoff International, 1979), p 120.

[10] C.F. Doebbler, 'A Human Rights Approach to Statelessness in the Middle East', pp 527–552.

[11] L. van Waas, *Nationality Matters: Statelessness Under International Law* (School of Human Rights Research Series, V. 29, 2008), pp 35–36.

[12] Article 1 of the 1930 Hague Convention.

[13] League of Nations, Protocol Relating to a Certain Case of Statelessness (12 April 1930), No. 4138. 179 LNTS 115.

[14] *M.O. Hudson,* 'Nationality, Including Statelessness', UN Doc. A/CN 4/50, Extract from the *Yearbook of the International Law Commission,* V. II (1952).

[15] Articles 8 and 9 of the Convention, for instance, prevent a wife who might lose her nationality upon marriage with a foreigner from being stateless by requiring that such consequence being conditional on the wife acquiring the nationality of the husband. As for children, Article 14 avoids statelessness among foundlings, namely a child with unknown parents, by entitling them to the nationality of their country of birth. Article 15 further safeguards the nationality of children born to stateless parents, or to parents of unknown nationality, by allowing the child to obtain the nationality of his or her country of birth subject to the law of that particular state of birth.

[16] League of Nations, Protocol Relating to a Certain Case of Statelessness (12 April 1930), No. 4138, 179 LNTS 115. Article 1 of the Protocol states that: 'In a State whose nationality is not conferred

The 1930 Hague Convention, however, had little impact on the eradication of all cases of both statelessness and double nationality. Among the reasons cited for its little influence include the fact that only a limited part of its 31 articles actually deals with statelessness, most of which are formulated in the negative, without giving equal importance to the grant of nationality,[17] the conflict between the positions of the states of emigration on the one hand, and those of immigration on the other, the division in the adherence to *jus soli* and *jus sanguinis*, and the primacy given by various delegations to the preservation of their own national law that impeded a shared understanding on many questions.[18] Although the 1930 Convention did not bear direct and concrete results, the principles introduced by the Convention served to be of significant guidance to a number of states' nationality laws, including the states that were not parties to the Convention and its related Protocols.[19]

2. Promulgation of the Right to a Nationality following the Birth of the United Nations and the Two Statelessness Conventions

The turmoil of World War II further led to the break-up of states and devastating mass denationalisation across Europe during the first half of the twentieth century. A vast number of people became stateless and were in dire need of state protection. States, therefore, not only had to avoid statelessness but also to react to the situation of statelessness. In the early work of the Commission of Human Rights and ECOSOC, the prevailing legal protection environment was understood to extend both to refugees and persons who did not enjoy the protection of any state, namely, stateless persons. The birth of the UN marked a turning point in the course of international legal development addressing both the refugees and stateless.[20]

---

by the mere fact of birth in its territory, a person born in its territory of a mother possessing the nationality of that State and of a father without nationality or of unknown nationality shall have the nationality of the said State'. The positive point that could be derived here is that it is not necessary for the father to prove his statelessness as the fact of his unknown nationality is enough to invoke the protection of this Article. However, the limited scope of this provision can be explained by the fact that statelessness of a child may not be prevented if the father has a nationality but cannot transmit it to the child. See further G.R. de Groot et al., *Protection Against Statelessness: Trends and Regulations in Europe* (2013), p 15. Retrieved from http://eudo-citizenship.eu/images/docs/eudocit_vink_degroot_statelessness_final.pdf [Accessed 1 April 2016].

[17] M. Stiller, 'Statelessness in International Law: A Historic Overview', at p 98.

[18] Ramaa Prasad Dhokalia, *The Codification of Public International Law* (UK: Manchester University Press, 1970), p 127.

[19] P. Weis, *Nationality and Statelessness in International Law*, 2nd Ed (The Netherlands: Sijthoff & Noordhoff International, 1979), pp 27–28. For instance, the previous principle of 'doctrine of subordination of the nationality of married women to their husband' had been changed by those states that upheld strongly to it. The same pattern could be seen in respect of expatriation and loss of nationality of origin as a consequence of naturalisation. See I. Brownlie, 'Relations of Nationality in Public International Law', p 300.

[20] UNHCR, *Information and Accession Package: The 1954 Convention relating to the Status of Stateless Persons and the 1961 Convention on the Reduction of Statelessness* (Revised 1999) (United Nations: Geneva, 1996), p 7; C.F. Doebbler, 'A Human Rights Approach to Statelessness in the Middle East', pp 527–552.

Among the subsequent highpoints was the promulgation of Article 15 of the 1948 Universal Declaration of Human Rights (UDHR) that contains an aspirational right to a nationality, together with the prohibition of arbitrary deprivation of nationality, as well as denial of the right to change one's nationality. Article 15 of UDHR provides that:

(1) Everyone has the right to a nationality.
(2) No one shall be arbitrarily deprived of his nationality nor denied the right to change his nationality.

Two forms of safeguards are underlined by this provision, the first being that every individual is entitled to a nationality, indirectly endorsing presumption against statelessness. Secondly, no one shall be subject to arbitrary deprivation of nationality, a limit intended to apply to the wide discretionary power held by states in determining the right of individuals to a nationality.

Following UDHR, the UN Secretary-General produced a Report on Statelessness, introducing UNHCR's mandate in relation to the right to a nationality.[21] A series of deliberations on the subject of statelessness took place. This resulted in the initiatives to create systematic legal norms on statelessness by ILC, the establishment of the Ad Hoc Committee on Statelessness and related problems by ECOSOC, and finally, the drafting committee for the presently known 1951 Refugee Convention, together with the Draft Protocol relating to the Status of Stateless Persons.[22]

The rights and protections of those who were rendered stateless are detailed in the 1951 Refugee Convention together with its 1967 Refugee Protocol, and in particular, the subsequently codified 1954 Statelessness Convention. Stateless refugees could expect to receive protection provided under the first Convention and its Protocol. The 1954 Convention that was modelled after the provisions in the 1951 Refugee Convention and the Draft Protocol is specifically intended to offer rights and protection to stateless persons.[23] The most important aspect of this treaty is its incorporation of the definition of the term 'stateless person' in its Article 1(1), which is considered to be the customary international law.[24]

After much deliberation and compromise, another treaty based on one of the original drafts prepared by ILC was adopted in 1961. Drafted principally to address administrative and technical causes of statelessness,[25] the 1961 Convention seeks to

---

[21] UNHCR, *The State of the World's Refugees: In Search of Solidarity* (2012), p 91.

[22] C.F. Doebbler, 'A Human Rights Approach to Statelessness in the Middle East', p 531; UNHCR, *Information and Accession Package: The 1954 Convention Relating to the Status of Stateless Persons and the 1961 Convention on the Reduction of Statelessness* (Revised 1999) (United Nations: Geneva, 1996), pp 7–10; L. van Waas, 'The UN Statelessness Conventions' in A. Edwards & L. van Waas (Eds.), *Nationality and Statelessness under International Law* (Cambridge: Cambridge University Press, 2014), pp 65–76.

[23] N. Robinson, *Convention relating to the Status of Stateless Persons: Its History and Interpretation*, (Institute of Jewish Affairs, 1955), pp 2–5.

[24] This definition is also applicable in interpreting the scope of the 1961 Convention. See G.R. de Groot et al., *Protection against Statelessness: Trends and Regulations in Europe* (2013), p 17.

[25] L. van Waas, *Nationality Matters: Statelessness under International Law* (School of Human Rights Research Series, V. 29, 2008), p 194.

prevent *de jure* statelessness, in particular, among children. Other than making sure that nationality is accessible to those who would otherwise be stateless, the 1961 Convention offers valuable safeguards against loss or deprivation of nationality, as well as in cases of transfer of territory, in the event that an individual is threatened by statelessness.[26] The significance of the 1961 Convention was highlighted by UNHCR as follows:

> Accession to the 1961 Convention equips States to avoid and resolve nationality-related disputes and mobilise international support to adequately deal with the prevention and reduction of statelessness.[27]

The 1961 Convention, however, took around eleven years to be launched and another twelve years to draw six ratifications in order for it to get into force.[28] This largely implies that nationality and sovereignty issues are highly sensitive in the era of sovereignty and state system.[29] The births of the 1954 Convention and subsequently the 1961 Convention represent the first concrete step to formulate dedicated rules of international law on the protection and prevention of stateless persons.[30]

3. UNHCR's Relevant Mandates

The original mandate of UNHCR was to oversee and address the situation of stateless persons who were refugees.[31] However, in the 1990s, cases of statelessness experienced a dramatic increase following the disintegration of the Soviet Union, the Socialist Republic of Yugoslavia, and Czechoslovakia, accompanied by the emergence of newly independent states. This phenomenon prompted UNHCR's Executive Committee to adopt a comprehensive Conclusion on the Prevention and Reduction of Statelessness in 1995.[32] The said Conclusion among others, acknowledges UNHCR's actions with regard to stateless persons as part of its statutory function, requires the

---

[26] C. A. Batchelor, 'Transforming International Legal Principles into National Law: The Right to a Nationality and the Avoidance of Statelessness', *Refugee Survey Quarterly*, V. 25(3) (2006): 8–25, at p 5.

[27] UNHCR, *Preventing and Reducing Statelessness: The 1961 Convention on the Reduction of Statelessness* (September 2010), p 2. Retrieved from http://www.unhcr.it/wp-content/uploads/2016/01/preventing_and_reducing_statelessness.pdf [Accessed 10 July 2013].

[28] The situation has changed significantly, thanks to the endless promotional efforts by UNHCR to attract new signatories to the said Convention. As of November 2014, UNHCR highlighted that there were 61 State Parties to the 1961 Convention during the launching phase of the 10-year campaign to end statelessness by 2024. See UNHCR, UN Conventions on Statelessness (2016). Retrieved from http:// www.unhcr.org/un-conventions-on-statelessness.html [Accessed 12 June 2016].

[29] L. van Waas, *Nationality Matters: Statelessness under International Law* (School of Human Rights Research Series, V. 29, 2008), pp 35–36; Tang Lay Lee, *Statelessness, Human Rights and Gender: Irregular Migrant Workers from Burma in Thailand* (The Netherlands: Martinus Nijhoff Publishers, 2005), pp 37–38.

[30] *A Study of Statelessness 1949,* UN Doc. E/1112; E/1112/Add.1 (New York: United Nations), p 43.

[31] See para 6(A) (11) of UNHCR Statute and Article 1(A)(2) of the 1951 Refugee Convention.

[32] M. Manly & S. Persaud, 'UNHCR and Responses to Statelessness', *Forced Migration Review (FMR)*, 1(32) (2009).

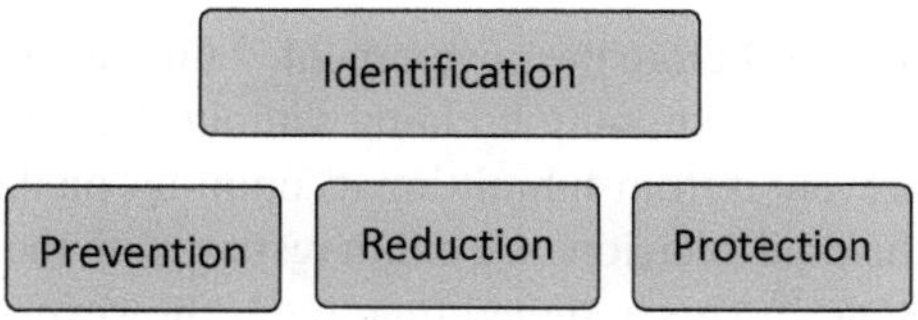

Fig. 3.1 UNHCR, Conclusion on Identification, Prevention and Reduction of Stateless Persons and Protection of Stateless Persons (2006)

body to promote accession to the two Statelessness Conventions and advise states on technical and legal matters pertaining to nationality legislation.[33]

A year later, the UN General Assembly (UNGA) reaffirmed UNHCR's global mandate on statelessness through its notable resolution, namely the UNGA Resolution A/RES/50/152 of 9 February 1996. Under paragraph 14 of the Resolution, the UNGA:

> (…) encourages the High Commissioner to continue her activities on behalf of stateless persons, as part of her statutory function of providing international protection and of seeking preventive action.[34]

Paragraph 15 requests the body to actively promote accession to the Statelessness Conventions and 'to provide technical and advisory services pertaining to the preparation and implementation of nationality legislation'.[35] Another major milestone in the expansion of UNHCR's global statelessness mandate was the adoption of a comprehensive conclusion addressing the four pillars of responding to statelessness, namely, through identification, prevention and reduction of statelessness, and the protection of stateless persons. Identification is indeed the first pillar that serves to be the foundation that helps address the other three pillars, as illustrated in Fig. 3.1.[36]

UNHCR's global mandate is complemented by its specific role under the 1961 Convention as the body 'to which a person claiming the benefit of this Convention may apply for the examination of his claim and for assistance in presenting it to the appropriate authority'.[37] As a result of oppositions to the establishment of a special tribunal and a disinclination to have UNHCR as the agency acting for the stateless

---

[33] UNHCR, Conclusion on Prevention and Reduction of Statelessness and Protection of Stateless No. 78 (XLVI), (1995); UNHCR, *The State of the World's Refugees: In search of Solidarity* (2012), pp 91–92.

[34] UNGA, Office of the United Nations High Commissioner for Refugees, General Assembly Resolution. UN Doc. A/RES/50/152, New York: UNGA' (9 February 1996), para 14.

[35] UNGA, Office of the United Nations High Commissioner for Refugees, General Assembly Resolution. UN Doc. A/RES/50/152, New York: UNGA (9 February 1996).

[36] UNHCR, Conclusion on Identification, Prevention and Reduction of Statelessness and Protection of Stateless Persons No 106 (LVII), General Assembly Document, A/AC.96/1035, Geneva: UNHCR (6 Oct 2006).

[37] See Article 11, the 1961 Convention; UNGA, UNHCR's Role under Article 11 of the 1961 Convention on the Reduction of Statelessness, Resolution 3274 (XXIV) (10 December 1974); M. Manly, 'UNHCR's Mandate and Activities to Address Statelessness' in A. Edwards & L. van Waas (Eds.), *Nationality and Statelessness under International Law* (Cambridge: Cambridge University Press, 2014), p 90.

persons before the government,[38] this supervisory role was translated into UNHCR's role of examining a claim without deciding on it. Nevertheless, the role does not prevent it from submitting its opinions on the interpretations of the Convention, with the final decision on a claim resting with the appropriate authority of the Contracting State.[39] This assigned function is, however, seldom invoked.[40]

It is important to highlight how prevention and reduction of statelessness occupies UNHCR's fundamental mandate responsibility. While its mandate on refugees requires the body to respond to refugee situations in the context of those who have crossed an international border, the mandate on statelessness assigns UNHCR a specific obligation to undertake preventive action. The activities under the purview of prevention include campaigning for the accession to the 1961 Convention and reform of nationality laws, law reform in the context of state succession, and prevention through civil registration. Prevention aspect is also pertinent given the active flows of migration and the related phenomenon of conflicts of law leading to statelessness.[41]

As part of the various initiatives to strengthen the international legal framework on statelessness, UNHCR has begun its expert meeting series since 2010, with the aim to develop and disseminate UNHCR's guidelines on topics and issues relating to statelessness. This exercise recognises the challenge inherent in statelessness as a deeply specialised yet vague zone of international law.[42]

The expert meetings which draw on the expertise and knowledge of specialists in the areas of international legal frameworks on statelessness, nationality and human rights address mainly five conceptual themes in relation to the two Statelessness Conventions: (i) the definition of a 'stateless person' in Article 1(1) of the 1954 Statelessness Convention; (ii) the concept of *de facto* statelessness; (iii) procedures for the determination of whether a person is stateless; (iv) the status in national law

[38] UNGA, Committee of the Whole, Summary Record of the Ninth Meeting, UN Doc. A/CONF.9/C.1/SR.9, UNGA: Geneva (7 April 1959). Retrieved from http://legal.un.org/diplomaticconferences/statelessness-1959/docs/english/Vol_2/10_a_conf-9_c-1_sr-9.pdf [accessed 3 May 2015], p 5; UNGA, Committee of the Whole, Summary of the Record of the Seventeenth Meeting, UN Doc. A/CONF.9/C.1/SR.17, UNGA: Geneva (13 April 1959), pp 2–9; L. van Waas, *Nationality Matters: Statelessness under International Law* (School of Human Rights Research Series V. 29, 2008), p 46.

[39] L. van Waas, *Nationality Matters: Statelessness under International Law* (School of Human Rights Research Series, V. 29, 2008), p 47; G.R. de Groot et al., *Protection against Statelessness: Trends and Regulations in Europe* (2013), p 34.

[40] L. van *Waas,* 'The UN Statelessness Conventions' in A. Edwards & L. van Waas (Eds.), *Nationality and Statelessness under International Law* (Cambridge: Cambridge University Press, 2014), p 77.

[41] M. Manly, 'UNHCR's Mandate and Activities to Address Statelessness' in A. Edwards & L. van Waas (Eds.), *Nationality and Statelessness under International Law* (Cambridge: Cambridge University Press, 2014), pp 103–104.

[42] The multitude of approaches between nationality laws of different countries and the vast range of issues and standards are part of the overall complexities. Prevention and reduction of statelessness, for instance, entails a different conception from that of the protection of stateless persons. See 'UNHCR's Mandate and Activities to Address Statelessness' in A. Edwards & L. van Waas (Eds.), *Nationality and Statelessness under International Law*, (Cambridge: Cambridge University Press, 2014), p 95.

to be conferred to stateless persons and the associated benefits; and (v) the scope of international legal safeguards for the prevention of statelessness among children at birth.[43] Such endeavours also took into account growing state practices and evolving responses to address protection gaps for stateless persons. The outcomes of such expert meetings significantly help clarify and develop the content and scope of the existing legal standards on statelessness.

3.3 Human Rights Instruments, Jurisprudence and Regional Norms on Protection of Children against Statelessness at Birth

The incorporation of the right to a nationality in international human rights instruments places limits on absolute sovereign discretion in the area of nationality. Regional human rights bodies have subsequently been at the forefront in growing the juris prudence on the right to a nationality.[44] Statelessness is tackled in three ways through the human rights instruments, namely; by legal recognition of the right of individuals to have a nationality; by facilitating the attainment of nationality; and through checks and limits on the capacity of states to withdraw nationality.[45]

The legal framework for protection against statelessness at birth is principally made up of the right to acquire a nationality for every child, and the safeguards through birth registration and nationality for avoidance of statelessness, both of which form the right to a legal identity, and the mechanisms to prevent statelessness under the framework of the 1961 Convention. The following subsections identify these norms and mechanisms, and explore their normative force and limitations, in trying to comprehend their capacity in protecting children against statelessness at birth.

(a) ***The Right to (Acquire) a Nationality for Every Child: Identification of Norms and Challenges***

The right of the child to acquire a nationality is clearly enshrined in Article 7 of CRC:

(1) *The child shall be registered immediately after birth and shall have the right from birth to a name, the right to acquire a nationality and, as far as possible, the right to know and be cared for by his or her parents.*
(2) *States Parties shall ensure the implementation of these rights in accordance with their national law and their obligations under the relevant international*

[43] UNHCR, *Strengthening the International Legal Framework on Statelessness: Expert Meeting Series* (2010). Retrieved from http://www.unhcr.org/4d78d5329.html [7 July 2014].

[44] J. Bialosky, 'Regional Protection of the Right to a Nationality', *Cardozo Journal of International & Comparative Law*, 24 (2015), p 153.

[45] C.A. Batchelor, 'Transforming International Legal Principles into National Law: The Right to a Nationality and the Avoidance of Statelessness', *Refugee Survey Quarterly*, 25(3), pp 8–25, at p 10.

instruments in this field, in particular where the child would otherwise be stateless.

Prior to CRC, Article 24 of ICCPR similarly promulgates the right of every child to acquire a nationality:

(2) *Every child shall be registered immediately after birth and shall have a name.*
(3) *Every child has the right to acquire a nationality.*

The provision on the right to acquire a nationality under ICCPR imposes upon the State Parties the duty to realise the acquisition of nationality when the child is born, through internal measures as well as cooperation with other states.[46]

The right to a nationality or to acquire it is equally upheld in reference to every child in other international and regional treaties, such as Article 29 of the 1990 International Convention on the Protection of the Rights of All Migrant Workers and Members of Their Families (ICMW),[47] Article 7 of the Covenant on the Rights of the Child in Islam (CRCI),[48] and Article 6 of the 1990 African Charter on the Rights and Welfare of the Child (ACRWC).[49]

A broad consensus among the states as to the universal right of children to acquire a nationality has, therefore emerged, consistent with the widespread ratification of ICCPR[50] and the almost universal acceptance of CRC.[51] Withdrawal of reservations to Article 7(1) on the right to acquire a nationality in recent times adds coherence to this right.[52] Other regional instruments provide for the right to a nationality of every 'person', instead of a 'child'. The instruments include the 1960 American Convention on Human Rights (AmCHR),[53] ECN,[54] and ASEAN Human Rights Declaration.[55] For AmCHR and ECN, avoidance of statelessness is additionally featured side by side with the right to a nationality.[56]

---

[46] UN Human Rights Committee, 7 April 1989, CCPR General Comment No 17.

[47] Article 24 (Rights of the Child), UN Doc. HRI/GEN/1/Rev. 6, Geneva: CCPR, para 8; See also UNGA, Office of the UN High Commissioner for Refugees, A/RES/61/137, 25 January 2007, para. 7.

[48] Adopted 18 December 1990, in force 1 July 2003, 2220 UNTS 3. Adopted June 2005, OIC/9-IGGE/HRI/2004/Rep. Final.

[49] Adopted 11 July 1990, in force 29 November 1999, CAB/LEG/24.9/49.

[50] There are 74 signatories and 168 parties to ICCPR as at 12 October 2016. See the status of acceptance at https://treaties.un.org/pages/ViewDetails.aspx?src=TREATY&mtdsg_no=IV-4&chapter=4&clang=_en.

[51] There are 140 signatories and 196 parties to CRC as at 12 October 2016. See the status of acceptance at https://treaties.un.org/Pages/ViewDetails.aspx?src=IND&mtdsg_no=IV-11&chapter=4&clang=_en.

[52] For example, Andorra on 1 March 2006; Switzerland on 1 May 2007; Tunisia on 23 September 2008; Liechtenstein on 1 October 2009; Thailand on 13 December 2010.

[53] Adopted 22 November 1969, in force 18 July 1978, OAS Treaty Series No. 36. See Article 20(1).

[54] Article 4(a).

[55] ASEAN Human Rights Declaration (Association of Southeast Asian Nations, 2012). Retrieved from http://www.refworld.org/docid/50c9fea82.html [9 September 2015]. See Article 18.

[56] See Article 20 (2) AmCHR and Articles 4(b) and Article 6(2) ECN.

The absence of the general right to a nationality in the European Convention on Human Rights (ECHR)[57] does not preclude the European Court of Human Rights from dealing with it. This occurs when the right to a nationality raises or leads to other issues under the Convention, typically involving contravention with any of its provisions.[58]

A case in point is Genovese *v.* Malta.[59] The case concerns Ben Alexander Genovese who was born out of wedlock to a British mother and a Maltese father in 1996. Genovese obtained his British nationality but was denied Maltese nationality under the (then) Maltese law. This was because a child born out of wedlock in a foreign country could not obtain Maltese nationality. In a majority six to one decision, the Court declared that the nationality law of Malta violates Articles 8 (on the right to respect for private and family life) and 14 (on prohibition of discrimination) of ECHR when it discriminated against the applicant who was denied Maltese citizenship on the basis that he was born out of wedlock.[60] In another decided case of Mennesson *v.* France,[61] a violation of Article 8 arose due to refusal of the French authorities to recognise the legal relationship between children born following a surrogacy treatment abroad and the couple (Mr. and Mrs. Mennesson), who had the said treatment.[62] The Court held that the children's rights to private life under Article 8 had been infringed by the prevention of recognition, and denial of the legal relationship between the children and their biological father, being himself a French national.[63]

Having discussed some of the important international legal reference points with respect to the international recognition of the right of the child to acquire a nationality, conceptually, it must be noted that the right to a nationality itself is not without gaps. Article 15(1) UDHR leaves open the question as to which nationality a person can lay his claim to.[64] The generality of the provision renders the identification of the duty bearers responsible for the conferment of nationality uncertain, in turn, reducing the prospect for the emergence of customary international law status with respect to

---

[57] Adopted 4 November 1950, in force 3 September 1953.

[58] See, for instance, *Abdulaziz, Cabales and Balkandi v. United Kingdom* (1985) 7 EHRR 471, para 59–60, in which the right of a non-citizen to enter or remain in a country was addressed by the Court.

[59] European Court of Human Rights (ECHR), Judgment of 11 October 2011, App. No. 53124/099 (*Genovese v. Malta*).

[60] See paras 33 & 34 of the decision of *Genovese v. Malta*.

[61] European Court of Human Rights (ECHR), Judgment of 26 June 2014, App. No. 65192/11 (*Mennesson v. France*).

[62] The reproductive technique was prohibited in France.

[63] See para 46 and 99 of *Mennesson v. France*. This judgment became the catalyst for amendments to relevant laws in Austria, Denmark, and Sweden. Sweden and Denmark now allow a child born to a citizen father to acquire their nationality, regardless of the place of birth of the child.

[64] M. Adjami & J. Harrington, 'The Scope and Content of Article 15 of the Universal Declaration of Human Rights', *Refugee Survey Quarterly,* V. 23(3) (2008), p 104.

the right to a nationality.[65] As observed by Hailbronner, both the rights to a specific nationality and to change nationality in order to acquire a new one have not attained customary international law status.[66]

In this vein, lack of clear-cut requirements over which state is responsible to grant nationality to children at birth and under what circumstances shall it take place, could plausibly hinder the substantive and procedural imperatives to ensure the respect for, and effective fulfilment of this right.[67] The ICCPR's General Comments No. 17 alludes to this when it states that:

> [s]pecial attention should also be paid, in the context of protection to be granted to children, to the right of every child to acquire a nationality, as provided for in Article 24, paragraph 3. While the purpose of this provision is to prevent a child from being afforded less protection by society and the State because he is stateless, it does not necessarily make it an obligation for states to give their nationality to every child born on their territory.[68]

The *travaux préparatoires* of the right to acquire a nationality under both ICCPR and CRC would reveal the stand taken by the majority of states against an absolute duty to confer nationality to every child born in the territory irrespective of the circumstances. The states were in favour of leaving the complex solutions to statelessness to be dealt with by other treaties, especially the 1961 Convention.[69] As a result, the original text of Article 24(3) was amended by the insertion of the word 'acquire' and deletion of the words 'from his birth'.[70] The drafting history of CRC further shows that the wording of Article 7(1) is correspondingly drafted based on the texts of sub-articles (2) and (3) of Article 24 ICCPR. The right 'to acquire' a nationality was retained instead of the right 'to a nationality', in order to avoid just any child who enters a state from an automatic entitlement to citizenship.[71]

Regardless of this position, the provision underlining the right to acquire a nationality under ICCPR still imposes upon the Contracting States the duty to realise the

---

[65] F. Costamagna, 'Statelessness in the Context of State Succession: An Appraisal under International Law', in A. Annoni & S. Forlati (Eds), *The Changing Role of Nationality in International Law* (Routledge, New York, 2013), p 20.

[66] K. Hailbronner, 'Nationality' in T.A. Aleinikoff & V. Chetails (Eds.), *Migration and International Legal Norms* (The Hague: T.M.C. Asser Press, 2003), p 77.

[67] A. Boll, *Multiple Nationality and International Law* (Leiden: Martinus Nijhoff, 2007), p 241; J.M.M. Chan, 'The Right to a Nationality as a Human Right', *Human Rights Law Journal*, 12 (1991), pp 1–14. The right to a nationality in Article 15 of UDHR not only lacks clarification but has also been weakened in ICCPR.

[68] UN Human Rights Committee, 7 April 1989, CCPR General Comment No 17: Article 24 (Rights of the Child), UN Doc. HRI/GEN/1/Rev. 6, Geneva: CCPR, para 8.

[69] S. Detrick, *A Commentary on the United Nations Convention on the Rights of the Child* (The Hague/Boston/London: Martinus Nijhoff Publishers, 1999), p 150.

[70] S. Detrick, *A Commentary on the United Nations Convention on the Rights of the Child* (1999), p 150.

[71] S. Detrick, *A Commentary on the United Nations Convention on the Rights of the Child* (1999), p 150.

acquisition of nationality when the child is born, through internal measures, as well as in cooperation with other states.[72]

(b) ***The Right to Acquire a Nationality for a Child Who Would Otherwise be Stateless***

Various human rights conventions directly or indirectly address the prevention of statelessness among women and children in their provisions. Article 13 of the 1930 Hague Convention provides that a child shall retain his nationality if he or she does not acquire the new nationality of his or her parents following naturalisation.[73]

Elimination of statelessness at birth particularly receives major approval from states. Many countries adopt rules of attribution of nationality at birth, followed by other rules providing for declaration and naturalisation procedures. This, in fact, implies a rank of importance, with birthright citizenship being the leading method of nationality attribution.[74]

Although birthright per se is not, however, a ground for an acquisition of nationality under customary international law,[75] according to Chan, there exists abundant support for the assertion that a norm of customary international law has emerged pertaining to the right of a stateless child to acquire nationality of the state of the child's birth.[76] Aside from the 1961 Convention, the elimination of statelessness at birth through an acquisition of nationality by way of providing for the right of the child at all times to have a name and a nationality[77] was earlier addressed in the 1973 Bern Convention of the International Commission of Civil Status[78] and various proposals by the Council of Europe, the 1959 UN Declaration of the Rights

---

[72] UN Human Rights Committee, 7 April 1989, CCPR General Comment No 17: Article 24 (Rights of the Child), UN Doc. HRI/GEN/1/Rev. 6, Geneva: CCPR, para 8; See also UNGA, Office of the UN High Commissioner for Refugees, A/RES/61/137 (25 January 2007), para. 7.

[73] See further A. Edwards, 'The Meaning of Nationality in International Law in an Era of Human Rights: Procedural and Substantive Aspects' in A. Edwards & L. van Waas (Eds.), *Nationality and Statelessness under International Law* (Cambridge: Cambridge University Press, 2014), p 24.

[74] P. V. Maarten & G.R. de Groot, *Birthright Citizenship: Trends and Regulations in Europe, Comparative Report*' (2010), p 3.

[75] T.A. Aleinikoff & V. Chetail (Eds.), *Migration and International Legal Norms* 2003 (T.M.C. Asser Press, 2003), p 21. See also K. Hailbronner, 'Nationality' in *Migration and International Legal Norms* (The Hague: T.M.C. Asser Press, 2003), p 78. Note that a regional customary international law could be said to exist pertaining to birthright citizenship in the Americas, where it has been shown that 30–35 sovereign nations in the Americas provide automatic birthright citizenship even to children of undocumented migrants. See K. Culliton-Gonzales, 'Born in the Americas: Birthright Citizenship and Human Rights', *Harvard Human Rights Journal*, 25 (2012), pp 131 & 179.

[76] J.M.M. Chan, 'The Right to a Nationality as a Human Right', *Human Rights Law Journal*, 12(1991), p 11.

[77] J.M.M. Chan, 'The Right to a Nationality as a Human Right', *Human Rights Law Journal*, 12(1991), p 11.

[78] J.M.M. Chan, 'The Right to a Nationality as a Human Right', p 11; Bern Convention of the International Commission of Civil Status to Reduce the Number of Cases of Statelessness, Bern (13 September 1973). See its Article 1 that provides that where a child would otherwise be stateless, the said child would acquire the nationality of its mother if the mother is a national of a Contracting State.

of the Child, particularly its Principle 3, and Article 8 of the UN General Assembly's Declaration on Social and Legal Principles relating to the Protection and Welfare of Children.[79]

Even though states are not required to apply the *jus soli* doctrine for every child born on their territory, the HR Committee appears to oblige states to confer nationality upon a child born in the territory who would be stateless.[80] The preference for an attribution of nationality *jus soli* could be seen in several Concluding Observations containing the relevant HR Committee's views on this matter. For instance, the HR Committee suggested for the State of Colombia to consider granting Colombian nationality on stateless children born in the said country.[81] The Committee also insisted that Syria grant its nationality to the Syrian-born children of stateless Kurds.[82]

In the drafting history of CRC, objections were raised against conferral of nationality by way of *jus soli* to children born without being granted nationality by other states at birth by countries whose *jus sanguinis* was more dominant and countries that did not grant automatic nationality to children born to foreign parents on their territories.[83] Concerns were also expressed that such a provision would generate a lot of reservations.[84] The delegations finally settled on a compromise through the adoption of the final draft of Article 7(2), explicitly obligating states to guarantee the implementation of this right, as suggested by the CRC Committee:

> States Parties shall ensure the implementation of these rights in accordance with their national law and their obligations under the relevant international instruments in this field, in particular where the child would otherwise be stateless.

The phrase 'in accordance with their national law' implies that both *jus soli* and *jus sanguinis* principles of nationality would be at par with each other.[85] Therefore, states

---

[79] UNGA, 3 December 1986, *Declaration on Social and Legal Principles relating to the Protection and Welfare of Children,* UN Doc. A/RES/41/85, New York: United Nations', Res/41/85. Article 8 states that 'The child should at all times have a name, a nationality and a legal representative. The child should not, as a result of foster placement, adoption or any alternative regime, be deprived of his or her name, nationality or legal representative unless the child thereby acquires a new name, nationality or legal representative'.

[80] J.M.M. Chan, 'The Right to a Nationality as a Human Right', *Human Rights Law Journal*, 12 (1991), p 5.

[81] Human Rights Committee, Concluding Observations: Colombia, A/52/40 vol. 1, Geneva: 1997, para 306, as cited in L. van Waas, *Nationality Matters: Statelessness under International Law* (School of Human Rights Research Series, V. 29, 2008), p 59.

[82] Human Rights Committee, Concluding Observations: the Syrian Arab Republic, A/60/40 vol. 1, Geneva: 2005, Section 94, para 19, as cited in L. van Waas, *Nationality Matters: Statelessness under International Law* (School of Human Rights Research Series, V. 29, 2008), p 59.

[83] S. Detrick, *A Commentary on the United Nations Convention on the Rights of the Child* (1999), p 124. The initial proposal in favour of *jus soli* attribution of nationality was suggested by the Australian representative who sought to align the right of the child to acquire a nationality as much as possible with prevention of statelessness under the 1961 Convention.

[84] S. Detrick, *A Commentary on the United Nations Convention on the Rights of the Child* (1999), p 151.

[85] S. Detrick, *A Commentary on the United Nations Convention on the Rights of the Child* (1999), p 151.

would be free to grant nationality to children based on their domestic legislation, including in cases involving children who would otherwise be stateless. Such freedom is only subject to their obligations in other instruments that address avoidance of childhood statelessness, in particular, the 1961 Convention.[86]

In the exercise of states' discretion over matters of nationality, including the right of every child to acquire a nationality, a number of guiding principles are to be observed, either by way of general principles, custom, or treaty obligations.[87] The following guiding principles shall be elaborated together with some arising issues bearing upon the normative safeguard against statelessness through the right to a nationality.

(i) The Prohibition of Arbitrary Deprivation of Nationality and Non-discrimination Principle

Previous studies highlight the major influence that the principle of non-discrimination has on informing the obligation of State Parties pursuant to Article 7 of CRC.[88] According to this principle,[89] childrenare to acquire a nationality regardless of the child's parents' or legal guardian's race, colour, sex, language, religion, political, or other opinion, national, ethnic, or social origin, property, disability, birth or other status.[90]

The prohibition of discrimination that is contained in other major human rights treaties, mainly ICCPR,[91] the 1965 Convention on the Elimination of Racial Discrimination (CERD),[92] the 1957 Convention of the Nationality of Married Women

---

[86] S. Detrick, *A Commentary on the United Nations Convention on the Rights of the Child* (1999), p 151.

[87] It must be clarified that the full array of international law on statelessness comprises not only the related treaties but also soft law standards and customary legal principles.

[88] Institute of Statelessness and Inclusion, *Addressing the Right to a Nationality through the Convention on the Rights of the Child, A Toolkit for Civil Society* (June 2016), p 8. Retrieved from http://www.institutesi.org/CRC_Toolkit_Final.pdf [Accessed 7 October 2016].

[89] The broad support for the rule of prohibition of non-discrimination promotes its status as 'a customary norm of a peremptory nature'. See A. Sironi, 'Nationality of Individuals in Public International Law: A Functional Approach' in A. Annoni & S. Forlati (Eds.), *The Changing Role of Nationality in International Law* (Oxon: Routledge, 2013), pp 54–55; M. Manly & L. van Waas, 'The Value of Human Security Framework in Addressing Statelessness' in A. Edwards & C. Frestman (Eds.), *Human Security and Non-Citizens: Law, Policy and International Affairs* (Cambridge: Cambridge University Press, 2010), p 64.

[90] See Article 2(1) CRC and HR Committee, A/HRC/31/29, p 3.

[91] See Articles 2 and 26 of ICCPR.

[92] International Convention on the Elimination of All Forms of Racial Discrimination (adopted 21 December 1965, in force 4 January 1969), 660 UNTS 195. Article 5(d) (iii) CERD specifically requires non-discrimination on the grounds of race, colour, descent, and national or ethnic origin in the enjoyment of the right to a nationality.

(CNMW),[93] and the 1978 Convention on the Elimination of All Forms of Discrimination against Women (CEDAW),[94] adds greater force to the regime of protection against statelessness.

The failure to abide by the prohibition of gender inequality in the conferral of nationality upon children in Article 9(2) and of inequality in the acquisition of nationality between children born within and out of wedlock[95] in implementing the right to acquire a nationality under Article 7[96] leads to arbitrary deprivation of nationality.[97] In *Genovese v. Malta*, the concept of private life embodied in Article 8 is held to be 'wide enough' to contain aspects of a person's social identity, with a right of nationality forming part of its components.[98] The Court found that the arbitrary denial of citizenship goes against a person's social identity, which is protected under the right to private life.

Even though the norm of non-discrimination is commanding in this regard, states may still choose not to be bound by this obligatory norm. For instance, the right to reserve such a broad-based concept of non-discrimination embodied in Article 2 of CRC is allowed, even if it may appear to be contrary to the object and purpose of the treaty.[99] Aside from Article 2, Article 7 of CRC itself is open to reservations by

[93] Convention on the Nationality of Married Women (adopted 29 January 1957, in force 11 August 1958), 309 UNTS 65. Articles 1 and 2 protect against loss of nationality of women from discriminatory effects resulting from their marriage to an alien and change, acquisition, or renunciation of nationality by the husband.

[94] Convention on the Eliminations of All Forms of Discrimination against Women (adopted 18 December 1979, in force 3 September 1981), 1249 UNTS 13. The right to a nationality is provided in its Article 5 as one of the rights that must be provided by states free from racial discrimination and subject to equality before the law. Articles 9(1) and (2) impose upon State Parties equality in respect of the right of men and women in acquiring, changing or retaining nationality, and in respect of conferral of nationality upon children.

[95] See HR Committee, General Comment No. 17 (1989).

[96] See HR Committee, A/HRC/31/29, p 3.

[97] UNGA, Secretary-General report on impact of the arbitrary deprivation of nationality on the enjoyment of the rights of children concerned, and existing laws and practices on accessibility for children to acquire nationality, inter alia, of the country in which they are born, if they otherwise would be stateless. HR Committee, A/HRC/31/29, 16 December 2015, para 8. Available at https://documents-dds-ny.un.org/doc/UNDOC/GEN/G15/286/02/PDF/G1528602.pdf?OpenElement; Institute on Statelessness and Inclusion, *Addressing the Right to a Nationality through the Convention on the Rights of the Child, A Toolkit for Civil Society*, p 8; A. Edwards, 'The Meaning of Nationality in International Law in an Era of Human Rights: Procedural and Substantive Aspects' in A. Edwards & L. van Waas (Eds.), *Nationality and Statelessness under International Law* (Cambridge: Cambridge University Press, 2014), p 25.

[98] See para 33 of the judgment.

[99] The Bahamas, Cook Islands, Luxemburg, Belgium, Malaysia and Qatar have entered their reservations on Article 2 relying on states' sovereignty in the conferment of nationality. See L.N. Coelho, *Reservations to the Convention on the Rights of the Child: the Committee's Approach*, Thesis, University of Amsterdam, p 4.

states, a mark of resentment against possible interference of international law in the sensitive domain of nationality.[100]

General Comment No. 15 by the Human Rights Committee (HR Committee) clarifies that the rights set forth in ICCPR shall apply to everyone, 'irrespective of reciprocity, and irrespective of his or her nationality or statelessness'.[101] As for aliens, exceptions apply with respect to Article 25 (right to participate in government) and Article 3 (expulsion of aliens).[102] Non-discrimination that may check and restraint state power in making distinctions between citizens and non-citizens can be restricted to non-citizens 'lawfully-staying in the territory', and could be applied subject to compelling reasons of national security of the state.[103] Article 2 of the 1985 Declaration on the Human Rights of Aliens[104] additionally maintains the prerogative of the state in controlling the entry of aliens, imposing any laws and regulations on their entry, and creating differences between nationals and aliens.[105] In light of these norms, protection against statelessness by way of conferral of citizenship *jus soli* on children of undocumented and irregular migrants born in the territory of the host state inevitably creates a point of tension with the power of the state to control access to rights, entry, and movement of aliens and their expulsion.

Globally, the ever-escalating waves of asylum seekers and low-wage irregular migrants are increasingly viewed as a threat to both the state sovereignty and security, prompting border policing to highly focus on these groups for control and scrutiny.[106]

---

[100] T.Y. Leinwand, 'Navigating Nationality: The Rights to Birth Registration and Nationality in Refugee Magnet States' (2014), p 127.

[101] UN Human Rights Committee, CCPR General Comment No. 15: The Position of Aliens under the Covenant, 27th session, 11 April 1986, p 127, para 1. Retrieved from http://www.refworld.org/docid/45139acfc.html [Accessed 13 October 2016].

[102] It is to be cautioned that the permissibility of distinctions in the treatment between citizens and non-citizens must be made in pursuit of a legitimate aim, based on an objective justification and is reasonably proportionate to the aims sought to be achieved. See South West Africa Case, Dissenting Opinion of Judge Tanaka (1966) ICJ Reports 6, p 313; and Belgian Linguistics Case (1968) ECHR, 23 July 1968; UN Human Rights Committee, CCPR General Comment No. 15: The Position of Aliens under the Covenant, 27th session, 11 April 1986, p 127 para 2. Retrieved from http://www.refworld.org/docid/45139acfc.html [Accessed 13 October 2016].

[103] See T.A. Aleinikoff, 'International Legal Norms and Migration: A Report' in T.A. Aleinikoff & V. Chetail (Eds.), *Migration and International Legal Norms* (The Hague: T.M.C. Asser Press, 2003), p 19.

[104] UN General Assembly, Declaration on the Human Rights of individuals who are not nationals of the Country in which they live: Resolution /adopted by the General Assembly, 13 December 1985, UN Doc. A/RES/40/144. Retrieved from http://www.refworld.org/docid/3b00f00864.html [Accessed 13 October 2016].

[105] Article 2 of the said Declaration provides that, 'Nothing in this Declaration shall be taken as legitimising the illegal entry into and presence in a State of any alien, nor shall any provision be interpreted as restricting the right of any State to promulgate laws and regulations concerning the entry of aliens and the terms and conditions of their stay or to establish differences between nationals and aliens'.

[106] P. Oberoi & E. Taylor-Nicholson, 'The Enemy at the Gates: International Borders, Migration and Human Rights', *Laws*, V. 2(3) (2013), pp 171–172.

Migration legal regime has, nevertheless, been demonstrated as inadequate to counterweight the effects of the lack of protection via the right to a nationality.[107] Take for instance ICMW, which contains some limits that impede the ability of children born to stateless, refugees, and undocumented migrants to be prevented from statelessness. This Convention guarantees the interrelated rights to a name, birth registration, and nationality for children of migrant workers in its Article 29, as follows:

> [e]ach child of a migrant worker shall have the right to a name, to registration of birth and to a nationality.

In principle, this right applies to both regular and irregular migrant workers as Article 29 is housed in the general section providing for the rights of all migrant workers. However, stateless persons and refugees are not covered in the scope of the Convention's application. A child born to a stateless regular or irregular migrant worker is, therefore, excluded from the Convention's benefits.[108] This is despite the stateless and refugee parents' capacity to meet the definition of a 'migrant worker'.[109] Another drawback is that, even though the rights provided by ICMW apply to families of migrant workers, the term 'migrant workers' referred to in Articles 1 and 5 does not envisage the situation of regular migrant workers who have some or all of family members who are undocumented.[110]

(ii) **The Principle of the Best Interests of the Child**

The principle of the best interests of the child provides that in all actions or decisions concerning the child in both public and private spheres, the child's best interests are to be assessed and taken into account as a primary consideration.[111] The Human Rights Council underscores that this principle must be respected by states in their administrative and legislative acts in the area of nationality, including in exercising the safeguards to prevent statelessness among children.[112] In the context of protection

---

[107] Tang Lay Lee, *Statelessness, Human Rights and Gender: Irregular Migrant Workers from Burma in Thailand* (Leiden: Martinus Nijhoff Publishers, 2005), pp 10 and 55–62.

[108] Article 3(d) of ICMW provides that the Convention is inapplicable to 'refugees and stateless persons unless such application is provided for in the relevant national legislation of, or international instruments in force for, the State Party concerned'.

[109] L. van Waas, *Nationality Matters: Statelessness under International Law* (School of Human Rights Research Series, V. 29, 2008), p 173; Tang Lay Lee, *Statelessness, Human Rights and Gender: Irregular Migrant Workers from Burma in Thailand* (2005), p 53.

[110] Tang Lay Lee, *Statelessness, Human Rights and Gender: Irregular Migrant Workers from Burma in Thailand*, (2005), p 57. Article 1 guarantees that ICMW applies to all migrant workers and members of their families without any distinction including on the basis of their nationality. Under Article 5, 'migrant workers and members of their families' are defined to be either documented or in a regular situation, or non-documented or in an irregular situation. Such may exclude regular migrant workers with some or all family members who are undocumented.

[111] CRC Committee, General Comment No. 14. 2013: The right of the child to have his or her best interests taken as a primary consideration (Art. 3, para. 1), UN Doc. No. CRC/C/GC/14, Geneva: CRC Committee.

[112] UN Human Rights Council, *Impact of the Arbitrary Deprivation of Nationality on the Enjoyment of the Rights of Children Concerned and Existing Laws and Practices on Accessibility for Children*

against statelessness for children, this denotes that children must acquire a nationality at birth or as soon after it, and must not be left stateless for a prolonged period of time,[113] without their nationality status determined.[114]

The regional tribunals that considered and applied this principle include *Yean and Bosico,* the *Kenyan Nubian case*, and *Mennesson v. France*. In *Yean and Bosico,*[115] the state, inter alia, acted arbitrarily and in a way contrary to the 'superior interest' of the child by increasing the requirements for registering the births of the Yean and Bosico children, leaving them stateless and in extreme vulnerability with regard to their enjoyment of rights.[116] In *Mennesson v. France,*[117] the best interests principle guided the decision that acknowledges the right to one's social identity as part of his or her private life. In the context of its application to the legal parent–child relationship, the margin of appreciation possessed by the state was held to be narrow when it comes to parentage, a paramount element of an individual's identity that implies the respect for the person's private life.[118] The court held that depriving a child of an established legal tie with his or her biological parent could not be said to be in the best interests of the child and went against the children's right to private life under Article 8 of ECHR.

The CRC Committee acknowledges that the concept of the child's best interests is a complicated one, yet flexible, and should be determined on a case-by-case basis.[119] The influence of this principle on the scope and substance of the right of children to acquire a nationality has nevertheless received a limited elaboration by the CRC Committee in their recommendations to State Parties.[120] It is thus legitimate to question whether decision-makers are in the first place equipped with the knowledge and tools to carry out such best-interest assessment, bearing in mind its purpose of ensuring the full and effective enjoyment of the rights in the CRC, and the short and long-term holistic development of the child.[121] Consider, for instance, the following complex situation:

---

to Acquire Nationality, inter alia, of the Country in Which They are Born, If They Otherwise Would be Stateless (2015), UN Doc. A/HRC/31/29, para 9, p 4. Retrieved from http://www.refworld.org/docid/56c42b514.html [Accessed 5 September 2016].

[113] See *Institute for Human Rights and Development in Africa (IHRDA) and Open Society Justice Initiative on behalf of Children of Nubian Descent in Kenya v. The Government of Kenya* (Decision: No 002/Com/002/2009), 22 March 2011 (*The Kenyan Nubian case*) and Guidelines No. 4.

[114] See *Mennesson v. France*, Decision of 26 June 2014.

[115] *Yean and Bosico v. Dominican Republic* (Series C, Case 130, 8 September 2005).

[116] *Yean and Bosico v. Dominican Republic*, para 166.

[117] *Mennesson v. France*, Decision of 26 June 2014.

[118] *Mennesson v. France,* Decision of 26 June 2014, p 3.

[119] General comment No. 14 (2013) on the right of the child to have his or her best interests taken as a primary consideration (Art.3, para 1), UN Doc. CRC/C/GC/14, Geneva: CRC (2013), para 32–34.

[120] Institute on Statelessness and Inclusion, *Addressing the Right to a Nationality through the Convention on the Rights of the Child, A Toolkit for Civil Society*, p 9.

[121] See para 84 of General Comment No. 14 (2013) pertaining to Article 3(1) CRC.

> The avoidance of statelessness—as a matter of principle—is always in the child's best interest. But in case the refugee child's nationality is unclear … her/his best interest would be served in the acquisition of *which* nationality? Should a host state pursue the widest possible application of the legal safeguards applicable to 'otherwise stateless' children and thus integrate as many refugee children as possible into its own community of nationals? Or should refugee children primarily be encouraged and helped to obtain a documentary proof of having inherited their parents' nationality (where this happens *ipso facto*)?[122]

Ending statelessness is undoubtedly a delicate process as it is not just a matter of granting a nationality, but rather finding the best nationality solution for a child in a given case. The CRC Committee has, in fact, encouraged the development of procedures and criteria to all relevant persons in authority for determining the best interests of the child and according them due deliberation as a primary consideration, including in the determination of statelessness.[123] In its General Comment No. 14 (2013) pertaining to Article 3(1) CRC, the elements in the child's best interests, including when they conflict, will have to be carefully balanced against each other to find a solution or a suitable compromise in the best interests of the child or children.[124] In doing so, the child's interests occupy a high priority, not merely one of several considerations, and thus must be attributed a greater weight through individualised procedures in all legislative, administrative, and judicial proceedings, and migration policies and programmes affecting children, including consular protection policies and services.[125]

(c) ***Other Regional Norms on the Right to a Nationality and Prevention of Childhood Statelessness***

Albeit lacking the enjoyment of extensive ratification, the 1961 Convention is reinforced by consistent regional norms adopting avoidance of statelessness at birth by means of nationality attributed on the basis of *jus soli*. Article 20(2) of AmCHR acknowledges the right of an otherwise stateless child to receive the nationality of her state of birth. Aside from reiterating the content of Article 15 of UDHR under Articles 4(a) and (c), the right to acquisition of nationality ex lege by children born

---

122 G. Gyulai, 'The Long-Overlooked Mystery of Refugee Children's Nationality' in Institute on Statelessness and Inclusion, *The World's Stateless Children* (2017). Retrieved from http://children.worldsstateless.org/3/migration-displacement-and-childhood-statelessness/the-long-overlooked-mystery-of-refugee-childrens-nationality.html [Accessed 5 July 2017].

123 Committee on the Rights of the Child, Concluding Observation: Turkmenistan, UN Doc. CRC/C/TKM/CO/2-4: CRC in Institute on Statelessness and Inclusion, *Addressing the Right to a Nationality through the Convention on the Rights of the Child, A Toolkit for Civil Society*, p 9.

124 General Comment No. 14 (2013) on the right of the child to have his or her best interests taken as a primary consideration (Art.3, para 1), para 81.

125 Committee on the Protection of the Rights of All Migrants Workers and Members of Their Families (CMW), Joint General Comment No. 3 (2017) of the Committee on the Protection of the Rights of All Migrant Workers and Members of Their Families and No. 22 (2017) of the Committee on the Rights of the Child on the General Principles regarding the Human Rights of Children in the Context of International Migration, 16 November 2017, CMW/C/GC/3-CRC/C/GC/22, para 28 and 32(b). Retrieved From http://www.refworld.org/docid/5a1293a24.html [Accessed 30 December 2017].

in the territory of the State Party who do not acquire at birth another nationality is underlined in Article 6(2) of ECN, in line with the duty of State Parties to avoid statelessness under Article 4(b). Article 6(4) of ACRWC also requires constitutional recognition of a child who would otherwise be stateless to acquire the citizenship of the country in which the child is born, if the child is not granted the nationality of any other state at birth.

Europe relatively displays sophisticated standards on prevention and reduction of statelessness, both in terms of norms and practices compared to other regions. The Council of Europe has been vigorous in their standard-setting endeavours in the field of nationality law. ECN, the 2006 European Convention on the Avoidance of Statelessness with respect to State Succession, Recommendation 2009/13 by Council of Europe elaborating the position of children under nationality law, are among the main instruments that set benchmarks in the area of children and their right to a nationality. In addition, various reports and studies on nationality and statelessness affecting children have been produced under the purview of the Council of Europe and its organs.[126]

In 2015, the African Committee of Experts (ACERWC) that monitors the implementation of ACRWC, took a remarkable stride by launching its General Comment to interpret the meaning, scope, and implementation by states of the rights of children guaranteed under Article 6 of the Charter. This pronouncement is indeed something that the CRC Committee could draw inspiration from, in terms of elaborating the scope and implementation of Article 7(1) of CRC. Premised on the international legal prohibition on discrimination pertaining to rules regarding nationality, ACERWC expresses its denunciation of the prevailing elements of gender, racial, and ethnic-related discrimination in the laws of several African countries.[127]

Echoing the guidance provided by UNHCR,[128] ACERWC urges states to acknowledge that a child is stateless if the child has been indicated not to be a national of another country, either through an expressed statement, or by way of its failure to reply to inquiries to ascertain that the said child is a national.[129] The Committee further issued many recommendations that adhere to the guidance. In some of them, it goes on to promote the provision of nationality attribution not only to children who are otherwise stateless, but also to children who exhibit the strongest connection to the state.[130]

---

[126] G.R. de Groot et al., *Practices and Approaches in EU Member States to Prevent and End Statelessness* (2015). Retrieved from http://www.europarl.europa.eu/RegData/etudes/STUD/2015/536476/IPOL_STU(2015)536476_EN.pdf [Accessed 13 January 2016]; G.R. de Groot et al., *Protection against Statelessness: Trends and Regulations in Europe* (2013). Retrieved from http://eudo-citizenship.eu/images/docs/eudocit_vink_degroot_statelessness_final.pdf [Accessed 1 April 2016].

[127] General Comment on Article 6 of ACRWC: The Right to a Name, Registration at Birth, and to Acquire a Nationality, ACERWC/GC/02, Addis Ababa: African Union, 2014, see para 6.

[128] UNHCR, *Handbook on Protection of Stateless Persons* (2014), p 17.

[129] ACERWC's General Comment No. 2 on Article 6, para 100.

[130] The recommendations can be found in paragraph 92 of ACERWC's General Comment No. 2 on Article 6 as extracted herein: (i) a child born in the State with one parent (either mother or father) also born in the State acquires the nationality of that State at birth; (ii) States to provide provisions giving

The rule that children who would otherwise be stateless be conferred nationality *jus soli* is strengthened further by the decision of *Kenyan Nubian case* that requires the said right to be accorded 'constitutional recognition'.[131] ACERWC heard this case brought on behalf of the Nubian children in Kenya for alleged violation of their rights to birth registration and to acquire a nationality at birth under Articles 6(2), (3) and (4) of ACRWC.[132]

The children of Kenyan Nubians inherit their parents' undocumented status and without identification documents, could not undertake their birth registration. The Nubians in Kenya who originated from Sudan and began to settle in Kenya since the time they were taken into the country by the British, acquired neither British nor Kenyan citizenship subsequent to the independence of Kenya in 1963. Birth registration certificates for Kenyan Nubian children who could obtain them, however, were not regarded proof of citizenship. Such reasons gave rise to statelessness among the affected children.

It was held by the Committee that the Kenyan Government violated Article 6(2) of ACRWC for failing to register the Nubian children. Further, there was a violation of Articles 6(3) and (4) of the Charter for the failure of the Kenyan Government to grant nationality to children who would otherwise be stateless by virtue of not being granted nationality anywhere. The principle of the best interests of the child upheld in Article 4 of the African Charter guided the interpretation of Article 6(1) of ACRWC, leading to the conclusion by the Court that children should have a nationality from birth.[133] The Court also ordered for legislative, administrative, and other measures to be taken to ensure that children of Nubian descent receive immediate registration after birth.[134]

Moving to SEA, obstacles to building strong regional norms on avoidance of statelessness could be attributed to the relatively weak human rights framework at

children born in their territory the right to acquire nationality after a period of residence that does not require the child to wait until majority before nationality can be confirmed (as recommended in the Kenyan Nubian case); (iii) children who are born in the territory of parents who are lawfully and habitually resident there to acquire nationality at birth (iv); and States to facilitate the acquisition of nationality by children who were not born in the territory but who arrived there as children and have been resident there for a large portion of their childhood.

[131] See *the Kenyan Nubian case.* Para 50 of the decision states: '...Therefore, while the African Committee is not suggesting that States Parties to the Charter should introduce the *jus soli* approach, in line with the best interests of the child principle, it is explaining the intent of Article 6(4) of the African Children's Charter that if a child is born in the territory of a State Party and is not granted nationality by another State, the State in whose territory the child is born, in this particular case Kenya, should allow the child to acquire its nationality.'

[132] *Institute for Human Rights and Development in Africa (IHRDA) and Open Society Justice Initiative on behalf of Children of Nubian Descent in Kenya v. The Government of Kenya* (Decision: No 002/Com/002/2009), 22 March 2011.

[133] See para 42 of *Institute for Human Rights and Development in Africa (IHRDA) and Open Society Justice Initiative on behalf of Children of Nubian Descent in Kenya v. The Government of Kenya* (Decision: No 002/Com/002/2009), 22 March 2011.

[134] *Institute for Human Rights and Development in Africa (IHRDA) and Open Society Justice Initiative on behalf of Children of Nubian Descent in Kenya v. The Government of Kenya* (Decision: No 002/Com/002/2009), 22 March 2011, para 69.

the ASEAN level, which is argued to be operating at the stage of 'courting rather than upholding the promotion and protection of human rights'.[135] As observed by the Institute on Statelessness and Inclusion:

> Unlike the Africa, the Americas and Europe, the Asia and Pacific region does not have a regional human rights framework, with its own treaty, court, and commission (or equivalent bodies). This lacuna means that there is a dearth of regional norms and jurisprudence which sets out the rights of all persons including the stateless. In the absence of such a regional framework, the importance of the UN framework is greater.[136]

Persuasion and publicity are seemingly the most favoured tools to advance human rights among the ASEAN Member States. Within ASEAN, the attempt to link the right to a nationality and avoidance of statelessness has also been compromised by how the text of Article 18 of the ASEAN Human Rights Declaration is couched. The provision of Article 18 reads, 'Every person has the right to a nationality as prescribed by law'. The phrase 'as prescribed by law' entails that the right to a nationality is eventually to be subject to domestic nationality regulations of the ASEAN Member States.

Notwithstanding the above, a number of existing human rights instruments of ASEAN, albeit constituting soft law, may serve to provide an important window for progressive actions to emerge toward realising the individual right to a nationality. For instance, the ASEAN Commission on the Promotion and Protection of the Rights of Women and Children (ACWC) issued the 2013 Declaration on the Elimination of Violence against Women and Violence against Children in ASEAN. This instrument acknowledges among others, the significance of preventing and protecting women and children in vulnerable situations, including stateless women and children from abuse and exploitation.[137] Meanwhile, the ASEAN Committee on the Protection and Promotion on the Rights of Migrant Workers (ACMW) in Article 2 of the ASEAN Declaration on the Protection and Promotion of the Rights of Migrant Workers 2007,[138] calls for close cooperation between receiving and sending states in finding solutions to cases of migrant workers, who have subsequently become undocumented through no fault of their own.[139]

---

[135] Yuyun Wahyuningrum, *The ASEAN Intergovernmental Commission on Human Rights: Origin, Evolution and the Way Forward*, Discussion Paper (Institute for Democracy and Electoral Assistance (IDEA), 12 December 2014), p 25.

[136] Institute on Statelessness and Inclusion, *The World's Stateless Children* (2017), p59. Retrieved from http://www.institutesi.org/worldsstateless17.pdf [Accessed 5 January 2018].

[137] ASEAN, *The Declaration on the Elimination of Violence Against Women and Elimination of Violence Against Children in ASEAN* (2004). Retrieved from http://aseanevaw.org/wp-content/uploads/2014/03/A4-declaration-eng.pdf [12 August 2015].

[138] ASEAN, *ASEAN Declaration on the Protection for the Protection and Promotion of the Rights of Migrant Workers,* Cebu City: Association of Southeast Asian Nations (13 January 2007).

[139] Article 2 under its General principles provides that 'The receiving States and the sending States shall, for humanitarian reasons, closely cooperate to resolve the cases of migrant workers who, through no fault of their own, have subsequently become undocumented'. See the text of the Declaration at http://www.ilo.org/dyn/migpractice/docs/117/Declaration.pdf.

The ASEAN Convention against Trafficking in Persons (ACTIP)[140] and the ASEAN Consensus on the Protection and Promotion of the Rights of Migrant Workers[141] could further provide leverage for the advent of more effective standards of protection for such vulnerable groups. Articles 15(3) and (4) of ACTIP adopt a mechanism of cooperation between Receiving and Requesting States in the verification of nationality or permanent residence status of the victim concerned and the issuance of travel documents or other necessary authorisation for repatriation and return of victims including the undocumented ones. As for the Consensus, General Principle 1(e) underlines the commitment of the Member States of ASEAN to 'uphold fair treatment with respect to gender and nationality, and protect the rights of migrant workers, particularly women, in accordance with the obligations of ASEAN Member States under appropriate international instruments to which they are parties.'

AICHR, ACWC, and ACMW possess their respective mandates to propose useful measures to resolve statelessness, including by ensuring undocumented and otherwise stateless children have access to legal identity documents, including a nationality. However, there are underlying limitations to their capabilities to enforce such measures, owing largely to resource constraints and non-binding force of their instruments.[142]

Outside ASEAN, the right to a nationality and protection of stateless persons are also dealt by the Asian-African Legal Consultative Council (AALCO), a forum established for research, training, exchange of views, and providing advice to governments on matters of international law.[143] Aside from its principles and articles adopted in relation to the rights of non-nationals including on nationality, its 2006 Resolution on 'Legal Identity and Statelessness' is considered pertinent for calling for avoidance of statelessness and taking measures to better address the issue of stateless persons.[144] The Resolution affirms the strong nexus between the legal bond of nationality and the legal identity of an individual. The Resolution encourages among others that its Member States review their nationality legislation for the purpose of reducing and avoiding statelessness and to actively cooperate in the identification of statelessness,

---

[140] *ASEAN Convention against Trafficking in Persons, Especially Women and Children*, 21 November 2015 (entered into force 8 March 2016). See the text of ACTIP at https://asean.org/wp-content/uploads/2012/05/APA-FINAL.pdf [Accessed 26 September 2018].

[141] ASEAN Consensus on the Protection and Promotion of the Rights of Migrant Workers, done in Manila, the Philippines on 14 November 2017. See the text of the Consensus at https://asean.org/storage/2012/05/16-ASEAN-Declaration-on-the-Protection-and-Promotion-of-the-Rights-of-Mipdf [Accessed 26 September 2018].

[142] Institute on Statelessness and Inclusion, *The World's Stateless Children* (2017), p 59.

[143] As of February 2019, it has 47 member countries. See the website of AALCO at http://www.aalco.int/scripts/view-posting.asp?recordid=3.

[144] See Asian-African Legal Consultative Organization (AALCO), *Resolution on the Half-Day Special Meeting on 'Legal Identity and Statelessness'*, 8 April 2006, RES/45/ SP.I. Retrieved from https://www.refworld.org/docid/44eaddc54.html [accessed 5 August 2017].

paying particular attention to 'establishing identity and acquiring relevant documentation for women, children, and families in instances of displacement, migration or trafficking'.[145]

(d) ***Specific Framework for Prevention and Reduction of Statelessness under the 1961 Convention***

The 1961 Convention was crafted to avoid future cases of statelessness through factors such as birth in the territory, descent from a national, habitual residence, and family ties, for purposes of nationality determination. Under Articles 1 to 4, states shall grant their nationality to children who would otherwise be stateless, through the link of birth in the territory or descent. The grant shall either be by automatic means/operation of law at birth, or, upon application.[146]

The term 'would otherwise be stateless' refers to a scenario whereby a child would be stateless unless a Contracting State with which he or she has a link through birth in the territory or birth to a national of that State grants that child its nationality.[147] The test of 'an otherwise stateless child' is, therefore, to determine whether the child has acquired the nationality of another state, either from his/her parents (*jus sanguinis* principle) or from the state on whose territory the child was born (*jus soli* principle), regardless of the situation of the parent(s). In other words, it is the nationality status of the child that is under inquiry, not of the parent(s).[148] Additionally, the object of elimination of statelessness at birth targets foundlings through the grant of nationality based on the presumption that they are nationals.[149]

In interpreting the provisions of the 1961 Convention in the context of prevention of statelessness among children, two important instruments have been adopted by UNHCR as the guidelines: (i) Interpreting the 1961 Statelessness Convention and Preventing Statelessness among Children (Dakar Conclusions)[150]; and (ii) Guidelines on Statelessness No. 4: Ensuring Every Child's Right to Acquire a Nationality through Article 1–4 of the 1961 Convention on the Reduction of Statelessness (Guidelines No. 4).[151] Throughout this book, frequent references are made to Guidelines No. 4 as the main interpretive guidelines, which are built upon several expert meetings, including Dakar Conclusions.

---

145 See para 3 and 4 of the Resolution.

146 The other areas where prevention of statelessness is targeted are avoidance of statelessness due to loss or renunciation of nationality under Articles 5 to 7; avoidance of statelessness due to deprivation of nationality under Articles 8 and 9; and avoidance of statelessness in the sphere of state succession under Article 10.

147 Para 18 Guidelines No. 4.

148 Dakar Conclusions, para 12; See also Guidelines No. 4, para 18.

149 Article 2 of the 1961 Convention. See further para VI of Guidelines No. 4 at p 12.

150 UNHCR, *Interpreting the 1961 Statelessness Convention and Preventing Statelessness among Children: Dakar Conclusions* (2011). Retrieved http://www.refworld.org/docid/4e8423a72.html [Accessed 12 August 2016].

151 UNHCR, *Guidelines on Statelessness No. 4: Ensuring Every Child's Right to Acquire a Nationality through Article 1–4 of the 1961 Convention on the Reduction of Statelessness* (2012). Retrieved from http://www.refworld.org/docid/50d460c72.html [Accessed 25 June 2016].

i. Protection against Statelessness for 'Otherwise Stateless Children' under the 1961 Convention: Principles, Mechanisms and Issues of Concern

The safeguard against statelessness under the 1961 Convention requires the Contracting States to provide in their nationality laws that children born on their territories acquire the nationality of the states concerned ex lege or by application, if they would otherwise be stateless.[152] The obligation arises only with respect to children who cannot obtain any other nationality.[153] As for children born to a Contracting State's national outside of its territory, the nationality of the Contracting State shall be granted if the nationality of one of the child's parents at the time of birth was that of the Contracting State.[154] Articles 1 and 4 of the 1961 Convention contain these two mechanisms of safeguard against statelessness.[155]

> Article 1:
>
> A Contracting State shall grant its nationality to a person born on its territory who would otherwise be stateless.
>
> Article 4:
>
> A Contracting State shall grant nationality to a person, not born in the territory of a Contracting State, who would otherwise be stateless if the nationality of one of his parents at the time of the person's birth was that of that State.

Determining 'An Otherwise Stateless Child': Possible Confusion

Other than having stateless parents, children would otherwise be stateless if their parent(s) who possess a nationality are unable to transmit such nationality to their children, including as a result of gender-discriminatory nationality provisions. As shall be illustrated, the determination of an 'otherwise stateless child' is not as straightforward and uncomplicated.

Firstly, the procedures involved in deciding whether a child is otherwise stateless might easily be confused with the process of statelessness status determination procedures, aiming at the identification and protection of stateless persons. As there

---

[152] Article 1(1) of the 1961 Convention.

[153] UNHCR, *Global Action Plan to End Statelessness* (2014), p 10.

[154] Article 4 (1) of the 1961 Convention.

[155] These provisions reflect a compromise between *jus soli* and *jus sanguinis* states. In the case of a Contracting State that adopts a strict *jus sanguinis* doctrine, Article 1 requires that the State provides for attribution of *jus soli* to benefit a child born on its territory who would otherwise be stateless. Correspondingly, based on Article 4, *jus soli* countries should introduce nationality *jus sanguinis* to a child born to its national abroad if the said child would otherwise be stateless. See L. van Waas, *Nationality Matters: Statelessness under International Law.* (School of Human Rights Research Series, V. 29), p 54. These two provisions are regarded as the cornerstone of strategies to prevent statelessness among children, including avoiding cases resulting from a conflict between *jus sanguinis* and *jus soli* doctrines. See Guidelines No. 4 at p 2. Bachelor further adds that by basing nationality upon place of birth and descent, the drafters indirectly suggest that these are ample grounds, 'genuine and effective' to connect an individual to a particular State, including a person who has received no nationality. See C. A. Batchelor, 'Statelessness and the Problem of Resolving Nationality Status', p 156 and p 162.

are other different manners in which a child may be rendered stateless,[156] it would be misguided if the interpretation of the scope of 'otherwise stateless' children were to be narrowed strictly to children born to stateless parents or parents of unknown citizenship, such as in Croatia, Czech Republic, Latvia, Macedonia, and Slovenia, as well as in half of the countries in West Africa.[157]

As such, if it is not clearly provided that 'otherwise stateless children' are not restricted to children of parents recognised as stateless,[158] it is feared that children born to parents not being stateless or officially determined to be stateless might be excluded from the protection envisaged under the 1961 Convention, despite not being able to acquire a nationality from their parents.

Next, requiring a person to prove the negative, namely, their lack of nationality elsewhere is likely to be problematic, especially for certain groups of individuals such as children born abroad to undocumented migrant parents and refugees. The Human Rights Council warned that:

> [c]hildren born in exile to refugee parents and children of undocumented migrants can be especially vulnerable to statelessness, owing to practical and procedural obstacles in their access to their parents' nationality.[159]

As further exemplified by Manby, the requirement is highly challenging against the background of individuals originating from countries with predominantly *jus sanguinis* nationality regimes, such as Africa and Asia.

> Requiring a person to prove their lack of nationality elsewhere is an impossible demand to place, especially in the African context, and especially when nationality laws are frequently drafted to allow indefinite transmission of nationality for generations born outside the country.[160]

Reduction Effect rather than Elimination—The Downsides of Nationality by Application

Based on Article 1(1) (a) and (b) of the 1961 Convention, the state of birth of an otherwise stateless person may choose to grant nationality under three modalities:

- automatically (ex lege or by operation of law) at birth to a person born on its territory (Article 1(1)(a)); or

---

156 G.R. de Groot et al., *Protection against Statelessness: Trends and Regulations in Europe*' (2013), p 42.

157 G.R. de Groot et al., '*Protection against Statelessness: Trends and Regulations in Europe*' (2013), p 42; See also HR Committee, A/HRC/31/29, p 8.

158 ECN, *Statelessness Determination and the Protection Status of Stateless Persons* (2013); European Network on Statelessness, *Preventing Childhood Statelessness in Europe: Issues, Gaps and Good Practices*' (2014), p 14. Italy, for instance, has been reported to only allow the child to acquire nationality by way of their safeguard if it is officially confirmed that the child's parent is stateless after conducting the statelessness determination procedure. See UNHCR, Guidelines on Statelessness No. 4, para 58.

159 See HR Committee, A/HRC/31/29, p 7.

160 B. Manby, *Citizenship and Statelessness in Africa: The Law and Politics of Belonging* (2015), p 459.

- by operation of law at a fixed age determined by domestic law, subject to conditions set by the domestic law (Article 1(1) (b)); or
- upon application in the case of a person born on the State's territory (Article 1(1)(b)). The application may be made subject to one or more of the conditions provided in Article 2, namely; (a) the period of lodging the application shall be fixed by the Contracting State, starting prior to the age of eighteen years, and ending before the age of twenty-one years[161]; (b) the residency requirement of being habitually resident in the Contracting State for a period fixed by that State, which must not exceed five years immediately prior to the lodging of the application nor ten years in all; (c) freedom from conviction of an offence against national security nor imprisonment sentence exceeding five years on a criminal charge; and (d) that the person has always been stateless.

It seems clear that the 1961 instrument allows for a relatively wide margin of state discretion in conferring nationality upon children. The preceding options afforded to the Contracting States reflect that a complete eradication of statelessness is not the aim and purpose of the 1961 Convention.[162] States may choose to decide at what age (for instance, in early childhood or later) and by what conditions, childrencan acquire citizenship upon application.[163] Further, the option to grant citizenship to otherwise stateless children by application and subject to the residency requirement, namely of fulfilling habitual residence, freedom from criminal conviction, and continuous statelessness experienced by children,[164] serves only to meet partial safeguards against statelessness.[165]

In line with the principle of the best interests of the child and the desired object of eradication of statelessness, Guidelines No. 4 underline that the preferred mechanism remains the ex lege or automatic conferral of nationality at birth to otherwise stateless children, as such would prevent even a brief period of statelessness for the child

[161] This is to enable the child who has reached the age of majority but has missed the deadline to still lodge an application with the State. See para 39 of Guidelines No. 4.

[162] The resolution 896 (IX) of the General Assembly of the UN adopted on 4 December 1954 (Resolution 896 (IX), Elimination or reduction of future statelessness, 504th plenary meeting, 4 December 1954), desired to adopt a Convention on elimination or at the minimum, reduction of statelessness. The UN Conference on the Elimination or Reduction of Future Statelessness which took place firstly in 1959 and subsequently in 1960 had settled on adopting the draft dealing with the Reduction of Statelessness as the working draft for further debate and discussion. Driven by the strong *jus soli* principle as the key principle to eliminate statelessness, the first draft was regarded to be less attractive to states adopting the traditional *jus sanguinis regime* and was therefore forsaken. Finally, the Convention on the Reduction of Statelessness was adopted on 30 August 1961 and came into force on 13 December 1975. See UNGA, United Nations Conference on the Elimination or Reduction of Future Statelessness, Summary Records, Sixth Plenary meeting, UN Doc. A/CONF.9/C.1/SR.9. UNGA: Geneva (31 March 1959), pp 1–3; See UNHR, Information and Accession Package: The 1954 Convention Relating to the Status of Stateless Persons and the 1961 Convention on the Reduction of Statelessness, (Revised 1999), United Nations: Geneva' (1996).

[163] Article 1(1)(b) of Dakar Conclusions.

[164] Article 1(1)(b) and Article 2 of Dakar Conclusions.

[165] See L. van Waas, *Nationality Matters: Statelessness under International Law* (School of Human Rights Research Series, V. 29, 2008), p 88.

concerned.[166] Another merit of this ex lege conferral system is that it shall avoid problems related to the application process, such as lack of knowledge, associated costs, or other practical challenges in meeting the procedures.[167] Admittedly, an automatic attribution of nationality may not be feasible in cases where access to nationality is politically sensitive and structural discrimination drives exclusion of certain marginalised groups. The plight of the Roma ethnics is an illustrative case in point. The state's attitude in renouncing any responsibility for their right to a legal identity including birth registration is well captured in the argument put forward by the Netherlands, in the case of Kalderas Gypsies v Federal Republic of Germany and Netherlands[168]:

> Whilst recognising that the legal position of stateless gypsies generally leaves much to be desired, the Government emphasised that no specific State could be designated as bearing a special legal responsibility towards an unlimited number of persons belonging to this group, either in connection with their wish to possess identity papers or with their wish to move freely from one country to another or to settle in a certain place. Consequently, no specific responsibility could be attributed to the state on whose territory the gypsies concerned chance to be at a given moment.[169]

Where states opt to grant nationality via the method of application to an otherwise stateless child, barriers commonly tend to surface. Certain procedures are put in place, which may not be able to be executed by, or, on behalf of the child. The requirement of submission of a birth certificate, for instance, could be in the realm of impossibility for children born to irregular migrant parents with no legal status in the country of birth, and where birth registration is made contingent on parents' proof of legal status. Furthermore, one can least expect hidden and marginalised parents to approach the relevant competent authorities for clarification and verification of their nationality. These usually entail irregular/undocumented migrants, including parents from

[166] Such is in line with the principle of the best interests of the child as a primary consideration upheld in Article 3 of the CRC and other regional standards such as Article 20 of the AmCHR and Article 6 of ACRWC. See further para 9, 34 and 5 of Guidelines No. 4.

[167] European Network on Statelessness, *Preventing Childhood Statelessness in Europe: Issues, Gaps and Good Practices* (2014), p 8. It is to be noted that the responsibility to grant nationality to an otherwise stateless child does not arise if the child born stateless could acquire a nationality by registration from the State of the nationality of his parent, or through other procedures such as a declaration or a right of option. However, the said responsibility is not engaged only when the child could acquire the nationality as soon after his birth, and when the State of the parent's nationality does not have the discretion to refuse the grant of nationality. See paras 24 and 25 of Guidelines No. 4.

[168] *Kalderas Gypsies v. the Federal Republic of Germany and the Netherlands*. Judgment of 6 July 1977, Application No. 7823/77–7824/77. The European Commission of Human Rights noted that ECHR contains no right to obtain identity papers. The Court dismissed the applications that the denial of birth registration and other identity documents to the Romanov applicants by Germany and the Netherlands constitutes a violation of ECHR, in particular of its Articles 3 and 14 concerning the respect for human dignity and their treatment on the basis that the applicants have not exhausted domestic remedies and that no *prima facie* case could be established as to the alleged events. See paras 60–69 and 70–79 of the judgment.

[169] Judgment of 6 July 1977, Application No. 7823/77–7824/77, *Kalderas Gypsies v. the Federal Republic of Germany and the Netherlands*, para 37.

mobile and rural backgrounds who lack awareness on the need for, or the procedures involved, in ascertaining their uncertain legal identity status. Similar implementation issues may affect women detainees or prisoners. These circumstances have, in fact, been described as an understudied problem.[170]

While UNHCR may provide training, technical, as well as operational support to states on issues related to statelessness following its mandate,[171] what it may do for populations of concern at risk of statelessness such as promoting birth registration and identity documents, disseminating information, and rendering legal advice on citizenship matters, should not be seen as challenging the prerogative of states with respect to acquisition and loss of nationality.[172] However, the extent to which such affected populations are aware of the mandate, and willing and able to turn to UNHCR for such assistance, is something that necessitates further investigation.[173]

Paragraph 26 of Guidelines No. 4 obligates the Contracting State to grant nationality through the safeguard in Article 1 should the child's parents be unable or have good reasons not to register their children with the state of their own nationality. According to the paragraph's footnote, this includes the inability to register due to parents' refugee status.[174] It is rather unclear as to whether such obligation would extend to others who are in comparable situations to that of refugees, such as those who fled from instability in their countries but never apply for a refugee status or may have their asylum applications rejected.[175] 'Good reasons' in this context remain a

---

[170] UNGA, 'Human Rights and Arbitrary Deprivation of Nationality', UN Doc. A/HRC/25/28, New York: UNGA (19 December 2013). Retrieved from http://www.refworld.org/pdfid/4b83a9cb2.pdf (3 April 2015); Human Rights Council, *13th Session, Agenda Item 3, Annual Report of the United Nations High Commissioner for Human Rights and Reports of the Office of the Commissioner and the Secretary General (A/HRC/13/34)* (2009), para 28, p 12. Retrieved from http://www.refworld.org/pdfid/4b83a9cb2.pdf [Accessed 20 January 2014].

[171] UNHCR, *Conclusion on Identification, Prevention and Reduction of Statelessness and Protection of Stateless Persons No 106 (LVII),* General Assembly Document A/AC.96/1035, Geneva: UNHCR (2006) (Conclusion No. 106 (LVII) on Identification, Prevention and Reduction of Statelessness and Protection of Stateless Persons).

[172] G.R. de Groot et al., *Protection against Statelessness: Trends and Regulations in Europe* (2013), p 35.

[173] UNHCR in its strategy to prevent and reduce statelessness in the migratory context appears to impose heavier obligations upon the state vis-à-vis the affected person of a migratory background in establishing the person's identity. One needs to examine the state's system and attitude as in whether: (i) national authorities have procedures in place to assist migrants having difficulties in establishing their identity, including their nationality (e.g. migrants without genuine or no travel identity documents); (ii) national authorities of the host state actively seek the cooperation of other countries for the verification of the nationality of migrants; (iii) the migrant's country of origin cooperates with other countries for verification of identities of persons abroad believed to be its nationals; (iv) there is a policy to assist such persons in obtaining the rights flowing from nationality, including the rights to obtain a passport and to return to their country. See E. Irwin & M. Manly, *Statelessness: An Analytical Framework for Prevention, Reduction and Protection* (2008), para 2.7, at p 14.

[174] See para 27 of Guidelines No. 4.

[175] B. Manby, *Nationality, Migration and Statelessness in West Africa: A Study for UNHCR and IOM* (2015), p 57.

question of subjectivity. Would ignorance, fear of the authorities, and lack of financial means amount to 'good reasons' for not registering the births of children?[176]

Children may also be registered at birth and determined as having 'unknown' or 'undetermined nationality', or their nationality status may be specified as being 'under investigation', particularly when the parents are undocumented or have disappeared.[177] Guidelines No. 4 attempt to fill this gap in the texts of the 1961 Convention. The Guidelines specify that when a State makes a finding that a child is 'of undetermined nationality', the State is required to make a determination of whether the child 'would otherwise be stateless' as soon as possible. Such period for purposes of Articles 1 and 4 should not exceed five years.[178]

The 1961 Convention and Guidelines No. 4 seem, however, not to impose a further duty upon the state to inform the affected persons on the need to lodge an application for a nationality within a certain period of time, as the law might prescribe. This is detrimental in the context of widespread lack of awareness and knowledge of the rules of nationality, and where the imposition of certain time limits that may invalidate one's application. It could also create space for undesirable interpretations by the state, to the detriment of otherwise stateless children.

To illustrate the possible effects of the above shortcoming is the application of the Serbian Law on Citizenship that adopts measures of prevention of statelessness at birth following its ratification of the 1961 Convention in 2011.[179] Under Article 13 of its Law on Citizenship, children who are otherwise stateless acquire citizenship by *jus soli* principle automatically by birth in the Serbian territory, without conditions attached. This applies to children born to unknown parents; parents whose nationality is unknown; stateless parents; and stateless children themselves. Even when the method of attribution of nationality was automatic, the competent body thought that submission of an appropriate request for acquisition of citizenship was necessary. Although the ex lege mode of attribution of citizenship under Article 13 does not prescribe an age limit (as opposed to an age-bound attribution of citizenship by application), the practice still shows that it is necessary to submit the application within a certain period of time, in this case, before a child reaches 18 as the authority interprets it.[180]

---

[176] M. Manly & S. Persaud, 'UNHCR and Responses to Statelessness', *Forced Migration Review* (FMR) (2009). The authors highlight that aside from complex nationality procedures often unknown to stateless people, the costs of travel and getting basic documents, registering births, or satisfying naturalisation procedures are obstacles to prevention and reduction of statelessness.

[177] G.R. de Groot, 'Children, Their Right to a Nationality and Child Statelessness' in A. Edwards & L. van Waas (Eds.), *Nationality and Statelessness under International Law* (Cambridge: Cambridge University Press, 2014), pp 159–160. The designation of unknown or undetermined nationality additionally places such children along the border between *de facto* and *de jure* stateless.

[178] UNHCR, Guidelines on Statelessness No. 4, para 22.

[179] The following illustration here is based on a real case handled by Praxis, a Serbian-based NGO. See European Network on Statelessness, *Preventing Childhood Statelessness in Europe: Issues, Gaps and Good Practices*' (2014).

[180] European Network on Statelessness, *Preventing Childhood Statelessness in Europe: Issues, Gaps and Good Practices* (2014).

Another problematic area is that the grant of nationality to an otherwise stateless child based on the application method under Article 1(1) (b) and Article 4(1), subject to the conditions in Article 2 and Article 4(2) of the 1961 Convention respectively, disqualifies children who may have had a previous nationality and subsequently rendered stateless. As required by Article 1(2) (d) and 4(2) (d) of the 1961 Convention, the child concerned must have always been stateless. A minimum period of 5 years to the maximum of 10 years of habitual residence immediately preceding the application that is imposed under Article 1(2) (b) of the 1961 Convention is also considered lengthy, potentially defeating the aim of reducing statelessness.[181] The child could be left stateless for a significant period of time, unless the state concerned opted to be guided by the best interests of the child principle, by keeping the period as short as possible, as suggested by UNHCR Guidelines No. 4, under paragraph 34.

Burden of Proof and Its Intricacies

In terms of the burden of proving whether a person would otherwise be stateless, paragraphs 20 and 21 of Guidelines No. 4 provide:

> '[i]n most legal systems a claimant bears the initial responsibility of substantiating his or her claim. Because of the difficulties that often arise when determining whether an individual has acquired a nationality, the burden of proof must be shared between the claimant and the authorities of the Contracting State to obtain evidence and to establish the facts as to whether an individual would otherwise be stateless'... The consequence of an incorrect finding that a child possesses a nationality would be to leave him or her stateless. Therefore, decision makers need to take into account Articles 3 and 7 of the CRC and adopt an appropriate standard of proof, for example that it is established to a "reasonable degree" that an individual would be stateless unless he or she acquires the nationality of the State concerned'.

The shared burden of proof with the initial burden resting on the claimant to prove his statelessness requires a contextual appreciation of the ability of the claimant as well as the state of application. The process of examining evidence of one's nationality is a complex exercise involving law, jurisprudence, practice and politics of a foreign country. The differential capacities of the applicants in proving lack of a nationality can present an enormous challenge in the area of the 'shared burden'. Challenges can be associated with factors such as the roles and obligations of diplomatic or consular office in providing assistance to undocumented/irregular migrants and refugees with respect to proof of nationality; agents of a state who could be disinterested participants and thus lack reliability, especially when the nationality law is politicised or uncertain[182]; and where an applicant has a limited fund and resources to hire skilled legal professionals to assist in establishing her claim.

In *Expelled Dominicans and Haitians v. Dominican Republic*, the Inter-American Court of Human Rights considered that the burden was on the Dominican Republic to not just show that the children born in its territory in this case could acquire

---

[181] G.R. de Groot, 'Children, Their Right to a Nationality and Child Statelessness' in A. Edwards & L. van Waas (Eds.), *Nationality and Statelessness under International Law* (Cambridge: Cambridge University Press, 2014), p 151.

[182] E. Fripp, *Nationality and Statelessness in the International Law of Refugee Status* (Oxford and Portland: Bloomsbury, 2016), p 81.

Haitian nationality, but, in fact, would be able to exercise any right to nationality in Haiti.[183] The Court, however, neither explained the approach to its burden of proof, nor enlightened on the degree of certainty in discharging the said burden. Acknowledging that the Court was in no position to conclude on the operation of Haitian law, it found that certain public information concerning Haitian legal frameworks led to its view that the person (Victor Jean) who was born abroad could be considered foreign under the Haitian 1984 law and the Constitutional Law of 1987, as the nationality of his father had never been established.[184] On the question of the same 'reasonable degree' from refugee law that should be applied in the domain of statelessness, Baluarte shed important light on the possible incongruence as follows:

> The principal challenge posed by a shared standard is that the language of the relevant conventions is not analogous. The 1951 Refugee Convention protects a person as a refugee when she demonstrates a well-founded fear of persecution in her country of nationality. The notion of a 'well-founded fear' implicitly refers to a level of risk. Indeed, much has been written on this formulation, and some have advanced the position that this suggests a one in a ten chance of persecution. The question is whether a 10% risk of statelessness is similarly sustainable as a standard of proof to find someone to be a stateless person.[185]

The above comparison demonstrates the lack of certainty in applying the shared standard in the case of determination of statelessness in the same way the standard is applied in making refugee status determinations.[186] A similar ambiguity can be present in the specific context of the reasonable standard of proof on a shared basis in determining 'otherwise stateless persons'. Clear and sufficient guidance on this point should be developed, in order to clarify the varied levels of threshold required, for the determination of stateless persons and otherwise stateless children.

Absence of Prohibition of Non-Discrimination on the Basis of Gender in Conferral of Nationality

Article 9 of the 1961 Convention merely prohibits discrimination that would amount to a deprivation of nationality on racial, ethnic, religious, or political grounds. Gender and marital status have been left out, thus creating a risk for children becoming stateless. Another major source of concern is in relation to parents' unrecognised marriages that often result in the ever-increasing incidences of children born out of wedlock. Pursuant to a compromise achieved between *jus soli* and *jus sanguinis* countries, Article 1(3) of the 1961 Convention on this point prescribes that:

> Notwithstanding the provisions of paragraphs 1(b) and 2 of this Article, a child born in wedlock in the territory of a Contracting State, whose mother has the nationality of that State, shall acquire at birth that nationality if it otherwise would be stateless.

---

[183] *Expelled Dominicans and Haitians v. Dominican Republic* (2014), p 297.

[184] *Expelled Dominicans and Haitians v. Dominican Republic* (2014), p 297.

[185] D.C. Baluarte, 'The Risk of Statelessness: Reasserting a Rule for the Protection of the Right to a Nationality', p 89.

[186] UNHCR, *UNHCR Handbook on Protection of Stateless Persons* (30 June 2014). Retrieved from http://www.unhcr.org/dach/wp-content/uploads/sites/27/2017/04/CH-UNHCR_Handbook-on-Protection-of-Stateless-Persons.pdf [Accessed 20 August 2017].

Jus soli attribution of nationality to a legitimate child who would otherwise be stateless must be granted by operation of law only if the child's mother has the nationality of that state in whose territory the child is born. This provision would only operate to curb statelessness if the state were to prevent the attribution of nationality through *jus sanguinis* maternal for children born out of wedlock.[187] The limited scope of the inequalities addressed here could be due to the fact that the provision was drafted during the time when most *jus sanguinis* states applied *jus sanguinis a patre*, allowing only male nationals to transfer citizenship to their children.[188]

To counter this imbalance, Guidelines No. 4 clarify that the safeguard contained in Article 1(3) of the 1961 Convention is likewise relevant in the context of the ability of children who would otherwise be stateless to immediately acquire the nationality of their fathers who are nationals. This interpretation is adopted in light of the gender equality principle promoted in ICCPR, CEDAW, and other relevant human rights treaties.[189] If the Contracting States act on this equality principle, then the situations that could render unmarital children stateless due to their inability to acquire a nationality from mothers who are stateless or foreigners in *jus sanguinis* states could be minimised. Challenges, however, remain as to the viability of this equality principle as traditional norms that prohibit paternity to be ascribed to 'illegitimate' children are still prevalent in many countries, predominantly due to cultural and/or religious reasons.[190]

Lack of Norms on Interstate Cooperation

In order to counter the risk of statelessness during state succession, the 1961 Convention prescribes a measure of interstate cooperation through inclusion of provisions in every treaty between Contracting States to ensure that no individual shall become stateless due to the transfer involved. For similar treaties with a non-party to the Convention, the Contracting State is to strive for such provisions to be included.[191] Beyond this specific setting, the 1961 Convention does not touch on the principle of interstate cooperation in the verification and confirmation of nationality or statelessness of a person. The task of identifying and determining an individual as an 'otherwise stateless' is presumably treated as a bilateral process between the individual making the claim and the relevant state authorities or institutions concerned. The lack of provisions addressing interstate mechanisms for prevention of statelessness appears to undermine the significance of securing the cooperation of other

---

[187] L. van Waas, *Nationality Matters: Statelessness under International Law* (School of Human Rights Research Series, V. 29, 2008), p 57.

[188] G.R. de Groot, 'Children, Their Right to a Nationality and Child Statelessness' in A. Edwards & L. van Waas (Eds.), *Nationality and Statelessness Under International Law* (Cambridge: Cambridge University Press, 2014), p 153.

[189] See para 4 of UNHCR, Guidelines on Statelessness No. 4.

[190] For instance, family names are prohibited to appear on identity cards of such children in Saudi Arabia. See B.L. Fisher, 'Why Non-Marital Children in the MENA Region Face a Risk of Statelessness', p 7.

[191] See Articles 10(1) and (2) of the 1961 Convention.

states connected to or having ties with the individual in question, for exchanges of information, including on nationality rules, policies, and practices.

ii. **Protection against Statelessness for Foundlings: Principles, Mechanisms, and Issues of Concern**

Article 2 of the 1961 Convention requires foundlings born to nationals of the Contracting State and in its territory to be considered its nationals should there exist no contrary proof in respect of their nationality.

Identical provisions can also be found in Article 14 of the 1930 Hague Convention,[192] Article 6(1) (b) of ECN, and Article 7(3) of CRCI.

In fact, the right of foundlings to a nationality has been supported by an overwhelming degree of state practice.[193] In March 2004, UNHCR issued a report based on its survey on statelessness that it conducted under the purview of its protection agenda. The report attests to the fact that state practice evidences strong compliance with the principle of prevention of statelessness among foundlings. In the report, it was quoted that 86.5% of the 74 states that responded to its questionnaire conferred nationality on, or, granted legal status to abandoned or orphaned children, while 8.1% provided no answer to the survey.[194]

The definition of 'foundling' is not, however, provided by the 1961 Convention. Its dictionary meanings include 'an infant that has been abandoned by its parents and is discovered and cared by others',[195] and 'an abandoned infant whose parents are not known'.[196] Strictly confining the word 'foundling' to newborn or infants, as suggested by the foregoing definitions, may leave older children who are not newborn or infants, yet are likewise found to be exposed or abandoned with no legal identity, outside the framework for prevention of statelessness.[197]

---

[192] Article 14 of the 1930 Hague Convention mentions both 'foundlings' and 'children of unknown parentage'.

[193] European Network on Statelessness, *Preventing Childhood Statelessness in Europe: Issues, Gaps and Good Practices* (2014), pp 20–21.

[194] UN Human Rights Council, *Human Rights and Arbitrary Deprivation of Nationality: Report of the Secretary-General* (14 December 2009), A/HRC/13/34, p 10. Retrieved 15 November 2014 from http://www.refworld.org/docid/4b83a9cb2.html.

[195] See Oxford Dictionaries (2015). Retrieved from http://www.oxforddictionaries.com/definition/english/foundling [Accessed 29 September 2016].

[196] See Collins English Dictionary (2015). Retrieved from http://www.collinsdictionary.com/dictionary/english/foundling?showCookiePolicy=true [Accessed 29 September 2016].

[197] This loophole has been pointed out in principle 9 of Recommendation CM/Rec (2009) 13 of the Committee of Ministers to Member States on the nationality of children (9 December 2009), para 24. It explains that varied approaches in national regulations are found in relation to foundlings. In some Member States, provisions on foundlings apply to all children below 18 with unknown parentage.For instance, Article 3(2) of the Kingdom Act on Netherlands Nationality (as in force on 13 April 2010) applies the term of 'foundlings' to all minors found abandoned on their territory. In other Member States, the similar provisions apply to newborn found abandoned, in line with the explanatory report to Article 6(1)(b) of ECN, *Statelessness Determination and the Protection Status of Stateless Persons* (2013).

Based on the object and purpose of the 1961 Convention, Guidelines No. 4 advise the State Parties to apply the provision of Article 2 to cases involving 'all young children who are not yet able to communicate accurately the information pertaining to the identity of their parents or their place of birth'.[198] The Contracting States are additionally allowed to apply their discretion under the 1961 Convention to determine an age limit for foundlings for the purpose of nationality attribution. Nonetheless, the said age determination must be based on the age when the child was found, and not when the said child came to the attention of the authority.[199]

What would then be the position if evidence were discovered that the foundling concerned was born abroad to a non-national parent? This issue is neither addressed in the text of the 1961 Convention nor the Guidelines on Statelessness No. 4. It appears that the nationality granted to the said child could be lost in such a circumstance. The relevant record of the preparatory negotiations of the 1961 Convention shows that 'the child would possess the nationality of the country in which he had been found until shown to be entitled to another nationality'.[200] Based on the foregoing *travaux preparatoires* of the 1961 Convention, the loss should thus be conditioned on the proof that the child possesses another state's nationality.[201]

iii. Prevention and Reduction of Statelessness through Prevention of Loss, Deprivation or Renunciation of Nationality

Article 7(3) of the 1961 Convention prohibits nationality from being lost as a result of departure, residence abroad, failure to register, or any similar ground. Although an automatic loss of nationality may affect both regular and irregular migrants, it is in the context of irregular migration and forced displacement that children are highly exposed to statelessness. The nature of irregularity of migrant parents and refugees may cause parents to be reluctant from staying in contact with the authorities including their states' representatives abroad, for registration or notification concerning their intention to keep their nationality. This situation calls for a closer attention of the relevant statelessness actors in light of today's contemporary refugee crisis that is taking place on a scale never imagined before.

Article 6 of this Convention, in particular, safeguards children from being affected by the statelessness of their parents as a result of loss or deprivation of nationality. The

---

198 See Guidelines No. 4, para 58. This is also in line with the object and purpose of Article 7 of CRC and Article 6(2) of ECN.

199 See Guidelines No. 4, para 58.

200 UNGA, Committee of the Whole, Summary Record of the Fifth Meeting of Committee 1, UN Doc. A/CONF.9/C.1/SR.5, UNGA: Geneva. (3 April 1959), p 10 as cited by G.R. de Groot in 'Children, Their Right to a Nationality and Child Statelessness' in A. Edwards & L. van Waas (Eds.), *Nationality and Statelessness under International Law* (Cambridge: Cambridge University Press, 2014), pp 144–168. See footnote 62 on p 162.

201 This is also in line with para 60 of UNHCR, Guidelines on Statelessness No. 4 and M. Freeman, *A Commentary on the United Nations Convention on the Rights of the Child, Article 3: The Best Interests of the Child.* Martinus Nijhoff Publishers, 2007); European Network on Statelessness, *Preventing Childhood Statelessness in Europe: Issues, Gaps and Good Practices*' (2014), pp 18–19. 388.

consequence of the said loss or deprivation shall not be extended to their children, if that would render them stateless. Such safeguard is also consistent with Article 8 of CRC that seeks to preserve the children's identity including their nationality.[202]

Articles 7(1) and (2) of the 1961 Convention do not permit renunciation of nationality if that could result in loss of nationality, including when another nationality of a foreign country is not acquired or assured prior to one's renunciation. Article 9 further entails a broad scope of obligations to avoid statelessness by forbidding the deprivation of nationality on racial, ethnic, religious, or political grounds, regardless of whether it would result in statelessness or not. Article 8 (1) strictly bars deprivation of a nationality if that would render a person stateless. Both provisions resonate with other norms on prohibition of deprivation of nationality in Article 15(2) UDHR and the norm against discriminatory termination of nationality in CERD that guarantees the enjoyment of the right to nationality 'without distinction as to race, colour, national, or ethnic origin'.[203]

Such anti-discriminatory norms are significant in preventing statelessness at birth that could potentially trigger displacement abroad of persons deprived of nationality and the inheritance of statelessness by their children.[204] The norms are also useful to curb administrative obstacles that prevent a child from securing his or her birthright citizenship, for instance, through refusal to register the birth of children born in a country's territory.[205]

(e) ***Beneficiaries to the Scheme of Protection against Statelessness at Birth for Purposes of Analysis***

Acknowledging that statelessness can affect children born to stateless parent(s) or to parent(s) holding a nationality, two broad categories of children who could not benefit from nationality *jus sanguinis* of their parents, therefore, emerge. The first category captures children who are born to unknown parents. Such entails foundlings, as well as older children abandoned by or separated from their parents, with no proof of parentage. Children would also be stateless if they are born to both stateless parents.[206] Children born to stateless refugees and migrants, as a result of losing

202 Article 8 CRC provides '(i) States Parties undertake to respect the right of the child to preserve his or her identity, including nationality, name and family relations as recognised by law without unlawful interference (ii) Where a child is illegally deprived of some or all of the elements of his or her identity, States Parties shall provide appropriate assistance and protection, with a view to speedily re- establishing his or her identity'.

203 The Committee on the Elimination of Racial Discrimination (2005), General Recommendation XXX on Discrimination against Non-Citizens, UN Doc. CERD/ CG/C/30, Geneva: CERD Committee, para 14; R. Donner, *The Regulation of Nationality,* 2nd Ed (Leiden: Martinus Nijhoff, 1994), pp 196–198.

204 Legal residence of the child/parent is often an added requirement for the eligibility to be granted a nationality. See also, Tang Lay Lee, *Statelessness, Human Rights And Gender: Irregular Migrant Workers from Burma in Thailand* (Leiden: Martinus Nijhoff, 2005).

205 *Yean and Bosico v. Dominican Republic* (Series C, Case 130, 8 Sep 2005), para 171.

206 The statelessness of the parents is determined in light of the legal criteria set out in Article 1(1) of the 1954 Convention and the relevant interpretative guidelines by UNHCR. As summarised by

nationality upon irregular migration, are included. These children would continue to be stateless unless they could acquire nationality *jus soli* of their birth countries.

The second category refers to other children who would otherwise be stateless for having parents who are unable or unwilling to confer nationality on their children, or are prevented from doing so. For the analysis herein, in the first sub-category are children who are born in the territory to at least a parent who may have a nationality and whose children may be able to acquire such parent's nationality by registration or other procedures imposed. However, when the parent is unable, unwilling, or has good reasons not to register his or her children with the state of the parent's nationality, the children would become otherwise stateless unless they could benefit from the *jus soli* legal safeguard, as formulated in the 1961 Convention.

These children may comprise those who are born abroad to non-stateless refugee parents. Yet, on account of the parents' refugee status, it is usually unreasonable to expect them to be in touch with the consular/governmental authority of their state of nationality, including for registering their children.[207] Being in contact with such authority may be too risky as this could expose them to continued persecution, and could be seen as an evidence of unfounded protection claim. In such a situation, the children are to acquire the nationality of the state of birth automatically, or at a later time by way of an application procedure, in order not to be left stateless.[208]

The second sub-category of 'otherwise stateless children' captures children born to parent(s) having a nationality, yet may be unwilling or unable to fulfil the required administrative requirements for their children to acquire a nationality. This is highly likely when the child's father refuses to institute the procedures required for the establishment of paternity or has abandoned his family. Lack of awareness to notify the authorities of the birth of his child abroad and to claim nationality within the time limit, the absence of consular services, and inability to prove the child's birth and paternity, are some of the possible and often interconnected factors that could

paragraph 19 of Guidelines No. 4, a Contracting State must accept that a person is not a national of a particular State if the authorities of that State refuse to recognise that person as a national. A State can refuse to recognise a person as a national either by explicitly stating that he or she is not a national or by failing to respond to inquiries to confirm an individual as a national. A Contracting State to the 1961 Convention cannot avoid the obligations to grant its nationality to a person who would otherwise be stateless under Articles 1 and 4 based on its own interpretation of another State's nationality laws where these conflict with the interpretation applied by the State concerned.

[207] See para 26 and footnote17 of Guidelines No. 4.

[208] See para 27 of Guidelines No. 4. As for children of refugees who are able to acquire nationality *jus sanguinis* of their parents by operation of law at birth, para 28 of Guidelines No. 4 links such children to their *de facto* stateless status. Such children, therefore, may enjoy the benefit housed in the Final Act of the 1961 Convention that is for them to be treated as stateless persons as far as possible. The states are nonetheless cautioned that it is undesirable for them to attribute nationality ex lege under Article 1(1) of the 1961 Convention in cases where such children could acquire the nationality of the states of origin of either of the refugee parents, in particular where either state (host state or state of origin) prohibits dual nationality. Instead, states are advised to allow the option for the refugee parents and their children to decide for themselves whether or not to acquire the nationality of the state of birth, in view of any plans that they may have for their durable solution, such as voluntary expatriation to the state of origin. See para 28 of Guidelines No. 4.

leave the affected children otherwise stateless.[209] Such reasons may further lead to another barrier for the child if the state of birth chooses to grant birthright citizenship to children by way of application, given that the child concerned may not be able to meet the application requirements independently.

The third sub-category of children who would otherwise be stateless consists of children born to parents of undetermined or unclear citizenship who are left with no other means of protection against statelessness.[210] A child may be registered with unknown or undetermined nationality, or his nationality status may be specified as being 'under investigation'. This could be administratively unavoidable due to difficulties involved in ascertaining a particular child's precise state of nationality, such as when the parents are undocumented or have disappeared. The said classification is certainly undesirable if prolonged, and, therefore, should only be maintained as a transitory measure for a short term.[211]

The fourth sub-category of children who would otherwise be stateless involves children born in a country or abroad, who are prevented from inheriting the mother's or father's citizenship due to gendered citizenship law. *Jus sanguinis* countries are commonly biased in terms of conferral of citizenship by parents upon their children.[212] Such countries typically differentiate between the ability of a child to inherit nationality on an equal basis from both parents based on the parents' gender, marital status, and nationality, as well as the place of birth of the child.

On this point, firstly, if the law of the Contracting State predominantly bestows nationality through one's paternal descent, marriage to a stateless man magnifies the risk of statelessness to the wife and her children. The risk would spread across generations if the law does not provide any exception that would enable the mother to pass on nationality to her children.[213] Secondly, marriage to a non-national can increase the risk of statelessness if the nationality of the mother's country is only conferred through the paternal line, yet the law of the father's country restricts nationality to a child born abroad.[214]

---

[209] R. Govil & A. Edwards, 'Women, Nationality and Statelessness: The Problem of Unequal Rights' in A. Edwards & L. van Waas (Eds.), *Nationality and Statelessness under International Law* (Cambridge: Cambridge University Press, 2014), pp 169–193.See p 177; ECN, *Statelessness Determination and the Protection Status of Stateless Persons* (2013); European Network on Statelessness, *Preventing Childhood Statelessness in Europe: Issues, Gaps and Good Practices* (2014), p 25.

[210] See G.R. de Groot et al., *Practices and Approaches in the EU Member States to Prevent and End Statelessness* (2015), p 28.

[211] See Recommendation 2009/13 on the Nationality of Children, p 21.

[212] R. Govil & A. Edwards,'Women, Nationality and Statelessness: The Problem of Unequal Rights' (2010), pp 174–175.

[213] R. Govil & A. Edwards, 'Women, Nationality and Statelessness: The Problem of Unequal Rights' (2014), p 176.

[214] R. Govil & A. Edwards, 'Women, Nationality and Statelessness: The Problem of Unequal Rights' (2014), p 177. Sometimes, the law may allow a citizen mother to pass on her nationality ex lege to her child born on a territory but restricts her ability to do so by operation of law if the child is born to a non-citizen father abroad.

Discrimination against the father could also arise in the context of his inability to transfer his nationality to a child born out of wedlock.[215] While recognition by the father can enable his nationality to be passed on to his children, this is not always made available under the law.[216]

The risk of statelessness is magnified for such children not only because of the lack of gender parity in nationality attribution system, but also due to common stigma and discrimination attached to illegitimacy. Parents may simply avoid birth registration fearing it could lead to official recognition of the 'illegitimate status',[217] resulting in the child to be without evidence of birth.

The circumstances that could give rise to children becoming otherwise stateless are not exhaustive. Advancement in reproductive technology now sees children born out of a surrogacy arrangement facing a heightened risk of statelessness if the country of nationality of the surrogate's mother does not allow attribution of nationality to the child, and the country of the commissioning mother likewise restricts nationality attribution as the commissioning mother is not the biological mother.[218] Inter-country adoption is another scenario that could expose children to be otherwise stateless. The risk of statelessness may be created if no concrete rules prescribe that the country of nationality of adoptive parents is to allow and facilitate for nationality acquisition by the adopted child and that revocation of an adoption does not lead to loss of the child's nationality acquired through adoption.[219]

In light of the numerous factors that could create 'otherwise stateless children', the analysis in the following chapter shall only concentrate on the prevention and reduction of statelessness at birth for the usual categories and sub-categories of children who would otherwise be stateless as depicted in Fig. 3.2. Surrogacy and adoption-related statelessness for instance, fall beyond the remit of this book.

---

[215] See the discussion on *Genovese v. Malta (*European Court of Human Rights (ECtHR), Judgment of 11 October 2011, and Application No. 53124/099) in the coming section concerning regional instrument.

[216] ECN, *Statelessness Determination and the Protection Status of Stateless Persons* (2013); European Network on Statelessness, *Preventing Childhood Statelessness in Europe: Issues, Gaps and Good Practices* (2014), p 24.

[217] In Malaysia, a national fatwa has ruled that a Muslim 'illegitimate' child (who includes a child born less than six months after the parents' marriage) cannot bear his father's name. Even if the father acknowledges the child and is present with the mother to register the child's birth, the National Registration Department would fill 'Tiada Maklumat' or 'No Information' in the column requiring the father's information. See N.A, 'Review for the Sake of the Child'. Retrieved from http://www.thestar.com.my/news/nation/2011/11/06/review-for-the-sake-of-the-child/ [6 Nov 2011].

[218] G.R. de Groot, 'Children, Their Right to a Nationality and Child Statelessness' in A. Edwards & L. van Waas (Eds.), *Nationality and Statelessness Under International Law* (Cambridge: Cambridge University Press, 2014), p 165.

[219] G.R. de Groot, 'Children, Their Right to a Nationality and Child Statelessness' in A. Edwards & L. van Waas (Eds.), *Nationality and Statelessness Under International Law* (Cambridge: Cambridge University Press, 2014), pp 163–165.

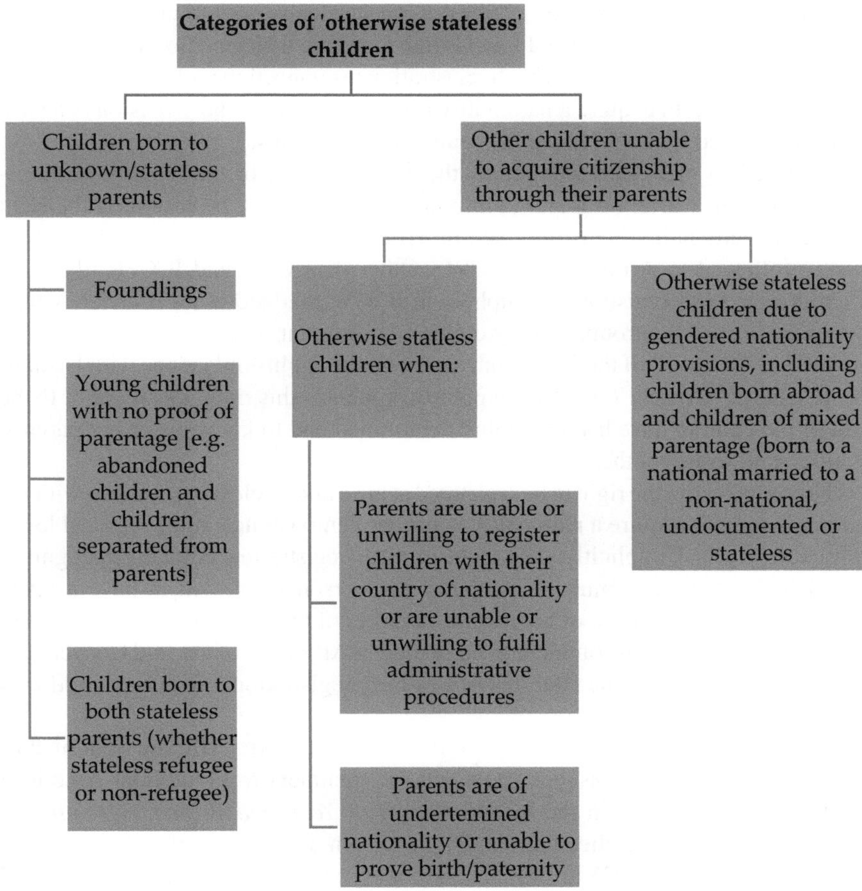

Fig. 3.2 Categories of 'otherwise stateless' children

(f) *The Right to Birth Registration as a Legal Safeguard against Statelessness*

The process of birth registration forms part of a broader civil registration system that entails free and universal recording of vital events, namely; births, deaths, adoptions, marriages, divorces, as well as other civil status occasions in the population.

UNICEF defines birth registration as:

> The continuous, permanent and universal recording within the civil registry of the occurrence and characteristics of birth, in accordance with the national legal requirements. It establishes the existence of a person under the law and lays the foundation for safeguarding civil, political, economic, social and cultural rights.[220]

---

[220] UN Human Rights Council, *Birth Registration and the Right of Everyone to Recognition Everywhere as a Person before the Law* (17 June 2014), p 23.

Birth registration has been proclaimed as an invaluable tool to prevent statelessness,[221] namely by acting as proof for children to realise their right to a nationality.[222] The important role of the right to birth registration in connection with children's fulfilment of their right to acquire a nationality is reflected in how the provisions on such rights are worded in the principal international instruments.

Article 24(2) of ICCPR safeguards the essential right of the child to be registered immediately after birth and to have a name, before the provision on the right to acquire a nationality is incorporated in Article 24(3). The similar trend is subsequently followed in Article 7(1) of CRC. Other than CRC and ICCPR, the right of children to birth registration is upheld in ICMW that addresses it under Article 29 to a more specific group, namely children of migrant workers. The right is also provided in Article 18 of the 2006 Convention on the Rights of Persons with Disabilities (CRPD).[223] Article 7 of CRCI explicitly proclaims this right, ideally prior to the right of the child to have his nationality determined and to know his or her parents, relatives, and foster mother.

The consensus on the right to be registered at birth and its close association with the children's right to acquire a nationality is further demonstrated at the regional level, both explicitly and implicitly. The right to birth registration is tacitly recognised in Article 18 AmCHR, enunciating that every person is entitled to have a given name and the family names of his parents or either of them. With the strong *jus soli* tradition in the American continent as embodied in Article 20 of the said Convention, it indirectly underscores the vital function of birth registration in securing children's right to a nationality.

Even with no explicit proclamation of the said right in AmCHR, the right of children to birth registration has received a detailed treatment from the Inter-American Court on Human Rights in the landmark case of *Yean and Bosico v. Dominican Republic*.[224] In this case, the children, Dilcia Oliven Yean and Violeta Bosico Cofi, each born in 1996 and 1985 to Dominican mothers and Haitian fathers, were denied birth certificates by the Registry Office, notwithstanding the *jus soli* principle of acquisition of nationality adopted by the Dominican law. The Court significantly pronounced that parents' migratory status is immaterial when it comes to access to birth registration. In light of Article 18 of AmCHR, the states are urged to not only safeguard the right to a name but also to facilitate the immediate registration of an individual after birth.[225]

In Europe, ECN does not expressly address the children's right to birth registration. Despite that, it could be inferred that the right to birth registration is highly relevant in view of the strong norms espoused by ECN on the right to a nationality at birth and

---

[221] UN Human Rights Council, *Birth Registration and the Right of Everyone to Recognition Everywhere as a Person before the Law* (17 June 2014), p 23.

[222] UNHCR, Guidance Note of the Secretary General (2011). Retrieved from http://www.refworld.org/pdfid/4e11d5092.pdf [12 April 2015].

[223] Adopted 13 December 2006, in force 13 May 2008, 2515 UNTS 3.

[224] Inter-American Court of Human Rights, Series C, Case 130, 8 September 2005.

[225] Inter-American Court of Human Rights, Series C, Case 130, 8 September 2005, para 183.

avoidance of statelessness.[226] The right to birth registration has also been regarded as implicitly recognised by Article 8 of ECHR in relation to the right to respect for family life.[227]

In contrast to the previous two regions, in Africa, the expression of the right to birth registration immediately after birth is clearly recorded and upheld in Article 6(2) of ACRWC. The law aside, the low rates of birth registration in Sub-Saharan Africa have been attributed to, among others, the region's geographic disparities and growing economic inequities, low awareness on the importance of birth registration, as well as lack of decentralised, well-managed and affordable birth registration systems.[228]

Unregistered children in the region are vulnerable to all sorts of exploitation, such as child marriage, trafficking, child labour, disinheritance, and recruitment into armed forces. The children are faced with a precarious situation in terms of their ability to acquire a nationality, exposing them to statelessness. This has led to the ACERWC holding a theme day on birth registration and the rights of the child in November 2012, as a prelude to the adoption of the General Comment on Article 6 of ACRWC.[229]

The right to birth registration is not explicitly provided in any of the human rights instruments of ASEAN. As part of its mandate to foster respect for the implementation of international human rights treaties ratified by the Member States of ASEAN, AICHR has partnered and collaborated with UNHCR and other UN bodies such as the United Nations Economic and Social Commission for the Asia Pacific (ESCAP) and UNICEF to identify, share, and disseminate good practices on birth registration among the Member States of ASEAN and states outside ASEAN.[230]

The ministers and representatives of members and associate members of ESCAP through its Ministerial Declaration in November 2014 entitled 'Get Every One in the Picture', proclaimed their shared vision that all people in Asia and the Pacific will benefit from universal and responsive civil registration systems by 2024. Three goals are to be achieved under this vision through a Regional Action Framework on

---

226 Articles 4(a) and (b) and 2(a) of ECN.

227 See the case *Marck v. Belgium* (Judgment of 13 June 1979, Application No. 6833/74, para 36–43 and the case heard by the European Commission on Human Rights, *Kalderas Gypsies v. the Federal Republic of Germany and the Netherlands* (Judgment of 6 July 1977, Application No. 7823/77–7824/77). In the case of *Marck v. Belgium* for instance, the European Court of Human Rights decided that conditions obstructing the registration of 'illegitimate' children were inexcusable.

228 UNICEF, *Eastern and Southern Africa: Birth Registration*. Retrieved from https://www.unicef.org/esaro/5480_birth_registration.html [Accessed 5 July 2017].

229 ACERWC's General Comment No. 2 on Article 6, see para 3.

230 See Article 1(7) of 2012 ASEAN Charter underlining the promotion and protection of human rights and fundamental freedoms, having regards to the rights and responsibilities of the Member States of ASEAN. This is further advanced by the AICHR's Terms of Reference, which spell out the enhancement of regional cooperation to promote and protect human rights and to uphold international human rights standards in UDHR and Vienna Declaration and Programme of Action, as well as the human rights instruments that bind the ASEAN Member States as part of the purposes of AICHR. See ASEAN, 'Terms of Reference of ASEAN Intergovernmental Commission on Human Rights' (2009), para 1.4 and 1.5. Retrieved from http://www.refworld.org/docid/4a6d87f22.html [12 October 2015].

Civil Registration. The goals are: (i) universal registration of vital events; (ii) every person to be provided with legal documentation to claim their identity, civil status and resultant rights; and (iii) accurate, complete and timely vital statistics to be produced and circulated. This Ministerial Declaration came about as a result of their finding that the majority of the countries in the region do not possess universal and responsive birth registration systems that meet international standards and recommendations.[231]

i. ***Identifying International Standards on Birth Registration Relevant to Achieving Prevention of Statelessness among Children***

The CRC Committee under its General Comment No. 7 on Implementing Child Rights in Early Childhood has pronounced a set of standards on birth registration.[232] Such standards have been adopted with more detailed elaboration by UNICEF in its guide to birth registration programming.[233]

The broad standards based on CRC's General Comment No. 7 have been reflected and echoed further in diffused resources addressing birth registration by various international bodies. A CRVS system that targets the elimination of non-discrimination and other barriers to birth registration could reduce the risk of statelessness, especially for the categories of children susceptible to being excluded from birth registration.[234] The extracted standards from such resources and their amplification in the following paragraphs are highly relevant to ensuring that every child has a free and universal access to a quality and responsive birth registration system.

Standard 1: Universal, Well-Managed, and Free (Access to and Process of Birth Registration and Issuance of Birth Certificate)

Based on General Comment No. 7 by the CRC Committee, birth registration entails a universal and well-managed registration system that is accessible to all and free of charge. UNICEF points out to non-discrimination being the fundamental principle of universality. Access to birth registration must be obtained by every person without regard to race, religion, national origin, sex, or, any other trait.[235] The Statistics Division of the United Nations Department of Economic and Social Affairs (UNSD)

---

231 Economic and Social Commission for Asia and the Pacific (UNESCAP), Resolution adopted by the Economic and Social Commission for Asia and the Pacific (2 June 2015), *Asian and Pacific Civil Registration and Vital Statistics, 2015–2024,* UN Doc. E/ESCAP/RES/71/14, New York: United Nations. Retrieved from http://www.unescap.org/sites/default/files/E71_RES14E.pdf. See Annex A, para 13, 29 and 30.

232 General Comment No. 7 (2005): Implementing Child Rights in Early Childhood, UN Doc. CRC/C/GC/7/Rev.1, Geneva: CRC, 2005, para 25.

233 UNICEF, *A Passport to Protection: A Guide to Birth Registration Programming* (2013).

234 The non-registration of several categories of children such as children born out of wedlock, children of minority groups, and children of refugee, asylum-seeking or migrant families and children born to parents working abroad has been a key concern of the CRC Committee. See J. Doek, 'The CRC and the Right to Acquire and to Preserve a Nationality', pp 23 and 27.

235 UNICEF, *A Passport to Protection: A Guidet to Birth Registration Programming* (2013), p 22; Committee on the Protection of the Rights of All Migrants Workers and Members of Their Families (CMW), Joint General Comment No. 4 (2017) of the Committee on the Protection of the Rights of All Migrant Workers and Members of Their Families and No. 23 (2017) of the Committee on

referred to the element of totality of birth registration, which requires the access to birth registration to be extended to residents who are abroad[236] and non-nationals.[237]

Significantly, vulnerable children including non-nationals, asylum seekers, refugees, and stateless children are specifically mentioned as children who should have an equal access to birth registration.[238] The importance of birth registration that meets this standard for otherwise stateless children and for the prevention and reduction of statelessness has been expressly recognised by the HR Council[239] and UNHCR.[240]

Birth certificates are to be provided free and easily, whether automatically after registration or through another application.[241] While UNICEF recommends birth record or certificate to be free,[242] UNHCR encourages states to consider free birth and death registration according to national laws and regulations.[243]

Entries and Confidentiality

In terms of entries, registration should include the individual's name, date, place of birth, as well as wherever possible, the name, age or date of birth, place of usual residence, and nationality of both parents.[244] Preservation of confidentiality constitutes a component of a quality birth registration system and should be made part of the civil registration law, together with privacy and data protection of the individuals.[245] The

---

the Rights of the Child on the General Principles regarding the Human Rights of Children in the Context of International Migration (16 November 2017), CMW/C/GC/3-CRC/C/GC/23, para 20. Retrieved from http://www.refworld.org/docid/5a1293a24.html [Accessed 30 December 2017].

236 United Nations, Department of Economic and Social Affairs, Statistics Division (UNSD), *Principles and Recommendations for a Vital Statistics System* (Revision 3) (2014). Retrieved from https://unstats.un.org/unsd/demographic/standmeth/principles/m19rev3en.pdf [Accessed 24 June 2016], para 296 at p 68.

237 United Nations, Department of Economic and Social Affairs, Statistics Division (UNSD), *Handbook on Training in Civil Registration and Vital Statistic Systems, Series F No. 84* (2002), para 33, at p 9. Retrieved from http://unstats.un.org/unsd/publication/SeriesF/SeriesF_84E.pdf [Accessed 24 June 2016].

238 UN Human Rights Council, *Birth Registration and the Right of Everyone to Recognition Everywhere as a Person before the Law* (17 June 2014).

239 UN Human Rights Council, *Birth Registration and the Right of Everyone to Recognition Everywhere as a Person before the Law* (17 June 2014).

240 UNHCR, Conclusion on Civil Registration No. 111 (LXIV), Doc. A/AC.96/1035, Geneva: UNHCR [17 October 2013].

241 UN Human Rights Council, *Birth Registration and the Right of Everyone to Recognition Everywhere as a Person before the Law* (17 June 2014), para II.5.

242 UNICEF, *A Passport to Protection: A Guide to Birth Registration Programming* (2013), p 118.

243 UNHCR, Conclusion on Civil Registration No. 111 (LXIV), Doc. A/AC.96/1035, Geneva: UNHCR (17 October 2013).

244 UN Human Rights Council, *Birth Registration and the Right of Everyone to Recognition Everywhere as a Person before the Law* (17 June 2014), para II.5.

245 UNSD, *Principles and Recommendations for a Vital Statistics System* (Revision 3) (2014), para 299; See also Committee on the Protection of the Rights of All Migrants Workers and Members of Their Families (CMW), Joint General Comment No. 4 (2017) of the Committee on the Protection of the Rights of All Migrant Workers and Members of Their Families and No. 23 (2017) of the

information on a birth certificate does not need to be as complete as the information kept on a birth record. States, therefore, may omit details that may be prejudicial to the individual such as ethnicity or race.[246] Unavailable information such as the name of one of the parents, or the parent's personal identification record (because they are not registered), should not detract a person from birth registration.[247]

Law to Provide Clear Directions

Compulsoriness of a country's civil registration through a legal framework has also been underlined as fundamental for the smooth and effective operation of the system.[248] However, the law has to be organic and not over-regulated. It must contain custom-designed provisions that meet some minimum requirements and must not be so detailed so as not to defeat the requirements of the continuous, permanent, compulsory, and universal system.[249]

Proof of Birth

As for proof of birth, states may require legal documents, medical certificates, witnesses, or a combination of such requirements. Documents are generally more reliable than witnesses and are required in most cases.[250] The registrar needs to determine whether a witness is necessary, or if the birth could be registered based on the report by the informant in the case of birth without medical certificates and medical attendance.[251] On the whole, the standard requires flexible rules of proof that avoid excessive documentation requirements.[252]

Standard 2: Birth Registration that is Flexible and Responsive to the Circumstances of Families

The CRC Committee gave an example of mobile registration as an illustration of states being responsive to the circumstances of parents.[253] UNSD recommends a

---

Committee on the Rights of the Child on the General Principles regarding the Human Rights of Children in the Context of International Migration, 16 November 2017, CMW/C/GC/3-CRC/C/GC/23, paras 20–21. Retrieved from http://www.refworld.org/docid/5a1293a24.html [Accessed 30 December 2017].

[246] UNICEF, *A Passport to Protection: A Guide to Birth Registration Programming* (2013), p 122.

[247] UNICEF, *A Passport to Protection: A Guide to Birth Registration Programming* (2013), p 122.

[248] UNSD, *Principles and Recommendations for a Vital Statistics System* (Revision 3) (2014), para 294, p 68.

[249] UNSD, *Handbook on Training in Civil Registration and Vital Statistic Systems, Series F No. 84* (2002), para 48, p 69.

[250] UNSD, *Handbook on Training in Civil Registration and Vital Statistic Systems, Series F No. 84* (2002), para 126, p 28.

[251] UNSD, *Handbook on Training in Civil Registration and Vital Statistic Systems, Series F No. 84* (2002), para 127, p 28.

[252] *UN Human* Rights Council, *Birth Registration and the Right of Everyone to Recognition Everywhere as a Person before the Law* (17 June 2014), para C 56–60.

[253] UNICEF, *A Passport to Protection: A Guide to Birth Registration Programming* (2013). See footnote 18.

simpler type of registration document where literacy is a problem.[254] Meanwhile, UNHCR urges states to adopt both simplified administrative procedures and where appropriate, integrate civil registration with other public services, including those relating to childbirth, maternal-infant care, immunisation, and education.[255]

Standard 3: Timely and Accurate Birth Registration with Facilitated Late Birth Registration

In principle, the period prescribed by law between the vital event and its registration must be as short as possible as the accuracy of information relating to age, sex, parentage, and nationality of the parents, will have consequences on the rights and obligations of the registered individual.[256] UNSD sets a maximum period of 30 days for birth registration to take place.[257] It then recommends one year as the grace period for late registration, namely, registration after the legally specified period, if there are extenuating circumstances.[258] Delayed registration after one year may require age assessment and the court process.

It is to be noted that awareness-raising for birth registration is not a one-off but an on-going process.[259] In light of this, states are required to facilitate late birth registration.[260] UNSD underscores the need for sound legislation by states to provide for timely reporting of events. The people must also be made aware of the content of such legislation. The law may make provision for late registration 'provided that the birth and its circumstances are duly proved to the Registrar.'[261]

The relevant regulations must provide for specific and different levels of proof and other requirements for legally authorised late and delayed registrations.[262] As for UNHCR, awareness campaigns or community outreach activities should be organised

---

254 UNSD, *Handbook on Training in Civil Registration and Vital Statistic Systems, Series F No. 84* (2002), para 34, p 8.

255 UNHCR, Conclusion on Civil Registration No. 111 (LXIV), Doc. A/AC.96/1035, Geneva: UNHCR (17 October 2013).

256 UNICEF, *A Passport to Protection: A Guide to Birth Registration Programming* (2013), p 25.

257 UNSD, *Handbook on Training in Civil Registration and Vital Statistic Systems, Series F No. 84* (2002).

258 UNSD, *Principles and Recommendations for a Vital Statistics System (Revision 3)* (2014), para 363, p 81; UNSD, *Handbook on Training in Civil Registration and Vital Statistic Systems, Series F No. 84* (2002), para 121.

259 UN Human Rights Council, *Birth Registration and the Right of Everyone to Recognition Everywhere as a Person before the Law* (17 June 2014), para B. 55.

260 UN Human Rights Council, *Birth Registration and the Right of Everyone to Recognition Everywhere as a Person before the Law* (17 June 2014), para 13.

261 UNSD, *Handbook on Training in Civil Registration and Vital Statistic Systems, Series F No. 84* (2002), para 34.

262 UNSD, *Handbook on Training in Civil Registration and Vital Statistic Systems, Series F No. 84* (2002), para 123. Retrieved from http://unstats.un.org/unsd/publication/SeriesF/SeriesF_84E.pdf [24 June 2016].

by states, together with measures, as appropriate, to ensure that rural or remote locations are reached, such as through mobile registration units.[263]

Recommendations and Standards developed via Concluding Observations: The Link between Birth Registration and Nationality

According to a study conducted by the Institute on Statelessness and Inclusion, in over four hundred recommendations on birth registration made by the CRC Committee in its numerous Concluding Observations up to September 2015, there are specifically thirteen recommendations in which birth registration is linked to nationality. In these recommendations, states are urged to ensure that birth registrations are free and universally accessible to everyone regardless of:

(i) the parents' residence status;
(ii) whether the parents are foreign nationals; and
(iii) whether the parents are, themselves, undocumented.[264]

For the specific categories of children vulnerable to statelessness, the link between unregistered children, including those born as undocumented children, and the creation of *de jure* statelessness has been highlighted in CRC's Concluding Observation to Japan.[265] The Committee recommended that Japan amend its nationality laws and regulations in line with Article 7 of CRC to make sure children are registered at birth and protected against *de jure* statelessness and consider ratifying the 1954 and 1961 Conventions.[266] Other than children of undocumented migrants, states are advised to fulfil birth registration to other marginalised groups that are disproportionately at risk of statelessness.[267] Among the precise categories of children highlighted to be in need of registration at birth are; (i) children born out of

263 UNHCR, Conclusion on Civil Registration No. 111 (LXIV), Doc. A/AC.96/1035, Geneva: UNHCR (17 October 2013), UNHCR, EXCOM Conclusions on Civil Registration, No. 111 (LXIX)(17 October 2013).

264 Institute on Statelessness and Inclusion, *Policy Paper on Realising the right of every child to acquire a nationality: An analysis of the work of the Committee on the Rights of the Child* (2015), p 16.

265 Committee on the Rights of the Child, Concluding Observations: Japan, UN Doc. CRC/C/JPN/CO/3: CRC (20 June 2010), para 45.

266 Committee on the Rights of the Child, Concluding Observations: Japan, UN Doc. CRC/C/JPN/CO/3: CRC (20 June 2010), para 46.

267 Institute on Statelessness and Inclusion, *Policy Paper on Realising the Right of Every Child to Acquire a Nationality: An Analysis of the Work of the Committee on the Rights of the Child* (2015), p 17.

wedlock[268]; (ii) refugee and asylum-seeking children[269]; (iii) stateless children[270]; and (iv) abandoned children.[271]

Through various other Concluding Observations, precise measures recommended by the CRC Committee include:

(i) abolishment of fees for birth registration, decentralising the birth registration system and identifying children who were not registered at birth[272];
(ii) children registered are to be issued birth certificates, regardless of their nationality, religion, and status at birth, and that birth registration is facilitated free of charge everywhere and under all circumstances[273];
(iii) mobile registration mechanism to be provided for remote areas[274];
(iv) states taking measures to ensure that birth registration is achieved, in particular among those children who are not registered due to parents' economic status, ethnicity and immigration status, beside ensuring timely birth registration for newborn, including conducting campaigns for children born in the State Party who remain unregistered[275]; and removing multiple and complex administrative barriers to birth registration and excluding the requirement of family

---

[268] Implementation of the Convention on the Rights of the Child: List of Issues Concerning Additional and Updated Information related to the Initial Report of Afghanistan, UN Doc. (CRC/C/AFG/1), Afghanistan: CRC, 56th Session (2 November 2010), para 34; United Nations Committee on the Rights of the Child, 35th Session, Concluding Observations: Indonesia, UN Doc. CRC/C/15/Add. 233, Indonesia: CRC (26 February 2004), para 38.

[269] Committee on the Rights of the Child, Concluding Observations: Germany, UN Doc. CRC/C/15/Add.226, Germany: CRC (26 February 2004), para 55(e); UN Committee on the Rights of the Child: Concluding Observation: Malaysia, UN Doc. CRC/C/MYS/CO/1, Malaysia: CRC (25 June 2007), para 33.

[270] Committee on the Rights of the Child. Concluding Observations: India, UN Doc. CRC/C/15/Add. 228, India: CRC (26 February 2004), paras 40–41.

[271] See Committee on the Rights of the Child, Concluding Observations on the Initial Report Submitted by Brunei Darussalam, UN Doc. CRC/C/15/Add. 219, Indonesia: CRC (27 October 2003), para 33.

[272] See, for instance, Committee on the Rights of the Child, Consideration of Report Submitted by Zambia, Concluding Observations, UN Doc. CRC/C/15/Add. 206, Zambia: CRC (2 July 2003), para 29.

[273] Committee on the Rights of the Child (CRC), Concluding Observations on the Combined Third and Fourth Periodic Reports of Indonesia, UN Doc. CRC/C/IDN/ CO/3-4, Indonesia: CRC (13 June 2014), para 28.

[274] See for instance Committee on the Rights of the Child, Concluding Observations: India, UN Doc. CRC/C/15/Add. 228, India: CRC (26 February 2004), para 39; Committee on the Rights of the Child. Concluding Observations: Myanmar, UN Doc. CRC/C/15/Add. 237, Myanmar: CRC (30 June 2004), para 35; UN Committee on the Rights of the Child, Consideration of Report Submitted by Zambia, Concluding Observations, UN Doc. CRC/C/15/Add. 206, Zambia: CRC (2 July 2003), para 29; Consideration of Reports Submitted by States Parties under Article 44 of the Convention, Concluding Observations: Cambodia, UN Doc. CRC/C/ KHM/CO/2-3, Cambodia: CRC (3 August 2011), para 37.

[275] Committee on the Rights of the Child, Consideration of Reports Submitted by States Parties under Article 44 of the Convention, Concluding Observations: Thailand, Report No. CRC/C/THA/CO/3-4, Thailand: CRC (17 February 2012), para 44.

household registration (hukou) attached to the birth registration of children of migrant workers.[276]

With regard to CRC's Concluding Observations on the right of children to acquire a nationality, the previous trend shows little inclination in favour of conferment of nationality *jus soli* in the event that a child would otherwise be stateless. Neither does it reveal specific measures that States Parties must adopt for prevention of statelessness, or in dealing with a conflict of nationality laws. In the Concluding Observations issued to Switzerland, for instance, the CRC Committee underlines its concern over the legal status of parents as a barrier to both birth registration and the right of children who would otherwise be stateless to acquire Swiss nationality. It is recommended that both birth registration and Swiss nationality be made available to children born on its territory regardless of the legal status of the parents, and in the latter case, if the children would otherwise be stateless.[277]

Better attention was given to anti-discrimination norms that could have negative effects on citizenship. Concerns over discriminatory practices in relation to citizenship at birth have been expressed among others, in relation to the Central African Republic,[278] Democratic Republic of the Congo,[279] and Liberia's citizenship law that restricts birth citizenship on racial grounds.[280] Whereas acquisition of Bhutanese citizenship that is subjected to both parents being of Bhutanese nationality raised a similar concern with the Committee that subsequently urged Bhutan to take all measures necessary to ensure 'no child is or risks being stateless, in accordance with Article 7 of the Convention'.[281] Another emphasis in the Committee's Concluding Observations was on the facilitated acquisition of nationality for reduction of stateless children.[282]

---

[276] Committee on the Rights of the Child, Concluding Observations on the Combined Third and Fourth Periodic Reports of China (including Hong Kong and Macau Special Administrative Regions), adopted by the Committee at its 64th session (16 September–4 October 2013), UN Doc. CRC/C/CHN/CO/3-4, China: CRC (4 October 2013), para 40.

[277] Committee on the Rights of the Child, Concluding Observations: Switzerland, CRC/C/CHE/CO/2-4, Section III D (4 February 2015), para 31, p 7.

[278] Committee on the Rights of the Child, Concluding Observations: Central African Republic, UN Doc. CRC/C/100 (14 November 2000), 435–6.

[279] Committee on the Rights of the Child, Concluding Observations: Democratic Republic of the Congo, UN Doc. CRC/C/108 (23 July 2001), 177–8.

[280] Committee on the Rights of the Child. Concluding Observations: Liberia, UN Doc. CRC/C/140 (27 September 2004), 334–5.

[281] Committee on the Rights of the Child. Concluding Observations: Bhutan, UN Doc. CRC/C/BTN/CO/2 (8 October 2008), para 34, p 7.

[282] See, for instance, Committee on the Rights of the Child, Concluding Observations: Czech Republic, UN Doc. CRC/C/15/Add. 201, Czech: CRC (18 March 2003), para 38; Committee on the Rights of the Child, Concluding Observations, Kazakhstan, UN Doc. CRC/C/15/Add. 213, Kazakhstan: CRC (10 July 2003), para 33; Committee on the Rights of the Child, Concluding Observations: Romania CRC/C/15/Add. 199, Romania: CRC (18 March 2003), para 33; Committee on the Rights of the Child, Concluding Observations: India, UN Doc. CRC/C/15/Add. 228, India: CRC (26 February 2004), para 66; Committee on the Rights of the Child. Concluding Observations: Myanmar, UN Doc. CRC/C/15/Add. 237, Myanmar: CRC (30 June 2004), para 65.

ii. ***The Right to Birth Registration and Prevention of Statelessness: Issues of Concern***

If birth registration is touted as a safeguard to prevent children from statelessness by helping establish a child's legal link of nationality to a state, it behoves one to question whether international norms on children's right to their legal identity and prevention of statelessness have been sufficiently developed to link birth registration with acquisition of nationality for avoidance of statelessness? In retrospect, the imposition of the duty to register children immediately after birth was not linked to the right of children to acquire a nationality. Instead, as commented upon by the HR Committee in its General Comment No. 17, the main reason of immediate birth registration is:

> to reduce the danger of abduction, the sale of or traffic in children, or of other types of treatment that are incompatible with the enjoyment of rights provided by the Covenant.[283]

As pointed out before, notwithstanding the primacy of prevention and reduction of statelessness upon which the 1961 Convention is premised, it is silent on the prevention of statelessness through children's right to universal birth registration. This is because the Convention itself was concluded in the period when the new sources of statelessness including lack of, or defective birth registration, were not the major causes of statelessness.[284] It seems only after three decades later that the UN system began to recognise and actively promote the nexus between birth registration and the prevention of statelessness, following UNHCR's mandates on the latter.[285]

In 2011, the third expert meeting convened by UNHCR addressed the importance of birth registration in the context of the scope of application of Articles 1–4 of the 1961 Convention. In drawing attention to children 'who would otherwise be stateless', paragraph 41 of Dakar Conclusions states that:

---

[283] UN Human Rights Committee, CCPR General Comment No. 17: Article 24 (Rights of the Child) (7 April 1989), UN Doc. HRI/GEN/1/Rev. 6, Geneva: CCPR, para 7.

[284] L. van Waas, *Nationality Matters: Statelessness under International Law* (Antwerp/Oxford/Portland: Intersentia, 2008).

[285] UNGA Resolution A/RES/63/241 of 13 March 2009, at para 12 where States are urged to intensify efforts to preserve the child's identity and in the area of birth registration; UNGA Resolution A/RES/67/149 of 20 December 2012, at para 23 where UNGA recognises birth registration as officially recording a child's legal identity and is pertinent in preventing and reducing statelessness and welcomes pledges by states to ensure all children are registered at birth; UNGA Resolution A/RES/68/141 of 28 January 2014, at para 26 where UNGA notes that the lack of civil registration and related documentation renders people vulnerable to statelessness and its associated risks, recognises its crucial importance in preventing and reducing statelessness and welcomes pledges by states to ensure all children are registered at birth; UN Human Rights Council, *Birth Registration and the Right of Everyone to Recognition Everywhere as a Person before the Law* (17 June 2014); UNHCR, Conclusion on Identification, Prevention and Reduction of Statelessness and Protection of Stateless Persons No. 106 (LVII), General Assembly Document, A/AC.96/1035, Geneva; UNHCR (Conclusion No. 106 (LVII) on Identification, Prevention, and Reduction of Statelessness and Protection of Stateless Persons) (2006), at para (h) where States are encouraged to facilitate birth registration and issuance of birth certificate; UNHCR, Conclusion on Civil Registration No. 111 (LXIV), Doc. A/AC.96/1035, Geneva: UNHCR (17 October 2013).

> While the rules set out in the 1961 Convention operate regardless of whether a child's birth is registered, registration of the birth provides a key form of proof which underpins implementation of the 1961 Convention and related human rights norms. CRC Article 7 specifically requires the registration of the birth of all children and applies irrespective of the nationality or residence status of the parents.[286]

Earlier, the connection between these two rights can be traced to the UN resolution entitled 'A World Fit for Children' that was adopted following the UNGA's Special Session on Children in May 2002. Aside from a birth registration system that a state creates and manages, the Resolution underlines that states must as well establish a system that allows children to acquire a nationality. This strongly implies that children must be prevented from statelessness at the earliest stage of birth.[287]

Universal birth registration has been subsequently incorporated into UNHCR's Global Strategic Priority.[288] Failure to register birth has been singled out as a source of statelessness by UNHCR.[289] Children are also to be registered immediately after birth without any discrimination on the basis that birth registration is essential to the reduction and prevention of statelessness.[290]

As for the HR Committee, despite urging states to cooperate in ensuring every child has a nationality when he is born so as not to be rendered stateless,[291] it has not specifically outlined how birth registration may be implemented so that children may have a certain nationality. Its concluding observations on a number of periodic reports within its ambit have merely highlighted its concerns on the lack of a nationality experienced by children who are registered at birth. In its Concluding Observation on Slovenia, the Committee mentions that:

> [...] while recognising that registration is distinct from conferral of nationality, it is also concerned that some children are registered at birth without a nationality.[292]

---

[286] See also Guidelines No. 4, para 55.

[287] UNGA, A World Fit for Children, General Assembly Resolution. UN Doc. GA/10022, New York: UNGA (11 October 2002). Retrieved from https://www.un.org/press/en/2002/ga10022.doc.htm [Accessed 5 July 2016].

[288] UNHC (Division of International Protection), UNHCR Action to Address Statelessness: A Strategy Note' (2010); UN Human Rights Council, *Birth Registration and the Right of Everyone to Recognition Everywhere as a Person before the Law* (17 June 2014), para 15.

[289] UNHCR, UNHCR's 2010–2011 Global Strategic Priorities (2009) http://www.unhcr.org/4abb45419.html, para 1.3.

[290] UNHCR, Conclusion on Civil Registration No. 111 (LXIV), Doc. A/AC.96/1035, Geneva: UNHCR (17 October 2013), para 13.

[291] General Comment No. 17, Article 24, Geneva: Right of Child (1989).

[292] See Human Rights Committee, Concluding Observations: Slovenia, A/60. 40 vol. 1, Geneva (2005), para 93 (15); Human Rights Committee, Concluding Observations: Kuwait: 2011, KWT/CO/2, para 12. The HR Committee stated its concern over children born in Kuwait to stateless parents who may not be able to acquire any nationality. Nonetheless, no further recommendation was made to remedy this drawback.

Absence of General Comment on Article 7 CRC Obviates Clear, Systematic, and Mutually Reinforcing Norms on the Scope and Implementation of Children's Rights to Birth Registration and Nationality

Despite the universal recognition of the role of birth registration in avoiding statelessness and ensuring the protection and enjoyment of children's rights, regrettably, CRC's detailed views and position on the scope of obligations intended by Article 7 CRC have not materialised in the form of its General Comment.[293]

In respect of its General Comment No. 7 on 'Implementing child rights in early childhood',[294] no guidance is made as to how children may exercise the right to birth registration in a way that could lead them to secure a nationality. For the major part of its work, the CRC Committee has approached issues surrounding the right to birth registration and its influence on the right to acquire a nationality under Article 7 CRC via its monitoring mechanism of Concluding Observations, by making non-binding comments and recommendations to the Contracting States of CRC.

As already demonstrated, the right of every child to be registered at birth has been clearly provided and guaranteed by various international legal instruments. An argument has been advanced that this right has crystallised into a norm of customary international law.[295] Unfortunately, the bulk of such detailed standards as to how states may fulfil the right to birth registration remain a web of loose and scattered directions. Without a systemic and mutually reinforcing approach to clearly define the scope on birth registration, followed by sufficient and clear guidance on the implementation of the said right that may assist in the acquisition of nationality by children, birth registration would remain under-inclusive and incomplete in its role to prevent and reduce statelessness.

The following are several of the issues of concern demonstrating the barriers to and the disconnect between birth registration and acquisition of nationality.

Which State's Duty to Register Birth?

Firstly, CRC and ICCPR do not expressly provide as to which country has the obligation to register the birth of a child. CRC's General Comment No. 7 only refers to

---

[293] S. Köhn, '"Soft Law" Entrepreneurship and the Right of the Child to a Nationality in an Era of Migration' (2012), p 68; N. Cantwell, 'The Origins, Development and Significance of the United Nations Convention on the Rights of the Child' (1992); S. Detrick et al., *The United Nations Convention on the Rights of the Child* (1992); C. Bierwirth, 'The Protection of Refugee and Asylum-Seeking Children: The Convention on the Rights of the Child and the Work of the Committee on the Rights of the Child' (2005); ECN, *Statelessness Determination and the Protection Status of Stateless Persons* (2013), p 7; P. Alston, 'The Historical Origins of the Concept of "General Comments" in Human Rights Law' in *The International Legal System in Quest of Equity and Universality* (Geneva: Graduate Institute of International Studies (2001)), pp 763–776; See further Z. Vaghri et al., 'CRC General Comment 7 Indicators Framework: A Tool for Monitoring the Implementation of Child Rights in Early Childhood', *Journal of Human Rights*, 10(2) (2011), pp 178–188.

[294] General Comment No. 7 (2005): Implementing Child Rights in Early Childhood, UN Doc. CRC/C/GC/7/Rev. 1, Geneva: CRC (2005), para 25.

[295] T.Y. Leinwand, 'Navigating Nationality: The Rights to Birth Registration and Nationality in Refugee Magnet States', *Columbia Journal of International Law* (2014), p 119.

'State parties' that are required to take all necessary measures to ensure all children are registered at birth.

> As a first step in ensuring the rights to survival, development, and access to quality services for all children (art. 6), the Committee recommends that States parties take all necessary measures to ensure that all children are registered at birth. This can be achieved through a universal, well-managed registration system that is accessible to all and free of charge.[296]

Generally, the duty to register birth principally falls upon the state in whose territory the child is born, notwithstanding the child's nationality.[297] However, in the context of migration, due to the susceptible position of irregular migrants, this may not sit well with the authorities of the host state that are concurrently trusted with the enforcement of immigration laws. In view of this, the idea of adopting the broader interpretation of extending the role of birth registration to the state of nationality of the parents seems practicable.[298] The CRC Committee has indeed proposed this approach once:

> With reference to the high number of overseas Filipino workers, the Committee is concerned about children born abroad to Filipino migrant workers. Due to the non-registration of these children, they are deprived of their right to name, nationality and identity as well as to basic services. The Committee recommends the State party to encourage and facilitate parents, irrespective of their residence status, to register their children born abroad.[299]

UNHRC's interpretations of Articles 3 and 7 on the duty of states to ensure that a child acquires a nationality at birth, or, immediately after birth, strongly resonate with CRC's call for the country of origin of migrants to complement the duty of birth registration of children of migrants in the host state. UNHCR on this point underscores that the obligation to ensure that a child acquires a nationality at birth or soon after birth is common to both the state of birth, as well as to all countries that could be linked to the child through parentage or residence.[300]

With respect to children born in exile in countries of refuge, it is even more compelling for the international norms to emphasise on the duty of the host states to register their births, considering the general unwillingness or inability of the refugee

---

[296] General Comment No. 7 (2005), Implementing Child Rights in Early Childhood, UN Doc. CRC/C/GC/7/Rev. 1, Geneva: CRC (2005), para 25.

[297] UNHCR, *Self-Study Module on statelessness* (2012), p 77. Retrieved from https://www.refworld.org/docid/50b899602.html [Accessed 5 July 2017]; United Nations, *Handbook on Civil Registration and Vital Statistics System: Preparation of a Legal Framework* (1998). Retrieved from http://www.uneca.org/sites/default/files/images/en-pages-from-handbook-on-civil-registration-and-vital-statistics-systems-preparation-of-a-legal-framework.pdf [Accessed 17 January 2016].

[298] L. van Waas, 'The Children of Irregular Migrants: A Stateless Generation', *Netherlands Quarterly of Human Rights* (2007), p 456.

[299] CRC Concluding Observations. The Philippines, UN Doc. CRC/C/15/Add. 258 (2005), paras 36 and 37. Other treaty bodies have not followed this approach. The idea has only been pursued in other CRC's concluding observations. See Committee on the Rights of the Child, Concluding Observations: The Philippines, UN Doc. CRC/C/15/Add. 259, The Philippines: CRC (21 September 2005), para 33.

[300] Guidelines No. 4, para 11.

parents to be in contact with the authorities of their respective countries of origin. For the purpose of establishing their identity and refugee status, the Contracting States to the 1951 Refugee Convention are to issue identity papers to any refugee in their territory who does not have a valid travel document. The formal proof of recognition that a person is considered a refugee in countries where there is no formal recognition of refugee status by UNHCR[301] is highly important in helping such children to be registered at birth and gain a legal identity.

Children with Unknown Parents without Legal Identity

While the rights of foundlings to birth registration and acquisition of nationality have long been guaranteed under international law,[302] the right to birth registration as well as the duty of implementing it for older children found separated from parents with an unknown place of birth and other identity information are not articulated in the existing standards. In advocating for every child to obtain legal documents, UNHCR promotes older children and adolescents to be able to obtain birth certificates.[303] The General Comment on Article 6 of ACRWC on this point stresses that proof of identity provided under a birth registration system may guard children whose identity cannot be established, such as abandoned, separated, and stateless children, against harmful practices including trafficking and sexual exploitation.[304]

Going on the basis that every 'child' instead of 'foundling' is entitled to have his or her birth registered,[305] and subsequently, the right to acquire a nationality, express standards and effective mechanisms for states to investigate and record such children's vital information are, therefore, required.

Birth Registration and Determination of a Nationality

The relationship between birth registration and acquisition of nationality calls for further development of norms to better inform states on how to design a more inclusive system that could optimise prevention of statelessness among children. Such illumination is particularly critical for children born to undocumented parents, stateless, refugees, as well as children born out of wedlock and children of unknown

---

[301] UNHCR, Identity Documents for Refugees (Ec/Scp/33) (1984), paras 6–7. Retrieved from http://www.unhcr.org/3ae68cce4.html [Accessed 1 April 2016].

[302] See the 1930 Hague Convention on Certain Questions relating to the Conflict of Nationality Laws; 1961 Convention on the Reduction of Statelessness; 2005 Covenant on the Rights of the Child in Islam.

[303] In its landmark document that provides for a Framework for the Protection of Children, out of its six overall goals, the fourth goal aims for children to obtain legal document. To this end, older children and adolescents should be able to obtain birth certificates, procedures for late birth registration must be in place and barriers to birth registration must be identified. See UNHCR, A Framework for the Protection of Children (2012), p 25. Retrieved from www.unhcr.org/protection/children/50f6cf0b9/framework-protection-children.html [accessed 8 December 2013].

[304] General Comment on Article 6 of ACRWC: The Right to a Name, Registration at Birth, and to Acquire a Nationality, ACERWC/GC/02, Addis Ababa: African Union (2014), para 18.

[305] The proposed indicator for Target 16.9 within Goal 16 of the 2030 Sustainable Development Goals ('SDG') that calls for a legal identity for all is the percentage of children under five whose births have been registered.

parents, given the multiple barriers experienced by them in accessing birth registration and acquiring a nationality.[306] For a state that has chosen to grant its nationality ex lege at birth to children who would otherwise be stateless,[307] it appears that birth registration itself can be the juncture where the state may determine whether a child is otherwise stateless, and thus grant a nationality if the finding is affirmative.[308]

Common statuses concerning a child's nationality often recorded in the birth certificate include; 'non-citizen', 'nationality undetermined', 'nationality unknown' or 'pending clarification'.[309] However, there seems to be no international guidance on what amounts to and distinguishes between 'non-citizen', 'nationality undetermined', or 'nationality unknown'. This could also be due to the absence of any international convention on the status of persons of unknown or undetermined nationality. States, therefore, arrive at any of such determinations according to their nationality laws and policies.[310]

UNHCR's guidance generally requires that the determination of whether a child 'would otherwise be stateless' be carried out as soon as possible, in order that the child's undetermined status is not prolonged. In the context of the application of Articles 1 and 4 of the 1961 Convention, it should not exceed five years. Within that timeframe, the child should be allowed to enjoy human rights on equal terms with other citizen children.[311] Nonetheless, if the child's birth certificate marks him as 'non-citizen', the said status could likely remain so for an uncertain period of time. This is also possible when there is no application made on behalf of the child for his nationality status to be determined.

In practice, a state's attribution of nationality may or may not reflect the child's true nationality. The lack of uniformity and certainty in the process of nationality attribution can be particularly pronounced in the case of refugee children's nationality, as illustrated below.

---

[306] M. Manly, 'UNHCR's Mandate and Activities to Address Statelessness' in A. Edwards & L. van Waas (Eds.), *Nationality and Statelessness under International Law* (Cambridge: Cambridge University Press, 2014), p 95.

[307] The grant of nationality to an otherwise stateless child is an obligation under Article 1(a) 1961 Convention for State parties. In the context of non-State parties, Malaysia and Indonesia, for instance, provide for ex lege acquisition of nationality at birth for children born in the territory who would otherwise be stateless. See the analysis of the nationality laws of these countries in chapter III.

[308] This is in comport with paragraph 11 of Guidelines No. 4 that states, '... a child must not be left stateless for an extended period of time: a child must acquire nationality at birth or as soon as possible after birth...'; See further UNHCR, *Nationality and Statelessness: Handbook for Parliamentarians No. 22* (2014), p 37; Concluding Observations: Slovenia, A/60.40 vol. 1, Geneva (2005), para 93 (15). Although it is to be noted that where nationality is acquired by operation of law by descent or place of birth, the rules in the 1961 Convention operate regardless of whether a child's birth is registered. See para 55 of Guidelines No. 4.

[309] See HR Committee, A/HRC/31/29, p 9.

[310] UNHCR, *Nationality and Statelessness: Handbook for Parliamentarians No. 22* (2014), p 37.

[311] UNHCR, Guidelines on Statelessness No. 4 (2012), para 22. Further, if the state decides to confer nationality at birth to an otherwise stateless child, the child designated with having an 'undetermined nationality' is required to be treated as having the nationality of the state of birth unless and until the possession of another nationality is proven. See para 23f, Guidelines No. 4.

> In some states (like Romania or Italy), state authorities automatically attribute the parents' nationality—(or the nationality indicated by the parents)—to the baby on birth certificates. As the birth certificate often serves as a key source of data for other official documents issued later, this practice may give the false impression that the nationality status of the refugee child is properly determined and that statelessness was effectively avoided. In other countries (like Hungary), children of foreign nationals are automatically registered as having an unknown nationality until such time as they can provide proof of acquisition of nationality. In some instances, this may be the correct conclusion at the time of the birth, but it can easily become a source of hardship, legal limbo and human rights violations if it persists for several years. Yet in other states (like France, the United Kingdom, or the Czech Republic) no information concerning nationality is entered on the birth certificate. What often lacks, under the various scenarios, is the proper and timely determination of the child's *real* nationality, which also allows for a conclusion of statelessness—and thus the application of the safeguards applicable for 'otherwise stateless' children—if the conditions are met.[312]

Substantive and Procedural Norms on Birth Registration

With regard to birth registration law, states could be better informed of which standards are to be incorporated into states' legislation, monitored, and legally enforced on the one hand and others that should be recommended on the other.[313] The methods and conditions to implement birth registration also call for adequate outlining.[314] For instance, procedures for late registration are noted to be onerous, leaving a large number of populations to remain unregistered.[315]

However, the methods of late and delayed birth registrations are not sufficiently clarified to inform states and the institutions involved. To balance out between preservation of accuracy and the need to avoid children remaining without a legal identity, pertinent questions relating to the kind of evidence that could be accepted by the Court or the designated authority for late registration cases, and the mechanisms to ensure fair and efficient processes, should form part of the international legal norms addressing birth registration system.[316]

The consequences of denial of birth registration also seem to be omitted in the procedural context of the standards on birth registration. Procedures for lodging complaints and the opportunity to appeal against refusal of birth registration are additionally found to be lacking in the international standards of a well-managed

---

[312] G. Gyulai, 'The Long-Overlooked Mystery of Refugee Children's Nationality' in Institute on Statelessness and Inclusion, *The World's Stateless Children* (2017). Retrieved from http://children.worldsstateless.org/3/migration-displacement-and-childhood-statelessness/the-long-overlooked-mystery-of-refugee-childrens-nationality.html [Accessed 5 July 2017].

[313] T.Y. Leinwand, 'Navigating Nationality: The Rights to Birth Registration and Nationality in Refugee Magnet States', *Columbia Journal of Transnational Law* (2014), p 114.

[314] L. van Waas, *Nationality Matters: Statelessness Under International Law* (School of Human Rights Research Series, V. 29, 2008).

[315] UNICEF, *A Passport to Protection: A Guide to Birth Registration Programming* (2013), p 24.

[316] Through legal aid programmes conducted by Norwegian Refugee Council, many cases of late birth registration and documentation in Cote d'Ivoire were tackled. Yet, the effectiveness of the programmes was affected by lack of advice and support to people who urgently needed them. See M. Manly & S. Persaud, 'UNHCR and Responses to Statelessness'.

universal birth registration.[317] Other than these, provisions on interstate cooperation wherever needed to assist in the identification of nationality, and on legal assistance and representation to marginalised communities, equally need further elucidation.

Immigration Control v. Best Interests of the Child

The core challenge of ensuring universal birth registration among the children of irregular and undocumented migrants can be attributed in many ways to contradictory objects between immigration control and protection of the best interests of the child. The tension is habitually reflected in the lack of separation between public service provisions and immigration control. In the UK, the experience of the Migrant Children's Project at Coram Children's Legal Centre reveals that a recognised relation between an agency or institution and the Home Office will clearly demonstrate reduced contact being made by children, young people, and families, due to their 'real or perceived fear.'[318]

The UN Committee on the Protection of the Rights of Migrant Workers and Members of Their Families and the CRC Committee on State Obligations regarding the human rights of children in the context of international migration in countries of origin, transit, destination, and return, have recently formulated their comments on ensuring the separation between birth registration and immigration enforcement.

In their joint general comment issued in 2017 on the rights to a name, identity, and a nationality under Article 29 of ICMW and Articles 7 and 8 of CRC, the two Committees expressly recognise the many negative consequences associated with the lack of birth registration, including the risk of becoming stateless for children born to parents in an irregular situation who are obstructed from acquiring nationality in the country of origin, and from accessing birth registration and nationality at the place of birth. Importantly, in urging states to ensure that all children are immediately registered at birth and issued birth certificates regardless of their migration status or that of their parents', states are required among others:

> to remove legal and practical obstacles to birth registration, including the prohibition of data sharing between health providers or civil servants responsible for registration with immigration enforcement authorities; and not requiring parents to produce documentation regarding their migration status.[319]

---

317 M. Manly & S. Persaud, 'UNHCR and Responses to Statelessness'.

318 Coram Children's Legal Centre, *Growing up in a Hostile Environment: The Rights of Undocumented Migrant Children in the UK'* (2013), p 15. Retrieved from https://www.childrenslegalcentre.com/wp-content/uploads/2013/11/Hostile_Environment_Full_Report_Final.pdf [Accessed 15 June 2016].

319 Committee on the Protection of the Rights of All Migrants Workers and Members of Their Families (CMW), Joint General Comment No. 4 (2017) of the Committee on the Protection of the Rights of All Migrant Workers and Members of Their Families and No. 23 (2017) of the Committee on the Rights of the Child on the General Principles regarding the Human Rights of Children in the Context of International Migration (16 November 2017), CMW/C/GC/3-CRC/C/GC/23, paras 20–2. Retrieved from http://www.refworld.org/docid/5a12942a2b.html [Accessed 30 December 2017].

This and other measures spelled out in the said joint general comment should authoritatively guide member states in addressing insufficient policy and legislative directions for service providers, immigration control personnel, and irregular migrants to prioritise the best interests of the child over migration control in the area of birth registration.

The prevailing norm concerning the legal recognition of a marriage between a man and a woman that is dependent on their possession of a valid proof of nationality and/or legal immigration status poses a related challenge in the area of birth registration and nationality acquisition. The right to marry and find a family for men and women of full age is enshrined in Article 16 of UDHR,[320] and is further recognised expressly in Article 23(2) of ICCPR.[321] Article 3 of the Convention on Consent to Marriage, Minimum Age for Marriage and Registration of Marriages 1962 provides in general terms that 'All marriages shall be registered in an appropriate official register by the competent authority'.[322]

Nevertheless, the general prohibition of discrimination on the basis of immigration status in the context of protecting the fundamental rights to family formation and unity is not unequivocally provided in ICMW.[323] Such prohibition is also absent from the list of rights to protect the undocumented migrants and their families.[324] There also seems to be paucity in the existing norms on birth registration of alternative proof of parentage that could be accepted for birth registration purposes, in particular, where lawful marriages are not possible due to the parents' immigration status. Such proof may include other forms of documentary or witness testimonial evidence, or the evidence of DNA.[325]

---

[320] This right is universally upheld without any limitation due to 'race, nationality or religion'. See Article 16(1) of UDHR that provides 'Men and women of full age, without any limitation due to race, nationality or religion, have the right to marry and to found a family (…)'.

[321] Article 23(2) of ICCPR provides that: 'The right of men and women of marriageable age to marry and to found a family shall be recognised'.

[322] United Nations Human Rights, 'Opened for Signature and Ratification by General Assembly Resolution 1763 A (XVII) of 7 November 1962'. Entry into force: 9 December 1964, Convention on Consent to Marriage, Minimum Age for Marriage and Registration of Marriages.

[323] Article 44 of ICMW provides for State Parties to take appropriate measures in protecting the unity of the families of migrant workers.

[324] See L. Berg, 'At the Border and Between the Cracks: The Precarious Position of Irregular Migrant Workers under International Human Rights Law', *Melbourne Journal of International Law*, 8(1) (2007), pp 1–34.

[325] In Montenegro and Serbia, problems of birth registration and confirmation of nationality are the impetus of an intergenerational lack of documentation among the most excluded and vulnerable Roma population, which may lead to their statelessness. Improvements have been in place since 2014, where the Ministry of Interior has allowed witness testimony or alternative forms of documentation (e.g. school certificates or vaccination records) to be submitted as evidence including for children born outside of health facilities. As a result, more than a dozen children were registered in the first 2 months of 2014 alone. In Serbia, a non-contentious procedure for the determination of time and place of birth (on the basis of witness testimony) for subsequent registration has been in place since 2012 to ensure that those who had no proof of birth are still registered. In Montenegro, this is a first vital step to avoid statelessness, after which a process of citizenship determination

UNHCR in its report found that, 'Challenges also arise in relation to registering children born out of wedlock to parents whose religious marriages have not been formally registered'.[326] Religious marriages that go unregistered are a common scenario for stateless, undocumented, and refugee parents, due to their lack of possession of valid travel documents and proof of legal residence.

A child who is unregistered owing to having no proof of her parents' marriage certificate consequently assumes the status of a child born out of wedlock. In view of the negative social stigma attached to illegitimacy and being registered without one's father's name,[327] the child's parents or mother are frequently dissuaded or unwilling to register the child's birth. In Vietnam, unmarried women have been reported to be reluctant to register their child out of shame or a mistaken belief that registration could only be done if the parents were married.[328] Even if the birth is registered, a child born out of wedlock risks a future of statelessness due to a possible lack of gender-neutral citizenship provisions in many countries. In Malaysia and Singapore for instance, children born out of wedlock in both countries are only entitled to their mothers' citizenship ex lege.[329]

(g) ***Emerging Framework for the Right to a Legal Identity Comprising the Rights to a Nationality and Birth Registration***

Having a name and birth registered is the precursor to acquiring one's legal personhood.[330] Aside from the rights to a name and to be registered at birth, the right to acquire a nationality links up with these two components to constitute an integral package of the rights forming a child's legal identity. Such legal identity must nevertheless be demonstrable so as to avoid social exclusion and political marginalisation.[331] Proponents of the rights-based approach to a legal identity regard it as a fundamental right of both 'intrinsic and instrumental value'.[332] The former relates

before the Ministry of Interior is carried out. See European Network on Statelessness, *Preventing Childhood Statelessness in Europe: Issues, Gaps and Good Practices* (2014), p 22.

326 UNHCR, *Ending Statelessness within 10 Years* (2014), p 10.

327 For instance, under the Malaysian registration system, the father's name is not recorded in the case of children born out of wedlock to a non-Muslim mother. For such children born toa Muslims, the child's name is followed by 'Abdullah' in some states in Malaysia, indicating the 'illegitimate' status of the child. See Meerah Dewi Raja Gopal, 'Does Illegitimacy Status of Children Matter? A Review on Malaysian Perspective', *International Journal of Applied Psychology*, 5(4) (2015), pp 109–114; Anon, 'Review for the Sake of the Child', *The Star Online*.

328 M.S. Pais, 'Birth Registration: Right from the Start', *UNICEF Innocenti Digest*, 9 (2002), pp 10–11.

329 See Article 14(1)(b) and Part II, Section 1(a), read with Section 17 of Part III of Second Schedule, Federal Constitution of Malaysia, Article 121(2)(c) read with Article 15(1) of the Third Schedule, Article 140, Constitution of the Republic of Singapore (1965).

330 J. Bhabha, 'Women, Children and Other Marginalised Migrant Groups' in B. Opeskin et al. (Eds.), *Foundations of International Migration Law* (Cambridge: Cambridge University Press, 2012), p 216; J. Doek, 'The CRC and the Right to Acquire and to Preserve a Nationality', p 31.

331 J. Bhabha (Ed.), *Children Without a State: A Global Human Rights Challenge* (2011), p 4.

332 C. Vandenabeele & C.V. Lao (Eds.), *Legal Identity for Inclusive Development* (Manila: Asian Development Bank, 2007), p 1.

to the value recognition of an individual existence as integral to human dignity. The latter, instrumental value refers to its function of unlocking the gate to other rights and benefits. This simple yet compelling formulation has repositioned the strategy to address birth registration by UNICEF and PLAN, from a bureaucratic procedure to a child rights issue.[333]

In a multi-country study on legal identity conducted under the purview of the Asian Development Bank (ADB), Vandenabeele and Lao explain the meaning of legal identity by contrasting it with physical personality. Legal identity has the purpose of providing an individual with official and state's recognition of his or her existence.[334] Stressing on the two key elements of one's legal identity, namely its function of allowing for the legal protection and enforcement of rights, and its form of official proof, ADB defines 'legal identity' as 'Official, government-issued identity documents that prove one's status as a person who can exercise rights and demand protection under the law'.[335]

Birth certificates are considered the official document preferred as the primary standard in establishing one's legal identity due to their record of age, place of birth and, familial relationship at the earliest stage.[336] However, the study demonstrates other types of identity documents that could be more significant in accessing benefits and opportunities, such as citizenship certificates, or family and lodging books.[337]

The concept of 'legal identity' has recently received global attention and recognition with the adoption of the United Nations Resolution entitled 'Transforming Our World: The 2030 Agenda for Sustainable Development'. Target 16.9 of Goal 16 of Agenda 30 of the Sustainable Development Goals (SDG) specifically underscores the aim of providing legal identity, including birth registration by 2030.[338] Unlike its predecessor, the Millennium Development Goals (MDGs), which did not address discrimination or deprivation that could inhibit equal access to development except for the aspect of gender-based discrimination, the SDG's key goal is to 'leave no one behind'. It henceforth aims for the achievement of universal access to legal identity to meet this ambitious goal.[339] While the right of everyone to a legal identity entails a wider scope beyond birth registration, birth registration of children under 5, however, remains the only indicator to monitor progress and implementation of

---

[333] C. Vandenabeele & C.V. Lao (Eds.), p 1.

[334] C. Vandenabeele & C.V. Lao (Eds.), p viii.

[335] C. Vandenabeele & C.V. Lao (Eds.), p vii.

[336] C. Vandenabeele & C.V. Lao (Eds.), p vii.

[337] C. Vandenabeele & C.V. Lao (Eds.), p vii.

[338] See United Nations, *Transforming Our World: The 2030 Agenda for Sustainable Development* (21 October 2015), General Assembly Resolution A/RES/70/1. UN Doc. 70/1, New York: United Nations.

[339] B. Oppenheim & B. M. Powell, *Legal Identity in the 2030 Agenda for Sustainable Development: Lessons from Kibera, Kenya* (2015). Retrieved from https://www.opensocietyfoundations.org/sites/default/files/legal-identity-2030-agenda-lessons-kibera-kenya-2051216.pdf [10 January 2010]. In this article, the authors argue that effective measures must stretch beyond birth registration given the range of identity documents that enables people to enjoy full and equal participation in society. See pp 3–4.

this commitment at the national level. Moreover, no nexus is drawn between birth registration and acquisition of nationality in the SDG.

This SDG target is resounded strongly by the shared vision of achieving three overarching goals between 2015 and 2024 via a regional action framework to bolster universal and responsive CRVS in Asia and the Pacific, launched at the Asia–Pacific ministerial meeting in Bangkok, Thailand in 2004.[340] Aside from universal CRVS, the goals target provision of the legal documentation of CRVS to claim and realise one's identity, civil status, and the resulting rights, as well as to meet the standard of accurate, complete, and timely vital statistics.[341]

Experts strongly agree that the significance of the concept of legal identity is nonetheless guaranteed by the provisions of the human rights to birth registration and nationality under Article 7(1) CRC, and by the following provisions[342]:

(i) Articles 6 and 7 of UDHR that uphold the right of everyone to be recognised before the law, to be equal before the law, and to be entitled without any discrimination to equal protection of the law[343]; and
(ii) Article 8 of CRC that protects the child's right to preserve his or her identity, including nationality, name, and family relations, as recognised by law without unlawful interference.[344]

Legal identity, which necessarily encompasses the provision of legal documentation to facilitate access to an accomplishment of certain rights and resultant duties, therefore, has been asserted as an indispensable concept that upholds UNHCR's mandate on the prevention and reduction of statelessness.[345]

---

340 UNESCAP, 'Regional Action Framework on Civil Registration and Vital Statistics in Asia and the Pacific' (2014).

341 UNESCAP, 'Regional Action Framework on Civil Registration and Vital Statistics in Asia and the Pacific' (2014).

342 I. G. López, T. B. Sejersen, N. Oakeshott, G. Fajth, T. Khilji & N. Panta, 'Civil Registration, Human Rights and Social Protection in Asia and the Pacific', p 77; D. Hodgson, 'The International Legal Protection of the Child's Right to a Legal Identity and the Problem of Statelessness', pp 256–257.

343 UN Human Rights Council, *Birth Registration and the Right of Everyone to Recognition Everywhere as a Person before the Law* (17 June 2014).

344 R. Govil, 'Statelessness, and Key Concepts', Presentation Slides; D. Hodgson, 'The International Legal Protection of the Child's Right to a Legal Identity and the Problem of Statelessness', p 256. Hodgson further underscores that Article 7 and 8 that specifically aim to protect the child's legal identity (as opposed to other aspects of a child's identity such as religious and cultural identities under Article 14 and 30 CRC respectively) are of considerable importance considering how they are positioned directly after the child's inherent right to life.

345 R. Govil, 'Is the Concept of Legal Identity Relevant to UNHCR's Statelessness Mandate?' *The Hague Colloquium on the Future of Legal Identity,* Johannesburg, South Africa, 21–24 April 2015.

3.4 Conclusion

This chapter has traced the development of the legal rules and norms underpinning the protection against statelessness at birth. The following have been identified to be applicable to avoidance of statelessness at birth:

(i) the rights of the child to birth registration and nationality that together form the elements of the right to a legal identity; and
(ii) the framework for prevention of statelessness through the right of the child to acquire a nationality for otherwise stateless children under the 1961 Convention, together with the Convention's measures for prevention of loss, deprivation, and renunciation of nationality.

The rules and norms constituting the overall legal framework have also been identified, together with the jurisprudence developed at both the international and regional levels. In doing so, the chapter has cast some light on the normative strengths and limits of the standards examined.

Although the right to a nationality is overall upheld within the different regional frameworks, it seems that the right to birth registration appears to be less explicit, except in the context of the African region. CRC has introduced a set of standards on birth registration to ensure universality, well-managed, free, timely, flexible, and responsive birth registration system, which has further been particularised by other guidelines issued by UN organisations such as UNICEF and UNSD. At the ASEAN level, the standards emerge and thrive predominantly within its soft law framework, limiting robust and cogent standard-setting efforts in the area of prevention and reduction of statelessness.

This chapter has also analysed the problems and challenges emanating from the normative components of the legal framework for the protection of children against statelessness at birth. The analysis has yielded the following findings in respect of each component addressed.

i. **The right to a nationality**

The specific nationality one is entitled to and the responsible state that has the duty to grant it, are the questions that have been sidestepped by UDHR and other subsequent treaties incorporating the said right. Individuals, including children, remain substantially vulnerable to state power and policy in effecting their right to a nationality. The broad competence of states in the determination, change, and renunciation of nationality is not, however, unconstrained when it comes to the prohibition of discrimination, arbitrary deprivation of nationality, and the obligation to prevent children from statelessness.

Various international and regional human rights instruments and jurisprudence have contributed to the strong notion that nationality is a human right of every child. Despite the right to acquire instead of the complete right to a nationality, as codified in ICCPR and CRC, the Contracting States are still obligated to implement and take every reasonable step through internal measures and in cooperation with other states, to realise the acquisition of nationality for every child.

The existing norms on prevention of statelessness, non-discrimination principle, and best interests of the child, are inevitably subject to competing paradigms shaped largely by the will of states in making distinctions between citizens and aliens, pursuing immigration control, state security, and other reasons adverse to the best interests of children to acquire a nationality at birth. The registration of birth and acquisition of nationality for children born abroad to migrants, particularly those lacking legal status, and children born in exile to asylum seekers and refugees, remain especially problematic.

ICMW unfortunately attracts little acceptance. Despite assuring the right to a nationality, its application scope jettisons stateless persons, refugees, and undocumented family members of migrant workers, signifying its inadequate role in preventing statelessness and protecting stateless persons. Stronger international legal norms on citizenship rooted in the evolving human rights law are, therefore, needed to ensure that non-citizens, particularly, children vulnerable to statelessness, do not become victims of exclusion and ill-treatment in the struggle for equality and non-discrimination through the right to acquire a nationality.

ii. The Right to Birth Registration and its Nexus with the Realisation of the Right to a Nationality

With regards to the interconnection between the two pivotal safeguards against statelessness at birth through nationality acquisition and birth registration, it must be borne in mind that the aspect of birth registration has been left out from the scope of the 1961 Convention. This constitutes a critical oversight leading to a significant loophole that undermines the criteria of proof of entitlement to and possession of nationality, under this legal framework.

The General Comment on the scope and implementation of the right to birth registration under Article 7 CRC has also not materialised. Birth registration and nationality acquisition as contained in Article 7 of CRC are not coherently integrated in practice for prevention of statelessness. The link between birth registration and nationality acquisition is articulated in diverse soft law instruments, including in international resolutions and conclusions by various organisations pursuing their own mandates. Such less strategic directions fail to carefully calibrate a birth registration system that is geared toward the fulfilment of the right to a nationality, undermining states in their understanding and implementation of the scope of children's right to a legal identity and avoidance of statelessness.

As for the international legal framework for the protection of children against statelessness at birth, the drawbacks highlighted have also been the subject of previous critiques. The international legal framework is not unequivocal in assigning which country or countries have the duty to register births. This does not augur well for children born abroad to non-citizen parents, particularly children of migrants often facing discrimination by their countries of birth and residence. Freedom of entering reservations to Articles 2 and 7 of CRC further affects fortification of the legal norm on non-discrimination, and the rights to birth registration and a nationality, jeopardising the already vulnerable position of such children of undocumented migrants, asylum seekers, and refugees.

There appears to be a friction in the existing norms on the right of older children found separated from parents and guardians without information on their whereabouts and legal identity to be registered. The expansion of the meaning of 'foundling' has occurred in the context of the right to a nationality under Article 2 of the 1961 Convention,[346] suggesting it to also encapsulate younger children, especially those who are not able to communicate information on their legal identity. This is perceived to be in line with the object and purpose of the 1961 Convention in avoiding statelessness.

The position of children of undetermined or unknown nationality is equally concerning. UNHCR's Guidelines No. 4 allow states a maximum period of 5 years to determine whether children would otherwise be stateless before the safeguards in Article 1 and 4 of the 1961 Convention operationalise. If citizenship at birth were granted, then the child of undetermined nationality shall be assumed to acquire the nationality of his state of birth until another nationality is proven. There is no similar guidance as to how questions of nationality should be determined for children designated as 'non-citizen'.

Furthermore, the norms on birth registration that are to be legislated and enforced on the one hand, and others suggested as recommendations on the other, are not distinguished in a clear fashion. Procedural aspects of birth registration including evidentiary requirements and mechanisms for late birth registration that meet the standards of substantive and procedural justice remain underdeveloped. The rights to lodge complaints and to appeal against denial of birth registration constitute another neglected aspect.

The lack of specific norms on the right of undocumented and irregular migrants to lawfully marry and register their marriages, and the prevailing immigration rules that limit this right, render children born of such unrecognised unions vulnerable to being unregistered at birth, and as a result, facing the risk of statelessness. In this specific scenario, the risk of statelessness flows both from the children's lack of proof of birth, and the lack of gender neutrality in citizenship attribution.

iii. **Prevention and Reduction of Statelessness: Issues and Challenges**

As the product of an international compromise between the preservation of sovereignty by states and the interest in preventing statelessness, the 1961 Convention adopted the text stipulating reduction, instead of elimination of statelessness. Thus, one could finally grasp the idea behind the sub-paragraphs affording states their discretion in imposing certain conditions in the current text of the 1961 Convention, which eventually renders statelessness a possibility.

[346] See UNHCR, Guidelines No. 4, para 57–58.

There is no prohibition in the 1961 Convention of gender discrimination in nationality legislation. In fact, 'gender' as a basis against which non-discrimination must operate is left out from Article 9 of the 1961 Convention. This has been partly offset by the rules requiring gender equality in the area of nationality, as prescribed by CEDAW and ICCPR.[347] The safeguard in Article 1(3) of the 1961 Convention is only useful to prevent statelessness among out-of-wedlock children born to stateless or non-citizen fathers as the principle of *jus sanguinis maternus* is adopted. Guidelines No. 4 make up for this gender imbalance by extending the safeguard to such otherwise stateless children and allowing them to also acquire the nationality from the father if the mother was stateless or non-citizen.

The effect of the discovery of proof of the nationality possessed by the parent(s) of a foundling is not addressed in the 1961 Convention. This could cause the foundling already conferred a nationality to lose it if the state of birth that conferred the said nationality decided to retract it without ensuring that the child has first acquired the nationality of his either parent.[348]

The drawback that could significantly compromise the implementation of the 1961 Convention stems from the lack of clarity about the process and criteria for determining and proving 'the otherwise stateless'. The procedures for the determination of an otherwise stateless child need to be carefully articulated to avoid confusion with the statelessness determination procedures. The complexity substantially lies further in the ambiguous aspect of the burden of proof, such as with whom it rests, the types of evidence that may be considered, and the quantum of the shared burden of proof.[349]

Differential capacities of the claimants in undergoing the procedures must be weighed in and addressed fairly in this respect. For refugees, unregistered asylum populations and undocumented migrants, the desire to remain hidden due to their precarious nature, low awareness and understanding of the procedures, insufficient resources to undergo the whole processes, and lack of consular protection, routinely function as the key barriers in overcoming issues surrounding their legal identity and status.

States are further not informed of what it means in practice by nationality 'at birth' or 'by operation of law' as the mode for the attribution of nationality in the case of children found to be otherwise stateless under Article 1(1)(a) of the 1961 Convention. This may lead to misinterpretation or deliberate action to set conditions for such attribution to be subject to an application process, and to a prescribed minimum and maximum age limits. The prescribed age to start an application for citizenship under Article 1(2)(a) that is beginning at the age of 18 until a maximum of 21 years, is also found to be inconsistent with the rights and principles underpinning protection against statelessness at birth, as children could still risk facing statelessness in their early childhood.

---

[347] See Guidelines No. 4, para 15.

[348] Refer to para 60, UNHCR, Guidelines on Statelessness No. 4.

[349] M. Wells-Greco, *The Status of Children from Inter-Country Surrogacy Arrangements: The Past, The Present, The Future* (2016), p 447.

Additionally, it can be observed that the normative frameworks of citizenship and prevention of statelessness do not consider the unique position of mobile lifestyle and often marginalised existence of the world's minority migratory populations, causing them and their children to be legally excluded from the existing frameworks. Finally, the opportunity to effectively prevent statelessness is weakened when the pragmatic duty of interstate cooperation receives no mention in the 1961 Convention, despite the highly transnational nature of matters concerning citizenship between two or more states.

Chapter 4
Statelessness in the ASEAN Member States

4.1 Introduction

The Association of Southeast Asian Nations or ASEAN is made up of ten member states with a population of over 600 million people and is considered to be one of the fastest growing regions in the world.[1] Since its formation in 1967, economic growth, social development, peace, and stability have been the objectives pursued by this regional pact. The ten countries of ASEAN are highly diverse in their histories, political and legal systems. According to Neher, '…no comparable area of the world has such a range of geographic, ethnic, linguistic, and religious diversity as does Southeast Asia'.[2] At the minimum, 32 ethnolinguistic groups can be found with at least four major ones in each state. The region is also a melting pot of the key world's belief systems, namely, Islam, Buddhism, Christianity, and Communism.[3] The diversity continues to be reflected in the level of economic development and its vast ideological distinctions and political systems.[4] Against this complex diversity, countries within ASEAN currently harbour some of the largest stateless populations in Asia, making it a key focus of the goal of ending statelessness within

---

[1] As of 2016, the estimated GDP of all ASEAN states amounted to approximately 2.57 trillion U.S. dollars. See Statista (The Statistics Portal), 'Gross Domestic Product of the ASEAN countries from 2008 to 2018 (in billion U.S dollars)'. Retrieved from https://www.statista.com/statistics/796245/gdp-of-the-asean-countries/ [Accessed 20 October 2018].

[2] See C. D. Neher. *Southeast Asia: Crossroads of the world* (Illinois: Northern Illinois University, Center for Southeast Asian Studies, 2000), p 7.

[3] Sukhumbhand Paribatra & C. Anan, 'Factors Behind Armed Separatism: A Framework for Analysis' in Lim Joo-Jock & S. Vani (Eds.), *Armed Separatism in Southeast Asia* (Pasir Panjang: Institute of Southeast Asian Studies, 1984), p 30.

[4] V. Dimitri & R. Michael, 'ASEAN's Regional Approach to Human Rights: The Limits of the European Model' in W. Benedek et al. (Eds.), *European Yearbook on Human Rights* (Medieninhaber: NWV Verlag GmbH, 2014).

R. M. Razali, *Safeguarding Against Statelessness at Birth*,
https://doi.org/10.1007/978-981-19-5371-2_4

10 years.[5] Myanmar alone had publicly reported figures of almost one million stateless people. A large network of migrants of mixed backgrounds are without identity documents and development benefits.

Apart from contemporary factors such as mobility of people and displacement across borders, statelessness traces much of its deep root to de-colonisation, other historic causes and international migration, as alluded to in the passage below:

> Until the middle of the twentieth century, the common distinction between internal and international migration meant little in the Asian context. Most migration took place within and across the boundaries of empires. In the twentieth century, internal migration within empires turned abruptly into international migration, as new states were formed and new borders were drawn.[6]

As an overture to a more robust assessment of the legal frameworks on nationality in Chap. 5, and on birth registration in Chap. 6, this chapter provides an overview of the manners of acquiring citizenship within the ASEAN Member States, the status of acceptance of the relevant human rights treaties by the countries and the regional engagement with the subject of statelessness.

Next, it proceeds to present a background analysis of statelessness, its magnitude, and common causes in the region. Highlighted in the discussion are the populations at risk of statelessness, including children. For purposes of identifying good practices, selected responses to address statelessness in general and childhood statelessness at the level of ASEAN Member States shall be presented before the final conclusion.

4.2 General Aspects of Citizenship and Human Rights Acceptance among ASEAN Member States

1. **Key Features of Citizenship in ASEAN**

Colonialism is the past hallmark of Southeast Asia, together with the blueprint that led to the formation of nation-states, comprising the boundaries of the states, the laws and regulations, the traditions, and the institutions.[7] The British were in Burma, Malaya (now Malaysia), Singapore, Brunei, and Sabah and Sarawak (now East Malaysia). The Dutch colonised Indonesia, the French ruled the Indo-China (Viet Nam, Cambodia, Laos), and the Philippines was made a territory of the United

---

[5] At the launch of the UNHCR's Global Action Plan to End Statelessness (2014–2024) in February 2015, 1,393,739 were reported to be persons of concern under UNHCR's statelessness mandate residing in SEA. See N. Oakeshott, 'The Search for Solutions to Statelessness in Southeast Asia: State Practice and Recent Developments' in L. van Waas & M.J. Khanna (Eds.), *Solving Statelessness* (AH Oisterwijk: Wolf Legal Publishers), pp 349–350.

[6] S.S. Amrith, *Migration and Diaspora in Modern Asia* (New York: Cambridge University Press, 2011), p 3.

[7] L. Suryadinata, *The Making of Southeast Asian Nations: State, Ethnicity, Indigenism and Citizenship* (World Scientific, 2014), p xix.

States. These countries became independent post-1945. Thailand remains the only country with no history of colonialism.

Nationhood and citizenship are indeed Western-derived concepts that have influenced Asian countries in the post-colonial twentieth century.[8] This legacy led to the manifestation of nation-states and the presence of national laws. The precedent for nationality laws in the ASEAN countries that can be attributed to the region's colonial experience gave rise to the combination of *jus sanguinis* and *jus soli* as the common mode of attribution and acquisition of nationality. However, similar to the position in Europe, the principle of *jus sanguinis* is more popular than *jus soli* in this region.[9]

In recent decades, intra-regional migration has featured as a prominent factor that shapes the socio-economic patterns of the ASEAN Member States. From 1.5 million, migrant stocks within the region tremendously climbed to 6.5 million between 1990 and 2013, equivalent to almost 70% of ASEAN's total migration at the end of 2014.[10] Huge economic disparities, the porosity of borders, and demographic shift have been identified as the main determinants of such a drastic rise in mobility.[11]

Despite the high level of intra-regional movement, an important characteristic of citizenship within ASEAN countries is the preponderance of indigenous populations qualifying for citizenship of their homeland. The non-indigenous, referring to descendants of foreign migrants such as Indian and Chinese, will only be eligible for citizenship automatically if a special law allows for it in reference to a specific ethnic group(s).[12] Except for Singapore, all the other states provide for automatic citizenship for their indigenous populations, excluding those who hold other citizenship.[13]

Four main modes of acquisition of nationality prevail among the Member States of ASEAN, namely, birth in the territory, descent, registration, and naturalisation. Single nationality is the norm. There is limited acceptance of dual nationality in Viet Nam (for 'Overseas Vietnamese',[14] Indonesia (until a child reaches 18 at which

---

[8] L. Suryadinata, *The Making of Southeast Asian Nations: State, Ethnicity, Indigenism and Citizenship* (World Scientific, 2014), p xviii.

[9] S. Jaghai, *Statelessness and Transnational Migration: The Role of States as Duty-Bearers to Address Statelessness in the ASEAN Region under International Law* (2015), p 18; O.W. Vonk, *Comparative Report: Citizenship in Asia*, p 9. Retrieved from http://cadmus.eui.eu/bitstream/handle/1814/50047/RSCAS_GLOBALCIT_Comp_2017_04.pdf?sequence=1&isAllowed=y [Accessed 10 April 2018].

[10] M. Tuccio, 'Determinants of Intra-ASEAN Migration', *Asian Development Review*, V. 34(1) (2017), pp 144–166, at p 144.

[11] M. Tuccio, 'Determinants of Intra-ASEAN Migration', *Asian Development Review*, p 144.

[12] L. Suryadinata, *The Making of Southeast Asian Nations: State, Ethnicity, Indigenism and Citizenship* (World Scientific, 2014), p 55.

[13] L. Suryadinata, *The Making of Southeast Asian Nations: State, Ethnicity, Indigenism and Citizenship* (World Scientific, 2014), p 57.

[14] See Articles 3(3) and 3(4) of the 2008 Nationality Law of Viet Nam. Dual citizenship is said to target (i) persons of Vietnamese origin who reside overseas as part of Vietnamese refugee diaspora who wish to reacquire their Vietnamese nationality and (ii) persons living in Cambodia who suffered persecution during the Khmer Rouge regime. See Lyma Nguyen, *Report on Citizenship Law:*

Table 4.1 Means of acquiring citizenship in the ASEAN Member States

	Jus soll subject to being otherwise stateless or other conditions/ restrictions	*Jus sanguinis*	Registration	Naturalisation
Brunei		X	X	X
Cambodia	X	X		X
Indonesia	X	X		X
Laos	X	X		X
Malaysia	X	X	X	X
Myanmar		X		X
The Philippines		X		X
Singapore		X	X	X
Thailand	X	X		X
Viet Nam	X	X		X

time the child needs to elect his or her citizenship),[15] Cambodia (since 1996), the Philippines,[16] and Thailand.

Table 4.1 presents an overview of such methods of acquisition of nationality within the ASEAN Member States.

2. Human Rights Acceptance and Regional Engagement with Statelessness

The ASEAN Human Rights Declaration (AHRD) reaffirms the general principle of the universality of human rights and the principle of non-discrimination. CRC, CEDAW, and CRPD are the most accepted human rights treaties among the ASEAN Member States. Notwithstanding this, reservations of important provisions in respect of the right to a nationality in the CRC and CEDAW have been entered by Malaysia and Brunei.

Malaysia places its reservations to the CRC on Articles 2 (the right of children against discrimination) and 7 (the right of children to a name, birth registration and to acquire a nationality). As for CEDAW, Malaysia reserves Article 9(2) on the obligation to grant women equal rights with men with respect to the nationality of their children. Aside from Article 9(2), Brunei also reserves Article 9(1) on the equality of the right of both women and men to acquire, change or retain their nationality.[17]

Vietnam (2007), p 2. Retrieved from http://cadmus.eui.eu/bitstream/handle/1814/47966/GLOBALCIT_CR_2017_13.pdf?sequence=1 [Accessed 10 July 2018].

[15] Under its reformed Nationality Law of 2006, Indonesia to some extent tolerates dual nationality for children born of mixed parentage in order to allow such children to defer the choice of nationality until they reach adulthood.

[16] Some Americans of Filipino origin are allowed to apply for dual citizenship under the Republic Act no. 9225 introduced in 2003.

[17] See UN Treaty Collection, Status as at 2016. http://treaties.un.org/Pages/viewDetails.aspx?src=TREATY&mtdsg_no=IV-8&chapter=4&lang=en#EndDec.

Table 4.2 Status of acceptance of human rights treaties among the ASEAN Member States

Country	ICCPR	CERD	CEDAW	CRC	CRPD	CMW	1954 Conv.	1961 Conv.
Brunei			x-	x-	x-			
Cambodia	x	x	x	x	x	#		
Indonesia	x	x	x-	x	x-	x		
Lao PDR	x-	x	x	x	x			
Malaysia			x-	x-	x-			
Myanmar			x-	x	x			
Philippines	x	x	x	x	x	x	x	
Singapore		x-	x-	x-	x-			
Thailand	x	x-	x-	x-	x			
Viet Nam	x	x-	x-	x	x			

Notes x: acceded and/or ratified, x-: acceded and/or ratified with relevant reservations, #: signed

Table 4.2 indicates the acceptance of the main human rights treaties by the ASEAN Member States.

In comparison to other regions, ASEAN Member States demonstrate the weakest level of acceptance of the two Statelessness Conventions. Thus far, only one country remains party to the 1954 Convention relating to the Status of Stateless Persons[18] (the 1954 Convention), namely, the Philippines that acceded to it in 2011. None, however, has ratified the 1961 Convention on the Reduction of Statelessness[19] (the 1961 Convention).[20] Vonk attributes the scarce studies on nationality in the region to this low level of acceptance of international treaties pertaining to nationality and a lack of regionally-produced judgments and jurisprudence on citizenship-related issues, in comparison to Europe, the Americas, and Africa.[21] A significant number of states comprising Cambodia, Indonesia, Lao PDR, the Philippines, Viet Nam, and Thailand are also parties to two other human rights conventions that contain safeguards against statelessness, namely, the International Convention on Civil and

[18] Convention relating to the Status of Stateless Persons (28 September 1954, in force 6 June 1960), 360 UNTS 117.

[19] Convention on the Reduction of Statelessness, New York (30 August 1961, in force 13 December 1975), 989 UNTS 175.

[20] The record stands in sharp contrast even to that of the African region and the global trend, witnessing a greater increase in the number of ratifications of the two Statelessness Conventions. At the end of 2014 and by early 2015, 23 out of 54 African countries became parties to the 1954 Statelessness Convention and 15 acceded to the 1961 Statelessness Convention. http://treaties.un.org/Pages/Treaties.aspx?id+5&subid=A&lang=en [Accessed 16 January 2015].

[21] O.W. Vonk, *Comparative Report: Citizenship in Asia*, p 2. Retrieved from http://cadmus.eui.eu/bitstream/handle/1814/50047/RSCAS_GLOBALCIT_Comp_2017_04.pdf?sequence=1&isAllowed=y [Accessed 10 April 2018].

Political Rights (ICCPR) and the Convention on Elimination of All Forms of Racial Discrimination (CERD).[22]

The human rights in the ASEAN Human Rights Declaration are mostly guaranteed to all 'persons', including those whose nationality is undetermined or who are stateless. The said document contains the right of a person 'to leave any country including his or her own and to return to his or her own country' under Article 15. The realisation of this right nevertheless differs between the ASEAN Member States, subject to the level of protection and integration offered by each individual state.[23]

The underpinning right to a nationality is set out in Article 18 of the said Declaration that provides, 'Every person has the right to a nationality as prescribed by law'.[24] In the drafting process, the proposals by a few representatives to further include the phrase 'so that no one shall be rendered stateless' to Article 18 did not find support. This is despite the recognition by ASEAN Member States of Article 15 UDHR and their considerable acceptance of Article 9 CEDAW and Article 7 of CRC.[25] In light of the region's strong adherence to the principle of state sovereignty and non-interference, as reflected in the first principle of the founding document of ASEAN, namely, the ASEAN Charter,[26] the application of the preceding rights is understandably subject to each state's interpretations and preferences.

AICHR and ACWC are both mandated with the promotion and protection of human rights regionally. ACWC was launched in 2010 as an intergovernmental body to develop policies and strategies to protect the rights of women and children and ensure their equitable development in the ASEAN Member States, pursuant to ASEAN's commitment to CEDAW and CRC.

Unlike its counterparts in Europe, Africa, and the American States, ASEAN promotes human rights but do not have the required mechanisms to institutionally enforce the states' human rights obligations. There is no forum to hear and act upon complaints relating to denial of birth registration, nationality, and breaches of human rights at the regional level. AICHR's and ACWC's establishments and mandates continue to reflect the inherent challenge of forging common consensus for solutions to statelessness within the region.[27]

---

[22] The right to a nationality is guaranteed under Article 24 of ICCPR and under Article 5 of CERD, the prohibition of racial discrimination is also prescribed to apply to the right to a nationality among others.

[23] N. Oakeshott, 'The Search for Solutions to Statelessness in Southeast Asia: State Practice and Recent Developments' in L. van Waas & M.J. Khanna (Eds.), *Solving Statelessness* (Wolf Legal Publishers, 2017), p 350.

[24] ASEAN Human Rights Declaration, 18 November 2012.

[25] Sripapha Petcharamesree, 'The ASEAN Human Rights Architecture: Its Development and Challenges', *The Equal Rights Review*, 11 (2013), p 54.

[26] The first principle if the ASEAN Charter (20 November 2007, entry into force 15 December 2008) mandates ASEAN and its Member States to act with 'respect for the independence, sovereignty, equality, territorial integrity and national identity of all ASEAN Member States'.

[27] See para 6.1 of the Terms of Reference of AICHR and para 7.1 of the Terms of Reference of ACWC that provides for decision-making to be based on consultation and consensus in accordance with the ASEAN Charter.

Table 4.3 Main features of AICHR and ACWC

AICHR	ACWC
Established on 23 Oct 2009 based on Article 14 of the ASEAN Charter	Established on 7 April 2010 based on ASEAN Social-Cultural Community Blueprint
No individual complaint	No individual complaint
Provides advice to ASEAN sectorial government upon request	Provides advice to ASEAN sectorial government upon request
Can obtain information on human rights issues from the Member States	Consults civil society organisations, women, and children
Consults stakeholders	Advocates on behalf of women and children and encourages the ASEAN Member States to improve their situations
Submits Annual Report	Submits Annual Report

Source Adapted from the presentation slides of Yuyun Wahyuningrum, entitled 'The Protection of Stateless Persons in ASEAN: Opportunities & Challenges', presented at the Global Forum on Statelessness, The Hague, September 2014

Membership-wise, these two sectoral bodies are mostly represented and coordinated by the states' respective ministries of foreign affairs instead of their national human rights institutions. Table 4.3 summarises the limited roles of these two organs, which stem from the Member States', preferences for less intrusive over binding and adversarial human rights mechanisms.[28]

ASEAN sectoral bodies mainly engage themselves in the efforts to address statelessness through the mechanisms of capacity building, promoting exchanges of good practices, and influencing states and aiding them with the implementation of the relevant global norms and standards.[29] This affirms that persuasion and publicity are the more palatable tools to advance human rights among the ASEAN Member States.

Progress at the subregional level of ASEAN in the area of the rights to nationality and birth registration has been noticeable through the activities of AICHR and ACWC. UNHCR has engaged with AICHR and ACWC to disseminate the importance of birth registration in avoiding statelessness, good practices in tackling statelessness as well as considering complementarities between ASEAN's prioritised policies and the eradication of statelessness.[30] Relevant ASEAN bodies have been recommended by ACWC, UNHCR, and other partners to undertake a regional study on issues of nationality in the region, capacity-building activities to promote gender and child sensitivity of government agencies, particularly on the protection of the

[28] Yvonne Xin Wang, 'Contextualizing Universal Human Rights: An Integrated Human Rights Framework for ASEAN', *Duke Journal of Comparative & International Law*, 25 (2014), p 407.

[29] N. Oakeshott, 'The Search for Solutions to Statelessness in Southeast Asia: State Practice and Recent Developments' in L. van Waas & M.J. Khanna (Eds.), *Solving Statelessness* (AH Oisterwijk: Wolf Legal Publishers, 2017), p 368.

[30] UNHCR, *Report of the Regional Workshop on Good Practices in Birth Registration* (2011).

right to a nationality for women and children, and support for efforts by countries in the region to achieve universal birth registration.[31]

In 2015, the ASEAN leaders formally inaugurated ASEAN Community by espousing the ASEAN Community Vision 2025. By 2025, ASEAN aims to create an inclusive, people-oriented, and people-centred community, a regional community that upholds, protects, and promotes the rights of every individual. In this light, there is a potential for integration of common policies among the ASEAN Member States through the interactions of its human rights discourse with the vision of ASEAN Community and the parallel global aim to achieve SDG. This could be realised through an analysis of cross-cutting inequalities among different classes, races, ethnic groups, and men and women, together with other drivers that distinguish groups of people from one another. For instance, along the trajectory of ASEAN Community building and the fuller realisation of the rights of peoples of ASEAN, ACWC during its 12th Meeting in Jakarta on 16–17 February 2016 suggested that ACWC Viet Nam 'lead an evaluation of the progress of initiatives in promoting the right to a nationality for women and children, and consider future steps in collaboration with UNHCR, ACWC Representatives and other related bodies'.[32] This then resulted in the adoption by ACWC of a project on the right to a nationality for women and children and the building of the ASEAN Community in its 2016–2020 work plan.

The Bali Process on People Smuggling, Trafficking in Persons and Related Transnational Crime is another platform to offer and generate dialogue, information sharing and cooperation at the Asia Pacific level on migration-related challenges, including those that lead to inequalities among refugees, asylum seekers, stateless persons, and persons of undetermined nationality. In recognition of the key role of birth registration and legal identity in the frameworks of the development agenda and the Ministerial Declaration of 'Getting Every One in the Picture' adopted by ESCAP, the Regional Support Office of the Bali Process issued a document entitled 'Bali Process Civil Registration Assessment Toolkit' in 2018. The toolkit was developed specifically to achieve the following aim:

[31] ACWC, UNHCR, MOLISA & UN WOMEN, 'Recommendations', Regional Workshop on Promoting the Right to a Nationality for Women and Children in the Implementation of CEDAW and CRC in ASEAN: ACWC-UNHCR Potential Partnership (2003), organised jointly by the ASEAN Commission on the Promotion and Protection of the Rights of Women and Children (ACWC), Ministry of Labour, Invalids and Social Affairs of Viet Nam (MOLISA), United Nations High Commissioner for Refugees (UNHCR) and United Nations Entity for Gender Equality and the Empowerment of Women (UN Women), Da Nang, Viet Nam, 19 August 2013. See the text at http://asean.org/wp-content/uploads/images/2013/socio_cultural/acwc/Recommendations%20Workshop%20on%20Right%20of%20Nationality_FINAL.pdf; UNHCR, *The Campaign to End Statelessness: Campaign Update* (2016). Retrieved from http://www.refworld.org/docid/571e23fb7.html [26 June 2016].

[32] Opening Remarks of H.E. Lily D. Purba, Chair of the ASEAN Commission on the Promotion and Protection of the Rights of Women and Children (ACWC) for the Workshop on the Rights to Nationality for Women and Children in the ASEAN Community 2016–2022, 23–22 September 2016, Da Lat, Viet Nam, September 2016 (on file with author).

> …to help interested States assess and improve their national civil registration system in order to record all of the births, deaths and marriages that occur in their territory among refugees, asylum seekers, stateless persons and persons of undetermined nationality.[33]

The toolkit, therefore, seeks to optimise the role of birth registration in the identity management system through the inclusion of the targeted populations in the population register and issuance of identity documents within a state's nationality or residency legal regimes in this region.

Other regional human rights instruments such as ACTIP and the recently concluded ASEAN Consensus on the Protection and Promotion of the Rights of Migrant Workers bode well for the materialisation of stronger regional standards of prevention and protection in the field of statelessness for the specific vulnerable groups of migrants and human trafficking victims at risk of statelessness.[34]

[33] See Regional Support Office, The Bali Process on People Smuggling, Trafficking in Persons and Related Transnational Crime, *Bali Process Civil Registration Assessment Toolkit.* Retrieved from https://www.baliprocess.net/regional-support-office/guide-on-assisting-and-interviewing-child-victims-of-trafficking/ [Accessed 5 October 2017].

[34] ACTIP was signed by ASEAN leaders at the 27th ASEAN Summit in November 2015. The instrument that as of February 2019 binds all ASEAN Member States except for Indonesia and Brunei establishes a legal framework to curb human trafficking. As outlined in Chap. 3, Articles 15(3) and (4) of ACTIP entail a mechanism of cooperation between Receiving and Requesting States in the verification of nationality or permanent residence status of the trafficking victims concerned and the issuance of travel documents or other necessary authorisation for repatriation and return. See ACTIP at https://asean.org/wp-content/uploads/2012/05/APA-FINAL.pdf (Accessed 26 September 2018). ASEAN Consensus on the Protection and Promotion of the Rights of Migrant Workers was signed at the 31st ASEAN Summit in Manila following years of negotiations among the ASEAN Member States for the implementation of the ASEAN Declaration on the Protection and Promotion of the Rights of Migrant Workers (Cebu Declaration). The Consensus, which is expected to be followed-up with concrete action plans is regarded as a key milestone in the contentious field of the protection and promotion of the rights of migrant workers in the region. General Principle 1(e) of the Consensus underlines the commitment of the Member States of ASEAN to fair treatment with respect to gender and nationality and protection of the rights of migrant workers, particularly women, in accordance with the international human rights obligations of the ASEAN Member States.

Table 4.4 Countries in Southeast Asia with stateless persons (2018)

Country	2018
Myanmar	620,939
Thailand	478,843
Brunei	20,863
Malaysia	9,631
Vietnam	34,110
Singapore	1,303
Philippines	1,068
Cambodia	57,444

Source UNHCR, Global Trends 2018[42]

4.3 Common Causes and Triggers of Statelessness in ASEAN

Acknowledging the discrepancy between reliable country-level data published by UNHCR and the estimates of the total number of stateless persons globally[35] due to gaps in both qualitative and quantitative information and data on stateless persons, including in SEA,[36] statelessness is nonetheless known to be widespread in the Asia Pacific.[37] The region is home to more than 40% of the world's identified stateless population.[38] SEA is particularly marked as a sub-region hosting a large population of stateless persons.[39]

UNHCR has flagged the presence of stateless populations in eight out of the ten ASEAN Member States. Lao PDR and Indonesia are the two countries for which UNHCR provides no data on stateless persons[40] meanwhile Singapore and The Philippines record stateless populations of less than 2000.[41] Table 4.4 represents the countries in SEA recording the presence of stateless persons as of 2018.

[35] UNHCR, 'Addressing Situations of Statelessness'. Retrieved from https://www.unhcr.org/4922d4370.pdf [Accessed 13 June 2017].

[36] N. Oakeshott & Bongkot Napaumporn, 'Statelessness in South East Asia', Regional Statelessness Course: South East Asia Focus, Presentation Slides.

[37] Caster, 'Eliminating Statelessness in Southeast Asia'. Retrieved from https://thediplomat.com/2016/05/eliminating-statelessness-in-southeast-asia/ [Accessed 20 May 2018].

[38] Institute on Statelessness and Inclusion, *Stateless persons in Asia and the Pacific* (2017). Retrieved from http://www.worldstateless.org/continents/asia/stateless-persons-in-asia-and-the-pacific [Accessed 20 July 2018].

[39] N. Oakeshott, 'The Search for Solutions to Statelessness in Southeast Asia: State Practice and Recent Developments' in L. van Waas & M.J. Khanna (Eds.), *Solving Statelessness* (AH Oisterwijk: Wolf Legal Publishers), p 347.

[40] UNHCR, *Global Trends* (2018). Retrieved from https://www.unhcr.org/en-my/statistics/unhcrstats/5d08d7ee7/unhcr-global-trends-2018.html [Accessed 20 December 2019], p 71.

[41] UNHCR, *Global Trends* (2018), pp 72–73.

[42] UNHCR, *Global Trends* (2018), pp 70–73.

The majority of the affected populations are not recent migrants but populations residing in the country in which they were born and have lived in protracted situations.[43] A clear example of such 'in situ' stateless populations would be the stateless Rohingya in Myanmar. Another noticeable in situ group is registered stateless people in Thailand among the Hill Tribes or non-Hill Tribes and different ethnic minorities who have developed their strongest ties to Thailand than any other country.[44]

Statelessness that is produced through multiple and oftentimes interrelated causes as described below, in many cases, has its flow-on effect on children across generations through the inheritance of the lack of nationality of their parents and the children's inability to register births and acquire a nationality.

1. **Common Causes**

a. ***Discrimination and Exclusion from/Withdrawal of Nationality***

Citizenship has been used as a political instrument in some countries in the South and SEA.[45] While it could be argued that the Rohingya were citizens of Burma under the first constitution drafted in 1947 and the 1962 Constitution drafted by the Socialist Revolutionary Council, racial, and ethnic discrimination saw the Muslim Rohingya concentrated in the northern part of Rakhine state (Arakan) being disqualified from citizenship as a result of an arbitrary change to Burma's 1982 Citizenship Law.[46] The exclusion of the Rohingyas and other long-term ethnic groups from a list of 135 national ethnic subgroups,[47] onerous evidentiary criteria for the application of the citizenship of Myanmar, together with an uneven application of the law led to their statelessness.[48] Arraiza in his article published in *Statelessness Working Paper Series* in 2017 exemplified the nativism-motivated exclusion and statelessness resulting from the fully-ethnicized citizenship regime and its subsequent uneven and

---

[43] N. Oakeshott & B. Napaumporn, 'Statelessness in South East Asia', Presentation Slides, Regional Statelessness Course: South East Asia Focus, organised by UNHCR. Bangkok, Thailand, 4–8 November 2013.

[44] UNHCR, *Campaign Update* (April 2016). Retrieved from http://www.refworld.org/docid/571e23fb7.html [Accessed 20 May 2018].

[45] J.W. Heffernan, 'Being Recognised as Citizens: A Human Security Dilemma in South and Southeast Asia' (2002), prepared for the Commission on Human Security.

[46] Su Yin Htun, 'Legal Aspects of the Right to Nationality Pursuant to Myanmar Citizenship Law', *Journal of Southeast Asian Human Rights*, 3(2) (2019), pp 279–280. See Section 11 of the Constitution of the Union of Burma 1947 that recognised as citizens among others, a person born within the Union one of whose grandparents or both of parents belong to the indigeneous races and every person born and who has resided in any Burmese territory for at least 8 years during the British Era and intends to reside permanently therein. Equality between citizens irrespective of birth, religion, sex or race is guaranteed in Section 13.

[47] After the military take-over in 1962, ethnic Rohingya who previously had parliamentary representation and held government posts in the 1950s were systematically denied their civil, economic and social rights by the new junta administration. See J. W. Heffernan, 'Being Recognised as Citizens: A Human Security Dilemma in South and Southeast Asia', p 13.

[48] K.G. Southwick, 'Myanmar's Democratic Transition: Peril or Promise for the Stateless Rohingya?', *Tilburg Law Review*, 19(1–2) (2014), p 264.

arbitrary implementation and practices by the military regime of General Ne-Win as follows:

> In order to implement the 1982 Law, Myanmar undertook, starting in 1989, a 'national verification' process to determine the citizenship status of its inhabitants and provided them with a colour-coded ID Card: pink means full citizenship, green naturalised citizenship and blue associate citizenship. While the 1982 law sought to create second-class citizens, not stateless persons in Rakhine, an uneven application of the law had statelessness as a consequence. Persons holding National Registration Cards proving citizenship were not given full citizenship even though they were legally entitled to it. Moreover, the communities refused to participate in a process which denied their right to identify themselves as they wished and identified them as 'Bengali' (in practice, foreigners). The Muslim community argued that they were already citizens and refused to participate in the 'national verification process' unless their self-identifier was included in their ID Cards. However, the policy in Rakhine State and elsewhere has been to deny such option while offering to provide temporary documentation with unclear legal status (first Temporary White Cards, more recently Interim Cards for National Verification) pending a decision on 'citizenship scrutiny'.[49]

The institutionalised discrimination and persecution of this ethnic group continues unabated, causing the stateless Rohingya to take flight from time to time to other neighbouring countries, including to the Middle East. The forced departure that occurred on 25 August 2017 following deadly clearance operations against Rohingya fighters known as 'Arsa', including the burning down of Rohingya villages, forced an estimated 687,000 refugees to seek shelter in Bangladesh within and outside of refugee camp areas.[50]

Aside from the Rohingyas, other ethnic groups such as Indians, Nepali and Chinese in Myanmar have also been rendered stateless under the 1982 Citizenship Law, although their numbers cannot be ascertained. The ability of stateless persons to prove their legal residence in Myanmar has been significantly curtailed when the authority announced the expiry of the temporary identification certificates (to prove their residence in Myanmar) in 2015. The newly issued temporary identification cards were largely viewed with distrust by the affected stateless people.[51]

Compared to other stateless populations such as those in Brunei and Thailand who enjoy significantly greater protection, including access to affordable government healthcare and education, the Rohingya refugees and asylum seekers continue to be the most marginalised stateless population. Such is due to the persistent persecution amounting to crimes against humanity and genocide against them, such as the commission of rape and torture, and denial of their human rights in both their countries of origin and destination.[52]

---

[49] J. Arraiza, 'Re-imagining Myanmar Citizenship in Times of Transition', *Statelessness Working Paper Series*, No 2017/1, p 4. Retrieved from http://www.institutesi.org/WP2017_01.pdf [Accessed 9 April 2018]. In Myanmar, the lack of identity documentation is a problem that affects more than 10 million people.

[50] Anon, 'Myanmar Rohingya: What You Need to Know about the Crisis' (24 April 2018). Retrieved from https://www.bbc.com/news/world-asia-41566561 [Accessed 20 August 2018].

[51] Institute on Statelessness and Inclusion, *The World's Stateless Children* (2017), p 65.

[52] N. Oakeshott, 'The Search for Solutions to Statelessness in Southeast Asia: State Practice and Recent Developments' in L. van Waas & M.J. Khanna (Eds.), *Solving Statelessness* (AH Oisterwijk:

The Thai revolutionary regime altered citizenship laws in the country when Decree No. 337 it proclaimed in 1972 eliminated the concept of acquisition of Thai nationality by birth and retracted nationality acquired by people by virtue of being born in Thailand before 1972.[53] The people of the Hill Tribe communities were impacted, henceforth considered illegal and without nationality. Those who were left out from the previous registration exercise conducted to document Thai nationals in the 1950s and the subsequent surveys also became stateless.[54]

The Chinese population being descendants of the Chinese immigrants to Brunei during the British colonial period in the late 1920s mostly remain without citizenship. Predominantly caused by the tightening of Brunei's citizenship regulations in 1984, most stateless Chinese in Brunei hold the legal status of 'permanent resident'. Restricted among others from owning land and accessing certain professions, many have chosen to emigrate to other countries.

Hundreds of thousands of ethnic Vietnamese who had been living in Cambodia fled the country during the violent persecution of the Lon Nol regime in the 1970s. During the subsequent rule of Khmer Rouge, around 170,000 of them were forcibly deported to Viet Nam. In the 1980s, the ethnic Vietnamese re-entered Cambodia without documents, mostly lost during their previous forced exodus from Cambodia.[55] For these immigrants who are considered 'irregular' or 'foreign residents' by Cambodian authorities, their citizenship status has remained an outstanding and politically contested issue until today.[56] Discriminatory practices begin even at the stage of access to birth registration, and consequently their access to nationality.[57]

Wolf Legal Publishers), p 350; Human Rights Council, Detailed Findings of the International Facts-Finding Mission on Myanmar, UN Doc A/HRC/42/CRP.5 (16 Sep 2019); Su Yin Htun, 'Legal Aspects of the Right to Nationality Pursuant to Myanmar Citizenship Law', *Journal of Southeast Asian Human Rights*, 3(2) (2019), 277–299; Equal Rights Trust, *Confined Spaces: Legal Protections for Rohingya in Bangladesh, Malaysia and Thailand*. Retrieved from http://www.equalrightstrust.org/ertdocumentbank/Confined%20Spaces_0.pdf [Accessed 30 December 2016].

[53] The preamble to the 1972 Revolution cited the disloyalty of persons born in the Thai Kingdom to alien fathers or mothers who unlawfully stayed in the country or permitted to stay in the Kingdom on exceptional grounds as the main motivation behind the deprivation of their nationality that was meant to preserve the Kingdom's national security.

[54] Institute on Statelessness and Inclusion, *Report of the Working Group: Submission to the Human Rights Council at the 25th Session of the Universal Periodic Review: Thailand* (2016). Retrieved from http://www.refworld.org/docid/57cd6be64.html [Accessed 21 September 2016]; P. Saisoonthorn, 'Development of the Concept of Nationality and Efforts to Reduce Statelessness in Thailand', *Refugee Survey Quarterly*, V. 25(3) (2006), pp 40–53.

[55] C. Sperfeldt, 'Report on Citizenship Law: Cambodia', *GLOBALCIT Report 2017/02* (2017). Available from http://cadmus.eui.eu/handle/1814/45084 (accessed 18 September 2018).

[56] A. Seiff & Chhay Channyda, 'Ethnic Vietnamese Still Adrift in Cambodia', *The Phnom Penh Post* (14 February 2013).

[57] C. Sperfeldt & Lyma Nguyen, 'A Boat Without Anchors: A Report on the Legal Status of Ethnic Vietnamese Minority Populations in Cambodia Under Domestic and International Laws Governing Nationality and Statelessness', *RegNet Research Paper No. 2014/50* (2012). Retrieved from SSRN: https://ssrn.com/abstract=2514121 or http://dx.doi.org/10.2139/ssrn.2514121 [Accessed 5 July 2018].

For children born of mixed parentage (to parents of two different nationalities) and/or born outside of the territory, gender-discriminatory nationality provisions could trigger their statelessness. Brunei and Malaysia are the two countries that still adopt gendered nationality laws. Beginning 1 June 2010, the Malaysian Government has relaxed the provision of its Federal Constitution concerning the application of Malaysian citizenship by children born abroad to a Malaysian woman and a foreign father. Somehow, the acquisition of nationality is yet to fully adhere to CEDAW. The grant of nationality is not automatic but by way of registration. It is also subject further to the discretion of the Federal Government upon birth registration of such children at an overseas Malaysian consulate, or at the National Registration Department of Malaysia.[58]

In Cambodia, Viet Nam, Singapore, Malaysia, and Indonesia, children may not be fully safeguarded against statelessness if they are born out of wedlock. This could be due to further administrative requirements to be met or lack of gender neutrality in nationality provisions. In Malaysia and Singapore, children born out of wedlock are only entitled to their mothers' citizenship ex lege.[59]

Under the nationality law of Brunei, only fathers are allowed to confer nationality on their children by operation of law in all situations. Access to Bruneian citizenship by children born abroad is restricted to those born of a father who was born in Brunei and, who must be accepted as belonging to any of the stated indigenous groups of the Malay race.[60] In addition, children of Bruneian mother born abroad cannot acquire citizenship by operation of law if they are born to a father who is not a citizen of Brunei by registration or naturalisation at the time of birth under the stated provisions.[61] As for Cambodia, its 1996 Nationality Law provides for a *jus sanguinis* acquisition of Khmer nationality at birth to any child whose parent has Khmer nationality, regardless of the child's place of birth.[62]

b. ***Deficiencies in Civil Registration***

A well-known factor that generates statelessness in the Asia and the Pacific countries is inadequate coverage of birth registration and dysfunctional or weak birth registration systems.[63] It is typical for birth registration rates to be below the completeness

---

[58] Official Portal of Ministryof Home Affairs Malaysia, 'Citizenship' (2010). Retrieved from http://www.moha.gov.my/index.php/en/?option=com_content&view=article&id=276:bahagian-kawalan-penapisan-filem-dan-penguatkuasaan&catid=63&lang=en [Accessed 30 December 2014].

[59] See Article 14(1)(b) and Part II, Section 1(a), read with Section 17 of Part III of Second Schedule, Federal Constitution of Malaysia; Article 121(2)(c) read with Article 15(1) of the Third Schedule, Article 140, Constitution of the Republic of Singapore (1965).

[60] Section 4 of Brunei Nationality Act, No. 4, 1961, Revised Edition (2002).

[61] Section 4 of Brunei Nationality Act, No. 4, 1961, Revised Edition (2002).

[62] Article 4(1) of the Cambodian Law on Nationality, Decree No. NS/RKM/1096/31, 1996.

[63] See C. Abouzahr et al., 'Towards a Research Agenda for Civil Registration and Vital Statistics in the Asia-Pacific Region' in *Asia-Pacific Population Journal,* 29(1) (2014). See pp 24–25 for the overall rapid assessment scores of 47 countries in Asia and Pacific region for 2010–2012.

level[64] of above 80%. In 2014, the rates of birth registration were 62.1% in Cambodia, 66.6% in Indonesia, 72.4% in Myanmar, and 74.8% in Lao PDR.[65] Despite being registered, 42% of children did not have a birth certificate in Lao PDR. In Cambodia, 11% did not possess a birth certificate while 10% of the children in Indonesia were without proof of birth.[66] The effects of not having a birth certificate can be detrimental, equivalent to not having been registered.[67] These shortcomings significantly expose children to statelessness as they leave them without evidence of parentage and vital facts to claim nationality under the law.[68]

In SEA, it has been reported that access to birth registration is not uniform with certain groups facing a greater lack of access to birth registration than others. Barriers to getting access to birth registration include parents' lack of awareness and understanding, neglect and oversight in conducting birth registration. Problems related to proof of nationality as a result of unregistered births affect particularly the region's minority populations, inaccessible, remote, or isolated communities, as well as those belonging to the migrant and refugee populations.[69]

Prior to the reformed Thai Civil Registration Act in 2008, birth registration was in practice facilitated for Thai nationals and non-nationals who had legal residence in Thailand.[70] Under that system, forty to sixty percent of the Hill Tribe communities comprising some 400,000 people of different ethnic and linguistic groups could be without Thai nationality for lacking documentation proof including birth certificates to claim their eligibility as citizens under the Thai law.[71] Lack of birth registration, the requirement of good behaviour and proof of subsequent domicile in Thailand, coupled with the burdensome application process, costs, and travel time, are among

---

[64] Completeness of birth registration refers to the percentage of children under five whose births were registered at the time of a survey. The numerator of the completeness level encompasses children whose birth certificates were sighted or seen by the interview concerned, or whose mothers or caretakers inform that the births have been registered. See the definition provided at http://www.indexmundi.com/facts/nigeria/completeness-of-birth-registration, as taken from UNICEF's *State of the World's Children*.

[65] UNICEF, *Unequal at Birth: Disparities in Birth Registration in East Asia and the Pacific* (2015), p 5.

[66] UNICEF, *Unequal at Birth: Disparities in Birth Registration in East Asia and the Pacific* (2015), p 6.

[67] UNICEF, *Unequal at Birth: Disparities in Birth Registration in East Asia and the Pacific* (2015), p 6. The dates of the respective data on the rate of possession of birth certificates herein were not provided by the UNICEF in their report.

[68] UNHCR, *Regional Expert Roundtable on Good Practices for the Identification, Prevention and Reduction of Statelessness and the Protection of Stateless Persons in South East Asia* (2011), Bangkok, p 3.

[69] L. van Waas, 'The Children of Irregular Migrants: A Stateless Generation', p 452.

[70] UNHCR, 'Ensuring Birth Registration for the Prevention of Statelessness', *Good Practice Paper - Action* 7, pp 23–25. Available from http://www.unhcr.org/ke/wp-content/uploads/sites/2/2017/11/Good-Practices-Paper-on-Ensuring-Birth-Registration-for-the-Prevention-of-Statelessness.pdf [Accessed 18 September 2018], p 23.

[71] K.P. Joy et al., 'A Global Crisis Writ Large: The Effects of Being "Stateless in Thailand" on Hill-Tribe Children' in *San Diego International Law Journal,* 10 (2008), p 498.

the factors that still preclude anyone who had failed to acquire Thai nationality from gaining it under the reformed Thai Nationality Act in 2008.[72]

Fear of enforcement additionally detracts parents in this region from birth registration of their children. According to the Indonesian National Socio-Economic Survey of 2007, many children born abroad to Indonesian migrants are at risk of statelessness in light of their irregular stay and parents' reluctance in registering their children due to fears of deportation.[73] Such a scenario also affects children born abroad to parents whose undocumented status may have persisted in their countries of origin such as children of descendants of Filipino refugees and economic migrants in Sabah.[74] There is also paucity in the existing regulations on birth registration in most of the ASEAN Member States in regard to alternative proof of parentage that could be accepted for implementation of birth registration, in particular where lawful marriages are not possible for parents with undocumented or irregular status.[75]

c. *Migration and Risk of Statelessness*

Statelessness also takes its toll on settlers among migrant workers imported from other parts of the world during the colonial period. To respond to the labour demands in the plantation sector in the first two decades of the twentieth century, Tamil labourers were brought to work on scattered plantations in Peninsular Malaysia. Rather than facing structural discrimination through instrumentalisation of citizenship such as in the case of the Rohingya and other ethnic groups in Myanmar, poverty, illiteracy, economic and social marginalisation of the labourers were the major factors behind their undocumented status and invisibility.

The workers lived on the estates in grouped houses and remained alienated and economically sidelined even after the British left the country upon independence in 1957.[76] In 2009, the number of stateless persons in West Malaysia stood at 40,000. This figure comprising primarily stateless Indians of Tamil origin decreased to 12,400 as of end of 2017, as a result of mapping, outreach, and registration programmes targeting such population.[77] Generations of these Indians of Tamil origin never had

---

[72] Institute on Statelessness and Inclusion, *Report of the Working Group: Submission to the Human Rights Council at the 25th Session of the Universal Periodic Review: Thailand.*

[73] Francis Teoh, 'The Underlying Issue of Statelessness' (25 August 2011). Retrieved from http://www.thejakartapost.com/news/2011/08/25/the-underlying-issue-statelessness.html [Accessed 10 March 2016].

[74] Rodziana Mohamed Razali, *Protection against Statelessness at Birth: International and Domestic Legal Frameworks of ASEAN Member States with a Special Case Study on Kota Kinabalu, Sabah* (2017), Chapter IV.

[75] Rodziana Mohamed Razali, *Protection against Statelessness at Birth: International and Domestic Legal Frameworks of ASEAN Member States with a Special Case Study on Kota Kinabalu, Sabah* (2017), Chapter III.

[76] T.J. Duraisingam, *International and Domestic Legal Analysis on the Protection of Stateless Persons Residing in Malaysia*, Thesis submitted in fulfillment of the Degree of Doctor of Philosophy, Faculty of Law, National University of Malaysia (2014), p 162.

[77] UNHCR, 'Ending Statelessness in Malaysia'. Retrieved from https://www.unhcr.org/en-my/ending-statelessness-in-malaysia.html [Accessed 20 July 2018].

their children's births registered, hence becoming 'stateless Malaysians' for lacking documentary proof to demonstrate that they are Malaysians.

Southeast Asia is unique as the region houses countries of origin (the Philippines, Indonesia, Myanmar, Viet Nam, Lao PDR, and Cambodia), destination (Singapore and Brunei), as well as countries of both origin and destination (Malaysia and Thailand).[78] Over the past years, the size of irregular migration denotes that the supply of migrants to meet thriving demands in the region outstrips regular migration channels.[79]

One of the ongoing problematic features of Southeast Asian countries that give rise to significant protection challenges is the prevalence of mixed migration movements.[80] Mixed migration can be seen in the movements of migrants from Myanmar into Thailand and Malaysia, including undocumented migrants from the southern Philippines into Sabah (in East Malaysia). While relatively a small percentage of their numbers are recognised as refugees or persons of concern to UNHCR, the overall outflows consist of a much larger size of migrants, blurring the distinctions between them. The region's lack of legal protection frameworks renders the legal and protection statuses for refugees and stateless irrelevant under the immigration regimes of their host countries. In the case of Malaysia, it has been argued that the country's policies and politics towards the refugees and asylum seekers are predominantly shaped by its geopolitical, security, economic, and ethnicity factors. Human rights concerns have not been central to these paradigms.[81]

Overlaying the populations of concern in Sabah are undocumented economic migrants from the Philippines and Indonesia. These migrants are largely characterised as low-skilled workforce belonging to the irregular category. Geographical proximity, historical links, well-established migration routes, high costs of legal employment, the existence of fake documentation manufacturers, and weak regulation and governance of documentation system have been among the aggregate factors behind their sustained inflows into Sabah.[82] It appears that the colonial borders drawn

[78] M.M.B. Asis, 'Borders, Globalization and Irregular Migration in Southeast Asia' in Aris Ananta & Evi Nurvidya Arifin (Eds.), *International Migration in Southeast Asia* (Pasir Panjang: Institute of Southeast Asian Studies, 2004), p 206.

[79] S. Kneebone, 'The Governance of Labor Migration In Southeast Asia', *Global Governance: A Review of Multilateralism and International Organizations*, 16(3) (2010), p 383.

[80] IOM defines 'mixed migration' as complex population flows which are often irregular and prompted by a multiplicity of factors involving refugees, asylum seekers, economic and environmental migrants and victims of trafficking among others. See IOM, 'Mixed Migration' at https://www.iom.int/files/live/sites/iom/files/Country/docs/Mixed-Migration-HOA.pdf (20 September 2018).

[81] Amarjit Kaur, 'Refugees and Refugee Policy in Malaysia', *UNEAC Asia Papers*, V. 8(1) (2007), p 77; K. McGahan, *Managing Migration: The Politics of Immigration Enforcement and Borders Controls in Malaysia* (2008), PhD Thesis, University of Wisconsin-Madison; A. Gurowitz, 'Migrant Rights and Activism in Malaysia: Opportunities and Constraints', *The Journal of Asian Studies*, V. 59(4) (2000), pp 863–888.

[82] G. Hugo, 'Indonesian Labour Migration to Malaysia: Trends and Policy Implications', *Southeast Asian Journal of Social Science*, V. 21(1) (1993), p 36; G. Hugo et al., 'Indonesian Labour Migration to Sabah: Causes and Implications' (2011); Teuku Afrizal & D. Wong, 'The Irregular

between East Malaysia and its neighbouring Indonesia and the Philippines cannot pervade and break the sense of communality rooted in the shared cultural, social, and familial ties between the common ethnic groups that have straddled across the boundaries between Indonesia, Sabah, and the Philippines for many centuries[83]

Another migration-related dimension of statelessness is trafficking. Trafficking has been part of the irregular cross-border mobility in ASEAN, albeit inconspicuous.[84] Estimates suggest the figures between 200,000 and 400,000 of trafficked victims annually throughout the region, largely involving women and children.[85] The Walk Free Foundation's Global Slavery Index 2016 reported that two-thirds' of the world's human trafficking victims or 25 million people are in East Asia and the Pacific.[86] Statelessness is both a cause and a consequence of smuggling and trafficking. The victims are predisposed to statelessness as smugglers and traffickers often confiscate their proof of identity and travel documents. On the other hand, stateless people who often live in extreme poverty and destitution are highly vulnerable to trafficking and smuggling due to their very limited capacity to access regular forms of migration.[87]

Among the ASEAN Member States, Cambodia and the Philippines are the only two countries that have become parties to the 1951 Refugee Convention. Meanwhile, the Philippines is the only country that has ratified the 1954 Statelessness Convention. In the rest of ASEAN Member States, immigration measures invariably described as being punitive and lacking durable solutions for longstanding refugees largely define the protection environment for refugees, asylum seekers as well as stateless persons.[88]

Labour Migration System from Indonesia to Peninsular Malaysia', Akademika 58 (Januari) (2001), pp 99–108; Azizah Kassim, 'International Migration: Prospect and Challenges in Malaysia' in Mohd Yaakub Johari & Chong Shu Yaw (Eds.), *Reinventing Sabah: Global Challenges and Policy Responses* (Sabah: Institute for Development Studies, 2003), p 43; K. Sadiq, 'When States Prefer Non-Citizens Over Citizens: Conflict Over Illegal Immigration into Malaysia', *International Studies Quarterly*, 49(1) (2005), p 102; A.M. Hilsdon, 'Migration and Human Rights: The Case of Filipino Muslim Women in Sabah, Malaysia', *Women's Studies International Forum* (2006), p 409.

[83] E. Laipson & A. Pandya (Eds.), *Migration Challenges in the Indian Ocean Littoral* (Washington DC: The Henry L. Stimson Center, 2010), p 58; Commissioners of Enquiry on Immigrants in Sabah, *Report of the Commission of Enquiry on Immigrants in Sabah* (2014), p 230. Retrieved from http://www.sapp.org.my/rci/RCI-Eng.pdf [Accessed 9 January 2016], p 230.

[84] A. Schloenhardt, 'Trafficking in Migrants in the Asia-Pacific: National, Regional and International Responses', *Singapore Journal of International & Comparative* Law, V. 5(2001), pp 696–747.

[85] G. Arnold, *Migration: Changing the World* (London: PlutoPress, 2012), p 221.

[86] M. Caballero-Anthony, 'A Hidden Scourge', *Finance and Development, IMF Quarterly* (September 2018). Retrieved from https://www.imf.org/external/pubs/ft/fandd/2018/09/pdf/fd0918.pdf [Accessed 19 January 2019].

[87] UNHCR and ASEAN Intergovernmental Commission on Human Rights, *Report of the Regional Workshop on Statelessness and the Rights of Women and Children* (19 November 2011), p 18. Retrieved from http://www.refworld.org/docid/50f674c42.html [Accessed 20 January 2014].

[88] S. Cheung, 'Migration control and the Solutions Impasse in South and Southeast Asia: Implications from the Rohingya Experience', *Journal of Refugee Studies,* 25(1) (2012), p 51.

Long-term solutions for refugees are extremely limited. Repatriation of refugees to their home countries is not a feasible option due to recurring violence and persecution, especially for those originating from Myanmar and unstable countries in the Middle East such as Syria and Palestine. Resettlement to a third country, on the other hand, has recently been possible only for a small number of refugees from SEA.[89]

Integration remains a contested solution for many protracted groups of refugees, asylum seekers and migrants. Refugees who are without any identity document and remain unregistered with any authority in their host countries including UNHCR are invisible and, therefore, most vulnerable to being left out from legal identity and basic rights. Some organisations like the Rohingya Society in Malaysia (RSM) have put the number of unregistered Rohingyas in Malaysia at 40,000.[90] While registered asylum seekers and refugees with UNHCR cards may be able to access birth registration, those remaining unregistered are in a parallel position with that of other irregular migrants. Without legal status, they can be excluded from civil registrations of marriage and birth, entrenching further their lack of identity and statelessness across generations.[91]

Migration presents an increased risk of statelessness when countries provide for an automatic loss of nationality for individuals who emigrate and take up long residence abroad.[92] A citizen or an associate citizen who leaves Myanmar permanently ceases to be a citizen.[93] Although this applies to any person without regards to their race, several ethnic groups like the Karen, Mon, Shan, and other ethnic groups who have fled the country due to conflicts are highly affected.[94] More often than not, countries of origin do not sufficiently inform their citizens of the risks that they face when moving and residing abroad.[95] Previously, the 1958 Citizenship Law of Indonesia

---

[89] A. Saltsman, 'A Real Durable Solution for Southeast Asia's Refugees', *The Diplomat*. Retrieved from http://thediplomat.com/2015/12/a-real-durable-solution-for-southeast-asias-refugees/ [Accessed 29 September 2016]. Of all the countries of origin that have submitted for resettlement from 2005 to 2014, Myanmar has topped the list as the country with the highest submissions, totalling 246,953 over the said ten years, followed by submissions from Iraq (175,585), Bhutan (109,411), Somalia (106,578) and Syria (27,196). See UNHCR, 'UNHCR Refugee Resettlement Trends 2015' (June 2015), p 25. Retrieved from http://www.unhcr.org/559e43ac9.pdf [Accessed 6 June 2016].

[90] Adam Bemma, 'Malaysia: A Rohingya Safe Heaven' (23 November 2017). Retrieved from https://www.aljazeera.com/news/2017/11/malaysia-rohingya-safe-haven-171122190637814.html [2 January 2018].

[91] Human Rights Watch, *World Report 2017 - Malaysia*, 12 January 2017. Retrieved from http://www.refworld.org/docid/587b583313.html [accessed 29 August 2017].

[92] L. van Waas, *Nationality Matters: Statelessness under International Law* (School of Human Rights Research Series. V. 29 (2008), p 78.

[93] Section 16 and 13 of the Myanmar Citizenship Law 1982.

[94] Tang Lay Lee, *Statelessness, Human Rights and Gender: Irregular Migrant Workers from Burma in Thailand* (Leiden: Martinus Nojhoff Publishers, 2005), p 158.

[95] UNHCR & Inter-Parliamentary Union (IPU), *Nationality and Statelessness. A Handbook for Parliamentarians* (2005), p 41. Retrieved from http://www.ipu.org/pdf/publications/nationality_en.pdf [Accessed 24 June 2016].

provided that Indonesians who lived abroad exceeding 5 years would lose their citizenship if they failed to register themselves with the Indonesian authorities.

From the perspective of migration management, most Asian governments treat temporary workers with limited rights, fearing the possible social effects of settlement. In Malaysia, temporary low and semi-skilled foreign workers are not allowed to bring their family members and are prohibited from getting married during the tenure of their employment. Despite these restrictions, family members are taken clandestinely by foreign workers into the country on tourist passports. With the tendency to overstay, they eventually end up being irregular migrants.[96] Marriages are contracted outside of the legal framework leading to births 'out of wedlock' which often go unregistered to avoid law enforcement repercussions. Where illegality tends to make their stay less temporary,[97] the affected children often grow up undocumented with an undetermined nationality for having no proof of births and legal identity, putting them at risk of statelessness.

d. ***Statelessness due to Nomadism or Mobile Lifestyle***

Scattered communities of sea nomads in the region include the Moken and related Moken of the Mergui Archipelago of Burma and the islands of southwest Thailand, *Bajau Laut* of the South China Sea and the *Orang Suku Laut* or the 'Tribe of Sea People' inhabiting the Riau-Lingga Archipelago, Batam and the coastal areas of Sumatra and Southern Johor and more recently Singapore.[98]

According to a report by the Human Rights Watch, many of the Moken living on Burma's islands and waters are largely unregistered. The effect of being unregistered and nomadic is their non-recognition as citizens by the Burmese government. Previously issued travel permits in the form of ID cards allowed them to sail freely, but the issuance has not been consistent since the passing of the 1982 Burmese Citizenship Act. Extortion, bribery, arbitrary arrest, and confiscation of property have been identified as part of the abusive treatment they received, including by the Burmese Navy.[99]

For the Moken in Thailand, many have not been able to benefit from the reform introduced via Thai Nationality Law in 2008 that should allow the stateless populations to register and acquire Thai citizenship. The main impediment is their lack of a birth certificate required by law to prove that they have resided in the country for a minimum of 10 years. Other related factors include significant periods spent outside

[96] Azizah Kassim, *Dasar Pekerja Asing di Malaysia: Perlunya Anjakan Paradigma* (Selangor: Universiti Kebangsaan Malaysia 2012), p 51.

[97] B. Garces-Mascarenas, 'Revisiting the Myth of Guest Worker Programs: The Case of Malaysia' in D.A. Arcarazo & A. Wiesbrock (Eds.), *Global Migration: Old Assumptions, New Dynamics* (Vol. 3) (Santa Barbara & Denver: Praeger, 2015), p 41.

[98] Institute on Statelessness and Inclusion, *The World's Stateless* (2014), p 86; C. Chou, 'Research Trends on Southeast Asian Sea Nomads', *Kyoto Review of Southeast Asia 'States, People, and Borders in Southeast Asia'*, Issue 7, (2006).

[99] Human Rights Watch, *Statelessness at Sea, The Moken of Burma and Thailand* (2015), p 4. Retrieved from https://www.hrw.org/report/2015/06/25/stateless-sea/moken-burma-and-thailand [Accessed 22 June 2016].

of Thailand due to sea nomadism, causing difficulty in proving residence requirement under the law, birth outside of health institution, and the failure of officials to comply with the relevant governmental directive to issue a birth certificate to every child, including the children of stateless persons.[100]

The next group of the migratory population, the *Bajau Laut,* who have now become increasingly semi-settled in coastal areas in certain parts of Sabah, particularly in its north-eastern region, continue to experience statelessness and its effects, including their lack of access to formal education and healthcare, and the threats of arrest, detention and deportation. Their figures are not accurately known[101] as there has been no comprehensive mapping carried out on their presence. Inability to access civil registration, the security risk that the authorities perceive coming from them, and lack of awareness on the importance of documentation and citizenship are the main drivers of their inter-generational statelessness.[102]

e. ***Absence of or Inadequate Safeguards to Prevent Statelessness in Nationality Laws***

i. **Statelessness due to Technical Causes**

The definition of 'statelessness' that denotes a situation where a person is not recognised by any state to be a national under the operation of the state's law,[103] is not provided by the majority of ASEAN Member States in their domestic laws except for Lao PDR and Viet Nam.[104] This creates a gap that could hinder the first pillar of addressing statelessness, namely, to identify and map out stateless persons particularly for reduction and protection purposes. The lack of a unified definition also leads to inaccuracies in the statistical information on stateless populations and may hinder common policies and strategies to tackle it.[105]

Furthermore, adequate safeguards are not in place to prevent statelessness through renunciation, loss or deprivation of nationality in this region. The nationality laws of

[100] Human Rights Watch, *Statelessness at Sea, The Moken of Burma and Thailand* (2015), p 9.

[101] Institute on Statelessness and Inclusion, *The World's Stateless* (2014), p 86.

[102] See H. Brunt, 'The Sustainable Development Agenda and Childhood Statelessness' in Institute on Statelessness and Inclusion, *The World's Stateless Children* (2017). Retrieved from http://www.institutesi.org/worldsstateless17.pdf [Accessed 30 January 2018], pp 290–294; H. Brunt, *A Position Paper on the Vulnerability of Bajau Laut (Sama Dilaut) Children in Sabah* (APRRN, March 2015). http://www.aprrn.info/1/images/PDF/Bajau_Laut_position_paper_FINAL.pdf [Accessed 7 September 2017].

[103] See Article 1(1) of the 1954 Convention.

[104] Article 7 of the Law on Lao Nationality, No. 06/90/PSA, 1990 and Article 3 of the Law on Vietnamese Nationality, Order No. 22/2008L-CTN, 2008.

[105] L. van Waas, *The Situation of Stateless Persons in the Middle East and North Africa* (2010). Retrieved from http://www.unhcr.org/protection/statelessness/4ce63e079/situation-stateless-persons-middle-east-north-africa-laura-van-waas.html [Accessed 20 May 2014], p 17.

Brunei Darussalam,[106] Lao PDR,[107] Malaysia,[108] Myanmar,[109] the Philippines,[110] Singapore[111], Thailand,[112] and Viet Nam[113] contain provisions that allow citizens to voluntarily renounce their citizenship despite rendering them stateless as a consequence.[114] For instance, a Malaysian citizen may renounce his Malaysian citizenship if he is already or about to become a citizen of another country.[115] Nonetheless, the person may encounter statelessness if after renouncing his or her Malaysian citizenship, the person is denied citizenship of the other country. Except for the nationality law of Cambodia that does not allow deprivation of nationality under any circumstances hence adhering to the international standards addressing nationality and avoidance of statelessness, the other ASEAN Member States still permit loss or withdrawal of citizenship in many different circumstances.[116]

Marriage to foreigners could also lead to renunciation of nationality. It has been reported that the arrangement of marriages between Vietnamese women and foreign men from China, the Republic of Korea, and Taiwan Province of China turned into a profitable cross-border marriage business, particularly between 2003 and 2008, with very minimal control from the Vietnamese Government.[117] Between 1995 and 2002, more than 50,000 marriages were entered into between Vietnamese women and foreign men and 10% of such marriages failed, leaving around 3,000 women stateless.[118] A considerable number of former economic Vietnamese brides who had

---

[106] Section 10 of Brunei Nationality Act, No. 4, 1961, Revised Edition (2002).

[107] Article 18 of the Law on Lao Nationality, No. 06/90/PSA (1990).

[108] Article 23, Federal Constitution of Malaysia (1957).

[109] Articles 14, 23, 55 of the 1982 Myanmar Citizenship Law.

[110] Section 1 of Commonwealth Act No. 63, Act providing for the ways in which Philippine citizenship may be lost or reacquired (as amended) (21 October 1936).

[111] Article 128 of the Constitution of the Republic of Singapore, Act 8/65 (1965).

[112] Section 13 and 14 of the Thai Nationality Act (No. 4) B.E. 2551 (2008).

[113] Article 27(1) of the Law on Vietnamese Nationality, Order No. 22/2008/L-CTN (2008).

[114] N. Oakeshott & Bongkot Napaumporn, 'Statelessness in South East Asia', Presentation Slide No. 14. Note that efforts have been taken by the Government of Viet Nam to reduce statelessness through its nationality provisions and the same is true for the nationality laws of Lao PDR, the Philippines, and Thailand.

[115] Article 23, Federal Constitution of Malaysia (1957).

[116] UNHCR, *Regional Expert Roundtable on Good Practices for the Identification, Prevention and Reduction Of Statelessness and the Protection of Stateless Persons in South East Asia* (2011), Bangkok. For instance, in the case of Malaysia, deprivation of nationality is provided in Articles 24 and 26 of the Federal Constitution. Under Article 26(2), the Government has the authority to deprive any woman who has been registered under Article 15 as a citizen for her marriage to a Malaysian citizen if the marriage has been dissolved, other than by death, within the span of two years from the date of the marriage.

[117] See International Organization for Migration (IOM), *Situation Report on International Migration in East and South-East Asia: Regional Thematic Working Group on International Migration Including Human Trafficking* (2008), p 105.

[118] See K. McKinsey, 'Divorce Leaves Some Vietnamese Women Broken-Hearted and Stateless' (14 February 2007). Retrieved from http://www.unhcr.org/45d324428.html [Accessed 12 June 2017].

married foreigners became stateless when they had to renounce their Vietnamese citizenship in order to acquire the nationality of the countries of their foreign husbands, yet in the end, failed to attain the new nationality.[119]

ii. **Lack of or Inadequate Safeguards against Statelessness for Stateless/Otherwise Stateless Children**

The dominant *jus sangunis* mode of acquisition of nationality in the ASEAN Member States causes certain categories of children to be highly vulnerable to statelessness. Without adequate safeguards and fallback provisions for such children to acquire the nationality of their birth country, their only hope is to rely on the nationality of their parents in order to avoid statelessness. Such heavy dependence proves problematic if their parents are unknown or untraceable, have become stateless, including when the parents have lost their nationality or renounced it, or are deprived of the right to confer nationality on their children.

In the case of foundlings or abandoned newborn and infants, their right to be safeguarded against statelessness at birth through nationality attribution of the country in whose territory they are found absent in the nationality laws of Brunei and Myanmar. Acquisition of nationality by way of *jus soli* legal safeguard is also not provided for children born to stateless parents in the nationality laws of Brunei, Singapore, and Myanmar.

4.4 Some Selected Best Practices Through Country-Level Responses

Certain ASEAN governments have come to realise that statelessness is a problem that can be resolved. Given the slight accession rates to the Statelessness Conventions compared to other regions in the world, as well as the lack of binding and enforceable regional frameworks addressing statelessness, the ASEAN Member States' policy responses have so far focused on improving civil registration systems, identifying and registering stateless persons, law reforms and reducing statelessness by facilitating naturalisation. Below are some of the good practice examples within the ASEAN Member States that are useful in addressing statelessness, including childhood statelessness.

1. **Civil Registration and Protection of Foundlings against Statelessness**

Thailand's civil registration law went through a reform in 2008 culminating in a universal birth registration system and withdrawal of its reservation to Article 7 CRC.[120] In 2014, UNICEF reports that Thailand has achieved 100% total registration

[119] K. McKinsey. 'Divorce Leaves Some Vietnamese Women Broken-Hearted and Stateless' (14 February 2007).

[120] UNHCR, 'Ensuring Birth Registration for the Prevention of Statelessness', p 25.

rate for male children, and 99% for female children under 5 years category as of 2012.[121] According to UNHCR:

> Reform in 2008 of the Civil Registration Act provided the legal foundation for non-discriminatory access to birth registration of all children born in Thailand, regardless of their parents' nationality or legal status. The reform also permitted late birth registration of individuals who had been born in the country but were not able to register their birth before 2008. Further, the amendments created a more flexible birth registration procedure under which births can be registered in any District Office, regardless of where in Thailand the birth occurred.[122]

Technically, birth registration in Thailand is connected to the household registration system, which is part of the overall administration of legal status and nationality of persons residing in Thailand. A 13-digit identification number is issued to create a personal record for every child registered, which will determine the person's nationality status and his or her rights. Subject to eligibility requirements under different policies issued through various Cabinet resolutions, Tor Ror 13 granted to foreign nationals staying on a temporary basis at an address in Thailand and Tor Ror 14 issued to those with the permanent right to reside in Thailand[123] may open up a pathway to Thai nationality that can benefit the children born to such registered persons.[124] The reformed framework has helped many people acquire Thai nationality. For those who are not eligible for Thai nationality, their birth certificates are crucial to prove and establish their legal identity, which is vital for their legal protection.[125]

Viet Nam is another country in SEA that records a high level of birth registration. UNICEF reports that the country has achieved 96% of its birth registration rate as of 2013.[126] In Viet Nam, birth registration is significantly eased when the procedures indicate the evidence of birth expected and allow for some degree of flexibility in the types of evidence required. There must be the birth-certifying paper by medical establishments, or written certification of witnesses if infants are born outside of

[121] UNICEF, 'Monitoring the Situation of Women and Children' (2014).

[122] UNHCR, *Ensuring Birth Registration for The Prevention of Statelessness*, p 25.

[123] UNESCO, *Citizenship Manual-Capacity Building on Birth Registration and Citizenship in Thailand: Citizenship Manual* (2008), p 29.

[124] UNESCO, *Citizenship Manual-Capacity Building on Birth Registration and Citizenship in Thailand: Citizenship Manual* (2008), p 29. For the legal framework on hill tribe status and its political evolution, see A. Pesses, *Highland Birth and Citizenship Registration in Thailand. Final Report on Karen Focus Group Discussions in Chiang Mai Province.* [Research Report] UNESCO; UNESCO Highland Birth and Citizenship Registration Promotion Project Funded by the United Kingdom Sustainable Development Programme. 2007. hal-01736494. Retrieved from https://hal.archives-ouvertes.fr/hal-01736494/document [Accessed 10 August 2019].

[125] UNHCR, *Ensuring Birth Registration for the Prevention of Statelessness*, p 25. See Articles 20 and 21 of Thai Civil Registration Act (No. 2) B.E 2551 (2008).

[126] UNICEF, *Unequal at Birth: Disparities in Birth Registration in East Asia and the Pacific.* Retrieved from http://www.unicef.org/eapro/Unequal_at_Birth_UNICEF_EAP.pdf [Accessed 7 July 2017].

medical establishments, or in the absence of witnesses, written pledges are necessary.[127] The birth registration for abandoned children and children born to surrogate mothers shall be stipulated in detail by the Government.[128] Furthermore, instructions relating to the registration of parent and child recognition are further provided where submission of declarations and evidence of proving father and child, or mother and child relationship must be furnished.[129] In the Philippines, no legislative safeguard is found to protect foundlings against statelessness. However, a welcome development in support of prevention of statelessness came in 2016 when the Supreme Court of the Philippines pronounced that foundlings are considered natural-born citizens of the country in which they are found based on the domestic law and relevant accepted principle of international law.[130]

2. **Migration-related Statelessness**

To avoid statelessness due to long-term migration abroad, the 2006 Indonesian Nationality Law was amended in 2006 with the effect that Indonesians living overseas would no longer lose their citizenship if that would render them stateless, and that those who had lost their citizenship may reacquire their Indonesian citizenship. The amended law provides that an Indonesian citizen will lose their citizenship due to:

> Living outside of the territories of the Rep. of Indonesia for 5 (five) consecutive years for non-official purposes, without legal reason and deliberately refuses to declare their intention to remain as Indonesian citizens before the 5 (five) year limit ends, and in each of the next 5 (five) years the said person fails to declare their retaining of their citizenship to the Indonesian Representatives Offices which the said person's residence is under their jurisdiction although the said Representative Office has duly informed them in writing, as long as the incumbent does not become stateless because of such negligence.[131]

No evidence can be found in the application of the nationality laws of the key receiving states of migrants in ASEAN that protect against statelessness for children of migrants and refugees born on their territory. Perceived as 'outsiders', there could be an underlying assumption that it is the state where the parents originate that should be responsible for granting nationality to the children of migrants.[132] In Malaysia where several cases of stateless children have been litigated, there is a strong

---

[127] Article 16(2) of Decree No. 60/2014/ QH13 of 20 November 2014 on Law on Civil Status Decree No. 60/2014.

[128] Article 16(1) and 16(3) Decree No. 60/2014/QH13 of 20 November 2014 on Law on Civil Status Decree No. 60/2014.

[129] Articles 24 and 25 of Decree No. 60/2014/QH13 of 20 November 2014 on Law on Civil Status Decree No. 60/2014.

[130] The decision of the Supreme Court of the Republic of the Philippines in *Grace Poe v. Commission of Elections and Elampro*, G.R. Nos. 221697 & 221698–700 promulgated on March 8, 2016, p 33.

[131] Paragraph i of Article 23 of the 2006 Law of the Republic of Indonesia Number 12 on Citizenship of the Republic of Indonesia.

[132] N. Oakeshott, 'The Search for Solutions to Statelessness in Southeast Asia: State Practice and Recent Developments' in L. van Waas and M.J. Khanna (Eds.), *Solving Statelessness* (AH Oisterwijk: Wolf Legal Publishers, 2017), p 350.

tendency to disproportionately place the difficult burden of proving statelessness on the claimant, on behalf of the affected children.[133]

3. **Registration and Protection of Stateless Persons**

Baseline data and statistics on stateless persons are hard to come by due to among others, difficulties in defining and quantifying 'stateless persons', geographical barriers, and lack of political will to recognise and address the problem.[134] Yet in several of the ASEAN Member States, government and NGO-led initiatives to survey, register or document stateless and at-risk of stateless persons have been implemented.

In 2005, the Thai Government adopted the 'National Strategy on Administration of Legal Status and the Rights of Persons', with the intent to ensure appropriate legal statuses for the different categories of non-nationals in Thailand.[135] Stateless persons are recorded in Thailand's civil registration status, issued an identity document and are entitled to access basic rights such as health insurance and other rights enjoyed by Thai citizens.[136] The regularisation through the right to a temporary stay is the first step under the Thai Government's initiatives to address statelessness in Thailand.[137] New commitments and initiatives have subsequently followed suit.

In 2006, pursuant to bilateral memoranda of understanding with Cambodia, Lao PDR and Myanmar, Nationality Verification Registration scheme was introduced through which migrant workers from these three countries could apply to register themselves to obtain a temporary legal residence status and be eligible for a work permit. This verification procedure was intended to function as a tool to prevent statelessness among the irregular workers and their children by providing evidence of nationality and the foundation for regularisation of their legal status.[138] By January

---

[133] See Rodziana Mohamed Razali, 'Addressing Statelessness in Malaysia: New Hope and Remaining Challenges', *Statelessness Working Paper Series No. 2017/9*, p 9. Retrieved from http://www.institutesi.org/forum/workingpapers.php [Accessed 30 March 2018].

[134] Rodziana Mohamed Razali, *Protection against Statelessness at Birth: International and Domestic Legal Frameworks of ASEAN Member States with a Special Case Study on Kota Kinabalu, Sabah* (2017), Chapter II and Chapter IV.

[135] N. Oakeshott, 'The Search for Solutions to Statelessness in Southeast Asia: State Practice and Recent Developments' in L. van Waas & M.J. Khanna (Eds.), *Solving Statelessness* (AH Oisterwijk: Wolf Legal Publishers), p 355.

[136] Under the Thai alien registration scheme (for persons without Thai nationality), migrants in Thailand with or without the legal permission to enter the country, together with people born in Thailand who are without Thai nationality are allowed to apply for a one-year temporary ID card under the Thai household registration system. The advantage of this system is that those registered including children whose nationality is unconfirmed may be eligible to have access to Thai citizenship via naturalisation regardless of the matrimonial status of the parents.

[137] Cabinet Resolution, Strategies to Address the Problem of Legal Status and Rights of Stateless Persons, 18 January 2005 and Cabinet Resolution on addressing the legal status of students and stateless persons born in Thailand, 7 December 2016. See Equal Rights Trust, *Confined Spaces: Legal Protections for Rohingya in Bangladesh, Malaysia and Thailand*, p 169.

[138] Institute on Statelessness and Inclusion, *The World's Stateless Children* (2017), p 68. It was further noted that the migrant workers still faced the practical barriers of accessing the necessary documents in their countries of origin such as Myanmar and others may refuse to participate to avoid being deported or returned to their countries.

2013, more than 1.5 million formerly undocumented migrant workers had their nationality verified.[139]

In 2016, the Royal Thai Government adopted the goal of 'zero statelessness' in line with the 10-year campaign to eradicate statelessness by 2024.[140] The Government has made significant headway by requiring all districts to identify and accord legal status to stateless students in the country, a move that would benefit some 65,000 students affected by statelessness.[141]

Malaysia, on the other hand, carried out mapping and registration of undocumented stateless Indians of Tamil descent in West Malaysia. The efforts have been initiated and mobilised by a local community organisation known as Development of Human Resources in Rural Areas or DHRRA, with the technical support by UNHCR and funding from the Malaysian Government.[142] Between 2014 and 2016, DHRRA's outreach programmes have aided in resolving lack of documentation and proof of citizenship resulting in the registration of 11,689 stateless persons, and acquisition of documentation confirming nationality for 545 applicants.[143]

In the southern Philippines, a mapping exercise carried out by UNHCR and the governments of Indonesia and the Philippines in 2012 and 2013 identified approximately 6,000 people of Indonesian descent living with uncertain or undetermined nationality.[144] Mostly living without legal status,[145] a verification of nationality by UNHCR in 2014 with the cooperation of both the Indonesian and Philippine governments[146] led to registration and confirmation of nationality of some of the affected persons of Indonesian descent.[147]

---

[139] N. Oakeshott, 'The Search for Solutions to Statelessness in Southeast Asia: State Practice and Recent Developments' in L. van Waas & M.J. Khanna (Eds.), *Solving Statelessness* (AH Oisterwijk: Wolf Legal Publishers), p 355. Those whose nationality could not be verified would be allowed access to basic rights and temporary residence if they could not be returned to any country of origin as former residents.

[140] See generally UNHCR, *#IBelong Campaign to End Statelessness* (2024). Retrieved from http://www.unhcr.org/ibelong-campaign-to-end-statelessness.html [Accessed 10 January 2015]; See also UNHCR, *I Am Here, I Belong, The Urgent Need to End Childhood Statelessness* (2015). Retrieved from http://www.unhcr.org/ibelong/wp-content/uploads/2015-10-StatelessReport_ENG16.pdf [Accessed 15 February 2016].

[141] UNHCR, *The Campaign to End Statelessness: Campaign Update* (2016).

[142] Rodziana Mohamed Razali, 'Addressing Statelessness in Malaysia: New Hope and Remaining Challenges', *Statelessness Working Paper Series No. 2017/9*, p 6. Retrieved from http://www.institutesi.org/forum/workingpapers.php [Accessed 30 March 2018].

[143] UNHCR, *The Campaign to End Statelessness: April 2016 Update.* Retrieved from http://www.unhcr.org/ibelong/wp-content/uploads/Campaign-Update-April-2016.pdf [Accessed 27 September 2018].

[144] UNHCR, 'Stateless in the Philippines: Indonesia descendants Feel Torn between Two Lands', www.unhcr.org/5416d3519.html [Accessed 10 August 2016].

[145] UNHCR, 'Stateless in the Philippines: Indonesia descendants Feel Torn between Two Lands', www.unhcr.org/5416d3519.html [Accessed 10 August 2016].

[146] UNHCR, 'Stateless in the Philippines: Indonesia descendants Feel Torn between Two Lands', www.unhcr.org/5416d3519.html [Accessed 10 August 2014].

[147] UNHCR, *The Campaign To End Statelessness: Campaign Update* (2016).

4. **Closing the Gaps arising from Technical Causes**

To respond to statelessness that arose due to conflict of laws in the previous 1998 Citizenship Law of Viet Nam affecting women marrying foreign nationals, the Vietnamese Government restored the Vietnamese citizenship to the affected women and their children.[148] Bilateral agreements were also entered into with the foreign states concerned, which culminated in the latter lifting their renunciation of nationality requirement prior to the conferral of the new citizenship. The Vietnamese Government also creates a condition requiring renunciation of citizenship to be subjected to a written confirmation that the applicant has already obtained a new nationality.[149]

5. **Protection against Discriminatory Laws Giving Rise to Statelessness**

i. **Race**

The nationality laws of Indonesia, Malaysia, the Philippines, Singapore, Thailand, and Viet Nam seem to largely comply with the prohibition of race discrimination. Indonesia removed the difference between 'native' and 'non-native' through its law reform in 2006, undertaken as part of its democratisation process post-Suharto regime.[150] This legislative reform reduces the earlier hurdle faced by Indonesian ethnic minorities of Chinese and Indian descent in confirming their nationality despite their long-established residence in Indonesia over many generations.

ii. **Gender**

In general, children originating from the ASEAN Member States who are born abroad are entitled to the citizenship of at least one of their parents by way of *jus sanguinis.* Therefore, there are no specific safeguards to children born abroad where one parent is a national.[151] However, lack of gender-sensitive nationality provisions can expose children to statelessness. Several countries in the region have taken the step to reform their nationality laws so as to bring them into compliance with Article 9 of CEDAW, such as Singapore, Indonesia, the Philippines, Thailand, Lao PDR, and Myanmar.[152]

Gender equality regarding the transmission of Thai nationality has been in place since 1992. Children born abroad to a Thai parent is entitled to Thai nationality.[153]

---

[148] Article 23(1)(f) of 2008 Nationality Law of Vietnam.

[149] UNHCR and ASEAN Intergovernmental Commission on Human Rights, *Report of the Regional Workshop on Statelessness and the Rights of Women and Children* (19 November 2011), pp 14–15; Lyma Nguyen, *Report on Citizenship Law: Vietnam*, p 16. Retrieved from http://cadmus.eui.eu/bitstream/handle/1814/47966/GLOBALCIT_CR_2017_13.pdf?sequence=1 [Accessed 10 July 2018].

[150] Law on Citizenship of the Republic of Indonesia, Decree No. 12, 2006.

[151] N. Oakeshott, 'An Analysis of Nationality Laws in South East Asia' (2013), Presentation Slides.

[152] UNHCR, 'Regional Statelessness Course: South East Asia Focus', 4–8 November 2013, Bangkok, Thailand.

[153] See Section 7 of the Thai Nationality Act 2008 (No. 4) B.E. 2551. 'The following persons acquire Thai nationality by birth: (1) a person born of a father or a mother of Thai nationality, whether within or outside the Kingdom of Thailand; (2) a person born within the Kingdom of Thailand except for the person under Section 7 bis paragraph one.

With the amendment to the Thai Nationality Act (No. 4) B.E. 2551 (2008), children born out of wedlock can now acquire the nationality of his or her Thai father. Section 6 of the Nationality Act 2008 reinterprets the definition of a 'father'. A father is someone whoever proved to be the father of the person according to ministerial regulations, even if he has not registered the marriage license.[154] The effect of this amendment is retrospective.[155]

6. **Reduction of Statelessness through Facilitated Naturalisation**

The Philippines and Viet Nam provide exemplary provisions for facilitated naturalisation for children of refugees born in their territories.[156] The refugees in the Philippines, being a signatory country to the 1951 Refugee Convention are able to obtain citizenship in the same manner as other non-citizens.[157] For children of refugees born in the Philippines, facilitated naturalisation may apply whereby the normal period of 10 years of continuous residence may be reduced to 5 years.[158] In the case of Viet Nam, the country has introduced a facilitated naturalisation procedure under its revised Law on Vietnamese Nationality in 2008. Foreign nationals may apply to be naturalised after 5 years of residence in the country and meeting other prescribed conditions.[159] By the end of 2012, former Cambodian refugees in Viet Nam were able to acquire Vietnamese citizenship. Generations of children born to former refugees were also able to benefit from Vietnamese nationality.[160]

---

[154] 'Father' in Section 7(1) means 'a person having been proved, in conformity with the Ministerial Regulation that he is truly the father of the person even though he did not register the marriage with the mother of the person or did not complete registration of legitimate child'.

[155] N. Oakeshott & Bongkot Napaumporn, 'Statelessness in South East Asia', Regional Statelessness Course: South East Asia Focus, Bangkok, Thailand, 4–8 November 2013, Presentation Slides.

[156] UNHCR, *Universal Periodic Review: The Philippines* (December 2011), p 2. Retrieved from http://www.refworld.org/pdfid/4ee07aa22.pdf [Accessed 20 July 2016]; UNHCR, *Submission by the United Nations High Commissioner for Refugees for the Office of the High Commissioner for Human Rights' Compilation Report - Universal Periodic Review: Socialist Republic of Vietnam* (June 2013), p 2. Retrieved from http://www.refworld.org/pdfid/51c946514.pdf [Accessed 23 June 2016].

[157] UNHCR, *Universal Periodic Review: The Philippines* (December 2011), p 2.

[158] See Section 3(5) of Act to Provide for the Acquisition of Philippine Citizenship by Naturalisation and to Repeal Acts Numbered Twenty-Nine Hundred and Twenty-Seven and Thirty-Four Hundred and Forty-Eight (Commonwealth Act No. 473, 1939).

[159] Article 19(1) of the Law on Vietnamese Nationality, Order No. 22/2008L-TN, 2008.

[160] UNHCR, *Submission by the United Nations High Commissioner for Refugees for the Office of the High Commissioner for Human Rights' Compilation Report – Universal Periodic Review: Socialist Republic of Vietnam*' (June 2013), p 1.

4.5 Conclusion

First and foremost, the legal frameworks for nationality in the ASEAN region are essentially shaped by the restrictive doctrine of *jus sanguinis* and single nationality, causing statelessness to be highly transmissible across many generations. Despite limits that exist pertaining to ratification or accession to international human rights treaties including the two statelessness conventions, it will be demonstrated in the next chapter that domestic nationality laws of the ASEAN member states broadly reflect, to varying degrees, their commitments to international standards on the right to a nationality and avoidance of statelessness.

As examined in this chapter, the global phenomenon of statelessness and the risks it presents stem from a set of dynamic causes that can be both intersecting and context-specific, ranging from gender and racial discrimination, ethnic persecution and denationalisation, gaps in nationality laws, weaknesses in civil registration regimes and administration and cross-border migration. Many persistent situations of statelessness in SEA are indeed the outcome of discriminatory legal regimes that exclude certain groups from nationality or do not provide for equal nationality rights. This has chiefly affected minority populations, migrants, women, and children.

Meanwhile, the post-colonial states in SEA continue to struggle to accommodate nationality for certain groups, such as those of the sea nomadic populations. Problems related to proof of nationality as a result of unregistered births are widespread among minorities, remote and isolated communities, as well as those belonging to migrant and refugee populations.[161] Exclusion from civil registration is concerning for children of unregistered asylum seekers and irregular migrants due to the risk of generating new cases of statelessness at birth. Gaps in the registration system such as in Thailand additionally exacerbate the effects of discriminatory nationality laws, particularly in mountainous areas and borderlands.

With technical assistance from UNHCR, the ASEAN human rights bodies, especially AICHR and ACWC have already implemented their mandates to address statelessness, especially by providing important platforms for dialogue, research, and advocacy to promote the right to a nationality for women and children. Such efforts undoubtedly require much weight to be placed on the universality of birth registration and elimination of discriminatory provisions in nationality laws. While the selected best practices offer valuable lessons for the ASEAN countries, the various causes of statelessness, especially the longstanding and protracted ones, certainly call for resource mobilisation and greater partnerships between actors both regionally and internationally. Long-term solutions should also be developed for in situ situations of statelessness, such as through access to legal status and facilitated naturalisation to reduce existing and prevent new cases of statelessness.

---

[161] L. van Waas, 'The Children of Irregular Migrants: A Stateless Generation', *Netherlands Quarterly for Human Rights*, 25 (2007), p 452.

Chapter 5
Assessment of Domestic Legal Frameworks for Nationality of ASEAN Member States

5.1 Introduction

This chapter and Chap. 6 shall focus on examining the availability and degree of protection against statelessness at birth under the domestic legal frameworks for, and to some extent, practices on nationality and birth registration in the ASEAN Member States. It is mainly pursued to grasp the different levels of strength of the protection against statelessness among children within the ten Member States of ASEAN.

The centrality of the analysis is set on identifying gaps and issues in the domestic frameworks addressing the two safeguards, which could undermine and obstruct the protection of children against statelessness at birth. Simultaneously, efforts are also made to highlight positive aspects of the laws, steps, and practices that have been pursued by the countries that benefit children in realising the right to their legal identity and avoidance of statelessness. This latter aspect would serve to identify lessons for each country, and contribute to developing more targeted actions by stakeholders at the domestic and regional levels of ASEAN, considering the patterns discovered and challenges encountered.

The intended evaluation of the nationality laws of the Member States of ASEAN as a safeguard against statelessness at birth shall be guided by the relevant international and regional standards on the right to a nationality generally, as recapitulated in the following Table 5.1, and by other more specific standards including those extricated from the previously discussed soft law instruments. Such standards shall be outlined in the respective sections of the analysis. Aside from nationality legislation, other related and accessible laws providing protection for children against statelessness may be examined together to provide a more inclusive assessment of the countries' frameworks.

R. M. Razali, *Safeguarding Against Statelessness at Birth*,
https://doi.org/10.1007/978-981-19-5371-2_5

Table 5.1 International and regional instruments providing for the right to a nationality

International Instruments	Regional Instruments
1948 Universal Declaration of Human Rights, Article 15	1969 American Convention on Human Rights, Article 20
1961 Convention on the Reduction of Statelessness, Article 1	1990 African Charter on the Rights and Welfare of the Child, Article 6
1966 International Covenant on Civil and Political Rights, Article 24	1997 European Convention on Nationality, Article 6
1979 Convention on the Elimination of All Forms of Discrimination against Women, Article 9	2005 Covenant on the Rights of the Child in Islam, Article 7
1989 Convention on the Rights of the Child, Article 7	2006 Council of Europe Convention on the Avoidance of Statelessness in relation to State Succession, Article 2
1990 International Convention on the Protection of the Rights of All Migrant Workers and Members of Their Families, Article 29	2012 ASEAN Human Rights Declaration, Article 18
2006 Convention on the Rights of Persons with Disabilities, Article 18	

The international standards are meant to function as a set of benchmarks to guide the review of the nationality frameworks in the process of evaluating the strengths of the protection offered against childhood statelessness through the domestic nationality laws, alongside the relevant policies and practices of the countries assessed. It must also be stated that the analysis is unable to incorporate decisions of the courts on many of the interpretations of the provisions, largely due to a limited access to case law reports from the linguistically diverse common and civil law jurisdictions of the Member States of ASEAN.

5.2 Categories of Children Examined and Applicable International Standards

The analysis shall proceed according to the specific categories of children unable to acquire nationality *jus sanguinis*, consisting of foundlings and young children separated from parents and children born in the country to stateless parents (stateless refugees and non-refugees) and other children who are otherwise stateless.

For the following category comprising other children who would otherwise be stateless, the subgroups of children examined are:

a. children born to refugee parents unable or unwilling to confer nationality on their children (non-stateless refugee parents);
b. children born to parents of unclear or undetermined nationality; and

c. children born abroad and born to parents unable to confer nationality due to gender discrimination or absence of parental recognition.

The applicable international standards are displayed in the following table and in each box preceding the analysis for each category of the children stated.

5.3 Country-Level Assessment

1. **Foundlings and Young Children Separated from Parents**

Relevant international standards:

(a) The 1930 Hague Convention [Article 14—Nationality of the country of birth for children whose parents are unknown]
(b) The 1961 Convention [Article 2—Foundlings are presumed born to nationals of the State Party on whose territory they are found]
(c) CRC [Article 3 – Best interests of the child principle]
(d) CRCI [Article 7(3) – Children of unknown descent shall have the right to a name, title, and nationality]
(e) Guidelines No. 4 [Paragraph 58—the safeguard to grant nationality to foundlings is to apply to all young children not yet able to communicate accurate information pertaining to the identity of their parents or their place of birth]
(f) Guidelines No. 4 [Paragraph 60—Loss of nationality of a foundling found born to non-citizens abroad to be subject to possession of another state's nationality]

Foundlings are prone to experiencing statelessness at birth if the law does not have a mechanism to automatically confer nationality upon them. Aside from abandoned infants, children risk being in legal limbo if their migrant parents pass away, disappear, or, have been arrested and later deported.[1] In Malaysia, for instance, children of parents who have been arrested and deported for immigration offences in Sabah

[1] Azizah Kassim, 'Development and International Migration in Malaysia: Patterns, Policy and Human Rights' in Abdul Rahman Embong (Ed.), *Social Science & Malaysian National Development: Proceedings of the National Seminar on 'Social Science and Malaysian National Development'* (Putrajaya: Malaysian Social Science Association, 2006), pp 107–147 & pp 143–146. According to the author, during the previous rooting out exercises termed 'Ops Nyah 2', some irregular migrants escaped and left no trace, leaving behind their children. Irregular migrants who were detained during the operations included undocumented children themselves.

could be at a heightened risk of statelessness due to separation from their parents. They are commonly associated with children living and working on the streets.[2]

a. ***Strong Safeguards for Foundlings and Children whose Parents' Parentage is Unknown or cannot be Determined***

Insome ASEAN countries, protection of foundlings against statelessness is not limited to newborns. Lao PDR attributes nationality *ex lege* to 'children', instead of just foundlings discovered in its territory and whose parents' identity is unknown.[3] Viet Nam uses both 'abandoned newborn' and 'children found in the Vietnamese territory whose parents are unknown' in its safeguard provision concerning foundlings who gain Vietnamese nationality by birth.[4] Indonesia applies its safeguard to 'children newly born and found in Indonesian territory' and whose parents are undetermined.[5] Aside from newborn, children born in an Indonesian territory whose parents' whereabouts are undetermined are also entitled to nationality at birth.[6] Cambodia also separates a child from a newborn. A child born from an unknown mother or father and a newly born child found in Cambodia obtain Khmer nationality.[7]

The preceding countries' provisions mirror the standards of protection of foundlings envisaged by Article 2 of the 1961 Statelessness Convention, the best interests of the child principle, and paragraph 58 of Guidelines No. 4. The use of the word 'children' indicates that children other than infants are also entitled to benefit from the safeguards.

Lao PDR expressly addresses the effects of the discovery of parents' alien nationality status. If there is evidence that indicates that the parent(s) of such children are, in fact, in possession of citizenship of another country, the children will be considered as alien citizens from birth.[8] Viet Nam, on the other hand, withdraws the citizenship of a child under 15 years who has acquired citizenship for having unknown parents if the child has found his parents, or for having either parent who holds a single foreign nationality.[9] Inconsistent with paragraph 60 of Guidelines No. 4 and Article 3 of CRC, both provisions in the nationality laws of Lao PDR and Viet Nam do not have regard for the possibility of the said children being unable to acquire the nationality of their parents, despite the parents having a certain nationality. Other countries simply do not address the effects of such discovery of a foundling's or younger child's parent(s) in possession of foreign nationality in their nationality laws.

---

[2] M. Lynch, *Futures Denied: Statelessness among Infants, Children and Youth* (Refugees International, 2008), p 9. However, it is to be cautioned that lack of evidence-based research into the extent of their statelessness or its risk precludes any direct conclusion that they are stateless.

[3] Article 12 of the Law on Lao Nationality, No.06/90/PSA, 1990.

[4] Article 18 of the Law on Vietnamese Nationality, Order No. 22/2008L-TN, 2008.

[5] Article 4(10) of the Law on Citizenship of the Republic of Indonesia, Decree No. 12, 2006.

[6] Article 4(11) of the Law on Citizenship of the Republic of Indonesia, Decree No. 12, 2006.

[7] Article 4(2)(b) of the Cambodian Law on Nationality, Decree No. NS/RKM/1096/31, 1996.

[8] Article 12 of the Law on Lao Nationality, No. 06/90/PSA, 1990.

[9] Article 18(2)(a) and (b) of the Law on Vietnamese Nationality, Order No. 22/2008L-CTN, 2008.

b. ***Partial Safeguards Concentrating on Foundlings***

Safeguards strictly limited to protecting foundlings (customarily referring to newborns or infants) can be found in the nationality laws of Malaysia and Singapore. In these two countries, the phrase 'any newborn child found exposed' is used.[10]

Although no legislative safeguard is found for foundlings in the Philippines, a positive development in this area took place in March 2016. In a local high-profile case, the Supreme Court of the Philippines declared that foundlings are considered natural-born citizens of the country.[11] This case involves a petition to declare Senator Grace Poe, who was a foundling (abandoned at a local church with unknown biological parents) to be disqualified from running for the country's presidency on the ground that she is not a natural-born citizen of the Philippines, a constitutional requirement for the highest office in the country. The Court's pronouncement is premised inter alia, on the consistent principle of protection against statelessness for foundlings, as evidenced in international law conventions and instruments and state practice on nationality, including in *jus sanguinis* countries in Asia. It adopts the generally accepted principle of international law 'to presume foundlings as having been born of nationals of the country in which the foundling is found'.[12]

c. ***Lack of or Minimal Safeguards***

The right of foundlings to be safeguarded against statelessness at birth through nationality attribution *ex lege* is nevertheless not found in the nationality laws of Thailand, Brunei, and Myanmar. Foundlings are subject to provisions under Article 7 bis of Thai Nationality Act 1965 (B.E. 2508). However, in Thailand, a Cabinet resolution passed on 7 December 2016 allows children born in Thailand who have lived in the country for not less than 10 years and have certification from relevant agencies under the Ministry of Social Development and Human Security to apply for Thai nationality.[13]

---

[10] Refer to the Federal Constitution of Malaysia, Supplementary provisions relating to citizenship, part III, Section 19B, and Third Schedule, Section 13 read with Article 140 of the Constitution of the Republic of Singapore (1965).

[11] See Decision of the Supreme Court of the Republic of the Philippines in *Grace Poe v. Commission of Elections and Elampro, G.R. Nos.* 221697 & 221,698–700 promulgated March 8, 2016.

[12] In such circumstances, the Court accepted the rule under the doctrine of incorporation, as opposed to the normal practice of transformation. See the Decision of the Supreme Court of the Republic of the Philippines in *Grace Poe v. Commission of Elections and Elampro*, G.R. Nos. 221697 & 221,698–700 promulgated March 8, 2016, p 32–33.

[13] See Ministry of Foreign Affairs of the Kingdom of Thailand, *Press Release: Thailand announces additional measures to fight statelessness* (2017), Retrieved from http://www.mfa.go.th/main/en/news3/6886/74222-Thailand-announces-additional- measures-to-fight-st.html [Accessed 20 December 2018].

2. **Children Born in the Territory to Stateless Parents and Other Children in the Category of Otherwise Stateless Children**

Relevant international standards:

(a) The 1961 Convention [Article 1]
(b) CRC [Article 7(1) in conjunction with Article 3(1)]
Guidelines No. 4 [Paragraph 27- The child of refugees who would otherwise be stateless shall either acquire the nationality of the (host) state *ex lege* or through the application procedure at a later time in order to avoid statelessness]

a. ***Strong Safeguards (without Additional Requirements Attached)***

Among the ASEAN Member States, Malaysia appears to provide the strongest safeguard against statelessness in its Federal Constitution for children who would otherwise be stateless born in its territory. Article 14(1) (b) read together with Section 1, paragraph (e) of Part II of the 2nd Schedule of the Constitution stipulates that 'every person born within the Federation who is not a citizen of any other country is a citizen of Malaysia by operation of law'. Not only the mode of conferral of nationality prescribed is *ex lege* or automatic but also the safeguard is subject to no further requirement under the law.

Despite echoing the highest standards under international law for protection against statelessness at birth, the full potential of this safeguard could be compromised by the content of Section 2(3) of Part III of the Second Schedule. Paragraph 1(e) of Section 1 therein treats a person as having at birth any citizenship that he acquires within a year afterward by virtue of any provision that corresponds to paragraph (c) of Section 1 in Part II. This period of up to 1 year within which a child's acquired citizenship is considered to have been obtained at birth slightly falls below the ideal standard for states to facilitate the acquisition of nationality immediately after birth, or as soon as possible following birth.[14] Legal provisions aside, how the authority interprets this provision and its practical utility in avoiding childhood statelessness is another matter that requires a separate analysis.

Article 15A of the Malaysian Federal Constitution may also function as a safeguard against statelessness. Article 15A deals with the special power of the Federal Government to register any person below the age of 21 under special circumstances. Despite that, the wide room of discretion afforded to the Minister in charge in allowing or disallowing the grant of citizenship under Article 15A invokes much uncertainty

[14] See G.R. de Groot, 'Children, Their Right to a Nationality and Child Statelessness' in A. Edwards & L. van Waas (Eds.), *Nationality and Statelessness Under International Law*, (Cambridge: Cambridge University Press, 2014), p 150.

as to how far the provision could protect children against statelessness at birth.[15] As such, the discretionary nature of the provision renders Article 15 not meeting the highest standard of protection against statelessness at birth by *ex lege* mode of conferral of nationality.

Indonesia similarly provides full protection by attributing citizenship *ex lege* to children born to both parents who were stateless at the time of birth without further conditions attached.[16] Nonetheless, both Malaysia and Indonesia lack the implementing mechanisms for statelessness status determination to render such provisions to be fully operational.

b. ***Partial Safeguards (with additional requirements)***

While the safeguards against 'otherwise stateless children' in Malaysia and Indonesia appear to be rather all encompassing and in line with Article 1(1) of the 1961 Statelessness Convention (namely, without conditions attached), the other ASEAN Member States mostly provide safeguards against statelessness to 'otherwise stateless children' with additional requirements.

In Lao PDR and Viet Nam,[17] children born in their territories who would otherwise be stateless could acquire nationality at birth if they are born to both parents who are stateless. Besides being born to stateless parents, the child's parents are further required to be permanently residing in the country and integrated into the Lao society and culture.[18] Similarly in Viet Nam, both of the parents are required to be permanent residents.

Despite the aforementioned restrictions, Lao PDR and Viet Nam have inserted their definitions of a 'stateless person' in their nationality laws. Lao PDR defines an *apatrid* or 'a stateless person' as 'an individual residing in the territory of the Lao People's Democratic Republic who is not a Lao citizen and who is unable to certify

[15] The chances of getting citizenship via Article 15A are very slim, even in cases involving children born to a Malaysian father and non-Malaysian mother before registration of the parents' marriage. The response time to an Article 15A application is also unduly long (between two to three years, and in some recent cases, such exceeds four years). This operates adversely against the ability to meet the deadline of 21 years as the maximum age allowed to be recognised as a Malaysian citizen under this provision. Most applications get rejected with no reason given. The court cases on Article 15A yield no precedent so far on protection against statelessness. Several cases due to be heard by the Federal Court were instead settled out of court when the Home Ministry decided to grant citizenship to the applicants. See I. Lim, 'Reality check for Malaysian-born stateless children on 'special citizenship' route', *malaymail*, Retrieved from https://www.malaymail.com/news/malaysia/2019/03/26/reality-check-for-malaysia-born-stateless-children-on-special-citizenship-r/1736436. malaymail.com/news/malaysia/2019/03/26/reality-check-for-malaysia-born-stateless-children-on-special-citizenship-r/1736436 [Accessed 20 June 2019]. Some of the court cases on the relevant provisions to avert statelessness in Malaysia have been highlighted in Rodziana Mohamed Razali, 'Addressing Statelessness in Malaysia: New Hope and Remaining Challenges', *Statelessness Working Paper Series No. 2017/9.*

[16] Article 4(11) of the Law on Citizenship of the Republic of Indonesia, Decree No. 12, 2006.

[17] See Article 11 of the Law on Lao Nationality, No. 06/90/PSA, 1990 and Article 17 of the Law on Vietnamese Nationality, Order No. 22/2008L-CTN, 2008.

[18] Article 11 of the Law on Lao Nationality, No. 06/90/PSA, 1990.

his nationality'.[19] The insertion of inability to certify one's nationality as an element of statelessness denotes that children born to such parents would automatically be able to benefit from the *jus soli* legal safeguard provided that the parents could fulfil the requirements under Article 11.[20] Echoing the definition in Article 1(1) of the 1954 Convention, a stateless person under the Law on Vietnamese Nationality is 'a person who has neither Vietnamese nationality nor foreign nationality'.[21]

In 2008, Thailand made a significant reform to its nationality law through Nationality Act 2008 (No. 4), B.E. 2551. Before the repeal of paragraphs 2 and 3 of Section 7 of the 1965 Nationality Act (B.E. 2508) by Section 7 of Thai Nationality Act 2008 (No. 4), B.E. 2551, the law excluded from the acquisition of Thai nationality at birth children born to alien parents with; (i) their fathers (natural or legal) and mothers having the permission to stay temporarily in Thailand; and (ii) parents having entered and stayed in Thailand without permission under Thai immigration law.

However, with the said amendment (which repealed Section 7, paragraphs (2) and (3)), the Minister of Interior is given the discretion to grant nationality to alien parents such as irregular migrants in the country,[22] if he deems appropriate, according to relevant rules decided by the Cabinet. The content of Section 7 stipulates that human rights considerations are factored into nationality provisions together with considerations of national security.[23]

It is important to highlight that the Thai Cabinet through its various resolutions allows for the possibility of stateless minorities to be recognised as lawful residents and given the right of permanent residence (PR), especially to those who have immigrated to Thailand and fully assimilated themselves.[24] It is possible for children born

---

[19] Article 7 of the Law on Lao Nationality, No. 06/90/PSA, 1990.

[20] UNHCR, *Regional Expert Roundtable on Good Practices for the Identification, Prevention and Reduction of Statelessness and the Protection of Stateless Persons in South East Asia* (2011), p 12.

[21] Article 3 of the Law on Vietnamese Nationality, Order No. 22/2008L-CTN, 2008.

[22] Refer to para (1) of Section 7 *bis* of the Thai Nationality Act 2008 (No.4) B.E. 2551.

[23] See Section 7 *bis* of para 3 as amended by the Nationality Act (No. 4) B.E. 2551 (2008) that reads: '…The person who is born within the Thai Kingdom and has not acquired Thai nationality under paragraph one shall reside in the Thai Kingdom under conditions stated in the Ministerial Regulation, but principles of national security and human rights have to be considered as well. Nevertheless, the person shall be deemed to have entered and resided in the Thai Kingdom without permission under the law on immigration when there is no such Ministerial Regulation still'.

[24] For instance, on 7 December 2016, the Thai Cabinet passed two resolutions to firstly provide through a Ministerial Regulation, the right to legally stay in Thailand for foreign children born in Thailand based on the rights of their parents and, secondly, to address nationality and status problem of stateless persons in Thailand. The latter allows foreign children born in Thailand to apply for Thai nationality taking into account that either their parents are from ethnic minority registered with the Ministry of Interior who have lived in Thailand for not less than 15 years, or that the children have received a bachelor's degree or equivalent even though their parents are from other groups. Additionally, children who are currently studying and abandoned children can apply for Thai nationality. However, for the latter, the children must have lived in Thailand for not less than 10 years and possess certification from relevant agencies under the Ministry of Social Development and Human Security. See Ministry of Foreign Affairs of the Kingdom of Thailand, *Press Release: Thailand announces additional measures to fight statelessness* (2017), Retrieved from http://www.mfa.go.th/main/en/news3/6886/74222-Thailand- announces-additional-measures-to-fight-st.html [Accessed 20 December 2018].

on Thai territory to parents who have a PR status to acquire Thai nationality.[25] Children born to stateless persons who qualify under the relevant Cabinet resolutions and other eligible stateless children such as students may also be permitted to acquire a certain legal status, such as permanent or temporary residence and Thai nationality.[26]

In the case of Cambodia, for children born to a foreign mother and father, Khmer nationality could only be obtained provided both parents were born and are living legally in Cambodia.[27] A considerable ambiguity around the requirement of legal residency is still present. Such arises from a lack of a clear and accessible system to provide 'immigrant aliens'[28] with any required residence or immigration documents, including how to prove legal residence for Cambodia's long-term residents such as the ethnic Vietnamese (classified as 'immigrant aliens' by Cambodian authorities).[29] The strict demand in the 1996 Nationality Law, therefore, precludes children born to any migrant parent who was born abroad and/or to any parent staying irregularly in Cambodia from acquiring citizenship at birth.

c. ***Lack of or Minimal Safeguards***

In the Philippines, the status of one's statelessness must be first determined by the country's Statelessness Determination Procedure. Once determined stateless, the person can apply for judicial or administrative naturalisation under the Philippine Law.

The Constitution of Singapore grants a general discretion to the Government to confer citizenship 'where it considers it just and fair and having regard to all circumstances of the case'.[30] There are no further requirements imposed in relation to the

---

[25] Section 7(2) of the Thai Nationality Act 2008 (No.4) B.E. 2551.

[26] Section 7(2) of the Thai Nationality Act 2008 (No.4) B.E. 2551. In pledging to meet 'zero statelessness' in Thailand by 2024, the Thai government has urged the districts in the country to identify stateless students and issue the eligible ones with legal status, ranging from Thai nationality to permanent or temporary residence. See N. Jedsadachaiyut & N. Al-Jasem, 'Overcoming Statelessness in Thailand One Case at a Time' (24 November 2016). Retrieved from http://www.unhcr.org/news/latest/2016/11/5836af624/overcoming-statelessness-thailand- case-time.html [Accessed 5 March 2017].

[27] Article 4(2)(a) of the Cambodian Law on Nationality, Decree No. NS/RKM/1096/31, 1996. Note that the previous 1954 Cambodian nationality law only required one parent to be born in Cambodia and without any legal residence requirement. See J. Mudrick, 'Revisiting Cambodia's Laws on Nationality and Immigration', *The Cambodia Daily*. Retrieved from https://www.cambodiadaily.com/opinion/revisiting-cambodias-laws-on-nationality-and-immigration-57,789/ [Accessed 17 November 2014].

[28] This term refers to aliens who are legally residing in Cambodia undertaking their professions, or aliens not included in any of the categories belonging to 'non-immigrant aliens' according to Article 4 of the Law on Immigration of 1994 (Promulgated by Decree No. 05/NS/1994 on 22 September 1994).

[29] C. Sperfeldt & Lyma Nguyen, 'A Boat Without Anchors: A Report on the Legal Status of Ethnic Vietnamese Minority Populations in Cambodia under Domestic and International Laws Governing Nationality and Statelessness'. *RegNet Research Paper No. 2014/50* (2012), p 33–34.

[30] Article 121(3) of the Constitution of the Republic of Singapore (1965).

exercise of this discretion, which could make it useful for avoidance of statelessness.[31] Brunei likewise has a general provision affording minors of any subject to be registered as a subject of His Majesty upon application[32] and for minors to be caused to be registered as the same in special circumstances as His Majesty thinks fit.[33] Section 6(1) and (2) may apply to adopted children of Bruneian citizens.[34] Yet, such discretionary-based provisions will not fully guarantee protection against statelessness at birth, just as in the case of Article 15A of the Malaysian Federal Constitution that empowers the Minister in charge to register any person under the age of 21 under special circumstances.

Myanmar and Brunei are countries of double *jus sanguinis* system. In both countries, acquisition of nationality at birth by automatic means can only be obtained by children of both parents who are nationals of the respective countries. The parents must also belong to one of the indigenous races required by the law of each country.[35] No specific safeguards exist in both countries for nationality to be granted to children born on their territories who would otherwise be stateless.

3. Children Born to Non-Stateless Refugee Parents Unable or Unwilling (for valid reasons) to Confer Nationality upon Children

Relevant international standards:
As for children of refugees who are able to acquire nationality *jus sanguinis* of their parents at birth, Guidelines No. 4, paragraph 28 recognises their *de facto* stateless status. (Comparable with paragraph 18 of Dakar Conclusions)

(i) Such children, therefore, may enjoy the benefit housed in the Final Act of the 1961 Convention, as they are not by law regarded as *de jure* stateless

[31] Ko Swan Sik, *Nationality and International Law in Asian Perspectives* (The Hague: T.M.C. Asser Institute, 1990), p 450–451.

[32] Article 6 (1) of the Brunei Nationality Act, No. 4 of 1961.

[33] Article 6 (2) of the Brunei Nationality Act, No. 4 of 1961.

[34] Section 6 (3) of the Brunei Nationality Act, No. 4 of 1961.

[35] See Sects. 5 and 7 of the 1982 Myanmar Citizenship Law and Section 4(1)(a) and (b) of the Brunei Nationality Act, No. 4 of 1961. Section 5 of the 1982 Myanmar Citizenship Law provides that 'Every national and every person born of parents, both of whom are nationals are citizens by birth'. Under section 3, 'Nationals belonging to the Kachin, Kayah, Karen, Chin, Burman, Mon, Rakhine or Shan and ethnic groups as have settled in any of the territories included within the State as their permanent home from a period anterior to 1185 B.E., 1823 A.D. are Burma citizens' i.e. they must prove that their ancestors have settled before the stated year. Section 7 additionally acknowledges two other types of citizenship, namely 'associate citizen' (further defined and elaborated in Sects. 23–41) and 'naturalised citizen' (further defined in Sects. 42 to 45). Section 4(1) (a) of the Brunei Nationality Act 4 of 1961 requires the person born in Brunei to be accepted as belonging to any of the indigenous groups of the Malay race, namely Belait, Bisayah, Brunei, Dusun, Kedayan, Murut or Tutong, or under section 4(1)(b), to be born to both parents who were born in Brunei and are members of any of the groups of people specified in the First Schedule to the Act.

(ii) It is further recommended that the states of birth offer such children the opportunity to acquire their nationality according to Article 1(1) of the 1961 Convention. States are reminded that it is undesirable to attribute nationality *ex lege* under Article 1(1) in cases where such children could acquire the nationality of the states of origin of the refugee parents, in particular where either state prohibits dual nationality

a. ***Minimal Safeguards***

i. Minimal Safeguards by Way of Access to Facilitated Naturalisation or Naturalisation

Viet Nam has introduced a facilitated naturalisation procedure under its revised Law on Vietnamese Nationality in 2008. Foreign nationals may apply to be naturalised after 5 years of residence in the country and meeting other prescribed conditions.[36] By the end of 2012, former Cambodian refugees in Viet Nam were able to acquire Vietnamese citizenship. Generations of children born to former refugees were also able to benefit from Vietnamese nationality.[37] For stateless persons who have resided for more than 20 years, the application fees for naturalisation, Vietnamese language certificate, and proof of renunciation of the previous nationality were not imposed.[38]

The refugees in the Philippines, a signatory to the 1951 Refugee Convention, are able to obtain citizenship in the same manner as other non-citizens.[39] The applicants must be 21 years and above and must meet other requirements, among others, language competency and real estate ownership/ having a profession or business in the Philippines.[40] Subject to any of the special qualifications provided such as having been born in the Philippines or being married to a Filipino woman, facilitated naturalisation may apply whereby the normal period of 10 years of continuous residence may be reduced to 5 years.[41] Children born to such naturalised parents are considered to be the Philippine citizens.[42]

Under Article ~~4~~9 (2) of the 2018 Cambodian Law on Nationality, any child who is born to a foreign mother and father who were born and living legally in the Kingdom

[36] Article 19(1) of the Law on Vietnamese Nationality, Order No. 22/2008L-TN, 2008.

[37] UNHCR, *Submission by the United Nations High Commissioner for Refugees for the Office of the High Commissioner for Human Rights' Compilation Report—Universal Periodic Review: Universal Periodic Review: Socialist Republic of Vietnam* (June 2013), p 1.

[38] Lyma Nguyen, *Report on Citizenship Law: Vietnam* (September 2017), p 17. Retrieved from http://cadmus.eui.eu/bitstream/handle/1814/47966/GLOBALCIT_ CR_2017_13.pdf?sequence = 1. [Accessed 7 September 2018].

[39] UNHCR, *Universal Periodic Review: The Philippines* (December 2011), p 2.

[40] Section 2 of Act to Provide for the Acquisition of Philippine Citizenship by Naturalisation and to Repeal Acts Numbered Twenty-Nine Hundred and Twenty- Seven and Thirty-Four Hundred and Forty-Eight (Commonwealth Act No. 473, 1939).

[41] Section 3(5) of Commonwealth Act No. 473, 1939.

[42] Section 15 of Commonwealth Act No. 473, 1939.

of Cambodia shall obtain Khmer nationality. Article 7, on the other hand, provides for the conditions of naturalisation of non-citizens. A minimum of 7 years of legal residence is required to start the naturalisation process. These two provisions should be applicable to refugees. Unfortunately, in practice, proof of legal residence for refugees in Cambodia can be problematic as refugees were reported not being issued with residency cards, despite Cambodia being one of the only two countries in SEA that have signed the 1951 Refugee Convention.[43] It has also not been demonstrated in the literature as to how the provision and practice of recognising dual nationality may benefit children born to refugees in the country.

ii. Minimal Safeguards through the Grant of Permanent Residence (PR)

On top of the lack of the legal frameworks governing refugees and stateless, Malaysia is not a signatory to ICCPR and places its reservation on Article 7 CRC on the right of children to acquire a nationality. In limited circumstances where local integration has been the approach to resolve refugee situations, as what has been pursued in the case of Filipino refugees fleeing the southern part of the Philippines in the 1970s and 1980s into Sabah, children born to either or both refugee parents stand a chance to acquire Malaysian citizenship *ex lege*.

This is possible for children born in lawful wedlock to a Filipino refugee parent, who, by virtue of holding IMM13, a legal residence permit issued under Regulation 11(10), Malaysian Immigration Regulations 1963, has been granted the status of Malaysian Permanent Resident by the Malaysian authority.[44] It is to be noted that the grant of PR is also a pre-condition for an application of naturalisation under Article 19 of the Federal Constitution. The refugees in Sabah holding IMM13 as such benefit from a more secure status as compared to those refugees in the Peninsula, including the Rohingya refugees, for the former's ability to reside with their dependents, work legally, and apply for the PR status after residing between 15 and 19 years in Sabah.[45]

[43] E. Pearson, 'Cambodia is not Safe for Refugees', *Human Rights Watch News*. https://www.hrw.org/news/2014/05/22/cambodia-not-safe-refugees [Accessed 16 March 2016]. It has been reported in the news quoted here that refugees originating from China (ethnic Uighurs) and Khmer Krom activists from Viet Nam were subject to forcible deportation to their countries of origin. Note that Cambodia became a State Party to the 1951 Refugee Convention in 1992.

[44] Article 14(1)(b), read together with Second Schedule, Part II, 1(a) to (d) of the Federal Constitution of Malaysia (1957).

[45] Commissioners of Enquiry on Immigrants in Sabah, *Report of The Commission of Enquiry on Immigrants in Sabah* (2014), p 234. Retrieved from http://www.sapp.org.my/rci/RCI-Eng.pdf [Accessed 9 January 2016]. At one time, local integration solution was almost attained in the Rohingya case in Malaysia. In 2004, the Government after its negotiation with UNHCR agreed to grant temporary residence permits to 10,000 Rohingya refugees residing in the country. Such would have allowed the Rohingya to be legally absorbed into the workforce that experienced a critical shortage, and for schools to accept the Rohingya children. Unfortunately, the implementation was aborted just days after it took off in August 2016. This was due to alleged corrupt practices on the part of local agencies and Rohingya volunteers involved in the implementation exercise outsourced to them, and the arrival of some 8,000 Rohingyas, triggered by the possibility of work permits. Further in 2010, the Government came up with another plan to issue identification cards without employment right. However, the Home Ministry rejected the proposal of issuing any card to illegals and due to this pushback, the idea was again dropped. For details, see C. Lewa, 'Asia's New Boat

While Thailand is a party to ICCPR[46] and CRC,[47] subject to section 7 of its 2008 Nationality Act, children born to migrant parents in its territory would be excluded from the acquisition of nationality at birth if their parents are not holders of PR or are staying irregularly without any residence status.

For the vast majority of the Burmese refugees in Thailand living in nine refugee camps near the Thai-Burma border, who might themselves have been rendered stateless under the law of Myanmar, neither resettlement nor local integration serves as a durable solution in their case. Mainly treated as having no legal status, the Thai Government had in the past accommodated access to Thai nationality for displaced persons in the country. However, for recently displaced persons such as the Karen and Karenni in the camps, they are merely entitled to protection and access to facilities in the camps so long as the situation in Burma does not permit repatriation.[48] In 2019, the Thai Government approved the National Screening Mechanism to identify those in need of protection. However, the regulation has been criticised for its failure to meet the international refugee legal definition and unclear policies in protecting refugees.[49]

iii. Other Minimal Safeguards

Naturalisation provisions are available in Brunei subject to at least 25 years of residence in the country and other prescribed requirements.[50] In Singapore, the period of residence for naturalisation is not less than 10 years.[51] For Brunei and Singapore, the discretionary provisions to grant citizenship appear to be helpful.[52] However, this may not be invoked if it would result in a dual nationality. Under Article 8(a) of the

People', *Forced Migration Review (FMR),* 30 (June 2008); S. Cheung, 'Migration Control and the Solutions Impasse in South and Southeast Asia: Implications from the Rohingya Experience', p 55.

[46] Acceded 29 October 1996. See UN Treaty Collection. Retrieved from https://treaties.un.org/Pages/ViewDetails.aspx?src=IND&mtdsg_no=IV-4&chapter=4&lang=en#EndDec.

[47] Acceded 27 March 1992, with reservation to the application of Article 22. See UN Treaty Collection, Retrieved from https://treaties.un.org/Pages/ViewDetails.aspx?src=IND&mtdsg_no=IV-11&chapter=4&lang=en#EndDec [Accessed 10 August 2015].

[48] For instance, displaced persons of Thai race and Burmese nationality identified with Yellow Card or with Blue Border who continued to settle in Thai territories after the demarcation of the boundary between Siam and Burma were approved for naturalisation if they entered Thailand before 10/02/1976. The children of Burmese displaced persons with Burmese Nationality ID Cards identified by their possession of Pink Cards were eligible for Thai citizenship if they were born between 24/12/1972–25/02/1976. See Pinkaew Laungaramsri, 'Crafting Citizenship: Cards, Colours and The Politics of Identification in Thailand', pp 1–31, p 14 and p 19; I. Brees, 'Refugee Business: Strategies of Work on the Thai–Burma Border', *Journal of Refugee Studies*, 21(3)(2008), p 384.

[49] T. Lewis and D.Davies, 'A new era for refugee protection in Thailand', (19 March 2020), *The Bangkok Post*, Retrieved from https://www.bangkokpost.com/opinion/opinion/1881970/a-new-era-for-refugee-protection-in-thailand-_ [Accessed 30 March 2020].

[50] Section 8 of Brunei Nationality Act 1961.

[51] Article 127 of the Constitution of the Republic of Singapore 1965.

[52] For Brunei, such refer to the registration of minors under Section 6 of the Brunei Nationality Act 4 of 1961, or non-minors' application to be registered as citizens subject to their prescribed period of lawful residence and other conditions listed. For Singapore, such refers to Article 121(3) of the Constitution of the Republic of Singapore 1965.

Myanmar Citizenship Law 1982, the President of the State or the Union Government may confer citizenship, including associate or naturalised citizenship when this is in the interest of the state. However, naturalisation is still subject to the category of citizenship of one's parents.[53]

4. Children Born to Parents of Unclear or Undetermined Nationality

Relevant international standards:

(a) The 1961 Convention [Articles 1 and 4]
(b) CRC [Article 7(1) in conjunction with Article 3(1)]
(c) Guidelines No. 4 [Paragraph 22—Immediate determination whether the child would otherwise be stateless; and Paragraph 23—States that grant their nationality to otherwise stateless children automatically are to treat children of undetermined nationality as possessing the nationality of the state of birth unless and until the possession of another nationality is proven]
(d) Council of Europe Recommendation 2009/13 on the Nationality of Children [Principle 1, paragraph 8 that states: 'Register children as being of unknown or undetermined nationality, or classify children's nationality as being "under investigation"' only for as short a period as possible']
(e) General Comment No. 17 to Article 24 ICCPR [Paragraph 8 on the duty of States to cooperate in order to ensure every child has a nationality when he is born]
(f) Recommendation 2009/13 on the Nationality of Children [Principle 1, paragraph 6—The duty of states to cooperate closely on issues of statelessness of children, including exchanging information on nationality legislation and public policies, and on nationality details in individual cases]
(g) AALCO Resolution of 8 April 2006 [Paragraph 4—States are encouraged to cooperate in identifying statelessness with the main objective of establishing identity and obtaining relevant documentation for women, children, and families affected by displacement, migration, and trafficking]

The lack of nationality determination procedures in the ASEAN Member States other than the Philippines may present an obstacle for children born to parents of undetermined nationality to acquire a nationality at birth. Children born to undocumented or irregular migrants, who may include asylum seekers, bear the biggest brunt of this lack of, or undetermined nationality status.

[53] S. Petcharamasree & B. Napaumporn, Legal Identity of All Women and Children in ASEAN: A Regional Synthesis. ASEAN (2020), p 50.

a. ***Strong Safeguards***

Indonesia seems to stand out among the rest of the ASEAN Member States for being the only country that expressly provides its full *jus soli* safeguard for children born in its territory whose parents are of undetermined citizenship at the time of birth. Its nationality law provides under Article 4 (9) that:

'A Citizen of the Republic of Indonesia is:

> Children born in Indonesian territory whose parents are of undetermined citizenship at the time of the child's birth'.[54]

b. ***Minimal Safeguards***

In the Philippines, other than determination of statelessness that could result in acquisition of nationality via a judicial or an administrative order, in practice, the Philippines initiated a nationality verification procedure. A mapping exercise carried out by UNHCR and the governments of Indonesia and the Philippines in 2012 and 2013, respectively, detected approximately 6,000 people of Indonesian descent living with uncertain or undetermined nationality.[55] Most of them were children, grandchildren and great-grandchildren whose ancestors moved there many generations ago. Living without legal status, they suffered from poor access to legal employment, particularly outside of their mixed community of Filipinos and Indonesians, and discriminatory treatment in their employment and immigration penalties.[56]

On a positive note, the outcome of the said mapping study carried out by UNHCR led both the governments of Indonesia and the Philippines to initiate verification of nationality of such persons of Indonesian descent in Mindanao.[57] In March 2014, a batch of 660 people in the southern Philippines had their citizenship confirmed via a confirmation and registration of persons of Indonesian descent.[58]

In the case of Thailand, subject to section 7 *bis* of the Thai Nationality Act 2008 (No. 4), B.E. 2551, children of migrant parents who are irregular are excluded from the acquisition of nationality at birth if their parents are not permanent residents or staying without any legal residence status.[59] A formal mechanism for nationality

---

[54] N. Oakeshott, 'Statelessness in the Asia Pacific: Introduction and Context', Presentation Slides.

[55] UNHCR, 'Stateless in the Philippines: Indonesia Descendants Feel eTorn between Two Lands', http://www.unhcr.org/5416d3519.html. [Accessed 10 August 2014].

[56] UNHCR, 'Stateless in the Philippines: Indonesia Descendants Feel Torn between Two Lands', http://www.unhcr.org/5416d3519.html. [Accessed 10 August 2014].

[57] UNHCR, 'Stateless in the Philippines: Indonesia Descendants Feel Torn between Two Lands', http://www.unhcr.org/5416d3519.html. [Accessed 10 August 2014].

[58] UNHCR, *The Campaign to End Statelessness: Campaign Update* (2016).

[59] Thai nationality may be available if the parents are registered with the temporary right to reside in Thailand leading to legal residence status, subject to eligibility and documentary requirements

verification exists, albeit for legalisation purposes leading to temporary travel documents being issued to migrant workers from the three countries with which Thailand has entered into bilateral agreements, namely Cambodia, Myanmar, and Lao PDR.

c. ***Lack of Safeguards***

In Malaysia, a temporary resident pass used to be issued to children born in the country to parents whose citizenship could not be ascertained during their birth registration. The pass, known as 'Kad Pengenalan Pemastautin Sementara' (temporary resident identity card) or 'MyKas' is regulated and issued according to Regulation 5(3) (c)(ii) of the National Registration Regulations 1990 (Amendment 2001).[60] The burden lies with the holder of this pass to prove his or her citizenship.[61] Prior to the expiry of the 5 years' validity period of MyKas, the holder may apply for renewal of the pass, subject to getting the approval from the Malaysian Registration Department. Unlike the grant of PR, which paves the way for naturalisation under Article 19 of the Federal Constitution, possessing MyKas as a temporary resident does not lead to acquisition of Malaysian citizenship. As such, children in possession of MyKas or born to holders of MyKas are not protected from statelessness through the acquisition of Malaysian citizenship.[62]

No safeguard against statelessness for children born to parents of undetermined citizenship can be found in Singapore, Brunei, and Viet Nam. On the whole, Indonesia, Thailand, and the Philippines appear to be ahead of other countries in the region with their respective initiatives as highlighted. Nonetheless, only Indonesia fully meets the standard of prevention and reduction of statelessness at birth for stipulating clearly that children born to parents of undetermined citizenship are automatically entitled to its citizenship *jus soli.*

---

announced via the relevant Cabinet resolutions. Such may include, for instance, the Hill Tribe population surveyed and classified as 'aliens' according to Project for Granting Alien Status to the Immigrants in 1995 who could fulfil the conditions for eligibility determined by the relevant Cabinet resolution(s).

[60] Jabatan Pendaftaran Negara, 'Kad Pengenalan Pemaustautin Sementara (MyKas)', Media Statement by Datuk Jariah Mohd Said, Ketua Pengarah Pendaftaran Negara (29 April 2013), https://www.astroawani.com/berita-pilihanraya/tiada-mykas-dikeluar-untuk-warga-asing-mengundi-jpn-13141. [Accessed 6 April 2016].

[61] Rodziana Mohamed Razali, *Protection against Statelessness at Birth: International and Domestic Legal Frameworks of ASEAN Member States with a Special Case Study on Kota Kinabalu, Sabah* (2017), p 201.

[62] See JPN, Portal Feedback, National registration Department. Retrieved from http://intranet.jpn.gov.my/emaklumbalas/publish.php?p=4 [Accessed 15 July 2016].

5. Children Born Abroad and Children Born Out of Wedlock (Parents Unable to Confer Nationality due to Gender Discrimination or Lack of Parental Recognition)

Relevant international standards:

(a) The 1961 Convention [Articles 1, 3 and 4]
(b) CRC [Article 7(1) in conjunction with Article 3(1)]
(c) CEDAW [Article 9(2)]
(d) Guidelines No. 4 [Paragraph 4 – on the ability of children who would otherwise be stateless to similarly acquire the nationality of their fathers who are nationals]

In countries that adopt the principle of *jus sanguinis*, nationality attribution and acquisition may differ according to several factors, such as the father's versus the mother's right to transfer nationality by descent, the requirement of whether one or both parents have to have the country's nationality, and the role that marital status of the parents plays in determining the child's entitlement to a nationality *jus sanguinis.*

Generally, children originating from the ASEAN Member States who are born abroad are entitled to the citizenship of at least one of their parents by way of *jus sanguinis.* Therefore, there are no specific safeguards for children born abroad where one parent is a national.[63] However, the lack of gender-sensitive nationality provisions can expose children born abroad and children born out of wedlock to the risk of becoming stateless.

a. ***Strong Safeguards***

Gender equality regarding the transmission of Thai nationality has been in place since 1992. Children born abroad to a Thai parent are entitled to Thai nationality.[64] With the amendment effected under the Thai Nationality Act (No. 4), B.E. 2551 (2008), children born out of wedlock can now acquire the nationality of his or her Thai father. Section 6 of the said Act provides a redefinition of 'father' to mean:

> a person having been proved, in conformity with the Ministerial Regulation, that he is truly the father of the person even though he did not register marriage with the mother of the person or did not do a registration of legitimate child.

This definition differs from the definition of 'father' in the previous Thai Nationality Act of 1965 that imposed a stricter requirement that a father must be legally

[63] N. Oakeshott, 'An Analysis of Nationality Laws in South East Asia', Presentation Slides.

[64] See Section 7 of the Thai Nationality Act 2008 (No. 4) B.E. 2551. 'The following persons acquire Thai nationality by birth: 1) a person born of a father or a mother of Thai nationality, whether within or outside the Kingdom of Thailand; 2) a person born within the Kingdom of Thailand except for the person under Section 7 bis, para one.

proved. Another positive aspect is that the effect of this amendment is retrospective.[65] As such, children born in and out of a registered marriage in the Kingdom to a Thai father or mother are entitled to Thai citizenship. A child born out of wedlock to a Thai father and an alien mother outside of Thailand may not however enjoy the same right to acquire citizenship automatically.[66]

In Singapore, children are safeguarded against statelessness as long as one parent is a citizen of Singapore. Article 121(2)(c) of the Constitution of the Republic of Singapore 1965 provides that a person born in Singapore after 16 September 1963 shall not be a citizen at the time of his birth if 'neither of his parents was a citizen of Singapore'. In Indonesia, dual nationality is tolerated whereby children born in or outside of the country may acquire Indonesian citizenship, including when the law of the country of birth abroad grants nationality by operation of law to the child.[67]

Except for Thailand, children, however, may not be fully safeguarded against statelessness in Cambodia, Viet Nam, Malaysia, Singapore, and Indonesia if they are born out of wedlock. This could be due to further administrative requirements to be met or as a result of gender discrimination, as shall be highlighted below.

b. ***Partial Safeguards***

In Viet Nam, a child is considered legitimate regardless of whether the parents are married or not.[68] In such a case, a child born out of wedlock is safeguarded against statelessness as long as either parent holds Vietnamese citizenship, or both parents are stateless with a PR status, or in the case of a stateless mother, she holds a PR status if the father is unknown.[69] However, where the child's mother is a non-citizen, undocumented or stateless without a PR status, an administrative procedure is necessary for recognition to be made by the father in order that the child may benefit from the father's Vietnamese citizenship. The father has to recognise or acknowledge the child by making and submitting a written confirmation to the competent state agencies that he is the biological father of the child. The decision of the competent state agencies on the determination of the father, mother, and child shall be recorded

---

65 N. Oakeshott & Bongkot Napaumporn, 'Statelessness in South East Asia', Presentation Slides, Regional Statelessness Course: South East Asia Focus, Bangkok, Thailand, 4–8 November 2013; L. K. Kerber, 'Birthright Citizenship: The Vulnerability and Resilience of American Constitutional Principle' (2011); J. Bhabha (Ed.), *Children Without a State: A Global Human Rights Challenge* (Cambridge, London, England: MIT Press, 2011), p 264.

66 S. Petcharamasree & B. Napaumporn, Legal Identity of All Women and Children in ASEAN: A Regional Synthesis. ASEAN (2020). Retrieved from https://asean.org/?static_post=legal-identity-women-children-asean-regional-synthesis. [Accessed 5 December 2020], p 45.

67 Article 4(12) Law on Citizenship of the Republic of Indonesia, Decree No. 12, 2006.

68 See Government of the United Kingdom, 'Legitimation and Domicile'. Retrieved from https://www.gov.uk/government/uploads/system/uploads/attachment_data/file/118568/legitimation-and-domicile.pdf. [Accessed 16 March 2015].

69 Articles 16 and 17 Law on Vietnamese Nationality, Order No. 22/2008/L-CTN, 2008.

in the civil status book of previous registration of the child's birth.[70] When the father refuses to recognise the child, then the child may be at risk of statelessness.[71]

In Cambodia, there must be recognition of a non-marital child or child born out of wedlock as a child born to a parent of Khmer nationality;[72] or alternatively, a court judgment can be obtained declaring that the child was born to a Khmer national or citizen.[73] A non-marital child in Cambodia could still be rendered at risk of statelessness if his Cambodian parent of Khmer nationality refuses to recognise him, and a court judgment is not obtained on the child's behalf to declare that he or she was born to a Khmer national.

As for Lao PDR, a child born to either parent who has Lao citizenship is considered a Lao citizen if the child is born in the country.[74] If born abroad, the child is a citizen only when either parent has a permanent address in the territory of the Lao PDR.[75] When a child is born to one parent who is a Lao citizen and the other an *apatrid* (a stateless person), the child is considered a Lao citizen at birth without regard to the child's place of birth.[76]

The law does not distinguish between marital and non-marital children born to either parent who is a Lao citizen in its territory. However, a father's affiliation to a non-marital child has to take place according to the rules stipulated under Article 30 of the Family Law of the Lao PDR No. 97/P 1990. Where the child is unable to acquire the nationality through his or her mother and the father refuses to submit a common request for a voluntary affiliation or disputes it, the child could face the risk of statelessness. However, the child's mother, caregiver, or guardian is still given the right to request the court to consider making a finding of affiliation.[77]

In Indonesia, children of mixed parentage (involving an Indonesian parent and an alien or stateless parent) may acquire citizenship in two situations, namely when the children are born in legal wedlock and out of wedlock. Under Article 4 of the Law of the Republic of Indonesia Number 12, 2006, children of mixed parentage who are born in a legal wedlock may acquire Indonesian citizenship if they are born:

(3) from an Indonesian father and an alien mother,
(4) from an alien father and an Indonesian mother,
(5) from an Indonesian mother and a stateless father, or where the child cannot acquire the father's citizenship based on the law of the father's country.

[70] Article 42 of Section 8, Decree No. 158/2005/ND-CP of December 27, 2005, on Civil Status Registration and Management (Decree No. 158/2005).

[71] Article 17(2) Law on Vietnamese Nationality, Order No. 22/2008/L-CTN, 2008.

[72] Article 9(1) of the Cambodian Law on Nationality, Decree No. NS/RKT/0618/008, 2018.

[73] Article 9(1) of the Cambodian Law on Nationality, Decree No. NS/RKT/0618/008, 2018.

[74] Article 10(1) of the Law on Lao Nationality, No.06/90/PSA, 1990.

[75] Article 10(2) of the Law on Lao Nationality, No.06/90/PSA, 1990.

[76] Article 10(2) of the Law on Lao Nationality, No.06/90/PSA, 1990.

[77] Article 30 (Replaced with Decree of the President of the Lao People's Democratic Republic on the Promulgation of the Law on Family Registration No. 21, 1992 (Family Registration Decree No 21/1992)).

For children of mixed parentage born out of wedlock, attribution of an Indonesian nationality under Article 4 is provided to:

(7) children born from an Indonesian mother,
(8) children born from an alien mother who is acknowledged by the Indonesian father as his natural child and the said acknowledgment is made before the child reaches 18 or before the child has married.

Article 5(a) further serves as a safety net provision for unmarried children of Indonesian citizens below 18 who are born out of wedlock and not legally adopted by their alien fathers. Under this provision, the law shall continue to consider them as Indonesian citizens.[78] Regrettably, children below 18 born out of wedlock and who have been married fall outside the scope of the safeguard under Article 4(8).

Parents' subsequent legal marriage is said to have the effect of legitimising an 'illegitimate' child in Indonesia provided the parents were married religiously.[79] As for Muslim spouses who are married according to religious rites without registering their marriage,[80] their child is ascribed to the mother on the child's birth certificate.[81] If the mother is stateless, then the child would also be stateless, unless the child prior to reaching 18 years old, acquires the Indonesian father's citizenship through the latter's claim of his paternity under Article 4(8) of the Law on Citizenship of the Republic of Indonesia, Decree No. 12, or, through scientific proof of fatherhood such as DNA evidence.

In the case of religious marriages, Article 49 of Undang-Undang Republik Indonesia,[82] Nomor 24 Tahun 2013 Tentang Perubahan Atas Undang-Undang Nomor

---

[78] Where this could result in dual citizenship of the child, the child is required to choose one citizenship upon reaching the age of 18. See Article 6(1) Law on Citizenship of the Republic of Indonesia, Decree No. 12, 2006, that reads, 'The Indonesian citizenship status of children as determined in Article 4 Law on Citizenship of the Republic of Indonesia, Decree No. 12, 2006 Items c, d, h and i, and Article 5 will effect in the dual citizenship of the child. Upon reaching the age of 18 (eighteen) or upon marriage, the child must choose one citizenship'.

[79] Article 50 of Undang-Undang Republik Indonesia, Nomor 24 Tahun 2013 Tentang Perubahan Atas Undang-Undang Nomor 23 Tahun 2006 Tentang Administrasi Kependudukan (Law 24 of 2013 on Population Administration).

[80] Known as 'kahwin siri' or 'nikah siri' in Indonesia. See *hukum online.com*, 'Pertanyaan: Perbedaan Perkahwinan Beda Agama Secara "Siri" dan di Luar Negeri', http://www.hukumonline.com/klinik/detail/cl2214/perbedaan-perkawinan-beda-agama-secara-siri-dan-di-luar-negeri.

[81] See Pasal 55 ayat (2) Peraturan Pemerintah No. 37 Tahun 2007 Tentang Pelaksanaan Undang-Undang No. 23 Tahun 2006 Tentang Administrasi Kependudukan.

[82] To be read with Article 43 (ayat 1), Undang-Undang No. 1 Tahun 1974 Tentang Perkahwinan and the decision of the Constitutional Court of the Republic of Indonesia No. 46/PUU-VIII/2010 dated 17 February 2012. Note that Article 43 (ayat 1) of the 1974 Law on Marriage provides that 'Anak yang dilahirkan di luar perkahwinan hanya mempunyai hubungan perdata dengan ibunya dan keluarga ibunya' ('A child born out of wedlock only has a legal relationship with his mother and the mother's family'). The decision of the Constitutional Court referred here provides a significant reinterpretation of the law by concluding that a child born out of wedlock does not only have a civil legal relationship (*hubungan pendata*) with the child's mother but also with the man (and his family) proven through science and technology and/or other evidence according to the law to be the child's biological father. See also R. Pramudatama, 'Constitutional Court Affirms "Illegitimate"

23 Tahun 2006 Tentang Administrasi Kependudukan (Law 24 of 2013 on Population Administration) provides that if there is a statutory declaration signed by the father proving that he is the father of the child, then the civil registry will furnish a certificate as evidence of this recognition by the father and mother that they are the parents of the child (*kutipan akta pengakuan anak*).[83] In practice, however, legalisation of marriages by the courts may still be needed for a birth certificate to be issued with the father's name to be on it, the absence of which shall affect the status of children born to unmarried parents or parents married religiously.[84]

In the Philippines, prior to and after the promulgation of the 1935 Constitution, non-marital children could only acquire the nationality of their Filipino mothers. The distinctions between marital and non-marital statuses have been watered down following the coming into effect of the 1973 Constitution. Under the 1973 Constitution, children born not only to Filipino mothers but also to Filipino fathers are entitled to be granted Philippine nationality.[85] This rule is preserved in the subsequent 1987 Constitution.[86]

The 1987 Constitution of the Philippines provides that a person born to a Filipino mother or father is a citizen of the country.[87] It appears that to avoid the risk of statelessness, an act of legitimation through the parents' subsequent marriage or the Filipino father's filiation, recognition, or admission of paternity may be required for the child to acquire Philippine citizenship through the paternal line, particularly if the mother is stateless or a non-national.[88] Otherwise, a non-marital child is under the parental authority of the mother and takes the mother's citizenship.[89]

Children's Rights', *Jakarta Post* (2012). Retrieved from http://thejakartapost.com/news/2012/02/18/constitutional-court-affirms-illegitimate-children-s-rights.html. [Accessed 22 June 2016].

[83] Article 49 Undang-Undang Republik Indonesia, Nomor 24 Tahun 2013 Tentang Perubahan Atas Undang-Undang Nomor 23 Tahun 2006 Tentang Administrasi Kependudukan (Law 24 of 2013 on Population Administration).

[84] A.L. Buffardi & Kwan Men Yon, *Realising the Right to Legal Identity: A case study as part of an evaluation as part of the Australia Indonesia Partnership for Justice* (July 2016) https://www.refworld.org/pdfid/57922cfd4.pdf [Accessed 8 January 2018].

[85] Article 111(1)(2) of the 1935 Commonwealth Constitution, the 1973 Constitution, and the 1986 Freedom Constitution.

[86] See Article IV(1)(2) of the 1987 Constitution of the Republic of the Philippines. See the analysis of the nationality status of illegitimate children under the different Constitutions of the Philippines in Ko Swan Sik, *Nationality and International Law in Asian Perspectives* (The Hague: T.M.C. Asser Institute, 1990), p 358–360.

[87] See Section 1(2) of Article IV of the 1987 Constitution of the Republic of the Philippines.

[88] Note that admission or recognition of paternity can be made by way of an Affidavit of Admission of Paternity and other enumerated public documents or a Private Handwritten Instrument in the handwriting of the father and duly signed by him. See Rules 2.1 and 2.2 of Republic Act 9255, an Act allowing illegitimate children to use the surname of their father, amending for the Purpose Article 176 of Executive Order 209, and Administrative Order No. 1, Series of 2016.

[89] The Republic of the Philippines vs Nora Fe Sagun, G. R. No. 187567 of 15 February 2012.

c. **Lack of or Minimal Safeguards**

Brunei and Malaysia still have nationality laws that are not in full compliance with CEDAW in respect of citizenship.[90] In both countries, automatic acquisition of nationality at birth for children born abroad can only be acquired if they are born to a citizen father of each country. Myanmar requires both parents to be nationals of the country[91] in order for their children to qualify as citizens in any of the citizenship categories prescribed under its Citizenship Law of 1982. Such rigidity certainly results in many children being excluded from access to its citizenship.[92] The risk of statelessness is magnified by the lack of any provision to grant Burmese citizenship to children born in the country, or to its nationals abroad who would otherwise be stateless.[93]

Lack of gender equality in the transfer of nationality to children adversely affects non-marital children, including those born to citizen and non-citizen parents following their parents' legally unrecognised marriages. In Malaysia, a child born in wedlock in its territory to either parent who is a Malaysian citizen or holder of Malaysian PR acquires citizenship *ex lege* or by operation of law at birth.[94] If the child is born in wedlock outside Malaysia, the law would confer citizenship *ex lege* only if the child's father is a Malaysian citizen. If the child's father is a non-citizen, the child may only acquire his or her Malaysian citizenship through registration at an overseas Malaysian consulate or National Registration Department in Malaysia. Such conferment of citizenship is subject to the discretion of the Home Minister.[95] Therefore, children born outside Malaysia to a Malaysian mother and a foreign or stateless father may be at risk of statelessness if the child could not get citizenship *jus soli* or through the method of registration. This is inconsistent with Article 9 (2) of CEDAW, Article 3 of the 1961 Statelessness Convention, paragraph 4 of Guidelines No. 4, and CRC's Articles 7 and 3.

On the other hand, if the child is born out of wedlock in Malaysia or out of an unregistered marriage, the child may acquire citizenship *ex lege* provided his or her mother holds Malaysian citizenship or has a PR, regardless of the father's citizenship.[96] Safeguards against statelessness at birth are therefore lacking in at

---

[90] Note that Brunei and Malaysia still maintain their reservation to Article 9(2) of CEDAW that confers an equal right to women and men to pass on nationality to their children.

[91] Article 345(a) of the Constitution of the Republic of the Union of Myanmar (2008).

[92] Consideration of reports submitted by States Parties under Article 44 of the Convention, Concluding Observations and Recommendations: Myanmar UN. Doc. CRC/C/MMR/CO/3–4. Myanmar: CRC, 14 March 2012, para 41(b).

[93] Consideration of reports submitted by States Parties under Article 44 of the Convention, Concluding Observations and Recommendations: Myanmar UN. Doc. CRC/C/MMR/CO/3–4. Myanmar: CRC, 14 March 2012, para 41(a).

[94] Article 14(1)(b) and Part II, Section 1(a), Federal Constitution of Malaysia.

[95] Article 14, part II, section 1(c) Federal Constitution of Malaysia; UNHCR, 'Background Note on Gender Equality, Nationality Laws and Statelessness' (2016). Retrieved from http://www.unhcr.org/4f5886306.pdf. [Accessed 23 June 2016].

[96] Section 17, Part III of Second Schedule of Federal Constitution of Malaysia. See also Murib Morpi, 'NRD Explains Law, Procedures on Birth Certificate, IC and Citizenship', *Borneo Post*

least two situations for Malaysia, firstly, as a result of the lack of gender neutrality in the transfer of nationality to children born abroad, and secondly, when children are born out of wedlock. In the second situation, the children could fall through the cracks if born to a stateless or non-Malaysian mother unable to confer her foreign nationality, regardless of the place of birth.

In Brunei, racial and double *jus sanguinis* conditions restrict a child born abroad from acquiring Bruneian citizenship at birth. A child may only acquire Bruneian citizenship if born to a father who is a subject of His Majesty (by virtue of the father being born to parents who were also born in Brunei and are members of any of the groups of the Malay race specified in the law); or born to a father who was born in Brunei and belonging to one of the listed groups of the Malay race, and was employed outside Brunei in the service of the Bruneian Government or a company registered in Brunei, or in any such special. circumstances as His Majesty thinks fit, provided that the birth of the child was registered at a Brunei Consulate or in Brunei within 6 months of its occurrence, or such longer period allowed by His Majesty.[97]

A marital or non-marital child of non-Malay parents is not entitled to Bruneian citizenship by operation of law.[98] A Muslim non-marital child shall not be ascribed to the biological father if born prior to 6 *qamariah* months from the date of the marriage.[99] The child, therefore, could face statelessness if he or she is not registered as a subject of His Majesty by virtue of an application of the parent or guardian (in relation to adoption, the 'parent' here refers to the child's adopter), or in such special circumstances as His Majesty thinks fit.[100]

In Singapore, the problem concerning non-marital children born of mixed parentage with one parent having Singaporean citizenship lies in the definition of the word 'parent' and 'father'. Article 15 (1) of the Third Schedule of the Constitution of the Republic of Singapore 1965[101] clearly stipulates that references to a person's father or to his parent or one of his parents shall be construed to refer to the child's mother. Similar to Malaysia, a child born out of wedlock in Singapore to a non-citizen undocumented or stateless mother is highly at risk of statelessness, regardless of the father's citizenship. The legal positions in Malaysia and Singapore for children born out of wedlock are clearly opposed to the international standards applicable to this category.

Online. Retrieved from http://www.theborneopost.com/2013/02/22/nrd-explains-laws-procedures-on-birth-certificate-ic-and-citizenship/. [Accessed 1 April 2014].

[97] See Section 4(1)(b) of the Brunei Nationality Act, No. 4, 1961, Revised Edition (2002).

[98] See Section 4(1) of the Brunei Nationality Act, No. 4, 1961, Revised Edition (2002).

[99] See Section 113 of the Islamic Family Law of Brunei (CAP 217) (Revised Edition 2012). Section 92 of the same statute provides: 'Custody of illegitimate children shall be on the mother and her relative, however, the Court may surrender the child to any party which it thinks appropriate, taking into consideration the welfare, care and education of the child', the Islamic Family Law Order, 1999, Brunei Darussalam, and 'Consideration of reports submitted by States Parties under Article 44 of the Convention, Combined second and third periodic reports of States Parties due in 2008: Brunei Darussalam', UN. Doc. CRC/C/BRN/2–3. Brunei: CRC, 13 July 2015, para 72, p 23.

[100] Sections 6(1) and (2) of the Brunei Nationality Act, No. 4 of 1961, Revised Edition (2002).

[101] Article 140, the Constitution of the Republic of Singapore (1965).

5.4 Summary of Findings

The findings of the preceding analyses shall be summarised in the following tables according to the following categories of the safeguards as described below:

(i) strong safeguards—where the relevant laws and/or practices comply with the international standards;
(ii) partial safeguards—where the relevant laws and/or practices addressing the safeguards fall short of the identified international standards, gaps/obstacles are identified, and/or not all otherwise stateless children are able to benefit from the safeguards; or
(iii) lack of or minimal safeguards—where the relevant laws and/ or practices do not incorporate any safeguard for stateless and otherwise stateless children, or where provisions that may facilitate access to a nationality later in life are identified, including by way of discretionary-based registration and naturalisation (through which children may derive citizenship from their parents) (Tables 5.2, 5.3, 5.4, 5.5 and 5.6).

5.5 Conclusion

In trying to gauge the levels of protection against statelessness at birth in the context of the nationality legal frameworks and related practices of the Member States of ASEAN, the results of the preceding analyses are further mapped in the following table.

Table 5.7 tracks the overall level of strength of the protection against statelessness at birth based on the respective findings for each of the categories of children examined.

The most safeguarded category of children against statelessness at birth is 'children born abroad'. Of the ten countries examined, 70 percent offer full safeguards for this category. Three countries (Malaysia, Brunei and Myanmar) offer minimal or no protection, due to gender and/or racial criteria in their nationality provisions.

The second most protected children are foundlings and young children with an unknown legal identity. Forty percent of the countries comply with the international standards in this area, with 30 percent of others providing partial safeguards, which could exclude young children with an unknown legal identity. Nonetheless, the results further reveal that not a single country safeguards such foundlings from losing their nationality upon proof of discovery of their parent(s)' foreign nationality.

Protection against statelessness for children born to stateless parents comes in third. Only 20 percent of the countries provide unconditional *jus soli* safeguards, 40 percent partially protect the affected children subject to the prescribed limitations, and the remaining 40 percent offer minimal or no safeguard, leaving such children highly vulnerable to statelessness.

For children born out of wedlock, half of the countries protect such children against statelessness, albeit partially, as unperformed administrative procedures relating to

Table 5.2 Protection against statelessness for foundlings and young children separated from parents

Countries with strong safeguards		Countries with partial safeguards		Countries with no or minimal safeguards	
		Malaysia	-Limited to foundlings (newborn)	Thailand	• Minimal safeguard by way of application and with further conditions of residence and certification as outlined in a Cabinet Resolution passed in 2016
				Myanmar	• No safeguard
Indonesia	• Safeguard covers newborn whose parents are undetermined, as well as children whose parents' whereabouts are undetermined at birth	Singapore	• Limited to foundlings (newborn)	Brunei	• No safeguard
Viet Nam	• Safeguard covers both abandoned newborn and children found with unknown parents	The Philippines	• Limited to foundlings • Safeguard exists through case law instead of legislation		
Cambodia	• Safeguard covers both abandoned newborn and children born of unknown mother or father				
Lao PDR	• Safeguard covers children (instead of just foundlings) whose parents' identity is unknown				

Additional Finding:
Countries with safeguards do not provide protection against the possibility of foundlings or children losing nationality acquired at birth and thus becoming stateless due to the discovery of their parent(s)' foreign nationality (i.e. for not being able to acquire their parent's foreign nationality)

Table 5.3 Protection against Statelessness at Birth for Children Born on the Territory to Stateless Parents and Others as Otherwise Stateless Children

Countries with strong safeguards		Countries with partial safeguards		Countries with no or minimal safeguards	
Malaysia	-Safeguard applies with no additional conditions	Lao PDR	-Safeguard applies if both parents are stateless and permanent residents	Singapore	-Minimal safeguard in the form of discretion of the Government to confer citizenship where it is just and fair having regards to circumstances of the case
Indonesia	-Safeguard applies with no additional conditions	Viet Nam	-Safeguard applies if both parents are stateless and permanent residents	The Philippines	-No safeguard
		Thailand	-Safeguard applies to children of alien parents with permanent residence (which may be granted to stateless persons) or with lawful residence in Thailand (where nationality can be granted to their parents following any Cabinet resolutions)	Myanmar	-No safeguard
		Cambodia	-Safeguard applies if both parents were born and have legal residence in Cambodia	Brunei	-Minimal safeguard in the form of discretion of His Majesty to cause any minor to be registered as a subject

Table 5.4 Children born to Non-Stateless Refugee Parents-Unable or Unwilling to Confer Nationality

Countries with strong safeguards	Countries with partial safeguards	Countries with no or minimal safeguards	
		The Philippines	• Minimal safeguard in the form of facilitated naturalisation (through which children may derive nationality)
		Viet Nam	• Minimal safeguard in the form of facilitated naturalisation (through which children may derive nationality)
		Malaysia	• Minimal safeguard for a child of either parent holding IMM13 residence permit, awarded to eligible refugees in Sabah, making them eligible to apply for permanent residence (PR) (a pre-condition for naturalisation). A child born to a PR holder in wedlock may obtain Malaysian citizenship *ex lege*
		Thailand	• No safeguard
		Lao PDR	• No safeguard
		Cambodia	• Minimal safeguard subject to the child concerned being born to refugee parents who were also born in Cambodia and living legally in the country, or through access to naturalisation (lack of proof of legal residence can be a hindrance)
		Indonesia	• No safeguard
		Singapore	• No safeguard
		Brunei	• No safeguard

Table 5.5 Children born to parents of unclear or undetermined nationality

Countries with full safeguards		Countries with partial safeguards		Countries with no or minimal safeguards
Indonesia	• Safeguard applies *ex lege* with no further conditions for a child born to parents of undetermined nationality		Thailand	• Minimal safeguard in the form of nationality verification procedures in the context of MoU with labour-sending countries, namely Myanmar, Lao PDR and Cambodia • No automatic provision for Thai nationality to be granted to a child of undetermined nationality except when born to parents with permanent residence/legal residence status
			The Philippines	• Minimal safeguard via determination of statelessness that may result in nationality acquisition based on judicial or administrative order • Minimal safeguard in practice through cooperation with Indonesia for nationality verification and confirmation • No provision for Philippine citizenship to be granted automatically
			Malaysia	• No safeguard
			Singapore	• No safeguard
			Viet Nam	• No safeguard
			Lao PDR	• No safeguard
			Cambodia	• No safeguard
			Myanmar	• No safeguard
			Brunei	• No safeguard

Table 5.6 Children born abroad (Marked with #) and Non-marital children (Marked with @)

Countries with full safeguards		Countries with partial safeguards		Countries with no or minimal safeguards	
				#Malaysia	• Gender inequality identified. Citizenship *ex lege* only for a child born abroad to a Malaysian citizen father. Minimal safeguard against statelessness in the form of discretionary provision of citizenship acquisition by registration
				@Malaysia	• Gender inequality identified. Citizenship *ex lege* for a non-marital child only if born to a Malaysian citizen mother or mother holding Malaysian PR status. Minimal safeguard against statelessness is available, but through the discretionary provision of citizenship by registration

(continued)

Table 5.6 (continued)

Countries with full safeguards		Countries with partial safeguards		Countries with no or minimal safeguards	
				#Brunei	• Minimal safeguard for a child born abroad if registered as a subject of His Majesty by virtue of the application of the parent or guardian of the child (in relation to adoption, the 'parent' refers to the child's adopter) or in such special circumstances as His Majesty thinks fit
				@Brunei	• Minimal safeguard for non-marital children if registered as a subject of His Majesty by virtue of the application of parent or guardian of the child (in relation to adoption, the parent refers to the child's adopter) or in such special circumstances as His Majesty thinks fit
#Thailand	• *Ex lege* Thai citizenship for a child born abroad as long as one parent is a Thai citizen			**#Myanmar** **@Myanmar**	No safeguard No safeguard
@Thailand	• No gender inequality for a non-marital child. Thai nationality may be acquired from mother or father who is a Thai national. The nationality may not be automatic if the child's mother is a non-national and the child is born outside Thailand				

(continued)

Table 5.6 (continued)

Countries with full safeguards		Countries with partial safeguards		Countries with no or minimal safeguards	
#Viet Nam	• No gender inequality in the conferral of nationality to a child born in Viet Nam and abroad, provided one parent is a Vietnamese citizen	**@Viet Nam**	• No gender discrimination for a non-marital child as long as one parent is a Vietnamese citizen • Recognition from a Vietnamese father is required if the mother is a non-national/stateless (without PR and unable to confer citizenship)		
#Cambodia	• No gender inequality in the conferral of nationality to a child born abroad provided one parent has a Khmer nationality	**@Cambodia**	• No gender discrimination for a non-marital child so long as parenthood is recognised by a Khmer parent or by a court judgment		
#Lao PDR	• No gender inequality for a child born abroad. *Ex lege* Lao citizenship if either parent has a permanent address in Lao PDR, or when one parent is stateless or *apatrid* and the other is a Lao citizen. Safeguard exists when both parents have permanent addresses outside Lao PDR, under which the child's nationality will be decided by both parents	**@Lao PDR**	• No gender inequality for a non-marital child if parenthood is recognised by a citizen father or by the Court. No safeguard in the absence of such recognition		

(continued)

Table 5.6 (continued)

Countries with full safeguards		Countries with partial safeguards		Countries with no or minimal safeguards	
#Indonesia	• No gender inequality for a child born abroad. *Ex lege* Indonesian citizenship if either parent is an Indonesian citizen	**@Indonesia**	No gender inequality for a non-marital child provided the mother is an Indonesian citizen, or if the mother is an alien/foreigner, the child is acknowledged by the Indonesian father before the child reaches 18 or is married		
#The Philippines	• No gender inequality for a child born abroad. *Ex lege* Philippine citizenship if either parent is a Philippine citizen	**@The Philippines**	• No gender inequality for a child born out of wedlock provided one parent is a Philippine citizen. However, legitimation (through subsequent marriage) or affiliation/declaration of paternity by the father may be required if the mother is stateless or non-national unable to confer citizenship		
#Singapore	• No gender inequality for a child born abroad. *Ex lege* citizenship of Singapore if either parent is a Singaporean citizen			**@Singapore**	• Gender inequality identified. Citizenship *ex lege* for a child born out of wedlock only if the mother is a Singaporean citizen

Table 5.7 Mapping of the overall degree of safeguards against statelessness at birth based on the nationality frameworks of the ASEAN member states

Categories of Children

Stronger Safeguards/ Protection	**Children Born Abroad**	7	0	3	10
	Foundlings and Young Children with Unknown Legal Identity	4	3	3	10
Weaker Safeguards/ Protection	**Children Born on the Territory to Stateless Parents (whether refugee or non-refugee parents)**	2	4	4	10
	Children Born out of Wedlock	1	5	4	10
	Children Born to Parents of Unclear/ Undetermined Nationality	1	0	9	10
	Children Born to Non-Stateless Refugee Parents Unable or Unwilling to Confer Nationality	0	0	10	10

affiliation or recognition of paternity could still leave such children unshielded against the risk of statelessness. Forty percent of the countries display either the absence of or minimal safeguards, with Malaysia and Singapore strictly restricting the acquisition of nationality through the maternal line. Meanwhile, Brunei and Myanmar have no express safeguard in the laws for this group. The only full protection with gender neutrality is offered by Thailand.

Falling into the second lowest class of children extremely lacking protection against statelessness are children born to parents of unclear or undetermined nationality. A striking 90 percent of the countries offer no or minimal protection, possibly suggesting the consequential widespread presence of such children in this subregion. Indonesia represents the polar opposite, being the only country that meets the standard of full safeguard for such children.

At the lowest rank is the category of children born to non-stateless refugee parents, who are unable or unwilling (for valid reasons) to confer nationality upon them. Ninety percent of the countries offer minimal protection, largely through facilitated naturalisation or naturalisation. In Cambodia, citizenship is granted for children of refugees born in Cambodia whose both parents were also born and have been living legally in the country. However, this provision lacks utility when proof of legal residence is not available for refugees in the country.

Chapter 6
Assessment of Domestic Legal Frameworks for Birth Registration of ASEAN Member States

6.1 Introduction

Despite the absence of the right of every child to birth registration in the ASEAN's regional human rights instruments, all of the Member States of ASEAN, except Malaysia, have committed themselves to be bound by the right to birth registration and to acquire a nationality under Article 7(1) of CRC. The similar obligation to provide for such rights in Articles 24(2) and (3) of ICCPR additionally binds Cambodia, Indonesia, Lao PDR, the Philippines, Thailand, and Viet Nam.

The regional trend of birth registration in the region sees countries like Thailand, Viet Nam, and the Philippines recording overall high registration and low-income differentials, but with sustained pockets of low registration. On the other end, countries like Indonesia, Myanmar, Lao PDR, and Cambodia on the whole experience low registration rates and high level of income gaps.[1]

The problems that surround birth registration in this region have serious implications for children, particularly those in marginalised circumstances, comprising children of migrants, asylum seekers, and refugees; children living and working on the streets including sexually exploited children; and children who are trafficked and sold. The CRC Committee has also expressed its serious concerns over statelessness and the inability of children to prove their legal identity and age.[2]

The aim of this chapter is to evaluate the extent to which children are able to exercise their right to birth registration, a safeguard to ensure that the risk of statelessness is reduced at the earliest possible stage of their childhood. To this end, it shall present a structural appraisal of the laws and to some degree, practices relating to birth registration in the ASEAN Member States. This assessment, however, shall be limited to the extent that data on the laws, practices, and related problems or issues

---

[1] L. Butt & J. Ball, 'Birth Registration in Southeast Asia: A Child's Foundation Right?', *Asian Population Studies*, 13(3) (2017), p 223.

[2] UNICEF, '*Unequal at Birth: Disparities in Birth Registration in East Asia and the Pacific*' (2015), p 12.

R. M. Razali, *Safeguarding Against Statelessness at Birth*,
https://doi.org/10.1007/978-981-19-5371-2_6

Table 6.1 Percentage of registered births of children under five in Southeast Asian countries, 2017

Thailand	100 (date differed from the standard definition/refer only to part of the country)
Viet Nam	96
Philippines	90
Lao PDR	75
Myanmar	81
Indonesia	73 (date differed from the standard definition/refer only to part of the country)
Cambodia	73
Timor-Leste	55

Source UNICEF (2017)[3]

on birth registration in the ASEAN Member States are accessible from the existing literature. Primary data on civil registration law in relation to Myanmar, for instance, are not available as there is no specific legal framework that governs CRVS in this country.

The analyses of the safeguards via birth registration are based on a set of general and specific standards and recommendations compiled from the main instruments of law and soft norms as summarised in Tables 6.1 and 6.2. The specific standards with the supporting explanations would serve to generally guide this assessment into how universal, free, timely, and facilitated access to birth registration could be achieved so that no child is left behind in exercising their right to a legal identity through birth registration.

6.2 International Standards on Birth Registration and Limitations

Tables 6.2 and 6.3 compile and summarise the general and specific standards and recommendations on birth registration, which serve to be largely the criteria against which the subsequent laws and practices governing birth registration in the Member States of ASEAN are assessed.

In terms of the limitations of the assessment in this chapter, the entries on birth certificates shall not be part of the analysis. The different forms of birth certificates of the countries may not be readily accessible, chiefly due to language barriers. The interpretations of the laws by the courts and the conflicts between law and practice in the area of birth registration are aspects worth a more detailed investigation beyond the work conceived in this chapter. Although we may see that some of the laws correspond with the relevant international standards, there might be implementation gaps, problems, and complexities that still contribute to the low birth rates in some

[3] UNICEF, *Birth Registration,* Retrieved from http://data.unicef.org/topic/child-protection/birth-registration/ [Accessed 7 July 2019].

Table 6.2 General standards on birth registration

International Documents underlining Universal Right to Birth Registration	Content
1966 International Covenant on Civil and Political Rights	Every child shall be registered immediately after birth and shall have a name [Article 24(2)]
1989 Convention on the Rights of the Child	The child shall be registered immediately after birth and shall have the right from birth to a name, the right to acquire a nationality […] [Article 7(1)]
1990 African Charter on the Rights and Welfare of the Child	Every child shall be registered immediately after birth [Article 6(2)] • Upheld in the Kenyan Nubian Case
1990 International Convention on the Protection of the Rights of All Migrant Workers and Members of Their Families	Each child of a migrant worker shall have the right to a name, to registration of birth and to a nationality [Article 29]
2005 Covenant on the Rights of the Child in Islam	A child shall, from birth, have right to a good name, to be registered with authorities concerned, to have his nationality determined and to know his/her parents, all his/her relatives and foster mother [Article 7]
United Nations Resolution entitled 'Transforming Our World: The 2030 Agenda for Sustainable Development'	'By 2030, provide legal identity for all, including birth registration' [Target 16.9 under Goal 16—'Promote peaceful and inclusive societies for sustainable development, provide access to justice for all and build effective, accountable and inclusive institutions at all levels'][a]

[a] See UN Economic and Social Affairs, *UN Economic and Social Affairs, Sustainable Development Knowledge Platform (2006).* Retrieved from http://www.tandfonline.com/doi/abs/10.1080/13504620500526362#.V5w3e_l96wU [Accessed 16 June 2016]

countries. For instance, a baseline study on legal identity in Indonesia revealed how the lack of marriage certificates impacts on the right of children to be registered at birth in Indonesia. As less than 50% of Indonesian couples obtain a marriage certificate, it is estimated that each year, over 2 million couples in Indonesia do not register their marriages. As a consequence, children from these marriages are not able to obtain a birth certificate with both the names of their parents.[4]

The specific component of the link between birth registration and how it may lead to an acquisition of nationality and access to rights and public goods such as healthcare and education is also beyond the scope of this analysis. Such would have required an in-depth investigation both into theory and practice of CRVS, nationality and welfare regimes in one functional gestalt. A combination of doctrinal and empirical tools of analysis in that context is necessary, including conducting interviews with participants and stakeholders to unearth how the laws and practices relating to

[4] C. Summer & Santi Kusumaningram, 'AIPJ Baseline Study on Legal Identity Indonesia's Missing Millions' (2014). Retrieved from http://www.cpcnetwork.org/wp-content/uploads/2015/02/AIPJ-PUSKAPA-BASELINE-STUDY-ON-LEGAL-IDENTITY-Indonesia-2013.pdf, p 18, para 29.

Table 6.3 Specific standards and recommendations on birth registration

CRC's General Comment No. 7 (2005): Implementing Child Rights in Early Childhood	Corresponding contents from soft law instrument
Standards derived from Paragraph 25 **Standard 1:**	
Universal, well-managed and free […] the Committee recommends that State Parties take all necessary measures to ensure that all children are registered at birth. This could be achieved through a universal, well-managed registration system that is accessible to all and free of charge. […] that all children should be registered at birth, without discrimination of any kind (Article 2)	***Totality and Compulsory nature of birth registration*** • Universal indicates totality and includes non-nationals and children born abroad.[a] Children born to foreigners, asylum seekers, refugees and undocumented immigrants qualify for birth registration in the same way as those born to citizens.[b] Geographical location, gender, religion or ethnicity should not be barriers to civil registration[c] • The link between birth registration and statelessness is reaffirmed, as such (to avoid statelessness), every child shall be registered immediately after birth, without discrimination of any kind[d] • A comprehensive law must guarantee continuity, permanence, universal coverage and compulsoriness of the civil registration system[e] • The law must be organic, not over-regulated, and so detailed so as to defeat the foregoing elements. Yet it must meet some minimum requirements[f] ***Confidentiality of sensitive content and information from irregular migrants*** • Preservation of confidentiality constitutes a component of a quality birth registration system.[g] The information on a birth certificate does not need to be as complete as the information kept on a birth record. That being said, states may omit details that may be prejudicial to the individual such as ethnicity or race[h] • Sensitive details prejudicial to an individual may be omitted or not displayed on a birth certificate and unavailable information such as the name of one of the parents or the parent's personal identification (because they are not registered) should not detract from birth registration[i] • The system should allow the registry authorities to guarantee confidentially to those in an irregular situation, so as to encourage them to register births. Details (submitted for birth registration) should not be shared with police and immigration authorities[j] ***Free Birth Registration*** • States to consider free birth and death registration in accordance with national laws and regulations[k] • Late registration should occur free of charge within a grace period of one year after birth. Late or delayed registration, if not free, should only incur a nominal fee. Variable fees for late registration should be applied on the understanding that rural areas should benefit from reduced fees[l] • Birth record or certificate is recommended to be free.[m] Not only must it be free but must be easily provided, either automatically issued or by an application.[n] The African Union makes it compulsory to be issued free of charge immediately after birth.[o] UNESCAP underlines that all people to be provided with legal documentation of CRVS to claim an identity, civil status and ensuring rights[p] ***Rules of proof to be flexible, i.e. that avoid excessive documentary requirements*** • A combination of witnesses and documents may be required as proof of birth, although documentary proof is generally more reliable[q] • The registrar needs to determine whether a witness is necessary or if the birth could be registered based on the report by the informant in the case of birth without medical certificates and medical attendance[r] • In a nutshell, rules of proof must be flexible and avoid excessive documentation requirements[s] • For children of undocumented migration status, proof of parental identity by non-documentary evidence should be explored by State Parties to prevent recurrence of the generational problem of unregistered persons[t]

(continued)

Table 6.3 (continued)

CRC's General Comment No. 7 (2005): Implementing Child Rights in Early Childhood	Corresponding contents from soft law instrument
Standard 2:	
Flexible and responsive to circumstances of families (…) An effective system must be flexible and responsive to circumstances of families, for example by providing mobile registration units where appropriate	***Mobile registration and decentralised system*** • The CRC Committee gave an example of providing mobile registration as an illustration of a responsive birth registration system. Decentralisation of the birth registration system and providing mobile services of birth registration are imperative for access in remote areas[u] ***Interoperability*** • Other solutions are to be sought for service delivery; for example, interoperability with existing services, such as health and education, and the use of new technology for vital event notification in overcoming geographical obstacles and costs[v] • Other alternative mechanisms to reach out to the remotest area include through mobile phone registration systems or health workers or community leaders[w] ***Simpler procedures of birth registration*** • A simpler type of registration document where literacy is a problem is recommended[x] • Registration must not only be physically accessible, but socially accessible too. Materials concerning registration must be provided in local and minority languages. Furthermore, the information must also be presented in a form that is comprehensible, and the forms to be filled are simple enough to ensure that those with low literacy levels can understand them[y]
Standard 3:	
Accurate, timely and facilitated late birth registration (…) The Committee also reminds State parties of the importance of facilitating late registration of birth and ensuring that children who have not been registered have equal access to healthcare, protection, education, and other social services	***Timely birth registration to ensure the accuracy of birth registration*** • The prescribed period by law between a vital event and its registration must be as short as possible as the accuracy of information relating to age, sex, parentage, and nationality of the parents affects the rights and obligations of the individual[z] • 'Immediately' after birth means as soon as possible, with due regard to cultural and local practice regarding maternity and infant rearing[aa] • UNSD suggests 30 days as the period for birth registration to take place[ab] • UNSD further recommends one year as the grace period for late registration, i.e. registration after the legally specified period, taking into account extenuating circumstances[ac] • Delayed registration after one year may require age assessment and court involvement[ad] • Incentives should be offered to families for timely birth registration[ae] ***Facilitated late birth registration*** • Awareness-raising on birth registration is not a one-off but an on-going process[af] • The law may make provision for late registration 'provided that the birth and its circumstances are duly proved to the Registrar'. The regulations must specify specific and different levels of proof required and other requirements for legally authorised late and delayed registration[ag] • Sound legislation is required to provide for timely reporting of events and the people must be aware of the content[ah] • Possible causes of delay (that are to be overcome) include complex requirements, lack of awareness or interest on the public, apathy, indifference, and ignorance. Community awareness and interest must be raised, for instance through education and campaign[ai]

Table 6.3 (continued)

[a]United Nations, Department of Economic and Social Affairs, Statistics Division (UNSD), *Handbook on Training in Civil Registration and Vital Statistic Systems, Series F No. 84* (2002), para 33, p 9; Department of Economics and Social Affairs (Statistics Division), *Principles and Recommendations for a Vital Statistic System* (2014), New York: UN Publications, para 296

[b]UN Human Rights Council. *Birth Registration and the Right of Everyone to Recognition Everywhere as a Person before the Law* (17 June 2014), para III.11; African Charter on the Rights and Welfare of the Child (adopted 11 July 1990, in force 29 November 1999), CAB/LEG/24.9/49, para 50

[c]Economic and Social Commission for Asia and the Pacific (UNESCAP), 2 June 2015, Resolution adopted by the Economic and Social Commission for Asia and the Pacific, *Asian and Pacific Civil Registration and Vital Statistics 2015–2024*, UN Doc. E/ESCAP/RES/71/14, New York: United Nations. Part B, II (13); Committee on the Protection of the Rights of All Migrants Workers and Members of Their Families (CMW), Joint General Comment No. 4 (2017) of the Committee on the Protection of the Rights of All Migrant Workers and Members of Their Families and No. 23 (2017) of the Committee on the Rights of the Child on the General Principles regarding the Human Rights of Children in the Context of International Migration, para 20

[d]UNHCR, 'Conclusion on Civil Registration No. 111 (LXIV)'. Doc. A/AC.96/1035. Geneva: UNHCR. [17 October 2013]

[e]UNSD, *Civil Registration and Vital Statistics Knowledge Base* (2015), para 62, p 15. Retrieved from http://unstats.un.org/unsd/demographic [Accessed 5 May 2016]; Department of Economics and Social Affairs (Statistics Division), *Principles and Recommendations for a Vital Statistic System* (2014), New York: UN Publications, para 294

[f]UNSD, *Civil Registration and Vital Statistics Knowledge Base* (2015), para 48, p 12. Retrieved from http://unstats.un.org/unsd/demographic [Accessed 5 May 2016]

[g]UNSD, *Principles and Recommendations for a Vital Statistics System* (Revision 3)(2014), para 299, p 68; See also Committee on the Protection of the Rights of All Migrants Workers and Members of Their Families (CMW), Joint General Comment No. 4 (2017) of the Committee on the Protection of the Rights of All Migrant Workers and Members of Their Families and No. 23 (2017) of the Committee on the Rights of the Child on the General Principles regarding the Human Rights of Children in the Context of International Migration, paras 20–21

[h]UNICEF, *A Passport to Protection: A Guide to Birth Registration Programming* (2013), p 22

[i]UNICEF, *A Passport to Protection: A Guide to Birth Registration Programming* (2013), p 22 and 122; General Comment on Article 6 of the ACRWC: The Right to a Name, Registration at Birth, and to Acquire a Nationality, ACERWC/GC/02, Addis Ababa: African Union, 2014, para 82

[j]General Comment on Article 6 of the ACRWC: The Right to a Name, Registration at Birth, and to Acquire a Nationality, ACERWC/GC/02, Addis Ababa: African Union, 2014, para 51

[k]UNHCR, Conclusion on Civil Registration No. 111 (LXIV), Doc. A/AC.96/1035, Geneva: UNHCR [17 October 2013]

Table 6.3 (continued)

[l]General Comment on Article 6 of the ACRWC: The Right to a Name, Registration at Birth, and to Acquire a Nationality, ACERWC/GC/02, Addis Ababa: African Union, 2014, para 81

[m]UNICEF, *A Passport to Protection: A Guide to Birth Registration Programming* (2013), p 118

[n]UN Human Rights Council, *Birth Registration and the Right of Everyone to Recognition Everywhere as a Person before the Law* (17 June 2014), para II.5

[o]General Comment on Article 6 of the ACRWC: The Right to a Name, Registration at Birth, and to Acquire a Nationality, ACERWC/GC/02, Addis Ababa: African Union, 2014, para 41

[p]Economic and Social Commission for Asia and the Pacific (UNESCAP), 2 June 2015, Resolution adopted by the Economic and Social Commission for Asia and the Pacific, *Asian and Pacific Civil Registration and Vital Statistics* 2015–2024, UN Doc. E/ESCAP/RES/71/14, New York: United Nations, Goal 2; UNESCAP, *Regional Action Framework on Civil Registration and Vital Statistics in Asia and the Pacific* (2014), p 14, Inter-American Court of Human Rights, Series C, Case 130, 8 September 2005

[q]United Nations, Department of Economic and Social Affairs, Statistics Division (UNSD), *Handbook on Training in Civil Registration and Vital Statistic Systems, Series F No. 84* (2002), para 126, p 28

[r]United Nations, Department of Economic and Social Affairs, Statistics Division (UNSD), *Handbook on Training in Civil Registration and Vital Statistic Systems, Series F No. 84* (2002), para 127, p 28

[s]UN Human Rights Council, *Birth Registration and the Right of Everyone to Recognition Everywhere as a Person before the Law* (17 June 2014), para C.56–60, p 13

[t]General Comment on Article 6 of the ACRWC: The Right to a Name, Registration at Birth, and to Acquire a Nationality. ACERWC/GC/02. Addis Ababa: African Union (2014), para 66

[u]General Comment on Article 6 of the ACRWC: The Right to a Name, Registration at Birth, and to Acquire a Nationality. ACERWC/GC/02. Addis Ababa: African Union (2014), para 73

[v]UN Human Rights Council, *Birth Registration and the Right of Everyone to Recognition Everywhere as a Person before the Law* (17 June 2014), para C. 56, p 13; UNHCR, *Conclusion on Civil Registration No. 111* (LXIV), Doc. A/AC.1035/96, Geneva: UNHCR [17 October 2013]

[w]General Comment on Article 6 of the ACRWC: The Right to a Name, Registration at Birth, and to Acquire a Nationality. ACERWC/GC/02. Addis Ababa: African Union, 2014, para 74

[x]United Nations, Department of Economic and Social Affairs, Statistics Division (UNSD), Handbook on Training in Civil Registration and Vital Statistic Systems, Series F No. 84 (2002), para 34, p 8

Table 6.3 (continued)

[y]UN Human Rights Council, Birth Registration and the Right of Everyone to Recognition Everywhere as a Person before the Law (17 June 2014), para C 56–60

[z]UNICEF, *A Passport yo Protection: A Guide to Birth Registration Programming* (2013), p 26

[aa]General Comment on Article 6 of the ACRWC: The Right to a Name, Registration at Birth, and to Acquire a Nationality, ACERWC/GC/02, Addis Ababa: African Union, 2014, para 79

[ab]UNSD, Civil Registry and Vital Statistics Knowledge Base (2015), para 121

[ac]UNSD, *Principles and Recommendations for a Vital Statistics System* (Revision 2014)(3), para 363; UNSD, *Civil Registration and Vital Statistics Knowledge Base* (2015), para 121

[ad]UNSD, *Civil Registration and Vital Statistics Knowledge Base* (2015), para 121

[ae]UNESCAP, *Regional Action Framework on Civil Registration and Vital Statistics in Asia and the Pacific* (2014), para 46, p 17

[af]UN Human Rights Council, Birth Registration and the Right of Everyone to Recognition Everywhere as a Person before the Law (17 June 2014), para B.55

[ag]UNSD, Civil Registration and Vital Statistics Knowledge Base (2015), para 123

[ah]United Nations, Department of Economic and Social Affairs, Statistics Division (UNSD), Handbook on Training in Civil Registration and Vital Statistic Systems, Series F No. 84. (2002), para 34

[ai]UNSD, Civil Registration and Vital Statistics Knowledge Base (2015), para 124–125, p 28

birth registration may or may not lead to a nationality acquisition and access to rights for the categories of children under study.

6.3 Country-Level Assessment

The following accounts contain the comparative summary of analyses of the laws on birth registration and to some extent, related practices by the ASEAN Member States according to the three main standards and their components. References to the specific laws relating to CRVS may be found in the tables of the mapping of safeguards according to each standard on birth registration.

1. **Analysis of laws (and practices) on birth registration for Standard 1: Universal, Well-Managed and Free Birth Registration**

In terms of non-discriminatory and total access to birth registration, the laws governing birth registration in six countries (Lao PDR, Viet Nam, Thailand, Indonesia, Malaysia, and the Philippines) reflect this standard in their laws by providing every child shall be registered at birth. Additional provisions address the rights of foundlings (who may include young children), and/or non-marital children and/or children born abroad to be registered with several laws outlining the processes involved. In the case of Viet Nam, an individual may conduct civil status registration at the civil status registration agency in his/her registered place of permanent or temporary residence or the place where he/she is living. For foreign residents including stateless persons, the civil status registration right and obligation, however, apply only to those permanently residing in Viet Nam.[5] Such may create a barrier to birth registration of children within irregular or informal migrant families who are without official proof of address[6] and foreign and stateless persons without permanent residence in the country.

Two other countries (Brunei and Singapore) prescribe birth registration to every child without further specifying access to birth registration for foundlings and non-marital children, rendering the level of protection to be generally echoing the standard. Cambodia limits access to birth registration for Cambodian citizens and non-citizens having legal and permanent residence status in Cambodia. The CRC Committee also voiced its concerns that children of irregular immigrants in Cambodia are not eligible for birth registration, and that families of Vietnamese origin are often turned away when they attempt to obtain a birth certificate for their children.[7] The low level of birth registration, particularly in remote areas and villages among children

[5] Article 6(1) of Decree No. 60/2014.

[6] K. Apland, B. K. Blitz, M. Lagaay, C. Hamilton, N. Indika, R. Lakshman, M. Lynch & E. Yarrow, 'Birth Registration and Children's Rights: A Complex Story', (2014), Retrieved from https://www.planusa.org/docs/birth-registration-rights-2014.pdf [Accessed 6 March 2015], p 26.

[7] Consideration of reports submitted by States parties under Article 44 of the Convention: Concluding Observations: Cambodia, UN Doc. CRC/C/KHM/CO/2–3, Cambodia: CRC, 3 August 2011, para 36.

in street situations, the 30-day limit to register a child after birth, sanctions for late registration, and the requirement of an address are cited as other issues affecting birth registration in Cambodia.[8] Although universality of birth registration has been introduced through B.E. 2551 in Thailand, low access to birth registration is still reported among children of migrant workers. A survey by the World Vision Foundation of Thailand (WVFT) found that 75% of migrant workers' children remain without a valid birth certificate. Lack of awareness on birth registration, knowledge and assistance to register, inability to communicate in Thai, and financial and logistical issues were cited as the contributing factors.[9]

In respect of the second component of the duty to preserve confidentiality, only two countries (Indonesia and the Philippines) meet the normal safeguard for prescribing the general duty to preserve information given for vital registration of events. The safeguards fall short of specifically requiring the duty not to reveal or share sensitive information of parents in irregular situations. The rest of other countries provide no express requirement for such duty of confidentiality in their laws.

On the third component of free birth registration, Viet Nam expressly exempts members of poor households and persons with disability from birth registration fees. Five other countries partially meet the standard, as delayed and/or late birth registration may be subject to fees. The remaining three countries do not provide free access to birth registration. Lao PDR and Thailand enact fees for birth registration from the start of the process, whereas the law in Singapore is silent on whether birth registration shall be free or subject to any fees. For Lao PDR, concerns were expressed by the CRC Committee over birth certificates that are not issued free of charge for all children born in the state territory.[10] Furthermore, despite being registered, 42% of the children were reported in 2015 as not having a birth certificate in the said country.[11]

As for the element of flexible rules of proof that avoid excessive documentary requirements, Viet Nam expressly specifies the types of evidence of birth required and accepts written evidence and pledges to prove birth. Indonesia, the Philippines, and Thailand are placed in the category of partially meeting the standard. The types of proof of birth are indicated in their laws, yet sufficient flexibility in the rules pertaining to proof is not reflected. The other five remaining countries either do not or minimally address this component in their laws.

---

[8] Concluding Observations on the report submitted by Cambodia under Article 8, para 1, of the Optional Protocol to the Convention on the Rights of the Child on the Involvement of Children in Armed Conflict, UN Doc. CRC/C/OPAC/KHM/ CO/1, Cambodia: CRC 23 February 2015, para 14(b).

[9] Dumrongkiat Mala, 'Migrants are Still Slow to Register Births' (24 August 2018). Retrieved from https://www.bangkokpost.com/news/general/1527374/migrants-are-still-slow-to-register-births [Accessed 20 September 2018].

[10] Consideration of reports submitted by State Parties under Article 44 of the Convention: Convention on the Rights of the Child: Concluding Observations: Lao People's Democratic Republic, UN Doc. CRC/C/LAO/CO/2, Lao: CRC, 8 April 2011, para 34.

[11] UNICEF, *Unequal at Birth: Disparities in Birth Registration in East Asia and the Pacific* (2015), p 6.

Analysis of the data on birth registration law and system in Myanmar is restricted as the legal framework addressing its CRVS has yet to be developed. It was further reported that Myanmar has yet to set up a single focal department to manage its CRVS. Administratively, registration of births and deaths is done at hospitals and township departments. Data on birth and death registration forms are then compiled by the Central Statistical Organisation and published in the country's statistical yearbook.[12]

As of 2016, the Special Rapporteur on the situation of human rights in Myanmar reported that the birth registration in some areas affected by conflict in Myanmar has not taken place for several years due to difficulties of accessing registration centres.[13] Regrettably, it was reiterated that birth registration remains 'alarmingly low' in Muslim communities in Rakhine state and in states like Kachin and Shan.[14] The issuance of birth certificates was said to have been halted by the Government of Myanmar since the mid-1990s to newly born Rohingya in the Northern Rakhine state. Furthermore, the signing of the country's controversial Population Control Healthcare Bill in 2015 would allow the authority to impose 36-month birth spacing for target groups, which highly likely include the persecuted minorities in the country[15] (Table 6.4).

2. **Analysis of laws (and practices) on birth registration for Standard 2: Birth Registration that is Flexible and Responsive to Circumstances of Families**

The second standard is made up of provisions of mobile registration, decentralised system of birth registration and its interoperability with other services (such as health and education) as collectively forming the first component, and simpler procedures being the second. As this standard addresses not only the substantive but also the operative aspects of birth registration, the assessment takes into consideration the relevant practices that substantiate it. Myanmar is included in the assessment where data on the relevant practices in the said country could be obtained.

On the first component, 70% of the countries (Brunei, Malaysia, the Philippines, Viet Nam, Indonesia, Thailand, and Singapore) reflect the international standard by having a decentralised birth registration system and/or mobile registration services

---

[12] Nyein Aye Tun, Role of Health Institutions in Vital Registration, Retrieved from https://shorturl.at/lrIZ7 [Accessed 19 July 2019].

[13] UN Human Rights Council, 14 March 2017, *Report of the Special Rapporteur on the Situation of Human Rights in Myanmar*, Doc. A/HRC/67/34. Retrieved from https://www.google.com/url?sa=t&rct=j&q=&esrc=s&source=web&cd=1&ved=2ahUKEwjJxfmfmLneAhVNwlkKHWnfBiwQFjAAegQIABAC&url=https%3A%2F%2Fwww.ohchr.org%2FEN%2FHRBodies%2FHRC%2FRegularSessions%2FSession342%FDocuments%2FA_HRC_67_34_EN.docx&usg = AOvVaw2Xbzj5g1o6HQjJ790 OxhqZ, para 33 at p 6.

[14] UNGA, *Promotion and Protection of Human Rights: Human Rights Situations and Reports of Special Rapporteurs and Representatives* (2016), UN Document A/71/361. New York: United Nations. See Item 69(c) of the provisional agenda.

[15] Nay Pyi Taw, 'Myanmar, Getting to the Goal of 100 Percent Birth Registration' (24 August 2015). Retrieved from http://www.unicef.org/myanmar/media_24526.html [Accessed 15 June 2016]. See also Anon, 'Myanmar Population Control Bill Signed into Law despite Concerns It Could be Used to Persecute Minorities', *ABC News*. Retrieved from http://www.abc.net.au/news/2015-05-24/myanmar-president-signs-off-on-controversial-population-law/6493198 [Accessed 30 June 2016].

Table 6.4 Mapping of birth registration safeguards for standard 1

Standard 1: Universal, well-managed and free birth registration	Totality of birth registration	Confidentiality of sensitive content, including information from irregular migrants	Free birth registration	Rules of proof to be flexible, i.e. that avoids excessive documentary requirements
Brunei	**Addressed** • Every live birth is to be registered[a]	**Not addressed**	**Addressed** • Birth registration is free within a brief period of 14 days • Free birth certificate is provided[b]	**Not addressed**
Lao PDR	**Addressed** • Every child shall be registered at birth, have a name and acquire a nationality[c] • Registrations of newborn, abandoned children[d] and births in a foreign country are specified[e] • Registration of acknowledgement of paternity is also included[f]	**Not addressed**	**Not addressed** • Fees prescribed by regulations are imposed for registration of vital events[g]	**Not addressed**
Cambodia	**Not addressed** • Access to civil registration is limited to Cambodian citizens and non-citizens with a legal[h] and permanent residence[i] in Cambodia • Specific provisions exist on registration of children born out of wedlock,[j] children born abroad[k] and abandoned babies and older children[l]	**Not addressed**	**Partially addressed** • No cost is imposed for registration within 30 days period but sanction (imposition of fee) may occur for late registration • Birth certificate is prescribed to be issued at no cost[m]	**Not addressed**

(continued)

Table 6.4 (continued)

Standard 1: Universal, well-managed and free birth registration	Totality of birth registration	Confidentiality of sensitive content, including information from irregular migrants	Free birth registration	Rules of proof to be flexible, i.e. that avoids excessive documentary requirements
Viet Nam	**Not addressed** • State agency to certify or record the civil status events in the civil status book of an 'individual', without pointing out to any restrictions as to race or nationality[n] • Detailed procedures on registrations of abandoned children and childrenborn to surrogate mothers are to be stipulated by the Government.[o] Recognition of parent-child relationship is further addressed[p] • Restrictions may apply to children within irregular or informal migrant families, foreign residents and stateless persons with no permanent residence[q]	**Not addressed** • No specific duty of confidentiality is prescribed under the law	**Strongly addressed** • The Prime Minister through a directive, prescribes that late birth registration must be free from any fee[r] Fees shall be exempted for members of the poor household and persons with disability[s]	**Strongly addressed** • Types of evidence of birth are specified • Rules of evidence appear flexible where they require written certification of witnesses for birth out of medical establishments, or written pledges that the birth was real in the absence of witnesses[t] • Marriage certificate is not prescribed as part of the procedures[u]
Thailand	**Addressed** • Every child regardless of the nationality status of the parents must be registered.[v] • Specific provision on the registration of abandoned children (newborn) exists[w]	**Not addressed**	**Not addressed** • Birth report (applicable for birth with or without professional delivery as the first step in the registration process) is subject to the imposition of a fee[x] • Minimal monetary penalty is maintained for late birth registration (as observed by the CRC Committee)[y]	**Partially addressed** • Provisions specify the requirement for a certificate confirming the birth (birth out of medical establishment) and delivery certificate (birth at a healthcare facility or by a professional)[z]

(continued)

Table 6.4 (continued)

Standard 1: Universal, well-managed and free birth registration	Totality of birth registration	Confidentiality of sensitive content, including information from irregular migrants	Free birth registration	Rules of proof to be flexible, i.e. that avoids excessive documentary requirements
Indonesia	**Addressed** • Aside from the general duty of every person residing in Indonesia to report vital events to the authority[aa], the relevant laws address birth registration for children found abandoned with no parental identity information and whereabouts[ab] • Acknowledgement of paternity[ac] including for children born out of religious marriage and their access to birth registration are provided in the relevant provisions[ad] • Indonesian citizens abroad are obligated to report the same to the authority of the said country in charge of population and civil registration and/or the representative of the Indonesian Government in that country[ae]	**Partially addressed** • Duty of state to preserve and protect data on vital registration of events is provided[af] • Yet no specific provision requires data concerning irregular migrants not to be shared with the enforcement authority	**Partially addressed** • Management and issuance of birth certificate is free[ag] • Penalty for late birth registration may be imposed as shall be determined by regulations at the district or provincial level[ah]	**Partially addressed** • Types of documentary requirements are specified in the relevant sub-regulations[ai]
Singapore	**Addressed** • Every child born alive must be registered[aj] • No specific provision on registration of foundlings and older children, abandoned and 'illegitimate' children	**Not addressed**	**Not addressed** • No prescription that birth registration is to be free • Prescription for the issuance of a birth certificate is not expressly provided	**Not addressed**

(continued)

Table 6.4 (continued)

Standard 1: Universal, well-managed and free birth registration	Totality of birth registration	Confidentiality of sensitive content, including information from irregular migrants	Free birth registration	Rules of proof to be flexible, i.e. that avoids excessive documentary requirements
Malaysia • Birth and Death Registration Act 1957 (Act 299)	**Addressed** • Every birth in the country is required to be registered[ak] • Specific provisions on the registration of abandoned children[al](newborn) and children born out of wedlock exist[am]	**Not addressed**	**Partially addressed** • No fee is imposed on the prescribed issuance of a birth certificate • Amendment to Section 12 of Act 299 provides that every birth reported after the expiration of 60 days from the date of birth shall not be registered except with the written authority of the Registrar general, subject to such fees and conditions for Late Birth Registration[an]	**Not addressed**
The Philippines	**Addressed** • Registration of every birth in the country and vital events abroad[ao] together with registration of foundlings[ap] and 'illegitimate'[aq] children are addressed in the legal framework	**Partially addressed** • Non-disclosure of the birth record is generally provided.[ar] However, preservation of information provided for birth registration to avoid immigration enforcement is not prescribed	**Partially addressed** • Birth registration is free[as] yet the issuance of certified or copies of birth transcripts may be subject to a fee.[at] No fee is indicated for delayed birth registration	**Partially addressed** • Detailed rules of evidencefor delayed registration are spelled out[au]
Myanmar	Unavailable civil registration law			

Table 6.4 (continued)

[a]United Nations, Department of Economic and Social Affairs, Statistics Division (UNSD), *Handbook on Training in Civil Registration and Vital Statistic Systems, Series F No. 84* (2002), para 33, p 9; Department of Economics and Social Affairs (Statistics Division), *Principles and Recommendations for a Vital Statistic System* (2014), New York: UN Publications, para 296

[b]UN Human Rights Council. *Birth Registration and the Right of Everyone to Recognition Everywhere as a Person before the Law* (17 June 2014), para III.11; African Charter on the Rights and Welfare of the Child (adopted 11 July 1990, in force 29 November 1999), CAB/LEG/24.9/49, para 50

[c]Economic and Social Commission for Asia and the Pacific (UNESCAP), 2 June 2015, Resolution adopted by the Economic and Social Commission for Asia and the Pacific, *Asian and Pacific Civil Registration and Vital Statistics 2015–2024*, UN Doc. E/ESCAP/RES/71/14, New York: United Nations. Part B, II (13); Committee on the Protection of the Rights of All Migrants Workers and Members of Their Families (CMW), Joint General Comment No. 4 (2017) of the Committee on the Protection of the Rights of All Migrant Workers and Members of Their Families and No. 23 (2017) of the Committee on the Rights of the Child on the General Principles regarding the Human Rights of Children in the Context of International Migration, para 20

[d]UNHCR, 'Conclusion on Civil Registration No. 111 (LXIV)'. Doc. A/AC.96/1035. Geneva: UNHCR. [17 October 2013]

[e]UNSD, *Civil Registration and Vital Statistics Knowledge Base* (2015), para 62, p 15. Retrieved from http://unstats.un.org/unsd/demographic [Accessed 5 May 2016]; Department of Economics and Social Affairs (Statistics Division), *Principles and Recommendations for a Vital Statistic System* (2014), New York: UN Publications, para 294

[f]UNSD, *Civil Registration and Vital Statistics Knowledge Base* (2015), para 48, p 12. Retrieved from http://unstats.un.org/unsd/demographic [Accessed 5 May 2016]

[g]UNSD, *Principles and Recommendations for a Vital Statistics System* (Revision 3)(2014), para 299, p 68; See also Committee on the Protection of the Rights of All Migrants Workers and Members of Their Families (CMW), Joint General Comment No. 4 (2017) of the Committee on the Protection of the Rights of All Migrant Workers and Members of Their Families and No. 23 (2017) of the Committee on the Rights of the Child on the General Principles regarding the Human Rights of Children in the Context of International Migration, paras 20–21

[h]UNICEF, *A Passport to Protection: A Guide to Birth Registration Programming* (2013), p 22

[i]UNICEF, *A Passport to Protection: A Guide to Birth Registration Programming* (2013), p 22 and 122; General Comment on Article 6 of the ACRWC: The Right to a Name, Registration at Birth, and to Acquire a Nationality, ACERWC/GC/02, Addis Ababa: African Union, 2014, para 82

[j]General Comment on Article 6 of the ACRWC: The Right to a Name, Registration at Birth, and to Acquire a Nationality, ACERWC/GC/02, Addis Ababa: African Union, 2014, para 51

[k]UNHCR, Conclusion on Civil Registration No. 111 (LXIV), Doc. A/AC.96/1035, Geneva: UNHCR [17 October 2013]

[l]General Comment on Article 6 of the ACRWC: The Right to a Name, Registration at Birth, and to Acquire a Nationality, ACERWC/GC/02, Addis Ababa: African Union, 2014, para 81

[m]UNICEF, *A Passport to Protection: A Guide to Birth Registration Programming* (2013), p 118

Table 6.4 (continued)

[n]UN Human Rights Council, *Birth Registration and the Right of Everyone to Recognition Everywhere as a Person before the Law* (17 June 2014), para II.5

[o]General Comment on Article 6 of the ACRWC: The Right to a Name, Registration at Birth, and to Acquire a Nationality, ACERWC/GC/02, Addis Ababa: African Union, 2014, para 41

[p]Economic and Social Commission for Asia and the Pacific (UNESCAP), 2 June 2015, Resolution adopted by the Economic and Social Commission for Asia and the Pacific, *Asian and Pacific Civil Registration and Vital Statistics* 2015–2024, UN Doc. E/ESCAP/RES/71/14, New York: United Nations, Goal 2; UNESCAP, *Regional Action Framework on Civil Registration and Vital Statistics in Asia and the Pacific* (2014), p 14, Inter-American Court of Human Rights, Series C, Case 130, 8 September 2005

[q]United Nations, Department of Economic and Social Affairs, Statistics Division (UNSD), *Handbook on Training in Civil Registration and Vital Statistic Systems, Series F No. 84* (2002), para 126, p 28

[r]United Nations, Department of Economic and Social Affairs, Statistics Division (UNSD), *Handbook on Training in Civil Registration and Vital Statistic Systems, Series F No. 84* (2002), para 127, p 28

[s]UN Human Rights Council, *Birth Registration and the Right of Everyone to Recognition Everywhere as a Person before the Law* (17 June 2014), para C.56–60, p 13

[t]General Comment on Article 6 of the ACRWC: The Right to a Name, Registration at Birth, and to Acquire a Nationality. ACERWC/GC/02. Addis Ababa: African Union (2014), para 66

[u]General Comment on Article 6 of the ACRWC: The Right to a Name, Registration at Birth, and to Acquire a Nationality. ACERWC/GC/02. Addis Ababa: African Union (2014), para 73

[v]UN Human Rights Council, *Birth Registration and the Right of Everyone to Recognition Everywhere as a Person before the Law* (17 June 2014), para C. 56, p 13; UNHCR, *Conclusion on Civil Registration No. 111* (LXIV), Doc. A/AC.1035/96, Geneva: UNHCR [17 October 2013]

[w]General Comment on Article 6 of the ACRWC: The Right to a Name, Registration at Birth, and to Acquire a Nationality. ACERWC/GC/02. Addis Ababa: African Union, 2014, para 74

[x]United Nations, Department of Economic and Social Affairs, Statistics Division (UNSD), Handbook on Training in Civil Registration and Vital Statistic Systems, Series F No. 84 (2002), para 34, p 8

[y]UN Human Rights Council, Birth Registration and the Right of Everyone to Recognition Everywhere as a Person before the Law (17 June 2014), para C 56–60

[z]UNICEF, *A Passport yo Protection: A Guide to Birth Registration Programming* (2013), p 26

[aa]General Comment on Article 6 of the ACRWC: The Right to a Name, Registration at Birth, and to Acquire a Nationality, ACERWC/GC/02, Addis Ababa: African Union, 2014, para 79

[ab]UNSD, Civil Registry and Vital Statistics Knowledge Base (2015), para 121

[ac]UNSD, *Principles and Recommendations for a Vital Statistics System* (Revision 2014)(3), para 363; UNSD, *Civil Registration and Vital Statistics Knowledge Base* (2015), para 121

Table 6.4 (continued)

[ad]UNSD, *Civil Registration and Vital Statistics Knowledge Base* (2015), para 121
[ae]UNESCAP, *Regional Action Framework on Civil Registration and Vital Statistics in Asia and the Pacific* (2014), para 46, p 17
[af]UN Human Rights Council, Birth Registration and the Right of Everyone to Recognition Everywhere as a Person before the Law (17 June 2014), para B.55
[ag]UNSD, Civil Registration and Vital Statistics Knowledge Base (2015), para 123
[ah]United Nations, Department of Economic and Social Affairs, Statistics Division (UNSD), Handbook on Training in Civil Registration and Vital Statistic Systems, Series F No. 84. (2002), para 34
[ai]UNSD, Civil Registration and Vital Statistics Knowledge Base (2015), para 124–125, p 28
[a]Section 12(1) of Births and Deaths Registration Act 1979 (Chapter 79) (Revised Edition 2013) Brunei
[b]Section 5(3) of Births and Deaths Registration Act 1979 (Chapter 79)(Revised Edition 2013) Brunei
[c]Article 3 of the Law on the Protection of the Rights and Interests of the Child No. 05/NA of 27 December 2006
[d]Article 9 and Article 20 of Decree of the President of the Lao People's Democratic Republic on the Promulgation of the Law on Family Registration No. 21, 1992
[e]Article 19 of the Law on the Protection of the Rights and Interests of the Child No. 05/NA of 27 December 2006
[f]Article 15 of the 9 Decree of the President of the Lao People's Democratic Republic on the Promulgation of the Law on Family Registration No. 21, 1992
[g]Article 6 of Decree of the President of the Lao People's Democratic Republic on the Promulgation of the Law on Family Registration No. 21, 1992
[h]Article 26 of Sub-Decree on Civil Status (Civil Registration) No. 103 of December 2000
[i]Article 17 of Sub-Decree on Civil Status (Civil Registration) No. 103 of December 2000
[j]Article 23 of Sub-Decree on Civil Status (Civil Registration) No. 103 of December 2000
[k]Article 26 of Sub-Decree on Civil Status (Civil Registration) No. 103 of December 2000
[l]Articles 19 and 20 of Sub-Decree on Civil Status (Civil Registration) No. 103 of December 2000
[m]Article 24 of Sub-Decree on Civil Status (Civil Registration) No. 103 of December 2000
[n]Article 2(2) of Decree No. 60/2014/QH 13 on Law on Civil Status of 20 November 2014. The right to birth registration, name and nationality of children below the age of 16 is recognised in Article 13 of the Children Law (Law No 102/ 2016/ QH13)
[o]Article 16(1) and 16(3) of Decree No. 60/2014/QH 13 on Law on Civil Status
[p]Articles 24 and 25 of Decree No. 60/2014/QH 13 on Law on Civil Status
[q]Article 6(1) of Decree No. 60/2014/QH 13 on Law on Civil Status
[r]Prime Minister's Directive 24 of 2007 (Directive 24/2007/CT-TTg of the Prime Minister on Fees for Public Services). See further UNHCR, *Submission by the United Nations High Commissioner for Refugees for the Office of the High Commissioner for Human Rights› Compilation Report—Universal Periodic Review: Socialist Republic of Vietnam* (June 2013), p 2
[s]Article 11(1) of Decree No. 60/2014/QH 13 on Law on Civil Status

Table 6.4 (continued)

[t]Article 16(2) of Decree No. 60/2014/QH 13 on Law on Civil Status
[u]Article 16 of Decree No. 60/2014/QH 13 on Law on Civil Status
[v]Section 16 of the Thai Civil Registration Act (No. 2) B.E. 2551 (2008). Under the old provisions of the Civil Registration Act B.E. 2534, only children born to Thai parents and migrant parents with legal status (PR status or temporary residential status) may be registered at birth
[w]See Article 19 of Thai Civil Registration Act B.E. 2534 as amended by Article 14 of Thai Civil Registration Act B.E. 2551 (2008)
[x]Rates of Fees, Thai Civil Registration Act (No. 2) B.E. 2551 (2008). According to the new rates of fees in B.E. 2551, birth report under Section 18 is charged 100 baht each copy
[y]UN Committee on the Rights of the Child, 'Consideration of Reports Submitted by States Parties under Article 44 of the Convention, Concluding Observations: Thailand', Geneva: CRC/C/THA/CO/3–4. Thailand: CRC, 17 February 2012, para 43
[z]UNESCO, *Citizenship Manual-Capacity Building on Birth Registration and Citizenship in Thailand: Citizenship Manual* (2008), p 10; see Section 16 of Thai Civil Registration Act (No. 2) B.E. 2551 (2008) that repeals and replaces Section 20 of Thai Civil Registration Act B.E. 253
[aa]Article 3, Peraturan Pemerintah No. 37 Tahun 2007 Tentang Pelaksanaan Undang-Undang No. 23 Tahun 2006 Tentang Administrasi Kependudukan
[ab]Article 28, Peraturan Pemerintah No. 37 Tahun 2007 Tentang Pelaksanaan Undang-Undang No. 23 Tahun 2006 Tentang Administrasi Kependudukan
[ac]Article 49, Peraturan Pemerintah No. 37 Tahun 2007 Tentang Pelaksanaan Undang-Undang No. 23 Tahun 2006 Tentang Administrasi Kependudukan
[ad]Article 49, Undang-Undang Republik Indonesia, Nomor 24 Tahun 2013 Tentang Perubahan Atas Undang-Undang Nomor 23 Tahun 2006 Tentang Administrasi Kependudukan (Law 24 of 2013 on Population Administration). For a religious marriage that is unregistered, the children may register their birth but they shall have their civil relationship only with their mothers. See Article 43(1) Undang- undang Republik Indonesia Nomor 1 Tahun 1974 Tentang Perkahwinan
[ae]Articles 4 and 29, Peraturan Pemerintah No. 37 Tahun 2007 Tentang Pelaksanaan Undang-Undang No. 23 Tahun 2006 Tentang Administrasi Kependudukan
[af]Chapter IX, Undang-Undang No. 23 Tahun 2006 Tentang Administrasi Kependudukan
[ag]Article 79A, Peraturan Pemerintah No. 37 Tahun 2007 Tentang Pelaksanaan Undang-Undang No. 23 Tahun 2006 Tentang Administrasi Kependudukan; Articles 1(9) and 5, Peraturan Pemerintah No. 37 Tahun 2007 Tentang Pelaksanaan Undang-Undang No. 23 Tahun 2006 Tentang Administrasi Kependudukan
[ah]E.g., Article 3(3) of para 2, Part 1, Chapter III, Peraturan Daerah Provinsi DKI Jakarta Nomor 3 Tahun 2012 Tentang Retribusi Daerah sebagaimana diubah dengan Peraturan Daerah Provinsi DKI Jakarta Nomor 1 Tahun 2015
[ai]Other sub-regulations may specify the procedures for birth registration, particularly the documentary requirements to be fulfilled. See, for instance, Article 52 of Peraturan Presiden Nomor 25 Tahun 2008 Tentang Pensyaratan dan Tata Cara Pendaftaran Penduduk dan Pencatatan Sipil
[aj]Section 9 of Registration of Births and Deaths Act (Chapter 267) (Revised Edition 1985)
[ak]Section 12 of the Birth and Death Registration Act 1957
[al]Section 9 of Birth and Death Registration Act 1957
[am]Section 13 of the Birth and Death Registration Act 1957

Table 6.4 (continued)

[an]Section 12 of the Birth and Death Registration Act 1957. The Government announced in 2017 that a fine of RM1,000 will be imposed for late registration after 60 days in Peninsular Malaysia under the new amendment to the Birth and Death Registration Act 1957 in 2016. See N.A., 'RM 1,000 fine for Late Registration' (2017), https://www.thestar.com.my/news/nation/2017/10/11/fine-for-late-birth-registration/ [Accessed 5 January 2018]. However, the rates for late birth registration listed as of November 2018 on the website of the National Registration Department of Malaysia are (i) RM5 for birth register search; (ii) RM10 for processing fee for late birth registration; and (iii) not exceeding RM50 for the penalty. See National Registration Department Malaysia, 'Home/ Late Registration of Birth (Peninsular)'. Retrieved from http://www.jpn.gov.my/en/maklumat-kelahiran/pendaftaran-lewat-kelahiran-2/#1458289648764-bf711d6d-f9ed [Accessed 27 November 2018]

[ao]Section 4 of the Civil Registry Law (Act No. 3753) and Administrative Order No. 1 Series of 1993 Implementing Rules and Regulations of Act No. 3753 and Other Laws on Civil Registration (Vol. 89, Number 2, Official Gazette; January 11, 1993 (Administrative Order No. 1 Series 1993); Rule 10 of Administrative Order No. 1 Series of 1993

[ap]Section 5 of the Civil Registry Law (Act No. 3753); Rules 27 to 29 of the Administrative Order No.1 Series 1993

[aq]Section 4 of the Civil Registry Law (Act No. 3753)

[ar]Rule 24 of Administrative Order No.1 Series 1993

[as]Rule 17 of Administrative Order No.1 Series 1993

[at]Rule 17(2) of Administrative Order No. 1 Series 1993

[au]See Rule 25 of Administrative Order No.1 Series 1993. The requirements include duly accomplished and signed certificate of live birth, affidavit for delayed registration, affidavit of two disinterested parties who might have witnessed the birth and certificate of marriage if the person is already married

and/or a registration system that interoperates with other services for the public. The rest three countries display an absence of or minimal fulfilment of the standard. The laws and practice in Lao PDR and Myanmar do not indicate provisions for the three elements, while Cambodia adopted mobile registration services during its previous birth registration campaign between 2004 and 2005, held with the support of Plan Cambodia, UNICEF, and the Child Rights Foundation. The campaign successfully resulted in the issuance of birth certificates to over 9.5 million Cambodian children and adults.[16]

In respect of simplicity of procedures, Viet Nam and Indonesia demonstrate this standard. The law relating to CRVS enforced in 2016 in Viet Nam creates a better level of simplicity, flexibility, and responsiveness to the communities, namely, through different means for submission of civil registration documents, including via the platform of an online civil registration service. The rest of the countries either minimally or do not exhibit this standard (Table 6.5).

3. **Analysis of laws (and practices) on birth registration for Standard 3: Accuracy, Timeline and Facilitated Late Birth Registration**

This standard is divided up into two components of (i) accurate and timely birth registration and (ii) facilitated birth registration. Under the first component, most countries partially reflect the recommended standards. Viet Nam provides for a longer timeframe than the recommended 30 days for birth registration while Thailand allows for a shorter period than 30 days, yet without prescribing an overdue period for registration that occurs after that. The Philippines requires that birth registration shall take place within 30 days from the time of birth without indicating the grace period of 1 year as suggested. In addition, the procedures for delayed registration after the prescribed period of 30 days are spelled out.[17]

Brunei and Singapore briefly prescribe 14 days as the initial period for birth registration (as opposed to the 30 days recommended by the standard). The countries further allow for late and/or delayed timeframes for birth registrations that are much shorter than the 1-year grace period recommended. Lao PDR, Cambodia seem to only provide for one applicable timeframe of 30 days after birth. Meanwhile, Indonesia, Malaysia, and Viet Nam specify that all births must be registered within 60 days.[18] (Previously, the initial period prescribed for births in Malaysia was 14 days.) In

[16] Plan International, *Count Me In: The global Campaign for Universal Birth Registration, Interim Campaign Report* (2005), p 11. According to a Cambodia's representative to the Regional Workshop to Evaluate Activities by ACWC (Viet Nam) relating to the Rights to a Nationality for Women and Children in the ASEAN Community and to Develop further Proposals for Collaboration for the 2016–2020 Workplan of the ASEAN Commission on the Promotion and Protection of the Rights of Women and Children held from 21 to 22 September 2016 in Dalat, Viet Nam, over 90% of birth certificates were issued in 2006, which is equivalent to 11, 828, 208 out of the total population of 12, 860, 124.

[17] See Rules 19 and 15, Administrative Order No. 1 Series of 1993.

[18] Article 32(1), Undang-Undang Republik Indonesia Nomor 24 Tahun 2013 Tentang Perubahan Atas Undang-Undang Nomor 23 Tahun 2006 Tentang Administrasi Kependudukan; Sect. 8 of the Birth and Death Registration Act 1957; Article 15 of Decree No. 60/2014.

Table 6.5 Mapping of birth registration safeguards for standard 2

Standard 2: flexible and responsive to circumstances of families	Mobile registration, decentralised system, and interoperability with other services such as healthcare and education	Simpler procedures
Brunei	**Addressed (partly in law and in practice)** • Decentralised birth registration is adopted[a] • Mobile registration is available in practice and interoperates with medical services[b]	**Minimally addressed** • Information may be given orally by persons unable to write[c]
Lao PDR	**Not addressed**	**Not addressed**
Cambodia	**Not addressed** • Decentralisation is not expressly reflected in the law • Mobile registration adopted during the period of birth registration campaign	**Not addressed**
Viet Nam	**Addressed** • The system is decentralised at the commune level[d] • Mobile registration is provided where necessary[e]	**Addressed** • The law requires the creation of favourable conditions for every individual to realise civil status registration.[f] • Documents of civil registration may be submitted physically, by post or electronically under the country's online civil registration system under the 2016 law.[g]
Thailand	**Addressed** • The system is decentralised at the district level[h] • Mobile registration is reflected in practice[i]	**Not addressed**
Indonesia	**Addressed** • The system is decentralised at the city or district level[j] • A circuit or mobile service for civil registry introduced in Aceh in 2005 following the tsunami. The policy pursuant to Law 24/2013 on Population Administration requires the government to conduct outreach to register people[k]	**Addressed** • Provision for assistance for those who are unable to implement civil registrationindependently exists[l]

(continued)

Table 6.5 (continued)

Standard 2: flexible and responsive to circumstances of families	Mobile registration, decentralised system, and interoperability with other services such as healthcare and education	Simpler procedures
Singapore	**Minimally addressed (only in practice)** • In practice, there is interoperability of birth registration services with hospitals and medical centres[m]	**Minimally addressed (only in practice)** • Registration by proxy with parents' letter of authorisation is possible[n]
Malaysia	**Addressed (partly in law and in practice)** • Birth registration system is decentralised in terms of the services (three laws govern birth registration systems according to the country's geographical regions)[o] • Mobile courts and birth registration are carried out, especially in Sabah and Sarawak[p]	**Not addressed**
The Philippines	**Addressed** • The civil registration system is decentralised at the level of municipality, district, and city[q] • Mobile registration exists in practice[r]	**Not addressed**
Myanmar	**Not addressed**	**Minimally addressed (in practice)** • An electronic platform for birth registration that operates in states and divisions has been created under a birth registration project[s]

[a]United Nations, Department of Economic and Social Affairs, Statistics Division (UNSD), *Handbook on Training in Civil Registration and Vital Statistic Systems, Series F No. 84* (2002), para 33, p 9; Department of Economics and Social Affairs (Statistics Division), *Principles and Recommendations for a Vital Statistic System* (2014), New York: UN Publications, para 296

[b]UN Human Rights Council. *Birth Registration and the Right of Everyone to Recognition Everywhere as a Person before the Law* (17 June 2014), para III.11; African Charter on the Rights and Welfare of the Child (adopted 11 July 1990, in force 29 November 1999), CAB/LEG/24.9/49, para 50

[c]Economic and Social Commission for Asia and the Pacific (UNESCAP), 2 June 2015, Resolution adopted by the Economic and Social Commission for Asia and the Pacific, *Asian and Pacific Civil Registration and Vital Statistics 2015–2024*, UN Doc. E/ESCAP/RES/71/14, New York: United Nations. Part B, II (13); Committee on the Protection of the Rights of All Migrants Workers and Members of Their Families (CMW), Joint General Comment No. 4 (2017) of the Committee on the Protection of the Rights of All Migrant Workers and Members of Their Families and No. 23 (2017) of the Committee on the Rights of the Child on the General Principles regarding the Human Rights of Children in the Context of International Migration, para 20

Table 6.5 (continued)

[d]UNHCR, 'Conclusion on Civil Registration No. 111 (LXIV)'. Doc. A/AC.96/1035. Geneva: UNHCR. [17 October 2013]

[e]UNSD, *Civil Registration and Vital Statistics Knowledge Base* (2015), para 62, p 15. Retrieved from http://unstats.un.org/unsd/demographic [Accessed 5 May 2016]; Department of Economics and Social Affairs (Statistics Division), *Principles and Recommendations for a Vital Statistic System* (2014), New York: UN Publications, para 294

[f]UNSD, *Civil Registration and Vital Statistics Knowledge Base* (2015), para 48, p 12. Retrieved from http://unstats.un.org/unsd/demographic [Accessed 5 May 2016]

[g]UNSD, *Principles and Recommendations for a Vital Statistics System* (Revision 3)(2014), para 299, p 68; See also Committee on the Protection of the Rights of All Migrants Workers and Members of Their Families (CMW), Joint General Comment No. 4 (2017) of the Committee on the Protection of the Rights of All Migrant Workers and Members of Their Families and No. 23 (2017) of the Committee on the Rights of the Child on the General Principles regarding the Human Rights of Children in the Context of International Migration, paras 20–21

[h]UNICEF, *A Passport to Protection: A Guide to Birth Registration Programming* (2013), p 22

[i]UNICEF, *A Passport to Protection: A Guide to Birth Registration Programming* (2013), p 22 and 122; General Comment on Article 6 of the ACRWC: The Right to a Name, Registration at Birth, and to Acquire a Nationality, ACERWC/GC/02, Addis Ababa: African Union, 2014, para 82

[j]General Comment on Article 6 of the ACRWC: The Right to a Name, Registration at Birth, and to Acquire a Nationality, ACERWC/GC/02, Addis Ababa: African Union, 2014, para 51

[k]UNHCR, Conclusion on Civil Registration No. 111 (LXIV), Doc. A/AC.96/1035, Geneva: UNHCR [17 October 2013]

[l]General Comment on Article 6 of the ACRWC: The Right to a Name, Registration at Birth, and to Acquire a Nationality, ACERWC/GC/02, Addis Ababa: African Union, 2014, para 81

[m]UNICEF, *A Passport to Protection: A Guide to Birth Registration Programming* (2013), p 118

[n]UN Human Rights Council, *Birth Registration and the Right of Everyone to Recognition Everywhere as a Person before the Law* (17 June 2014), para II.5

[o]General Comment on Article 6 of the ACRWC: The Right to a Name, Registration at Birth, and to Acquire a Nationality, ACERWC/GC/02, Addis Ababa: African Union, 2014, para 41

[p]Economic and Social Commission for Asia and the Pacific (UNESCAP), 2 June 2015, Resolution adopted by the Economic and Social Commission for Asia and the Pacific, *Asian and Pacific Civil Registration and Vital Statistics* 2015–2024, UN Doc. E/ESCAP/RES/71/14, New York: United Nations, Goal 2; UNESCAP, *Regional Action Framework on Civil Registration and Vital Statistics in Asia and the Pacific* (2014), p 14, Inter-American Court of Human Rights, Series C, Case 130, 8 September 2005

[q]United Nations, Department of Economic and Social Affairs, Statistics Division (UNSD), *Handbook on Training in Civil Registration and Vital Statistic Systems, Series F No. 84* (2002), para 126, p 28

[r]United Nations, Department of Economic and Social Affairs, Statistics Division (UNSD), *Handbook on Training in Civil Registration and Vital Statistic Systems, Series F No. 84* (2002), para 127, p 28

Table 6.5 (continued)

[s]UN Human Rights Council, *Birth Registration and the Right of Everyone to Recognition Everywhere as a Person before the Law* (17 June 2014), para C.56–60, p 13

[t]General Comment on Article 6 of the ACRWC: The Right to a Name, Registration at Birth, and to Acquire a Nationality. ACERWC/GC/02. Addis Ababa: African Union (2014), para 66

[u]General Comment on Article 6 of the ACRWC: The Right to a Name, Registration at Birth, and to Acquire a Nationality. ACERWC/GC/02. Addis Ababa: African Union (2014), para 73

[v]UN Human Rights Council, *Birth Registration and the Right of Everyone to Recognition Everywhere as a Person before the Law* (17 June 2014), para C. 56, p 13; UNHCR, *Conclusion on Civil Registration No. 111* (LXIV), Doc. A/AC.1035/96, Geneva: UNHCR [17 October 2013]

[w]General Comment on Article 6 of the ACRWC: The Right to a Name, Registration at Birth, and to Acquire a Nationality. ACERWC/GC/02. Addis Ababa: African Union, 2014, para 74

[x]United Nations, Department of Economic and Social Affairs, Statistics Division (UNSD), Handbook on Training in Civil Registration and Vital Statistic Systems, Series F No. 84 (2002), para 34, p 8

[y]UN Human Rights Council, Birth Registration and the Right of Everyone to Recognition Everywhere as a Person before the Law (17 June 2014), para C 56–60

[z]UNICEF, *A Passport yo Protection: A Guide to Birth Registration Programming* (2013), p 26

[aa]General Comment on Article 6 of the ACRWC: The Right to a Name, Registration at Birth, and to Acquire a Nationality, ACERWC/GC/02, Addis Ababa: African Union, 2014, para 79

[ab]UNSD, Civil Registry and Vital Statistics Knowledge Base (2015), para 121

[ac]UNSD, *Principles and Recommendations for a Vital Statistics System* (Revision 2014)(3), para 363; UNSD, *Civil Registration and Vital Statistics Knowledge Base* (2015), para 121

[ad]UNSD, *Civil Registration and Vital Statistics Knowledge Base* (2015), para 121

[ae]UNESCAP, *Regional Action Framework on Civil Registration and Vital Statistics in Asia and the Pacific* (2014), para 46, p 17

[af]UN Human Rights Council, Birth Registration and the Right of Everyone to Recognition Everywhere as a Person before the Law (17 June 2014), para B.55

[ag]UNSD, Civil Registration and Vital Statistics Knowledge Base (2015), para 123

[ah]United Nations, Department of Economic and Social Affairs, Statistics Division (UNSD), Handbook on Training in Civil Registration and Vital Statistic Systems, Series F No. 84. (2002), para 34

[ai]UNSD, Civil Registration and Vital Statistics Knowledge Base (2015), para 124–125, p 28

[a]Section 12(1) of Births and Deaths Registration Act 1979 (Chapter 79) (Revised Edition 2013) Brunei

[b]Section 5(3) of Births and Deaths Registration Act 1979 (Chapter 79)(Revised Edition 2013) Brunei

[c]Article 3 of the Law on the Protection of the Rights and Interests of the Child No. 05/NA of 27 December 2006

Table 6.5 (continued)

[d]Article 9 and Article 20 of Decree of the President of the Lao People's Democratic Republic on the Promulgation of the Law on Family Registration No. 21, 1992
[e]Article 19 of the Law on the Protection of the Rights and Interests of the Child No. 05/NA of 27 December 2006
[f]Article 15 of the 9 Decree of the President of the Lao People's Democratic Republic on the Promulgation of the Law on Family Registration No. 21, 1992
[g]Article 6 of Decree of the President of the Lao People's Democratic Republic on the Promulgation of the Law on Family Registration No. 21, 1992
[h]Article 26 of Sub-Decree on Civil Status (Civil Registration) No. 103 of December 2000
[i]Article 17 of Sub-Decree on Civil Status (Civil Registration) No. 103 of December 2000
[j]Article 23 of Sub-Decree on Civil Status (Civil Registration) No. 103 of December 2000
[k]Article 26 of Sub-Decree on Civil Status (Civil Registration) No. 103 of December 2000
[l]Articles 19 and 20 of Sub-Decree on Civil Status (Civil Registration) No. 103 of December 2000
[m]Article 24 of Sub-Decree on Civil Status (Civil Registration) No. 103 of December 2000
[n]Article 2(2) of Decree No. 60/2014/QH 13 on Law on Civil Status of 20 November 2014. The right to birth registration, name and nationality of children below the age of 16 is recognised in Article 13 of the Children Law (Law No 102/ 2016/ QH13)
[o]Article 16(1) and 16(3) of Decree No. 60/2014/QH 13 on Law on Civil Status
[p]Articles 24 and 25 of Decree No. 60/2014/QH 13 on Law on Civil Status
[q]Article 6(1) of Decree No. 60/2014/QH 13 on Law on Civil Status
[r]Prime Minister's Directive 24 of 2007 (Directive 24/2007/CT-TTg of the Prime Minister on Fees for Public Services). See further UNHCR, *Submission by the United Nations High Commissioner for Refugees for the Office of the High Commissioner for Human Rights› Compilation Report—Universal Periodic Review: Socialist Republic of Vietnam* (June 2013), p 2
[s]Article 11(1) of Decree No. 60/2014/QH 13 on Law on Civil Status
[t]Article 16(2) of Decree No. 60/2014/QH 13 on Law on Civil Status
[u]Article 16 of Decree No. 60/2014/QH 13 on Law on Civil Status
[v]Section 16 of the Thai Civil Registration Act (No. 2) B.E. 2551 (2008). Under the old provisions of the Civil Registration Act B.E. 2534, only children born to Thai parents and migrant parents with legal status (PR status or temporary residential status) may be registered at birth
[w]See Article 19 of Thai Civil Registration Act B.E. 2534 as amended by Article 14 of Thai Civil Registration Act B.E. 2551 (2008)
[x]Rates of Fees, Thai Civil Registration Act (No. 2) B.E. 2551 (2008). According to the new rates of fees in B.E. 2551, birth report under Section 18 is charged 100 baht each copy
[y]UN Committee on the Rights of the Child, 'Consideration of Reports Submitted by States Parties under Article 44 of the Convention, Concluding Observations: Thailand', Geneva: CRC/C/THA/CO/3–4. Thailand: CRC, 17 February 2012, para 43
[z]UNESCO, *Citizenship Manual-Capacity Building on Birth Registration and Citizenship in Thailand: Citizenship Manual* (2008), p 10; see Section 16 of Thai Civil Registration Act (No. 2) B.E. 2551 (2008) that repeals and replaces Section 20 of Thai Civil Registration Act B.E. 253
[aa]Article 3, Peraturan Pemerintah No. 37 Tahun 2007 Tentang Pelaksanaan Undang-Undang No. 23 Tahun 2006 Tentang Administrasi Kependudukan

Table 6.5 (continued)

[ab] Article 28, Peraturan Pemerintah No. 37 Tahun 2007 Tentang Pelaksanaan Undang-Undang No. 23 Tahun 2006 Tentang Administrasi Kependudukan

[ac] Article 49, Peraturan Pemerintah No. 37 Tahun 2007 Tentang Pelaksanaan Undang-Undang No. 23 Tahun 2006 Tentang Administrasi Kependudukan

[ad] Article 49, Undang-Undang Republik Indonesia, Nomor 24 Tahun 2013 Tentang Perubahan Atas Undang-Undang Nomor 23 Tahun 2006 Tentang Administrasi Kependudukan (Law 24 of 2013 on Population Administration). For a religious marriage that is unregistered, the children may register their birth but they shall have their civil relationship only with their mothers. See Article 43(1) Undang- undang Republik Indonesia Nomor 1 Tahun 1974 Tentang Perkahwinan

[ae] Articles 4 and 29, Peraturan Pemerintah No. 37 Tahun 2007 Tentang Pelaksanaan Undang-Undang No. 23 Tahun 2006 Tentang Administrasi Kependudukan

[af] Chapter IX, Undang-Undang No. 23 Tahun 2006 Tentang Administrasi Kependudukan

[ag] Article 79A, Peraturan Pemerintah No. 37 Tahun 2007 Tentang Pelaksanaan Undang-Undang No. 23 Tahun 2006 Tentang Administrasi Kependudukan; Articles 1(9) and 5, Peraturan Pemerintah No. 37 Tahun 2007 Tentang Pelaksanaan Undang-Undang No. 23 Tahun 2006 Tentang Administrasi Kependudukan

[ah] E.g., Article 3(3) of para 2, Part 1, Chapter III, Peraturan Daerah Provinsi DKI Jakarta Nomor 3 Tahun 2012 Tentang Retribusi Daerah sebagaimana diubah dengan Peraturan Daerah Provinsi DKI Jakarta Nomor 1 Tahun 2015

[ai] Other sub-regulations may specify the procedures for birth registration, particularly the documentary requirements to be fulfilled. See, for instance, Article 52 of Peraturan Presiden Nomor 25 Tahun 2008 Tentang Pensyaratan dan Tata Cara Pendaftaran Penduduk dan Pencatatan Sipil

[aj] Section 9 of Registration of Births and Deaths Act (Chapter 267) (Revised Edition 1985)

[ak] Section 12 of the Birth and Death Registration Act 1957

[al] Section 9 of Birth and Death Registration Act 1957

[am] Section 13 of the Birth and Death Registration Act 1957

[an] Section 12 of the Birth and Death Registration Act 1957. The Government announced in 2017 that a fine of RM1,000 will be imposed for late registration after 60 days in Peninsular Malaysia under the new amendment to the Birth and Death Registration Act 1957 in 2016. See N.A., 'RM 1,000 fine for Late Registration' (2017), https://www.thestar.com.my/news/nation/2017/10/11/fine-for-late-birth-registration/ [Accessed 5 January 2018]. However, the rates for late birth registration listed as of November 2018 on the website of the National Registration Department of Malaysia are (i) RM5 for birth register search; (ii) RM10 for processing fee for late birth registration; and (iii) not exceeding RM50 for the penalty. See National Registration Department Malaysia, 'Home/ Late Registration of Birth (Peninsular)'. Retrieved from http://www.jpn.gov.my/en/maklumat-kelahiran/pendaftaran-lewat-kelahiran-2/#1458289648764-bf711d6d-f9ed [Accessed 27 November 2018]

[ao] Section 4 of the Civil Registry Law (Act No. 3753) and Administrative Order No. 1 Series of 1993 Implementing Rules and Regulations of Act No. 3753 and Other Laws on Civil Registration (Vol. 89, Number 2, Official Gazette; January 11, 1993 (Administrative Order No. 1 Series 1993); Rule 10 of Administrative Order No. 1 Series of 1993

[ap] Section 5 of the Civil Registry Law (Act No. 3753); Rules 27 to 29 of the Administrative Order No.1 Series 1993

[aq] Section 4 of the Civil Registry Law (Act No. 3753)

[ar] Rule 24 of Administrative Order No.1 Series 1993

[as] Rule 17 of Administrative Order No.1 Series 1993

[at] Rule 17(2) of Administrative Order No. 1 Series 1993

[au] See Rule 25 of Administrative Order No.1 Series 1993. The requirements include duly accomplished and signed certificate of live birth, affidavit for delayed registration, affidavit of two disinterested parties who might have witnessed the birth and certificate of marriage if the person is already married

Table 6.5 (continued)

[a]Section 16 of Births and Deaths Registration Act 1979 (Chapter 79) (Revised Edition 2013) Brunei

[b]The CRC Committee in one of its Concluding Observations has noted and commended the work of Brunei's 'Flying Doctor Teams' in ensuring registration of children. The teams employ helicopters to reach remote areas and communities to both provide medical services and ensure birth registration. See United Nations Committee on the Rights of the Child, 'Concluding Observations on the Initial Report Submitted by Brunei Darussalam', UN Doc. CRC/C/15/Add.219, Indonesia: CRC, 27 October 2003, para 33; UN Human Rights Council, *Birth Registration and the Right of Everyone to Recognition Everywhere as a Person before the Law* (17 June 2014), para 79

[c]Section 5(1) of Births and Deaths Registration Act 1979 (Chapter 79) (Revised Edition 2013) Brunei

[d]The People's Committees of communes, wards, or district townships (known as the commune-level People's Committees) of the places of residence of fathers or mothers, as well as an overseas Vietnamese diplomatic mission or consular office, shall be the civil status registration agency. See Article 4(1) and Article 13 of Decree No. 60/2014

[e]Article 15(2) of Decree No. 60/2014

[f]Article 15(2) of Decree No. 60/2014

[g]See Article 9 of Decree No. 60/2014. See also Vietnam Law and Legal Forum, 'New Law on Civil Status' (5 August 2015). Retrieved from http://vietnamlawmagazine.vn/new-law-on-civil-status-4028.html [Accessed 6 October 2016]

[h]Parents or the official concerned must report the birth to the local registrar, which can include the village headmen. See Article 4, Thai Civil Registration Act (B.E. 2534) (1991). See further Section 6 of the Thai Registration Act (No. 2) B.E 2551 (2008)

[i]S. Heap & C. Cody. 2009. The Universal Birth Registration Campaign. *Force Migration Review 32*

[j]See Article 1(7) of Peraturan Pemerintah No. 37 Tahun 2007 Tentang Pelaksanaan Undang-Undang No. 23 Tahun 2006 Tentang Administrasi Kependudukan on the definition of 'Instansi Pelaksana'

[k]A.L. Buffardi & Kwan Men Yon, *Realising the Right to Legal Identity: A case study as part of an evaluation as part of the Australia Indonesia Partnership for Justice* (July 2016) https://www.refworld.org/pdfid/57922cfd4.pdf [Accessed 8 January 2018]

[l]See Section 57 of Peraturan Pemerintah No. 37 Tahun 2007 Tentang Pelaksanaan Undang-Undang No. 23 Tahun 2006 Tentang Administrasi Kependudukan

[m]Immigration and Checkpoints Authority Singapore Government, 'Checkpoints Authority'. Retrieved from https://www.ica.gov.sg/page.aspx?pageid=144 [Accessed 7 October 2016]

Table 6.5 (continued)

[n]Immigration and Checkpoints Authority Singapore Government, 'Checkpoints Authority'. Retrieved from https://www.ica.gov.sg/page.aspx?pageid=144 [Accessed 7 October 2016]
[o]Peninsular Malaysia (Birth and Death Registration Act 1957 (Act 299)), Sabahn (Sabah Birth and Death Registration Ordinance 1951 (Cap. 123)) and Sarawak (Sarawak Birth and Death Registration Ordinance 1951 (Cap. 10)). Under Section 7(1) Act 299, the birth of every child born in Malaysia shall be registered by the Registrar for the registration area in which the child was born
[p]A. Geraldine, 'Mobile Court: 10 Years On' (26 November 2017), *NST Online*. Retrieved from https://www.nst.com.my/news/nation/2017/11/307588/mobile-court-10-years [Accessed 20 December 2017]
[q]Section 3 of the Civil Registry Law (Act No. 3753)
[r]Mobile registration is available where civil registration is not accessible, for instance, to people vulnerable to armed conflicts and displacement in the Autonomous Region of Muslim Mindanao (ARMM). This is not reflected in the main legislation, but may be authorised through Executive Orders, such as through the Office of the Regional Governor, Executive Order No. 21, Series of 2012, Extending the Implementation of Free Birth Registration and Its Area of Coverage and Target Beneficiaries with DSWD-ARMM as Lead Implementing Agency
[s]In 2013, UNICEF Myanmar was reported working with the Government of Myanmar under the purview of its EU-funded multi-country birth registration project. Apart from providing technical advice, the project has created an electronic platform that adds real-time data as part of the permanent archive of birth registration that operates in all states and divisions in Myanmar. See Nay Pyi Taw, 'Getting to the Goal of 100% Birth Registration' (2015). Retrieved from http://www.unicef.org/myanmar/media_24526.html [Accessed 15 June 2016].

Malaysia and Indonesia, every birth reported after the expiration of 60 days from the date of birth shall not be registered except with the consent of the respective authorities, subject to such fees and conditions for late/delayed birth registration.[19] For the second component of facilitated birth registration, Viet Nam and Indonesia no longer subject late birth registration to court procedures.

Additionally, Viet Nam provides that 'publicity and transparency shall be ensured in civil status registration procedures'.[20]

Late birth registration is not subject to court procedures in Thailand. Somehow, the law does not clarify proof of birth registered after 30 days, which shall be further investigated. The Philippines may require the court process in the case of late birth registration, as there is a duty to file a complaint with the Prosecutor's Office. The law does spell out detailed procedures and evidence expected of late registrants, including furnishing an accomplished affidavit, sworn statements of the whereabouts of the mother, and the types of documentary evidence to be shown, such as baptismal certificate, school records, and medical records.[21]

In Malaysia (Peninsular), late registration is subject to some prescribed fee and will not involve court proceedings, but shall be referred to the Registrar General and subject to further conditions imposed. Nevertheless, its procedures and requirements for late and delayed birth registrations are not provided in the law. In Thailand, birth registration after 30 days shall be investigated with no court procedures required, yet the related procedures and evidence are not stipulated.

The last three countries minimally meet the standard. Brunei subjects its birth registration after 1 year to court procedures, without providing for facilitation of the registrants in respect of the rules and procedures involved. Cambodia instantly involves the court for birth registration that takes place after 30 days, similarly without addressing any facilitation in respect of the requirements of evidence and procedures. Meanwhile, the law in Lao PDR is silent on late and delayed birth registrations (Table 6.6).

6.4 Conclusion

Table 6.7 extrapolates the overall patterns of observance of the standards applicable to ensure birth registration that is universally accessible, flexible, and responsive to circumstances of families, as well as accurate, timely, and facilitated.

Legal provisions exist to ensure totality and universality of birth registration in seven out of the nine countries examined. The majority of the countries, however, do not address the standard on confidentiality of sensitive content, which may jeopardise

[19] Article 32(1), Undang-Undang Republik Indonesia Nomor 24 Tahun 2013 Tentang Perubahan Atas Undang-Undang Nomor 23 Tahun 2006 Tentang Administrasi Kependudukan; Sect. 12 of the Birth and Death Registration Act 1957.

[20] Article 5(7) of Decree No. 60/2014.

[21] Rule 25 of Administrative Order No. 1 Series 1993.

Table 6.6 Mapping of birth registration safeguards for standard 3

Standard 3: Accurate, timely, and facilitated late birth registration	Timely birth registration	Facilitated late birth registration
Brunei	**Partially addressed** • Prescribed initial period of 14 days is relatively brief compared to 30 days recommended[a] • Late registration period that starts after 14 days and within 42 days is too short compared to the grace period of 1 year for late registration. It is also subject to a prescribed fee[b]	**Partially addressed** • Delayed registration after 42 days may be subject to an inquiry and proceeding before a Magistrate[c] • Requirements as to proof of late and delayed registrations are not specified under the law
Lao PDR	**Partially addressed** • Prescribed initial period is 30 days from birth,[d] yet the law is silent on late and delayed registrations	**Not addressed**
Cambodia	**Partially addressed** • Prescribed initial period is 30 days from birth[e] • No prescribed period for late/delayed registration	**Partially addressed** • Prescribed initial period is 30 days from birth[f] • No prescribed period for late/delayed registration
Viet Nam	**Partially addressed** • Prescribed initial period is 60 days,[g] longer than the recommended period of 30 days • No prescribed period for late/ delayed registration	**Partially addressed** • Publicity and transparency shall be ensured in civil status registration procedures[h] • No court involvement is specified but fees may be imposed[i]
Thailand	**Partially addressed** • Prescribed initial period is relatively brief, i.e. within 15 days, yet reporting after 15 days and before 30 days is not considered overdue[j] • No prescribed period for late/delayed registration	**Partially addressed** • Requirements of proof for registration after 30 days are not specified but there shall be further investigations conducted into the identity of the person making the report, the parents, and the cause of delay[k] • No court involvement is specified but fine may be imposed[l]

(continued)

Table 6.6 (continued)

Standard 3: Accurate, timely, and facilitated late birth registration	Timely birth registration	Facilitated late birth registration
Indonesia	**Partially Addressed** • Prescribed period is 60 days[m] • For a birth that occurs abroad, it must be reported within 30 days to the authority in charge after the return of such Indonesian citizens to Indonesia[n]	**Addressed** • Procedures and requirements of proof for regulation including for late/delayed registration are spelled out in other regulations • Late registration requires the approval of the head of the authority in charge (Head of Population Administration and Civil Registration Office at the concerned district)[o] • Delayed registration after 1 year is not subject to court hearing.[p]Even so, the penalty may still be imposed for late birth registration, as shall be determined by regulations at the district or provincial level[q]
Singapore	**Partially addressed** • Prescribed initial period of 14 days[r] is relatively brief compared to 30 days recommended • Delayed registration after 14 days and within 42 days, and late registration after 42 Days[s] are much shorter than the grace period of 1 year as suggested	**Partially addressed** • Delayed registration is subject to a prescribed fee.[t] The registrar and its deputy are responsible to procure the best available information on birth reported after 42 days[u] • Birth after 42 days (Late Registration) is subject to the truth of the fact being decided by a Magistrate[v] • No provision addresses facilitated late birth registration. Procedures and requirements of proof for late and delayed birth registrations are not spelled out

(continued)

Table 6.6 (continued)

Standard 3: Accurate, timely, and facilitated late birth registration	Timely birth registration	Facilitated late birth registration
Malaysia(the Peninsula)	**Partially addressed** • The amended 60 days as the total period of registration before late registration period exceed the 30 days recommended[w] • However, there is no grace period of 1 year for late birth registration as recommended. Late registration begins immediately after the 60 days' registration period[x]	**Partially addressed** • Late registration is subject to the written authority of the Registrar, and to such fees and conditions for late registration[y] • Late registration is not subject to court procedures (unlike the situation in Sabah) • No provision addresses facilitated late birth registration. Procedures and requirements of proof for late birth registration are not spelled out
The Philippines	**Partially addressed** • Prescribed initial period for registration is 30 days as recommended[z] • Delayed registration occurs after the initial period of 30 days. The grace period of 1 year for delayed registration is not adopted	**Addressed** • Detailed rules of evidence and procedures for delayed registration are provided[aa] • Delayed registration may be subject to investigation and court procedures, even though the action shall not suspend or stop the registration[ab]
Myanmar	Unavailable civil registration law	

[a]United Nations, Department of Economic and Social Affairs, Statistics Division (UNSD), *Handbook on Training in Civil Registration and Vital Statistic Systems, Series F No. 84* (2002), para 33, p 9; Department of Economics and Social Affairs (Statistics Division), *Principles and Recommendations for a Vital Statistic System* (2014), New York: UN Publications, para 296

[b]UN Human Rights Council. *Birth Registration and the Right of Everyone to Recognition Everywhere as a Person before the Law* (17 June 2014), para III.11; African Charter on the Rights and Welfare of the Child (adopted 11 July 1990, in force 29 November 1999), CAB/LEG/24.9/49, para 50

[c]Economic and Social Commission for Asia and the Pacific (UNESCAP), 2 June 2015, Resolution adopted by the Economic and Social Commission for Asia and the Pacific, *Asian and Pacific Civil Registration and Vital Statistics 2015–2024*, UN Doc. E/ESCAP/RES/71/14, New York: United Nations. Part B, II (13); Committee on the Protection of the Rights of All Migrants Workers and Members of Their Families (CMW), Joint General Comment No. 4 (2017) of the Committee on the Protection of the Rights of All Migrant Workers and Members of Their Families and No. 23 (2017) of the Committee on the Rights of the Child on the General Principles regarding the Human Rights of Children in the Context of International Migration, para 20

Table 6.6 (continued)

[d]UNHCR, 'Conclusion on Civil Registration No. 111 (LXIV)'. Doc. A/AC.96/1035. Geneva: UNHCR. [17 October 2013]

[e]UNSD, *Civil Registration and Vital Statistics Knowledge Base* (2015), para 62, p 15. Retrieved from http://unstats.un.org/unsd/demographic [Accessed 5 May 2016]; Department of Economics and Social Affairs (Statistics Division), *Principles and Recommendations for a Vital Statistic System* (2014), New York: UN Publications, para 294

[f]UNSD, *Civil Registration and Vital Statistics Knowledge Base* (2015), para 48, p 12. Retrieved from http://unstats.un.org/unsd/demographic [Accessed 5 May 2016]

[g]UNSD, *Principles and Recommendations for a Vital Statistics System* (Revision 3)(2014), para 299, p 68; See also Committee on the Protection of the Rights of All Migrants Workers and Members of Their Families (CMW), Joint General Comment No. 4 (2017) of the Committee on the Protection of the Rights of All Migrant Workers and Members of Their Families and No. 23 (2017) of the Committee on the Rights of the Child on the General Principles regarding the Human Rights of Children in the Context of International Migration, paras 20–21

[h]UNICEF, *A Passport to Protection: A Guide to Birth Registration Programming* (2013), p 22

[i]UNICEF, *A Passport to Protection: A Guide to Birth Registration Programming* (2013), p 22 and 122; General Comment on Article 6 of the ACRWC: The Right to a Name, Registration at Birth, and to Acquire a Nationality, ACERWC/GC/02, Addis Ababa: African Union, 2014, para 82

[j]General Comment on Article 6 of the ACRWC: The Right to a Name, Registration at Birth, and to Acquire a Nationality, ACERWC/GC/02, Addis Ababa: African Union, 2014, para 51

[k]UNHCR, Conclusion on Civil Registration No. 111 (LXIV), Doc. A/AC.96/1035, Geneva: UNHCR [17 October 2013]

[l]General Comment on Article 6 of the ACRWC: The Right to a Name, Registration at Birth, and to Acquire a Nationality, ACERWC/GC/02, Addis Ababa: African Union, 2014, para 81

[m]UNICEF, *A Passport to Protection: A Guide to Birth Registration Programming* (2013), p 118

[n]UN Human Rights Council, *Birth Registration and the Right of Everyone to Recognition Everywhere as a Person before the Law* (17 June 2014), para II.5

[o]General Comment on Article 6 of the ACRWC: The Right to a Name, Registration at Birth, and to Acquire a Nationality, ACERWC/GC/02, Addis Ababa: African Union, 2014, para 41

[p]Economic and Social Commission for Asia and the Pacific (UNESCAP), 2 June 2015, Resolution adopted by the Economic and Social Commission for Asia and the Pacific, *Asian and Pacific Civil Registration and Vital Statistics* 2015–2024, UN Doc. E/ESCAP/RES/71/14, New York: United Nations, Goal 2; UNESCAP, *Regional Action Framework on Civil Registration and Vital Statistics in Asia and the Pacific* (2014), p 14, Inter-American Court of Human Rights, Series C, Case 130, 8 September 2005

[q]United Nations, Department of Economic and Social Affairs, Statistics Division (UNSD), *Handbook on Training in Civil Registration and Vital Statistic Systems, Series F No. 84* (2002), para 126, p 28

[r]United Nations, Department of Economic and Social Affairs, Statistics Division (UNSD), *Handbook on Training in Civil Registration and Vital Statistic Systems, Series F No. 84* (2002), para 127, p 28

Table 6.6 (continued)

[s]UN Human Rights Council, *Birth Registration and the Right of Everyone to Recognition Everywhere as a Person before the Law* (17 June 2014), para C.56–60, p 13

[t]General Comment on Article 6 of the ACRWC: The Right to a Name, Registration at Birth, and to Acquire a Nationality. ACERWC/GC/02. Addis Ababa: African Union (2014), para 66

[u]General Comment on Article 6 of the ACRWC: The Right to a Name, Registration at Birth, and to Acquire a Nationality. ACERWC/GC/02. Addis Ababa: African Union (2014), para 73

[v]UN Human Rights Council, *Birth Registration and the Right of Everyone to Recognition Everywhere as a Person before the Law* (17 June 2014), para C. 56, p 13; UNHCR, *Conclusion on Civil Registration No. 111* (LXIV), Doc. A/AC.1035/96, Geneva: UNHCR [17 October 2013]

[w]General Comment on Article 6 of the ACRWC: The Right to a Name, Registration at Birth, and to Acquire a Nationality. ACERWC/GC/02. Addis Ababa: African Union, 2014, para 74

[x]United Nations, Department of Economic and Social Affairs, Statistics Division (UNSD), Handbook on Training in Civil Registration and Vital Statistic Systems, Series F No. 84 (2002), para 34, p 8

[y]UN Human Rights Council, Birth Registration and the Right of Everyone to Recognition Everywhere as a Person before the Law (17 June 2014), para C 56–60

[z]UNICEF, *A Passport yo Protection: A Guide to Birth Registration Programming* (2013), p 26

[aa]General Comment on Article 6 of the ACRWC: The Right to a Name, Registration at Birth, and to Acquire a Nationality, ACERWC/GC/02, Addis Ababa: African Union, 2014, para 79

[ab]UNSD, Civil Registry and Vital Statistics Knowledge Base (2015), para 121

[ac]UNSD, *Principles and Recommendations for a Vital Statistics System* (Revision 2014)(3), para 363; UNSD, *Civil Registration and Vital Statistics Knowledge Base* (2015), para 121

[ad]UNSD, *Civil Registration and Vital Statistics Knowledge Base* (2015), para 121

[ae]UNESCAP, *Regional Action Framework on Civil Registration and Vital Statistics in Asia and the Pacific* (2014), para 46, p 17

[af]UN Human Rights Council, Birth Registration and the Right of Everyone to Recognition Everywhere as a Person before the Law (17 June 2014), para B.55

[ag]UNSD, Civil Registration and Vital Statistics Knowledge Base (2015), para 123

[ah]United Nations, Department of Economic and Social Affairs, Statistics Division (UNSD), Handbook on Training in Civil Registration and Vital Statistic Systems, Series F No. 84. (2002), para 34

[ai]UNSD, Civil Registration and Vital Statistics Knowledge Base (2015), para 124–125, p 28

[a]Section 12(1) of Births and Deaths Registration Act 1979 (Chapter 79) (Revised Edition 2013) Brunei

[b]Section 5(3) of Births and Deaths Registration Act 1979 (Chapter 79)(Revised Edition 2013) Brunei

[c]Article 3 of the Law on the Protection of the Rights and Interests of the Child No. 05/NA of 27 December 2006

Table 6.6 (continued)

[d]Article 9 and Article 20 of Decree of the President of the Lao People's Democratic Republic on the Promulgation of the Law on Family Registration No. 21, 1992

[e]Article 19 of the Law on the Protection of the Rights and Interests of the Child No. 05/NA of 27 December 2006

[f]Article 15 of the 9 Decree of the President of the Lao People's Democratic Republic on the Promulgation of the Law on Family Registration No. 21, 1992

[g]Article 6 of Decree of the President of the Lao People's Democratic Republic on the Promulgation of the Law on Family Registration No. 21, 1992

[h]Article 26 of Sub-Decree on Civil Status (Civil Registration) No. 103 of December 2000

[i]Article 17 of Sub-Decree on Civil Status (Civil Registration) No. 103 of December 2000

[j]Article 23 of Sub-Decree on Civil Status (Civil Registration) No. 103 of December 2000

[k]Article 26 of Sub-Decree on Civil Status (Civil Registration) No. 103 of December 2000

[l]Articles 19 and 20 of Sub-Decree on Civil Status (Civil Registration) No. 103 of December 2000

[m]Article 24 of Sub-Decree on Civil Status (Civil Registration) No. 103 of December 2000

[n]Article 2(2) of Decree No. 60/2014/QH 13 on Law on Civil Status of 20 November 2014. The right to birth registration, name and nationality of children below the age of 16 is recognised in Article 13 of the Children Law (Law No 102/ 2016/ QH13)

[o]Article 16(1) and 16(3) of Decree No. 60/2014/QH 13 on Law on Civil Status

[p]Articles 24 and 25 of Decree No. 60/2014/QH 13 on Law on Civil Status

[q]Article 6(1) of Decree No. 60/2014/QH 13 on Law on Civil Status

[r]Prime Minister's Directive 24 of 2007 (Directive 24/2007/CT-TTg of the Prime Minister on Fees for Public Services). See further UNHCR, *Submission by the United Nations High Commissioner for Refugees for the Office of the High Commissioner for Human Rights› Compilation Report—Universal Periodic Review: Socialist Republic of Vietnam* (June 2013), p 2

[s]Article 11(1) of Decree No. 60/2014/QH 13 on Law on Civil Status

[t]Article 16(2) of Decree No. 60/2014/QH 13 on Law on Civil Status

[u]Article 16 of Decree No. 60/2014/QH 13 on Law on Civil Status

[v]Section 16 of the Thai Civil Registration Act (No. 2) B.E. 2551 (2008). Under the old provisions of the Civil Registration Act B.E. 2534, only children born to Thai parents and migrant parents with legal status (PR status or temporary residential status) may be registered at birth

[w]See Article 19 of Thai Civil Registration Act B.E. 2534 as amended by Article 14 of Thai Civil Registration Act B.E. 2551 (2008)

[x]Rates of Fees, Thai Civil Registration Act (No. 2) B.E. 2551 (2008). According to the new rates of fees in B.E. 2551, birth report under Section 18 is charged 100 baht each copy

[y]UN Committee on the Rights of the Child, 'Consideration of Reports Submitted by States Parties under Article 44 of the Convention, Concluding Observations: Thailand', Geneva: CRC/C/THA/CO/3–4. Thailand: CRC, 17 February 2012, para 43

[z]UNESCO, *Citizenship Manual-Capacity Building on Birth Registration and Citizenship in Thailand: Citizenship Manual* (2008), p 10; see Section 16 of Thai Civil Registration Act (No. 2) B.E. 2551 (2008) that repeals and replaces Section 20 of Thai Civil Registration Act B.E. 253

[aa]Article 3, Peraturan Pemerintah No. 37 Tahun 2007 Tentang Pelaksanaan Undang-Undang No. 23 Tahun 2006 Tentang Administrasi Kependudukan

Table 6.6 (continued)

[ab] Article 28, Peraturan Pemerintah No. 37 Tahun 2007 Tentang Pelaksanaan Undang-Undang No. 23 Tahun 2006 Tentang Administrasi Kependudukan

[ac] Article 49, Peraturan Pemerintah No. 37 Tahun 2007 Tentang Pelaksanaan Undang-Undang No. 23 Tahun 2006 Tentang Administrasi Kependudukan

[ad] Article 49, Undang-Undang Republik Indonesia, Nomor 24 Tahun 2013 Tentang Perubahan Atas Undang-Undang Nomor 23 Tahun 2006 Tentang Administrasi Kependudukan (Law 24 of 2013 on Population Administration). For a religious marriage that is unregistered, the children may register their birth but they shall have their civil relationship only with their mothers. See Article 43(1) Undang- undang Republik Indonesia Nomor 1 Tahun 1974 Tentang Perkahwinan

[ae] Articles 4 and 29, Peraturan Pemerintah No. 37 Tahun 2007 Tentang Pelaksanaan Undang-Undang No. 23 Tahun 2006 Tentang Administrasi Kependudukan

[af] Chapter IX, Undang-Undang No. 23 Tahun 2006 Tentang Administrasi Kependudukan

[ag] Article 79A, Peraturan Pemerintah No. 37 Tahun 2007 Tentang Pelaksanaan Undang-Undang No. 23 Tahun 2006 Tentang Administrasi Kependudukan; Articles 1(9) and 5, Peraturan Pemerintah No. 37 Tahun 2007 Tentang Pelaksanaan Undang-Undang No. 23 Tahun 2006 Tentang Administrasi Kependudukan

[ah] E.g., Article 3(3) of para 2, Part 1, Chapter III, Peraturan Daerah Provinsi DKI Jakarta Nomor 3 Tahun 2012 Tentang Retribusi Daerah sebagaimana diubah dengan Peraturan Daerah Provinsi DKI Jakarta Nomor 1 Tahun 2015

[ai] Other sub-regulations may specify the procedures for birth registration, particularly the documentary requirements to be fulfilled. See, for instance, Article 52 of Peraturan Presiden Nomor 25 Tahun 2008 Tentang Pensyaratan dan Tata Cara Pendaftaran Penduduk dan Pencatatan Sipil

[aj] Section 9 of Registration of Births and Deaths Act (Chapter 267) (Revised Edition 1985)

[ak] Section 12 of the Birth and Death Registration Act 1957

[al] Section 9 of Birth and Death Registration Act 1957

[am] Section 13 of the Birth and Death Registration Act 1957

[an] Section 12 of the Birth and Death Registration Act 1957. The Government announced in 2017 that a fine of RM1,000 will be imposed for late registration after 60 days in Peninsular Malaysia under the new amendment to the Birth and Death Registration Act 1957 in 2016. See N.A., 'RM 1,000 fine for Late Registration' (2017), https://www.thestar.com.my/news/nation/2017/10/11/fine-for-late-birth-registration/ [Accessed 5 January 2018]. However, the rates for late birth registration listed as of November 2018 on the website of the National Registration Department of Malaysia are (i) RM5 for birth register search; (ii) RM10 for processing fee for late birth registration; and (iii) not exceeding RM50 for the penalty. See National Registration Department Malaysia, 'Home/ Late Registration of Birth (Peninsular)'. Retrieved from http://www.jpn.gov.my/en/maklumat-kelahiran/pendaftaran-lewat-kelahiran-2/#1458289648764-bf711d6d-f9ed [Accessed 27 November 2018]

[ao] Section 4 of the Civil Registry Law (Act No. 3753) and Administrative Order No. 1 Series of 1993 Implementing Rules and Regulations of Act No. 3753 and Other Laws on Civil Registration (Vol. 89, Number 2, Official Gazette; January 11, 1993 (Administrative Order No. 1 Series 1993); Rule 10 of Administrative Order No. 1 Series of 1993

[ap] Section 5 of the Civil Registry Law (Act No. 3753); Rules 27 to 29 of the Administrative Order No.1 Series 1993

[aq] Section 4 of the Civil Registry Law (Act No. 3753)

[ar] Rule 24 of Administrative Order No.1 Series 1993

[as] Rule 17 of Administrative Order No.1 Series 1993

[at] Rule 17(2) of Administrative Order No. 1 Series 1993

[au] See Rule 25 of Administrative Order No.1 Series 1993. The requirements include duly accomplished and signed certificate of live birth, affidavit for delayed registration, affidavit of two disinterested parties who might have witnessed the birth and certificate of marriage if the person is already married

Table 6.6 (continued)

[a]Section 16 of Births and Deaths Registration Act 1979 (Chapter 79) (Revised Edition 2013) Brunei

[b]The CRC Committee in one of its Concluding Observations has noted and commended the work of Brunei's 'Flying Doctor Teams' in ensuring registration of children. The teams employ helicopters to reach remote areas and communities to both provide medical services and ensure birth registration. See United Nations Committee on the Rights of the Child, 'Concluding Observations on the Initial Report Submitted by Brunei Darussalam', UN Doc. CRC/C/15/Add.219, Indonesia: CRC, 27 October 2003, para 33; UN Human Rights Council, *Birth Registration and the Right of Everyone to Recognition Everywhere as a Person before the Law* (17 June 2014), para 79

[c]Section 5(1) of Births and Deaths Registration Act 1979 (Chapter 79) (Revised Edition 2013) Brunei

[d]The People's Committees of communes, wards, or district townships (known as the commune-level People's Committees) of the places of residence of fathers or mothers, as well as an overseas Vietnamese diplomatic mission or consular office, shall be the civil status registration agency. See Article 4(1) and Article 13 of Decree No. 60/2014

[e]Article 15(2) of Decree No. 60/2014

[f]Article 15(2) of Decree No. 60/2014

[g]See Article 9 of Decree No. 60/2014. See also Vietnam Law and Legal Forum, 'New Law on Civil Status' (5 August 2015). Retrieved from http://vietnamlawmagazine.vn/new-law-on-civil-status-4028.html [Accessed 6 October 2016]

[h]Parents or the official concerned must report the birth to the local registrar, which can include the village headmen. See Article 4, Thai Civil Registration Act (B.E. 2534) (1991). See further Section 6 of the Thai Registration Act (No. 2) B.E 2551 (2008)

[i]S. Heap & C. Cody. 2009. The Universal Birth Registration Campaign. *Force Migration Review 32*

[j]See Article 1(7) of Peraturan Pemerintah No. 37 Tahun 2007 Tentang Pelaksanaan Undang-Undang No. 23 Tahun 2006 Tentang Administrasi Kependudukan on the definition of 'Instansi Pelaksana'

[k]A.L. Buffardi & Kwan Men Yon, *Realising the Right to Legal Identity: A case study as part of an evaluation as part of the Australia Indonesia Partnership for Justice* (July 2016) https://www.refworld.org/pdfid/57922cfd4.pdf [Accessed 8 January 2018]

[l]See Section 57 of Peraturan Pemerintah No. 37 Tahun 2007 Tentang Pelaksanaan Undang-Undang No. 23 Tahun 2006 Tentang Administrasi Kependudukan

[m]Immigration and Checkpoints Authority Singapore Government, 'Checkpoints Authority'. Retrieved from https://www.ica.gov.sg/page.aspx?pageid=144 [Accessed 7 October 2016]

Table 6.6 (continued)

[n]Immigration and Checkpoints Authority Singapore Government, 'Checkpoints Authority'. Retrieved from https://www.ica.gov.sg/page.aspx?pageid=144 [Accessed 7 October 2016]

[o]Peninsular Malaysia (Birth and Death Registration Act 1957 (Act 299)), Sabahn (Sabah Birth and Death Registration Ordinance 1951 (Cap. 123)) and Sarawak (Sarawak Birth and Death Registration Ordinance 1951 (Cap. 10)). Under Section 7(1) Act 299, the birth of every child born in Malaysia shall be registered by the Registrar for the registration area in which the child was born

[p]A. Geraldine, 'Mobile Court: 10 Years On' (26 November 2017), *NST Online*. Retrieved from https://www.nst.com.my/news/nation/2017/11/307588/mobile-court-10-years [Accessed 20 December 2017]

[q]Section 3 of the Civil Registry Law (Act No. 3753)

[r]Mobile registration is available where civil registration is not accessible, for instance, to people vulnerable to armed conflicts and displacement in the Autonomous Region of Muslim Mindanao (ARMM). This is not reflected in the main legislation, but may be authorised through Executive Orders, such as through the Office of the Regional Governor, Executive Order No. 21, Series of 2012, Extending the Implementation of Free Birth Registration and Its Area of Coverage and Target Beneficiaries with DSWD-ARMM as Lead Implementing Agency

[s]In 2013, UNICEF Myanmar was reported working with the Government of Myanmar under the purview of its EU-funded multi-country birth registration project. Apart from providing technical advice, the project has created an electronic platform that adds real-time data as part of the permanent archive of birth registration that operates in all states and divisions in Myanmar. See Nay Pyi Taw, 'Getting to the Goal of 100% Birth Registration' (2015). Retrieved from http://www.unicef.org/myanmar/media_24526.html [Accessed 15 June 2016].

[a]Section 12(1) of Births and Deaths Registration Act 1979 (Chapter 79) (Revised Edition 2013) Brunei

[b]Section 14 of Births and Deaths Registration Act 1979 (Chapter 79) (Revised Edition 2013) Brunei

[c]Section 15 of Births and Deaths Registration Act 1979 (Chapter 79) (Revised Edition 2013) Brunei

[d]Article 9 of Decree of the President of the Lao People's Democratic Republic on the Promulgation of the Law on Family Registration No. 21, 1992

[e]Article 17 Sub-Decree on Civil Status (Civil Registration) No. 103 of December 2000

[P] Parents or guardian who fail to report and have a baby recorded in a civil status book after the 30 days are required to directly request for a judgment from the relevant provincial or municipal court. See Article 25 Sub-Decree on Civil Status (Civil Registration) No. 103 of December 2000

[f]Article 15 of Decree No. 60/2014

[g]Article 5(7) of Decree No. 60/2014

[h]Article 11(1) of Decree No. 60/2014

Table 6.6 (continued)

[i]Article 18, Thai Civil Registration Act 1991, B.E. 2534. This is further explained in UNESCO, *Citizenship Manual—Capacity Building on Birth Registration and Citizenship in Thailand: Citizenship Manual* (2008), p 10
[j]See UNESCO, Citizenship Manual—Capacity Building on Birth Registration and Citizenship in Thailand: Citizenship Manual (2008), p 11
[k]See UNESCO, Citizenship Manual—Capacity Building on Birth Registration and Citizenship in Thailand: Citizenship Manual (2008), p 11
[l]Article 47 of the Thai Civil Registration Act, B.E. 2534 (1991)
[m]Articles 27(1) and 32(1), Peraturan Pemerintah No. 37 Tahun 2007 Tentang Pelaksanaan Undang-Undang No. 23 Tahun 2006 Tentang Administrasi Kependudukan
[n]Article 29(4), Undang-Undang Republik Indonesia Nomor 24 Tahun 2013 Tentang Perubahan Atas Undang-Undang Nomor 23 Tahun 2006 Tentang Administrasi Kependudukan
[o]Article 32(1), Undang-Undang Republik Indonesia Nomor 24 Tahun 2013 Tentang Perubahan Atas Undang-Undang Nomor 23 Tahun 2006 Tentang Administrasi Kependudukan
[p]The old Article 32(2), Undang-Undang 23 Tahun 2006 providing for registration beyond one year from birth to being subjected to the decision of the District Court was repealed by Article 32, Undang-Undang 24 Tahun 2014
[q] E.g. Article 3(3) of para 2, Part 1, Chapter III, Peraturan Daerah Provinsi DKI Jakarta Nomor 3 Tahun 2012 Tentang Retribusi Daerah sebagaimana diubah dengan Peraturan Daerah Provinsi DKI Jakarta Nomor 1 Tahun 2015
[r] Section 9 of Registration of Births and Deaths Act (Chapter 267) (Revised Edition 1985)
[s] Section 23(1) of Registration of Births and Deaths Act (Chapter 267) (Revised Edition 1985)
[t] Section 17 of Registration of Births and Deaths Act (Chapter 267) (Revised Edition 1985)
[u] Section 23(1) of Registration of Births and Deaths Act (Chapter 267) (Revised Edition 1985)
[v] Section 23(3) of Registration of Births and Deaths Act (Chapter 267) (Revised Edition 1985)
[w] Section 8 of Birth and Death Registration Act 1957 (Act 299)
[x] Section 12 Birth and Death Registration Act 1957 (Act 299)
[y] Section 12 of Birth and Death Registration Act 1957 (Act 299)
[z] Rule 19 of Administrative Order No. 1 Series 1993
[aa] Rule 25 of Administrative Order No. 1 Series 1993
[ab] Rule 15 of Administrative Order No. 1 Series 1993

Table 6.7 Mapping of the overall degree of safeguards against statelessness at birth based on the birth registration frameworks of the ASEAN Member States

Standards on birth registration/Degree of observance	Components	Addressed	Partially addressed	Not addressed or minimally addressed	Total
Standard 1: Universal, well-managed, and free birth registration	1.1 Totality of birth registration	7	2	0	9
	1.2Confidentiality of sensitive content, including information from irregular migrants	2	4	3	9
	1.3 Free birth registration	1	4	4	9
	1.4 Rules of proof to be flexible, avoiding excessive documentation requirements	1	3	5	9
Standard 2: Flexible and responsive to circumstances of families—practices of states considered to some extent	2.1 Mobile registration, decentralised system, and interoperability with other services	7	0	3	10
	2.2 Simpler procedures	2	0	8	10
Standard 3: Accurate, timely and facilitated birth registration	3.1 Timely birth registration	0	9	0	9
	3.2 Facilitated late birth registration	5	3	1	9

Note: Where '9' represents the total number of countries, Myanmar is not included in the analysis

the prospect for ensuring a trusted CRVS system for vulnerable populations, particularly irregular and undocumented migrants, and asylum seekers. Birth registration is not entirely free for most of the countries as delayed and late registrations are often subject to fees. Rules of proof that ensure documentary requirements are not excessive, which are important to eliminate barriers to universal birth registration, are highly visible in one country, and moderately for three others. In the other five countries, such rules are not addressed.

For flexible and responsive birth registration that caters for the situations of remote locations and persons with disabilities through mobile registration, seven countries seem to be requiring or implementing the said mechanism. For simplified birth registration to help address language barriers and illiteracy, only two countries reflect this in their laws. Meanwhile, the prescribed periods that meet timely birth registration are partially observed in most of the countries. Late birth registration is facilitated strongly in two countries, especially through their detailed rules of evidence and/or procedures. The rest of the countries examined do not clearly provide provisions to meet the said standard in their laws.

Chapter 7
Conclusion and Paths Forward

7.1 Conclusion

This book has dealt with the complex scope of protection against statelessness at birth. Statelessness is indisputably a challenging arena due to its dynamic concept and intersecting nature with other contested subjects, particularly refugees and irregular migrants. The discussion has demonstrated how prevention of statelessness at birth is fraught with many theoretical and practical challenges.

Chapter 2 looks at the key concepts around 'statelessness', a term which is surrounded by ambiguities. The legalistic approach to defining nationality has been subject to critiques. One that has been highlighted is its lack of protection utility, which leads to another form of *de facto* statelessness. Persons with undetermined nationality and with no proof of nationality are adversely affected. Schism in scholarship and discourse on who is and what amounts to 'a stateless person' has had its impact on the coherence of the international legal framework for the protection of the stateless persons under the 1954 Convention.

The concept of 'at risk of statelessness' subsequently entered the parlance to cover a wider range of individuals confronted with varying degrees of risk of statelessness and circumstances that render them vulnerable to being without any nationality. Prevention of statelessness becomes the pre-emptive strategy to curb the phenomenon. The 1961 Convention offers innovative mechanisms to accomplish this. The acquisition of nationality based on *jus soli* (for children born in the territory) and *jus sanguinis* (for children born abroad) dictate the dual strategies of prevention of statelessness. However, confounding the problem is the obscurity and complexity underlying the terminologies of 'at risk of statelessness' and 'otherwise stateless', both of which are not defined by the 1961 Convention. Yet 'children at risk of statelessness' and 'otherwise stateless children' need to be identified and targeted for prevention strategies devised under the said Convention.

Modernisation and globalisation have altered the scenes against which statelessness arises. International migration intensifies existing causes of statelessness.

R. M. Razali, *Safeguarding Against Statelessness at Birth*,
https://doi.org/10.1007/978-981-19-5371-2_7

Together with state-backed discrimination and exclusionary policies towards minorities, including undocumented migrants, refugees, asylum seekers and other non-citizens perceived as outsiders or aliens, lack of birth registration and means to prove and establish one's nationality are factors that lead to childhood statelessness. The right to a legal identity, comprising one's name, birth registration, and nationality stands in good stead with the right of the child to acquire a nationality and to be prevented from statelessness. However, better consensus should be forged around the meaning, conceptualisation, and utility of the right to a legal identity in ways that meaningfully prevent, tackle and eliminate statelessness.

The progress of human rights and international relations has shown that states are no longer the exclusive protector of an individual's rights. Aside from the basic right to a nationality espoused by UDHR, the protection of this right is directed to apply specifically to children under the 1930 Hague Convention, CRC, ICCPR, and a host of other international and regional instruments. The right to a nationality is further secured by international human rights principles of prohibition of arbitrary deprivation of nationality, non-discrimination, the best interests of the child principle, and the duty of states to prevent statelessness, particularly for children who would otherwise be stateless. Prior to UDHR, avoidance of statelessness has been the subject of international treaty provisions, notably the 1930 Hague Convention. Nonetheless, the 1961 Convention remains the most devoted instrument targeting children as the principal beneficiary under the formulated rules on prevention of statelessness at birth, by attributing nationality to 'foundlings' and 'children who would otherwise be stateless'.

Birth registration, being the other safeguard to protect children against statelessness at birth is a fundamental right that is equally upheld in various international and regional instruments, in parallel with the right of the child to acquire a nationality. However, its functionality is impaired by the lack of coherence and gaps in its substantive and procedural standards to be able to effectively connect it with the object of prevention of statelessness.

The right to birth registration lends its support largely through soft law substantive and procedural norms across international and regional instruments. As Chaps. 2 and 3 unveil, the norms comprising principles and standards on birth registration have been randomly expounded by different international organisations pursuing their respective mandates and goals. Regionally, the jurisprudence of the Inter-American Court of Human Rights and ACRWC explicitly endorse and prescribe the universality of birth registration. As for the other regions examined, regional norms on the right to birth registration appear to be less expressive.

Chapter 3 subsequently reveals that the right to a nationality promulgated by UDHR and other ensuing treaties is deprived of its substantive value, consequently devolving upon states a wide spectrum of discretion on nationality attribution and loss, without the existing regulations and principles addressing which nationality one is entitled to, and which country is obligated to grant it. ICCPR and CRC have, to some degree, undermined the total scheme of prevention of children from becoming stateless with the adoption of the right to acquire, instead of the complete right to a nationality.

The argument remains that the widespread international consensus on the obligation of states to ensure children acquire a nationality if they would otherwise be stateless does not suffice to guarantee the fulfilment of such protection to the affected children where the acquisition of nationality as the remedy is incompatible with national policies.

Marginalised groups of non-citizens with irregular status are particularly susceptible to the prospect of enduring statelessness. Up until today, international human rights law provides fewer directives on how such conflicting dichotomies of state sovereignty and interests on the one hand, and protection against statelessness on the other, can be reconciled so as not to jeopardise the international commitment to protect children against statelessness and its dire repercussions.

Further substantive and procedural shortcomings have been identified as desensitising and undermining the nexus between the right to birth registration and fulfilment of the right to a nationality. The scope of the substance and implementation of the right to birth registration reveal various gaps. Its normative development is diffused through a rich mixture of instruments and mechanisms, thus preventing a holistic framework and a systematic implementation. The instrumental value of the right to birth registration in avoiding statelessness is not optimised when it is not jointly addressed with the acquisition of nationality, despite the two featuring together in ICCPR, CRC and many other instruments.

Despite the inventive 'manual' that informs states of the mechanics to prevent statelessness via the 1961 Convention, statelessness is still accommodated to some extent. The application-based nationality safeguard embodied in Article 1(1)(b) and any of the conditions that it can be subjected to under Article 1(2)[1] are clear examples of the reduction, rather than the elimination 'path' taken by the drafters of the Convention.

Guidelines No. 4 have considerably contributed to procedural clarity concerning the implementation of the 1961 Convention. However, the different interpretations and import of the key concepts underpinning statelessness coupled with the lack of systematic methodology for identification and determination of a child who 'would otherwise be stateless' present the initial stumbling block to the realisation of an effective protective strategy.

The 1961 Convention did not foresee the regulation of birth registration and the resulting problems arising from the delicate connection between the lack of proof of one's nationality and statelessness as an outcome. Legal gaps in addressing and overcoming the dilemma of undetermined nationality are part of the consequences. The principle of the prohibition of discrimination against children in exercising birth registration on the basis of parents' immigration status has permeated the American and African regional treaty and judicial frameworks.[2] Elsewhere including in SEA, such significant norm is still evidently scant.

---

[1] E.g. the late age requirement to start the application process and the condition that the person must always be stateless. See Articles 1(2)(a) and 1(2)(d) of the 1961 Convention.

[2] See the case of *Yean v. Bosico*; *The Kenyan Nubian Case* and Article 6(2) ACRWC.

Meanwhile, the norms on inter-state cooperation in the area of prevention of statelessness appear rudimentary. In so far as the existing inter-state mechanism is concerned, the 1961 Convention has only perceived it to apply in the context of requiring a Contracting State to secure a treaty with a non-Contracting State, with a provision that ensures no person is rendered stateless following a transfer of territory.[3]The ICCPR's General Comment No. 17 on the 'Rights of the Child' requires inter-state cooperation in ensuring every child acquires a nationality when he or she is born in order to prevent the child from being stateless and having less or no protection as a result.[4] Even so, cooperation as a requirement to prevent statelessness in the preceding instruments lacks depth in both substance and implementation.[5]

Chapter 4 maps out the main causes of statelessness within the ASEAN Member States and provides an overview of the Member States' responses to the problem. Statelessness in the region has multiple causes that are often interrelated. The phenomenon has its roots in the establishment of post-colonial states alongside national borders and identity and in the ongoing challenges relating to the treatment of minorities, management of large-scale undocumented migration, as well as the lack of universal birth registration and legal safeguards through nationality provisions, strong institutions and accountable governance. Many children have struggled to acquire a nationality due to the strict *jus sanguinis* nationality provisions in ASEAN member states. This is especially so when they are born to unknown parents (including foundlings), have no proof of parentage, or are born to stateless parents and parents of undetermined nationality.

The responses to statelessness, including the reforms undertaken by the ASEAN Member States during the past decade or so have gradually resulted in a reduction of statelessness. While the Philippines has been the only state to subscribe to the 1954 Convention and introduce a statelessness determination procedure, Thailand and Viet Nam demonstrate that political will and targeted actions constitute the key recipe for potential solutions to the problem.

Statelessness has also made its way onto the human rights agenda of ASEAN. ASEAN sectoral bodies mainly engage themselves in the efforts to address statelessness through the mechanisms of capacity building, promoting peer to peer exchanges of good practices, influencing states, and aiding them in the implementation of the relevant global norms and standards. Lack of binding force of the regional human rights instruments, among others, makes it inherently challenging for common consensus to be built towards designing and pushing for solutions to statelessness and its implications within the region.

Chapter 5 demonstrates that in the sphere of nationality provisions in the ASEAN Member States, a closer look at the patterns of safeguards would evince an overall orientation in favour of extending protection via nationality acquisition to four groups

[3] See Article 10(1) of the1961 Convention.

[4] Human Rights Committee, General Comment No. 17: Article 24 (Rights of the Child), UN Doc. HRI/GEN/1/Rev. 9 (Vol. I) (Geneva: CCPR), para 8.

[5] L. van Waas, *Nationality Matters: Statelessness under International Law* (School of Human Rights Research Series, V. 29 (2008), p 196.

of stateless and otherwise stateless children, namely; (i) Children Born Abroad; (ii) Foundlings and Young Children with Unknown Legal Identity (iii) Children Born in the Territory to Stateless Parents; and (iv) Children Born Out of Wedlock (non-marital children). About 60–70% of the countries examined oscillate between providing partial safeguards to full safeguards against statelessness for these groups of children. On the other extreme, a glaring deficit in the availability of nationality safeguards affects two categories of 'otherwise stateless children', namely (i) Children Born to Parents of Unclear/ Undetermined Nationality; and (ii) Children Born to Non-Stateless Refugee Parents Unable or Unwilling to Confer Nationality.

Chapter 6 conducts an analysis into the extent of compatibility of the ASEAN member states' legal provisions and practices on birth registration as a safeguard against statelessness against the relevant international norms and standards. The outcome shows that the standard of a universal, well-managed, and free birth registration is generally observed in respect of totality of birth registration. Birth registration is proven to be universal in most of the countries examined (except for Cambodia and Viet Nam where certain non-citizens are excluded). The laws in six countries go further to ensure access to birth registration for certain categories of children highly vulnerable to being left out from birth registration, namely foundlings and young children without a legal identity and non-marital children.

Two critical components of the standards are not observed in the national legal frameworks of most if not all of the countries. Firstly, one addressing the preservation of confidentiality, which is absent in most of the legislative contents examined, and secondly, the prohibition of the sharing of data relating to the irregular status of parents or registrants with immigration enforcement authorities.

Furthermore, more than half of the countries do not indicate the types of proof of birth required, much less provide flexibility in evidentiary requirements. This lack of transparency creates further difficulty to registrants, and may encourage arbitrary discretionary exercise and inconsistent treatment in accepting or rejecting evidence of birth registration.

Varied trends can be seen in the area of free birth registration. Majority of the countries impose fees for late and delayed birth registration. Brief timeframes for birth registration, combined with the imposition of fees for late and delayed birth registration, as encountered in Malaysia, Singapore, and Brunei, are clear disincentives for birth registration among the poor, as well as communities in rural and remote places.

The standard of flexible and responsive birth registration through decentralisation of the system is common for 70 percent of the countries. The lack of decentralisation of birth registration and mobile registration is a serious concern especially in Lao PDR and Cambodia, where populations of rural districts and isolated villages reside. Simpler procedures are reflected only to a minimal degree in the legislation. Viet Nam and Indonesia stand out in this context when the laws stipulate for the need to create favourable conditions for birth registration, including through online registration.

The initial period for birth registration prescribed is usually below the recommended 30 days. The grace period of one year before the start of late registration is invariably not adopted. Late birth registration is not facilitated in half of the countries examined, raising valid concerns over the capacity of rural and uneducated populations to undergo such legal formalities without appropriate assistance. Indeed, most of the countries subject the process to court procedures yet do not pay sufficient regard to the facilitation of the process, such as through providing clear procedural and evidentiary requirements. The right of appeal against refusal of birth registration is found to be completely absent in the laws of the countries assessed.

7.2 Configuring Paths Forward

It appears that the prevailing norms still restrict the meaning of nationality within the parameters set by the state competence.[6] Dissatisfactions surrounding this position have not managed to wear down the conventional understanding of nationality, as neither the right to a specific nationality nor to change one's nationality has crystallised into international customary law to affect the status quo.[7]

An interpretative instrument on the scope of Article 7 and 8 CRC is long overdue to clarify the intent of the provisions in light of a legal identity for all, best interests of the child, and non-discrimination principles.

The protection through an automatic conferment of nationality for otherwise stateless children should be supported by clear and authoritative guidelines and jurisprudence that guarantee it as a human rights standard that cannot simply be trumped by states' wide margin of appreciation in favour of political, security, economic, cultural and ideological visions. Where prevention of statelessness at birth cannot be secured, human rights call upon states to activate protection, including by further easing the process for an attainment of nationality, such as through simplification of rules on proof of nationality and facilitated naturalisation. Lessons can be borrowed from Thailand's nationality law reform that has factored in human rights considerations, and from Viet Nam, in respect of facilitated naturalisation procedures.

The exclusion from the scope of the ICMW of stateless and refugees under Article 3(d) should be revisited with a view to ensuring the maximum benefit intended through its Article 29. The exclusion of these groups appears paradoxical to the rights to a name, registration of birth, and to a nationality provided in that Article to 'each child of a migrant worker', and applicable universally to all migrant workers and members of their families.[8]

---

[6] See International Law Commission, *Articles on Diplomatic Protection with Commentaries* (2006), p 32–33. See other critics of 'genuine and effective link' concept in A. Edwards, 'The Meaning of Nationality in International Law in an Era of Human Rights: Procedural and Substantive Aspects' in A. Edwards & L. van Waas (Eds.), *Nationality and Statelessness under International Law* (Cambridge: Cambridge University Press,2014), p 34.

[7] K. Hailbronner, *Nationality in Public International Law and European Law* (2006), p 37. Retrieved from http://www.eudo-citizenship.eu/docs/chapter1_Hailbronner.pdf [Accessed 6 April 2015] .

[8] In the same context of migration, the UN Human Rights Council has urged states to promote the human rights and fundamental freedoms of all migrants, particularly children. This shall apply regardless of the child's migration status and that of his/ her parents or family members. See UN

The normative development around the right to birth registration is diffused through a rich mixture of instruments and mechanisms, undermining a more systematic implementation and a holistic framework to reinforce its content. The instrumental value of the right to birth registration in preventing statelessness is not optimised when it is not jointly addressed with the acquisition of nationality. What is needed is for some form of convergence of the complex jigsaw of norms and standards to be contemplated, particularly in light of the increasing global consensus on the universal right to birth registration and the push for a worldwide commitment to realise the right to a legal identity, and other robust standard-setting measures undertaken by the relevant international and regional organisations in this regard. The General Comment on Article 6 of the ACRWC is a luminous guide that has been developed on this point, strategically consolidating and clarifying the norms and standards that connect the two rights in the spirit of prevention of statelessness.

The responsibility of registering births must be provided as equally resting with both the country of birth of the child and the country of origin of his or her migrant parents. Questions of proof of birth, accessible methods, and mechanisms of birth registration must be carefully regulated and elaborated, alerting states to the special circumstances including the risk of statelessness involving vulnerable populations such as migrants, refugees, foundlings, separated children with unknown identity, children born out of wedlock and nomadic or migratory populations.

A firewall must always exist to prevent migration enforcement actions from interfering with the duty to register every birth. The set of compulsory standards that are to be legislated and other supporting recommendations should be clearly articulated. Procedural oversights relating to the right to appeal against refusal of birth registration and procedures for delayed and late birth registration are to be amply enunciated and widely published. An example of a more hands-on approach to assist states in translating the required standards on birth registration into legal documents would be through a template bill on birth registration and a template birth registration certificate. These templates should embody the minimum rules and standards that states must comply with and additional standards that are recommended to enhance the quality and effectiveness of birth registration and certification. Best practices presenting comparable or better ways to achieve universal birth registration should be annotated for states to draw lessons from.

Birth registration campaigns and capacity building assisted by donors, and mobilised through strategic collaborations with international and regional bodies should be bolstered. Such have proved to be highly successful in increasing birth registration rates in Cambodia and are slowly effecting change in Myanmar.

Mindful that attracting ratification of and compliance with the 1961 Convention among the Contracting States is an uphill struggle that often loses out to state sovereignty and national interests,[9] it is thus hard to imagine how any amendment

Human Rights Office of the High Commissioner, *Migration and Human rights: Improving Human Rights- Based Governance of International Migration.* Retrieved from www.ohchr.org/Documents/Issues/Migration/MigrationHR_improvingHR_Report.pdf [13 March 2016].

[9] European Network on Statelessness, *No Child Should be Stateless* (2015).

or supplementary protocol to the Convention could earn the same level of existing support that it has so far garnered. It is proposed that non-treaty instruments, such as the relevant interpretive guidelines and conclusions, are best sustained in order to forge common trends and progress towards achieving the targeted standards in this area. In fact, soft law instruments have become a source of reference in drafting national legislation and developing regional and international jurisprudence.[10]

Soft law is also extremely useful to reflect and codify existing state practices, which could, over a period of time, crystallise into customary international law.[11] Furthermore, within ASEAN, the hard law approach through treaty-based instruments has hardly been an attractive medium to harness consensus in the area of human rights. In light of the foregoing observations, common grounds among the member states of ASEAN should be identified to foster shared norms, while promoting their compliance with the standards in 'under-safeguarded' areas, based on what has been tracked in Chaps. 5 and 6.

It is further submitted that the international standards on the prevention and reduction of statelessness could be further improved by considering inter alia, the following suggestions.

1. Promoting all states to provide the definition and procedures for the determination of 'a stateless person' in their relevant nationality laws, according to the established rules and guidance in the area of statelessness and its prevention. More effective ways must, however, be explored as to how a pragmatic approach that considers both the text and application of the law on citizenship could be adopted by states.
2. Hidden, marginalised and illiterate groups such as those among undocumented populations and asylum seekers are to be targeted for assistance in establishing their nationality. It must be prescribed unequivocally that their immigration status must not be divulged to the authorities to their detriment. Substantive issues such as the types of evidence and the burden of proof must be clarified and made to be understood by both the responsible agencies as well as the populations at risk. Where consular or diplomatic assistance is not available or accessible by such populations at risk, there should arise a duty on the part of the host state to inform and assist them in contacting the relevant authority of their states with whom links on the basis of descent or other relevant grounds could be identified, for reasons of nationality clarification and verification.
3. Effective methods of inter-state cooperation must be explored and developed, and the associated procedures studied, published, and disseminated to states. While ACTIP requires State Parties to undertake verification of nationality or permanent residence, and the proper issuance of documentation for victims of

[10] M. Wells-Greco, *The Status of Children from Inter-Country Surrogacy Arrangements: The Past, The Present, The Future* (2016), p 500.

[11] D. Shelton (Ed), *Commitment and Compliance: The Role of Non-Binding Norms in the International Legal System* (Oxford University Press, 2003); D. Shelton, 'Soft Law', *Handbook of International Law* (Routledge Press, 2008), p 8. Retrieved from https://scholarship.law.gwu.edu/cgi/viewcontent.cgi?article=2048&context=faculty_publications [Accessed 19 August2016].

trafficking, AALCO Resolution encourages cooperation between its Member States for purposes of establishing identity and acquiring relevant documentation for women, children and families in the wider scope of displacement, migration and trafficking. This prescribed cooperation must be strongly promoted to apply across other circumstances necessitating verification of one's nationality based on reasonable links to a particular state(s) for prevention of statelessness. Principle 6 of the Council of Europe Recommendation 2009/13 is exemplary for calling upon states to cooperate in exchanging information, particularly on acquisition or non-acquisition of a certain foreign nationality to prevent statelessness. One area where inter-state cooperation is significantly impactful is in relation to mapping initiatives of populations of undetermined nationality and verification of their nationality. Bilateral cooperation between the Governments of the Philippines and Indonesia steered and facilitated by UNHCR, is a shining model that could be replicated elsewhere.[12]

4. Evidentiary rules for proving the marriage of parents, the birth of a child, and questions surrounding paternity must also be clearly formulated, in light of religious and social values at play. The decision of the Constitutional Court of Indonesia No. 46/ PUU-VIII/2010 dated 17 February 2012 declaring the existence of civil relationship between a biological father and his non-marital child and the procedure of confirmation of a religious marriage by a religious court/ tribunal/authority or known as *Itsbat Nikah* in Indonesia are examples of forward-looking measures that could ensure that children do not simply end up being stateless. For Muslims, the role of 'fatwa' is highly pertinent in protecting non-marital children from deprivation of their right to a nationality, and the attendant victimisation of being 'without rights' through no fault of their own.

Regional harmonisation at the ASEAN level in the area of nationality through a single overarching framework would be highly controvertible given the countries' diverse political, economic, social, and legal systems. Based on the patterns of protection against statelessness via domestic nationality provisions discovered within the ASEAN Member States, actors and stakeholders in the field including AICHR, ACWC, and UNHCR are recommended to strategically design programs and actions both regionally and individually with the states to advocate for the following.

1. Adherence to customary international rules and norms and general principles of international law in the area of protection against childhood statelessness, highlighting the relevant best practices. Such include the enactment of the international legal definition of 'a stateless person', following the examples of the Philippines, Viet Nam, and Laos; explicit legislative recognition of the customary international legal right of foundlings to an automatic nationality, especially for Thailand, Brunei, the Philippines, and Myanmar; elimination of discrimination in the conferral of nationality between men and women, as still practised in

[12] See European University Institute & Robert Schuman Centre for Advanced Studies, *European Union Democracy Observatory on Citizenship* (2016). Retrieved from http://eudo-citizenship.eu/about [Accessed 26 June 2016].

Malaysia and Brunei; and prohibition of arbitrary denial of nationality and the right to birth registration as imposed on the Rohingyas in Myanmar and ethnic Vietnamese in Cambodia.

2. Adherence to full safeguards among countries already offering minimal to moderate safeguards. Such examples include; removal of limits or gaps in relation to *jus soli* safeguards for otherwise stateless children born on the territory (such could refer to the requirements of parents' statelessness and permanent residence status in Lao PDR and Viet Nam, and the condition that parents must be born and have legal residence in Cambodia); redefinition of 'foundling' in the existing legislation to cover minors and young children with unknown legal identity (for Malaysia and Singapore); prevention of loss of foundling's bestowed nationality upon discovery of his/her parent's foreign nationality; and removal of double *jus soli* rule for the relevant safeguard to apply to children born to non-stateless refugee parents who would otherwise be stateless (for Cambodia).
3. Identification of further cooperation and standard-setting where existing rules, norms, and standards are not adequate to protect children against statelessness at birth. This may be necessary for instance, where a non-marital child could be left unprotected against statelessness when the child's father fails or refuses to perform recognition of paternity, affiliation, or legitimation of the child, and where such procedures do not automatically confer nationality upon the child.

The states' adherence to the international standards in the area of nationality for all the categories of stateless and otherwise stateless children should be consistently promoted towards progressively meeting the standard of full safeguards against statelessness at birth. The approach of solidifying the international standards and norms on birth registration and guiding the states on their implementation that takes into special consideration the need of every child to have a nationality, is equally recommended for improvements in the area of birth registration within the ASEAN Member States.

The best practice examples presented in Chap. 4 hold valuable lessons for intercountry and cross-regional learnings. Long-term solutions for long-standing situations of statelessness should importantly be placed on the agenda of ASEAN and its regional and international partners. Certainly, there are national policy concerns and preferences that should not be disregarded so that appropriate context-specific strategies can be sensibly developed when engaging with the ASEAN Member States. Last but not least, capacity building, practical cooperation, and exchange of good practices should, over the course of time, translate into a more stable regional consensus, such as via a declaration or a framework of actions to address statelessness in this subregion.[13]

[13] UNHCR, *Campaign Update* (April 2016). Retrieved from http://www.refworld.org/docid/571e23fb7.html [Accessed 12 July 2016].

References

Books, Periodical Journals, Reports, Newspaper Articles

Abby Seiff & Chhay Channyda. 2013, 14 February. Ethnic Vietnamese Still Adrift in Cambodia. *The Phnom Penh Post.*

Abigaël Pesses, *Highland Birth and Citizenship Registration in Thailand. Final Report on Karen Focus Group Discussions in Chiang Mai Province.* [Research Report] UNESCO; UNESCO Highland Birth and Citizenship Registration Promotion Project Funded by the United Kingdom Sustainable Development Programme. 2007. hal-01736494. Retrieved from https://hal.archives-ouvertes.fr/hal-01736494/document [Accessed 10 August 2019].

ACWC, UNHCR, MOLISA & UN WOMEN. 2013, 19 August. Recommendations. Regional Workshop on Promoting the Right to a Nationality for Women and Children in the Implementation of CEDAW and CRC in ASEAN: ACWC-UNHCR Potential Partnership. Organised jointly by ASEAN Commission on the Promotion and Protection of the Rights of Women and Children (ACWC), Ministry of Labour, Invalids and Social Affairs of Viet Nam (MOLISA), United Nations High Commissioner for Refugees (UNHCR) and United Nations Entity for Gender Equality and the Empowerment of Women (UN Women), Da Nang, Viet Nam.

Adam Bemma. 2017, 23 November. Malaysia: A RohingyaSafe Heaven? Retrieved from https://www.aljazeera.com/news/2017/11/malaysia-rohingya-safe-haven-171122190637814. html [Accessed 2 January 2018].

Adam Saltsman. 2015. A Real Durable Solution for Southeast Asia's Refugees. *The Diplomat.* Retrieved from http://thediplomat.com/2015/12/a-real-durable-solution-for-southeast-asias-refugees/ [Accessed 1 April 2016].

African Commission on Human and Peoples' Rights. 2014. *African Commission on Human and Peoples' Rights - the Right to Nationality in Africa.* Retrieved from http://www.refworld.org/docid/54cb3c8f4.html [Accessed 15 March 2015].

Alec Paxton. 2012. Finding a Country to Call Home: A Framework for Evaluating Legislation to Reduce Statelessness in Southeast Asia. *Pacific Rim Law & Policy Journal,* V. 21.

Alice Edwards & Laura van Waas. 2014. *Nationality and Statelessness under International Law.* Cambridge: Cambridge University Press.

Alice Edwards. 2014. The Meaning of Nationality in International Law in an Era of Human Rights: Procedural and Substantive Aspects. In Alice Edwards & Laura van Waas (Eds.), *Nationality and Statelessness under International Law.* Cambridge: Cambridge University Press.

Alice Sironi. 2013. Nationality of Individuals in Public International Law: A Functional Approach. In Alessandra Annoni & Serena Forlati (Eds). *The Nationality in International Law.* Oxon: Routledge.

R. M. Razali, *Safeguarding Against Statelessness at Birth*,
https://doi.org/10.1007/978-981-19-5371-2

Allison Harvey. 2010. Statelessness: The 'De Facto' Statelessness Debate. *Immigration, Asylum and Nationality Law*, V. 24.
Alfred M. Boll. 2007. *Multiple Nationality and International Law.* Leiden: Martinus Nijhoff.
Amarjit Kaur. 2007. Refugees and Refugee Policy in Malaysia. *UNEAC Asia Papers,* V. 18 (1).
Amy Gurowitz. 2000. Migrant Rights and Activism in Malaysia: Opportunities and Constraints. *The Journal of Asian Studies,* V. 59 (4).
Andreas Schloenhardt. 2001. Trafficking in Migrants in the Asia-Pacific: National, Regional and International Responses. *Singapore Journal of International & Comparative Law,* V. 5.
Andrew J. Harding & James Chin. 2014. *50 Years of Malaysia: Federalism Revisited.* Marshall Cavendish International Asia Pte Ltd.
Anne-Marie Hilsdon. 2006. Migration and Human Rights: The Case of Filipino Muslim Women in Sabah, Malaysia. *Women's Studies International Forum.*
Anne L. Buffardi & Kwan Men Yon, *Realising the Right to Legal Identity: A case study as part of an evaluation as part of the Australia Indonesia Partnership for Justice* (July 2016) https://www.refworld.org/pdfid/57922cfd4.pdf [Accessed 8 January 2018].
Annemarieke Vermeer-Künzli. 2014. Diplomatic Protection and Consular Assistance of Migrants. In V. Chetail & C. Bauloz (Eds.), *Research Handbook on International Law and Migration.* London: Edward Elgar Publishing.
Anon. 2011, 6 November. Review for the Sake of the Child. *The Star Online.* Retrieved from http://www.thestar.com.my/news/nation/2011/11/06/review-for-the-sake-of-the-child/ [Accessed 10 February 2015].
Anon. 2016, 6 January. Pairin (Deadline Missed) Vows Report This Year. *Daily Express.* Retrieved from http://www.dailyexpresscom.my/news.cfm?NewsID=105610. [Accessed 10 August 2015].
Anon. 2015, 24 May. Myanmar population control bill signed into law despite concerns it could be used to persecute minorities. *ABC News.* Retrieved from http://www.abc.net.au/news/2015-05-24/myanmar-president-signs-off-on-controversial-population-law/6493198 [Accessed 30 June 2016].
Anon. 2018, 24 April. 'Myanmar Rohingya: What You Need to Know about the Crisis'. Retrieved from https://www.bbc.com/news/world-asia-41566561 [Accessed 20 August 2018].
Aris Ananta & Evi Nurvidya Arifin. 2004. *International Migration in Southeast Asia.* Institute of Southeast Asian Studies.
Asia Pacific Refugee Rights Network. *Statelessness.* Retrieved from http://aprrn.info/wiki/tiki-index.php?page=Statelessness [Accessed 19 April 2015].
Asian-African Legal Consultative Organisation. 2006, 8 April. Resolution on the Half-Day Special Meeting on Legal Identity and Statelessness. Res/45/Sp.1.
Audrey Macklin. 2007. Who is the Citizen's Other? Considering the Heft of Citizenship. *Theoretical Inquiries in Law* 8(2): 334–366.
Avila Geraldine. 2017, 26 November. Mobile court: 10 Years On. Retrieved from https://www.nst.com.my/news/nation/2017/11/307588/mobile-court-10-years [Accessed 20 December 2017].
Azizah Kassim. 2003. International Migration: Prospect and Challenges in Malaysia. In Mohd Yaakub Johari & Chong Shu Yaw (Eds.), *Reinventing Sabah: Global Challenges and Policy Responses.* Sabah: Institute for Development Studies.
Azizah Kassim. 2005. Cross-Border Movement of Foreign Workers in Malaysia: A Comparative Analysis. *Master Builders Journal,* 3rd Quarter: 78–91.
Azizah Kassim. 2006. Development and International Migration in Malaysia: Patterns, Policy and Human Rights. In Abdul Rahman Embong (Ed.), *Social Science & Malaysian National Development: Proceedings of the National Seminar 'Social Science and Malaysian National Development,* Putrajaya: Malaysian Social Science Association.
Azizah Kassim & Ragayah Mat Zin. 2011. Policy on Irregular Migrants in Malaysia: An Analysis on Its Implementation and Effectiveness. *Discussion Paper Series No. 2011–34.* Philippine Institute of Development Studies.
Azizah Kassim. 2012. *Dasar Pekerja Asing di Malaysia: Perlunya Anjakan Paradigma.* Selangor: Universiti Kebangsaan Malaysia.

Azizah Kassim. 2015. Pendatang Asing Tanpa Izin (Pati) Sebagai Musuh Nombor Dua Negara? In Zarina Othman & Nor Azizan Idris (Eds.), *Migrasi dan Keselamatan.* Kuala Lumpur: Dewan Bahasa dan Pustaka.

Azizah Kassim. 2005. Illegal Immigrants and the State in Sabah: Conflicting Interests and the Contest of Will. In Azizah Kassim (Ed.), *Proceedings of Seminar on States Response to the Presence and Employment of Foreign Workers in Sabah,* Kuala Lumpur: Perpustakaan Negara Malaysia.

Bastian Vollmer. 2011. *Irregular Migration in the UK: Definitions, Pathways and Scale.* Retrieved from http://migrationobservatory.ox.ac.uk/briefings/irregular-migration-uk-definitions-pathways-and-scale [Accessed 12 December 2014].

Ben Oppenheim & Brenna Marea Powell. 2015. *Legal Identity in the 2030 Agenda for Sustainable Development: Lessons from Kibera, Kenya.* Retrieved from https://www.opensocietyfoundations.org/sites/default/files/legal-identity-2030-agenda-lessons-kibera-kenya-2051216.pdf [Accessed 10 January 2010].

Betsy L. Fisher. 2015. Why Non-Marital Children in the Mena Region Face a Risk of Statelessness. *Harvard Human Rights Journal Online*, 28(1): 4–5.

Betsy L. Fisher. 2015. The Operation of Law in Statelessness Determinations under the 1954 Statelessness Convention, *Wisconsin International Law Journal*, V. 33.

Bill Berkeley. 2009. Stateless People, Violent States. *World Policy Journal* 26(1): 3–15.

Bongkot Napaumporn. 2011, 26–27 February. *Experience in Solving Statelessness and Nationalitylessness in Thailand: Identification, Prevention, Reduction and Protection.* The International Symposium on Human Rights and Support for the Stateless People around the World: Japan's Role. Osaka, Japan.

Brad K. Blitz & Maureen Lynch. 2011. *Statelessness and Citizenship: A Comparative Study on the Benefits of Nationality.* Edward Elgar Publishing.

Brad K. Blitz. 2011. Neither Seen nor Heard: Compound Deprivation among Stateless Children. In Jacqueline Bhabha (Ed.), *Children without a State: A Global Human Rights Challenge.* Cambridge, Massachusetts: MIT University Press.

Bridget Wooding. 2008. Contesting Dominican Discrimination and Statelessness. *Peace Review* 20 (3): 366–375.

Bronwen Manby. 2015. *Citizenship and Statelessness in Africa: The Law and Politics of Belonging.* PhD Thesis, University of Maastricht.

Bronwen Manby. 2015. *Nationality, Migration and Statelessness in West Africa: A Study for UNHCR and IOM.* Retrieved from http://www.unhcr.org/ecowas2015/Nationality-Migration-and-Statelessness-in-West-Africa-REPORT-EN.pdf [Accessed 16 December 2015].

Bronwen Manby, Ayalew Getachew & Julia Sloth-Nielson. 2017. The Right to a Nationality in Africa: New Norms and New Commitments. In Laura van Waas & Melanie Khanna (Eds.), *Solving Statelessness,* AH Oisterwijk: Wolf Legal Publishers.

Caitlin Wake & Tania Cheung. 2016 (June). *Livelihood strategies of Rohingya Refugees in Malaysia: We Want to Live in Dignity.* London: Humanitarian Policy Group.

Carla Abouzahr, Harbitz Mia, Fu Haishan & Mitra Raj Gautam. 2014. Towards a Research Agenda for Civil Registration and Vital Statistics in the Asia-Pacific Region. *Asia-Pacific Population Journal,* 29(1): 1–137.

Carla Abouzahr. 2014. A Development Imperative: Civil Registration and Vital Statistics Systems in the Asia-Pacific Region. *Asia-Pacific Population Journal,* 29 (1): 1–137.

Carol A. Batchelor. 2002, 8–9 January. The International Legal Framework Concerning Statelessness and Access for Stateless Persons. Contribution to the European Union Seminar on the Content and Scope of International Protection, organised by the General Directorate on Immigration and Foreigners of the Spanish Ministry of Internal Affairs.

Carol A. Batchelor. 1995. Stateless Persons: Some Gaps in International Protection. *International Journal of Refugee Law,* 7(2): 232–259.

Carol A. Batchelor. 1998. Statelessness and the Problem of Resolving Nationality Status. *International Journal of Refugee Law,* 10 (1–2): 156.

Carol A. Batchelor. 2000. Developments in International Law: The Avoidance of Statelessness through Positive Application of the Right to a Nationality. *1st European Conference on Nationality – Trends and Developments in National and International Law on Nationality.* Strasbourg, 18–19 October 1999.

Carol A. Batchelor. 2006. Transforming International Legal Principles into National Law: The Right to a Nationality and the Avoidance of Statelessness. *Refugee Survey Quarterly,* 25 (3): 8–25.

Caroline Vandenabeele & Christine V. Lao (Eds.). 2007. *Legal Identity for Inclusive Development.* Manila: Asian Development Bank.

Cate Summer & Santi Kusumaningram. 2014. *AIPJ Baseline Study on Legal Identity Indonesia's Missing Millions.* Research Report under Australia Indonesia Partnership for Justice. Retrieved from http://www.cpcnetwork.org/wp-content/uploads/2015/02/AIPJ-PUSKAPA-BASELINE-STUDY-ON-LEGAL-IDENTITY-Indonesia-2013.pdf [Accessed 18 September 2017].

Chris Lewa. 2008, June. Asia's New Boat People. *Force Migration Review (FMR)* 30.

J.M.M. Chan. 1991. The Right to a Nationality as a Human Right. *Human Rights Law Journal,* 12: 1–14.

Christoph Bierwirth. 2005. The Protection of Refugee and Asylum-Seeking Children, the Convention on the Rights of the Child and the Work of the Committee on the Rights of the Child. *Refugee Survey Quarterly,* 24 (2): 98–124.

Christoph Sperfeldt & Lyma Nguyen. 2012. A Boat without Anchors: A Report on the Legal Status of Ethnic Vietnamese Minority Populations in Cambodia under Domestic and International Laws Governing Nationality and Statelessness. *RegNet Research Paper,* 2014/50. Retrieved from SSRN: https://ssrn.com/abstract=2514121. https://doi.org/10.2139/ssrn.2514121 [Accessed 5 July 2018].

Clark D. Neher. 2000. *Southeast Asia: Crossroads of the World.* Illinois: Northern Illinois University, Center for Southeast Asian Studies.

Clifford Sather. 1997. *The Bajau Laut: Adaptation, History and Fate in a Maritime Fishing Society of South-Eastern Sabah.* New York: Oxford University Press.

Commissioners of Enquiry on Immigrants in Sabah. 2014. *Report of the Commission of Enquiry on Immigrants in Sabah.* Retrieved from http://www.sapp.org.my/rci/RCI-Eng.pdf [Accessed 9 January 2016].

Committee on the Rights of the Child. 2012. *Report of the 2012 Day of General Discussion: The Rights of All Children in the Context of International Migration.* Retrieved from http://www2.ohchr.org/english/bodies/crc/docs/discussion2012/DGD2012Outline.pdf [Accessed 3 March 2013].

Coram Children's Legal Centre. 2013. *Growing Up in A Hostile Environment: The Rights of Undocumented Migrant Children in the UK.* Retrieved from https://www.childrenslegalcentre.com/wp-content/uploads/2013/11/Hostile_Environment_Full_Report_Final.pdf [Accessed 15 June 2016].

K. Culliton-Gonzales. 2012. Born in the Americas: Birthright Citizenship and Human Rights. *Harvard Human Rights Journal,* 25:127–182.

Curtis F. Doebbler. 2002. A Human Rights Approach to Statelessness in the Middle East. *Leiden Journal of International Law,* 15(3): 527–552.

Cynthia Chou. 2006. Research Trends on Southeast Asian Sea Nomads. *Kyoto Review of Southeast Asia. Issue 7. States, People, and Borders in Southeast Asia.*

David C. Baluarte. 2017. The Risk of Statelessness: Reasserting a Rule for the Protection of the Right to a Nationality, *Yale Hum. Rts. & Dev. LJ,* 19(47): 47–94.

David Owen. 2013. Citizenship and the Marginalities of Migrants. *Critical Review of International Social and Political Philosophy,* 16(3): 326–343.

David Weissbrodt & Collins Clay. 2006. The Human Rights of Stateless Persons. *Human Rights Quarterly,* 28 (1): 245–276.

G. R. de Groot, Peter Vink Maarten & Olivier Willem Vonk. 2013. *Protection against Statelessness: Trends and Regulations in Europe.* Retrieved from http://eudo-citizenship.eu/images/docs/eudocit_vink_degroot_statelessness_final.pdf [Accessed 1 April 2016].

G.R. de Groot. 2014. Children, Their Right to a Nationality and Child Statelessness. In Alice Edwards & Laura van Waas (Eds.), *Nationality and Statelessness under International Law,* pp 144–168. Cambridge: Cambridge University Press.

G. R. de Groot, Katia Swider & Olivier Willem Vonk. 2015. *Practices and Approaches in EU Member States to Prevent and End Statelessness.* Retrieved from http://www.europarl.europa.eu/RegData/etudes/STUD/2015/536476/IPOL_STU(2015)536476_EN.pdf [Accessed 13 January 2016].

Dimitri Vanoverbeke & Michael Reiterer. 2014. ASEAN's Regional Approach to Human Rights: The Limits of the European Model? Retrieved from https://www.researchgate.net/publication/264484877_ASEANs_Regional_Approach_to_Human_Rights_The_Limits_of_the_European_Model [Accessed 9 May 2016].

Dinah Shelton (Ed.). 2003. *Commitment and Compliance: The Role of Non-Binding Norms in the International Legal System.* Oxford University Press.

Dinah Shelton. 2008. *Regional Protection of Human Rights.* New York: Oxford University Press.

Dinah L. Shelton. 2008. Soft Law. In *Handbook of International Law.* Routledge Press. Retrieved from http://scholarship.law.gwu.edu/cgi/viewcontent.cgi?article=2048&context=faculty_publications [Accessed 19 August 2016].

Douglas Hodgson. 1993. The International Legal Protection of the Child's Right to a Legal Identity and the Problem of Statelessness. *International Journal of Law, Policy and the Family,* 7(2): 255–270.

Dumrongkiat Mala. 2018. Migrants are still slow to register births. Retrieved from https://www.bangkokpost.com/news/general/1527374/migrants-are-still-slow-to-register-births [Accessed 20 September 2018].

ENS. 2013. *Statelessness Determination and the Protection Status of Stateless Persons.* Retrieved from http://www.refworld.org/pdfid/53162a2f4.pdf [Accessed 27 June 2016].

Economic and Social Research Council (ESRC). Researcher Development Initiative (RDI) and Institute of Education, University of London (IOE), the Research Ethics Guidebook. Retrieved from www.ethicsguidebook.ac.uk [Accessed 5 February 2015].

Equal Rights Trust. 2016. *Confined Spaced: Legal Protections for Rohingya in Bangladesh, Malaysia and Thailand.* Retrieved from http://www.equalrightstrust.org/ertdocumentbank/Confined%20Spaces_0.pdf [Accessed 30 December 2016].

Elain Pearson. 2014, 22 May. Cambodia is Not Safe for Refugees. *Human Rights Watch News.*

Ellen Laipson & Amit Pandya. 2010. *On the Move: Migration Challenges in the Indian Ocean Littoral.* Washington DC: The Henry L. Stimson Center.

Emilie Irwin & Mark Manly. 2008. *Statelessness: An Analytical Framework for Prevention, Reduction and Protection.* Retrieved from http://www.unhcr.org/49a271752.html [Accessed 21 March 2016].

Eric Fripp. 2016. *Nationality and Statelessness in the International Law of Refugee Status.* Oxford and Portland: Bloomsbury.

ESCAP. 2012. *Asia Pacific Population Journal,* No.1, 2014. UNICEF 29 (16 & 20).

European Network on Statelessness. 2013. *Statelessness Determination and the Protection Status of Stateless Persons.* Retrieved from http:// www.refworld.org/pdfid/53162a2f4.pdf [Accessed 24 July 2015].

European Network on Statelessness. 2014. *Preventing Childhood Statelessness in Europe: Issues, Gaps and Good Practices.* Retrieved from http://www.statelessness.eu/blog/prevention-statelessness-birth-%E2%80%93-adequate-nationality-law-inconsistent-implementation [Accessed 12 February 2015].

European Network on Statelessness. 2015. *No Child Should Be Stateless.* Retrieved from http://www.statelessness.eu/sites/www.statelessness.eu/files/ENS_NoChildStateless_final.pdf [Accessed 10 January 2016].

European University Institute & Robert Schuman Centre for Advanced Studies. 2016. *European Union Democracy Observatory on Citizenship.* Retrieved from http://eudo-citizenship.eu/about [Accessed 26 June 2016].

Forced Migration Online (FMO). 2012. *What Is Forced Migration*? Retrieved from www.forcedmigration.org/about/whatisfm [Accessed 12 December 2015].

Francesco Costamagna. 2013. Statelessness in the Context of State Succession: An Appraisal under International Law. In Alessandra Annoni & Serena Forlati (Eds.), *The Changing Role of Nationality in International Law*. New York: Routledge.

Francis Teoh. 2011, 25 August. The Underlying Issue of Statelessness: Retrieved from http://www.thejakartapost.com/news/2011/08/25/the-underlying-issue-statelessness.html [Accessed 10 March 2016].

Government of the United Kingdom. (No Year) Legitimation and Domicile. Retrieved from https://www.gov.uk/government/uploads/system/uploads/attachment_data/file/118568/legitimation-and-domicile.pdf [Accessed 16 March 2015].

Blanca Garces-Mascarenas. 2015. Revisiting the Myth of Guest Worker Programs: The Case of Malaysia. In Diego Acosta Arcarazo & Anja Wiesbrock (Eds.), *Global Migration: Old Assumptions, New Dynamics (Vol. 3)*. Santa Barbara & Denver: Praeger.

Guy Arnold. 2012. *Migration: Changing the World*. London: Pluto Press.

Gábor Gyulai. 2012. Statelessness in the EU Framework for International Protection. *European Journal of Migration and Law*, 14(3): 279–295.

Gabor Gyulai. 2014. The Determination of Statelessness and the Establishment of a Statelessness-Specific Protection Regime. In Alice Edwards & Laura van Waas (Eds.), *Nationality and Statelessness under International Law*. Cambridge: Cambridge University Press.

Gabor Gyulai. 2017. The Long-Overlooked Mystery of Refugee Children's Nationality. In Institute on Statelessness and Inclusion, *The World's Stateless Children*. Retrieved from http://children.worldsstateless.org/3/migration-displacement-and-childhood-statelessness/the-long-overlooked-mystery-of-refugee-childrens-nationality.html [Accessed 5 July 2017].

Geoffrey Benjamin. 1986. Achievements of Gaps in Orang Asli Research. *Akademika 35*: 7–46.

Geraldine van Bueren. 1998. *The International Law on the Rights of the Child*. Martinus Nijhoff Publishers.

Government of the United Kingdom. Legitimation and Domicile. Retrieved from https://www.gov.uk/government/uploads/system/uploads/attachment_data/file/118568/legitimation-and-domicile.pdf [Accessed 16 March 2015].

Graeme Hugo, Sayed Mahadi, Syed Abdul Razak & Ahmad Hashimi Mohammad. 2011. *Indonesian Labour Migration to Sabah: Causes and Implications*. In Konferensi antara Universiti Seborneo Kalimantan ke 6 (KABOKA 6), 24 Mei 2011, Universitas Palangka Raya, Palangka Raya, Kalimantan Tengah, Indonesia. (Unpublished).

Graeme Hugo. 1987. Postwar Refugee Migration in Southeast Asia: Patterns, Problems, and Policies. *Refugees: A Third World Dilemma*. New Jersey: Rowan and Littlefield.

Graeme Hugo. 1993. Indonesian Labour Migration to Malaysia: Trends and Policy Implications. Trends and Policy Implications', *Southeast Asian Journal of Social Science*, 21(1): 36–70.

Graeme Hugo. 2004. International Migration in Southeast Asia since World War. *International Migration in Southeast Asia*, 2: 28–70.

Graeme Hugo. 2005. *Migration in the Asia-Pacific Region: A paper prepared for the Policy Analysis and Research Programme of the Global Commission on International Migration*. Retrieved from https://www.iom.int/jahia/webdav/site/myjahiasite/shared/shared/mainsite/policy_and_research/gcim/rs/RS2.pdf [Accessed 16 March 2015].

Harald Bauder. 2012. Jus Domicile: In Pursuit of a Citizenship of Equality and Social Justice. *Journal of International Political Theory*, 8(1–2): 184–196.

Haro Fredrik van Panhuys. 1959. *The Role of Nationality in International Law*. Leyden: A.W. Sythoff.

Heather Alexander. 2017. *The Nationality and Statelessness of Nomads*. Retrieved from https://www.academia.edu/34503088/The_Nationality_and_Statelessness_of_Nomads [Accessed 20 August 2019].

Helen Brunt. 2014. *A Position Paper on the Vulnerability of Bajau Laut (Sama Dilaut) Children in Sabah*. Retrieved from http:// rightsinexile.tumblr.com/post/115241976092/a-position-paper-on-the-vulnerability-of-bajau [Accessed 20 August 2015].

Helen Brunt. 2017. The Sustainable Development Agenda and Childhood Statelessness. In Institute on Statelessness and Inclusion, *The World's Stateless Children*. Retrieved from http://children.worldsstateless.org/3/childhood-statelessness-and-the-sustainable-development-agenda/introduction.html [Accessed 20 August 2018].

Helen Brunt. 2017. *Stateless at Sea*. In Institute on Statelessness and Inclusion, the *World's Stateless Children*. Retrieved from http:// www.institutesi.org/worldstateless17.pdf [Accessed 30 January 2018].

Hugh Massey. 2010. *UNHCR and De Facto Statelessness*. Retrieved from http://www.refworld.org/docid/4bbf387d2.html [Accessed 16 December 2013].

Human Rights Watch. 2015. *Statelessness at Sea, the Moken of Burma and Thailand*. Retrieved from https://www.hrw.org/report/2015/06/25/stateless-sea/moken-burma-and-thailand [Accessed 22 June 2016].

Ian Brownlie. 1963. Relations of Nationality in Public International Law. *British Yearbook of International Law*, 39: 284.

Ida Lim. 2019. 'Reality check for Malaysian-born stateless children on 'special citizenship' route', *malaymail*, Retrieved from https://www.malaymail.com/news/malaysia/2019/03/26/reality-check-for-malaysia-born-stateless-children-on-special-citizenship-r/1736436 [Accessed 20 June 2019].

Immigration and Checkpoints Authority Singapore Government. Checkpoints Authority. Retrieved from https://www.ica.gov.sg/page.aspx?pageid=144 [Accessed 7 October 2016].

Inge Brees. 2008. Refugee Business: Strategies of Work on the Thai– Burma Border. *Journal of Refugee Studies*, 21 (3): 380–397.

Institute on Statelessness and Inclusion. 2016. *Report of the Working Group: Submission to the Human Rights Council at the 25th Session of the Universal Periodic Review: Thailand*. Retrieved from http://www.refworld.org/docid/57cd6be64.html [Accessed 21 September 2016].

Institute on Statelessness and Inclusion. 2017. *Stateless Persons in Asia and the Pacific*. Retrieved from http://www.worldsstateless.org/continents/asia/stateless-persons-in-asia-and-the-pacific [Accessed 20 September 2018].

Institute on Statelessness and Inclusion. 2014. *The World's Stateless*. Retrieved from http://www.instituesi.org/worldstateless.pdf [Accessed January 10, 2015].

Institute on Statelessness and Inclusion. 2015. *Policy Paper on Realising the Right of Every Child to Acquire a Nationality: An Analysis of the Work of the Committee on the Rights of the Child*. Retrieved from http://www.institutesi.org/CRC_nationality_paper.pdf [Accessed 12 August 2015].

Institute on Statelessness and Inclusion. 2016. *About Statelessness – Causes of Statelessness*. Retrieved from http://www.institutesi.org/world/causes.php [Accessed 17 April 2016].

Institute on Statelessness and Inclusion. 2016. *Submission to the Human Rights Council at the 25th Session of the Universal Periodic Review on 2–13 May 2016*. Retrieved from http://www.institutesi.org/ourwork/humanrights.php [Accessed 3 August 2016].

Institute on Statelessness and Inclusion. 2016. *Addressing the Right to a Nationality through the Convention on the Rights of the Child, a Toolkit for Civil Society*. Retrieved from http://www.institutesi.org/CRC_Toolkit_Final.pdf [Accessed 7 October 2016].

Institute on Statelessness and Inclusion. 2017. *The World's Stateless Children*. Oisterwijk: Wolf Legal Publishers. Retrieved from http:// www.institutesi.org/worldsstateless17.pdf [Accessed 5 January 2017].

International Labour Office. 2010. *International Labour Migration. A Rights-Based Approach*. Retrieved from http://www.ilo.org/wcmsp5/groups/public/---ed_protect/---protrav/---migrant/documents/publication/wcms_208594.pdf [Accessed 23 November 2013].

International Law Commission. 2006. *Articles on Diplomatic Protection with Commentaries*: Retrieved from http://untreaty.un.org/ilc/ guide/9_8.htm [Accessed 1 April 2016].

International Organization for Migration & UN Country Team in Thailand. 2011. *Thailand Migration Report 2011.* Retrieved from http://reliefweb.int/report/thailand/thailand-migration-report-2011 [Accessed 7 October 2014].
International Organization for Migration (IOM). 2008. *Situation Report on International Migration in East and South-East Asia: Regional Thematic Working Group on International Migration Including Human Trafficking.* Retrieved from http://publications.iom.int/bookstore/index.php?main_page=product_info&products_id=315 [Accessed 13 December 2014].
International Organization for Migration. 2015. *10 Years in Myanmar (2005–2014).* Retrieved from https://www.iom.int/sites/default/files/country/docs/myanmar/IOM-10-Years-in-Myanmar.pdf [Accessed 29 September 2016].
International Union for Child Welfare. 1947. *Stateless Children; a Comparative Study of National Legislations and Suggested Solutions to the Problem of Statelessness of Children,* 1st Ed. Geneva: International Union for Child Welfare.
Ivan Shearer & Opeskin Brian. 2012. Nationality and Statelessness. In Brian Opeskin, Richard Perruchoud & Jillyanne Redpath-Cross (Eds.), *Foundations of International Migration Law.* Cambridge: Cambridge University Press.
Jaap Doek. 2006. The CRC and the Right to Acquire and to Preserve a Nationality. *Refugee Survey Quarterly,* 25(3): 26–32.
Jabatan Pendaftaran Negara. 2013, 29 April. Kad Pengenalan Pemaustautin Sementara (MyKas). Media Statement by Datuk Jariah Mohd Said, Ketua Pengarah Pendaftaran Negara. https://www.astroawani.com/berita-pilihanraya/tiada-mykas-dikeluar-untuk-warga-asing-mengundi-jpn-13141 [Accessed 6 April 2016].
Jacqueline Bhabha. 2009. Arendt's Children: Do Today's Migrant Children Have a Right to Have Rights? *Human Rights Quarterly,* 31(2): 410–451.
Jacqueline Bhabha (Ed). 2011. *Children without a State: A Global Human Rights Challenge.* Cambridge, Massachusetts: MIT Press.
Jacqueline Bhabha. 2012. Women, Children and Other Marginalised Migrant Groups. In Brian Opeskin, Richard Perruchoud & Jillyanne Redpath-Cross (Eds.), *Foundations of International Migration Law.* Cambridge: Cambridge University Press.
Jacqueline Bhabha. 2017. The importance of nationality for Children. In Institute on Statelessness and Inclusion, *The World's Stateless Children.* Retrieved from http://www.institutesi.org/worlds stateless17.pdf [Accessed 30 January 2018].
Jacqueline Joudo Larsen. 2010. Migration and People Trafficking in Southeast Asia. *Trends and Issues in Crime and Criminal Justice,* 401: 1.
James A. Goldston. 2006. Holes in the Rights Framework: Racial Discrimination, Citizenship, and the Rights of Noncitizens. *Ethics & International Affairs,* 20 (3): 321–347.
James Chin. 2013. A Brief History of the Malay Peninsular and Northern Borneo and the Formation of Malaysia. In Phillip Mathews (Ed.), *The Chronicle of Malaysia 1963–2013,* pp 15–31.
Jason E. Tucker. 2014. Questioning De Facto Statelessness by Looking at De Facto Citizenship. *Tilburg Law Review,* 19(1–2): 276–284.
Jeff Mudrick. 2014, 30 April. Revisiting Cambodia's Laws on Nationality and Immigration. *The Combodia Daily.* Retrieved from https://www.cambodiadaily.com/opinion/revisiting-cambodias-laws-on-nationality-and-immigration-57789/ [Accessed 20 October 2015].
Jill Stein. 2014. *The Prevention of Child Statelessness at Birth under the Convention on the Rights of the Child: The Committee's Role & Potential.* Graduate Dissertation, Leiden University.
Jo Boyden & Hart Jason. 2007. The Statelessness of the World's Children. *Children & Society,* 21(4): 237–248.
John W. Heffernan. 2002. Human Security Dilemma in South andSoutheast Asia. Commission on Human Security. Retrieved from http://www.humansecurity-chs-org/activities/research/citize nship_asia.pdf.
Jonathan Bialosky. 2015. Regional Protection of the Right to a Nationality. *Cardozo Journal of International & Comparative. Law,* 24(1): 153–192.

Jonathan Todres. 2003. Birth Registration: An Essential First Step toward Ensuring the Rights of All Children. *Human Rights Brief*, 10 (3): 32–35.

Jorge V. Tigno. 2004. *Foreign Workers, Refugees, and Irregular Immigrants: Political Challenges and Perspectives for Asia Europe Cooperation*. Quezon City: Council for Asia-Europe Cooperation and Institute for Strategic and Developmental Studies.

Jorge V. Tigno. 2004. Irregular Migration From and Within. In Council for Asia-Europe Cooperation (Ed.), *Asia Foreign Workers, Refugees and Irregular Immigrants: Political Challenges and Perspectives for Asia-Europe Cooperation*. Manila: The Council for Asia-Europe Cooperation and Institute for Strategic and Development Studies.

Jose-Maria Arraiza. 2017. Re-imagining Myanmar Citizenship in Times of Transition. *Statelessness Working Paper Series*, No 2017/1. Retrieved from http://www.institutesi.org/WP2017_01.pdf [Accessed 9 April 2018].

Joy K. Park, John E. Tanagho & Mary E. Weicher Gaudette. 2008. A Global Crisis Writ Large: The Effects of Being Stateless in Thailand on Hill-Tribe Children. *San Diego International Law Journal*, 10: 495.

Julian Clifton, Greg Acciaioli, Helen Brunt, Wolfram Dressler, Micheal Fabinyi & Sarinda Singh. 2014. *Statelessness and Conservation: Exploring the Implications of an International Governance Agenda. Tilburg Law Review 19(1–2)*: 81–89.

Julius G. Getman. 1985. Contributions of Empirical Data to Legal Research. *Journal of Legal Education*, 35(4): 489–494.

Jyothi Kanics. 2017. Migration, Forced Displacement and Childhood Statelessness. Retrieved from http://children.worldsstateless.org/3/migration-displacement-and-childhood-statelessness/migration-forced-displacement-and-childhood-statelessness. html [Accessed 7 February 2018].

Kamal Sadiq. 2005. When States Prefer Non-Citizens over Citizens: Conflict over Illegal Immigration into Malaysia. *International Studies Quarterly*, 49 (1): 101–122.

Kara Apland, Brad K. Blitz, Dawn Calabia, Mark Fielder, Carolyn Hamilton, Nuwan Indika, Rajith Lakshman, Maureen Lynch & Elizabeth Yarrow. 2014. *Birth Registration and Children's Rights: A Complex Story* (Report). Plan International. Retrieved from https://www.planusa.org/docs/birth-registration-rights-2014.pdf [Accessed 6 March 2015].

Karn Sermchaiwong. 2008. *Member of the Sub-Committee on Ethnic Problems of the National Human Rights Commission*. Birth Registration in Thailand. Presentation Slides. Retrieved from http://slideplayer.com/slide/5821035/ [Accessed 6 April 2015].

Katherine G. Southwick. 2014. Myanmar's Democratic Transition: Peril or Promise for the Stateless Rohingya? *Tilburg Law Review*, 19 (1-2): 261–275.

Katie Hunt. 12 November 2017. Rohingya Crisis: How We Got Here. *CNN*. Retrieved from https://www.cnn.com/2017/11/12/asia/rohingya-crisis-timeline/index.html [Accessed 12 November 2017].

Katrina Navallo. *Filipino Migrants in Sabah: Marginalized Citizens in the Midst of Interstate Disputes*. Retrieved from https://www.academia.edu/6364345/Filipino_Migrants_in_Sabah_Marginalized_Citizens_in_the_Midst_of_Interstate_Disputes [Accessed 10 October 2015].

Kay Hailbronner. 2003. Nationality. In T.A. Aleinikoff & V. Chetail (Eds.), *Migration and International Legal Norms*. The Hague: T.M.C. Asser Press.

Kay Hailbronner. 2006. Nationality in Public International Law and European Law. Retrieved from http://www.eudo-citizenship.eu/docs/chapter1_Hailbronner.pdf [Accessed 6 April 2015].

Kevin McGahan. 2008. *Managing Migration: The Politics of Immigration Enforcement and Border Controls in Malaysia*. PhD Thesis, University of Wisconsin-Madison.

Khoo Ying Hooi. 24 March 2014. Long Way to Go on Human Rights. *The Malaysian Insider*. Retrieved from https://umexpert.um.edu.my/file/publication/00011588_104700.pdf [Accessed 23 May 2015].

Kim Rubenstein & Daniel Adler. 2000. International Citizenship: The Future of Nationality in a Globalized World. *Indiana Journal of Global Legal Studies, 7* (2): 519–548.

Kitty McKinsey. 2007, 14 February. Divorce Leaves Some Vietnamese Women Broken-Hearted and Stateless. Retrieved http://www.unhcr.org/45d324428.html [Accessed 20 September 2014].

Ko Swan Sik. 1990. *Nationality and International Law in Asian Perspectives.*The Hague: T.M.C. Asser Institute.
Lai Ah Eng, Francis Leo Collins & Brenda Yeoh. 2013. *Migration and Diversity in Asian Contexts.* Pasir Panjang: Institute of Southeast Asian Studies.
Laura Bosch. *Birth Registration Problems in Complex Migration Context – Case Studies from The Netherlands.* Retrieved from http://children.worldsstateless.org/3/migration-displacement-and-childhood-statelessness/birth-registration-problems-in-complex-migration-contexts-case-studies-from-the-netherlands.html [Accessed 20 January 2018].
Laura van Waas & Mark Manly. 2014. The State of Statelessness Research: A Human Rights Imperative. *Tilburg Law Review: Journal on International and Comparative Law,* 19 (1–2): 3–10.
Laura van Waas. 2007. The Children of Irregular Migrants: A Stateless Generation. *Netherlands Quarterly of Human Rights,* 25: 437–458.
Laura van Waas. 2008. *Nationality Matters: Statelessness under International Law.* School of Human Rights Research Series, V. 29.
Laura van Waas. 2008. *Nationality Matters: Statelessness under International Law,* Antwerp/Oxford/Portland: Intersentia.
Laura van Waas. 2009. Statelessness: A 21st Century Challenge for Europe. *Security and Human Rights,* 20 (2): 133–146.
Laura van Waas. 2010. *The Situation of Stateless Persons in the Middle East and North Africa.* Retrieved from http://www.unhcr.org/protection/statelessness/4ce63e079/situation-stateless-persons-middle-east-north-africa-laura-van-waas.html [Accessed 20 May 2014].
Laura van Waas. 2014. The UN Statelessness Conventions. In A. Edwards & L. van Waas (Eds.), *Nationality and Statelessness under International Law,* p 64–87. Cambridge: Cambridge University Press.
Laura van Waas. 2015. The Right to a Legal Identity or the Right to a Legal ID. *ENS' Blog.* Retrieved from http://www.statelessness.eu/blog/right-legal-identity-or-right-legal-id [Accessed 17 March 2016].
Laurie Berg. 2007. At the Border and between the Cracks: The Precarious Position of Irregular Migrant Workers under International Human Rights Law. *Melbourne Journal of International Law,* 8 (1): 1–34.
Leo Suryadinata. 2014. *The Making of Southeast Asian Nations: State, Ethnicity, Indigenism and Citizenship.* World Scientific.
Leslie Butt & Jessica Ball. 2017. Birth Registration in Southeast Asia: a child's foundation right? *Asian Population Studies,* 13(3): 223–225.
Linda K. Kerber. 2011. Birthright Citizenship: The Vulnerability and Resilience of American Constitutional Principle. In Jacqueline Bhabha (Ed.), *Children without a State: A Global Human Rights Challenge.* Cambridge, London, England: MIT Press.
Luca Bicocchi & Michele LeVoy. 2008. *Undocumented Children in Europe: Invisible Victims of Immigration Restrictions.* Retrieved from http:// picum.org/picum.org/uploads/publication/Undocumented%20 Children%20in%20Europe%20EN.pdf. [Accessed 17 December 2015].
Lucía González López, Tanja Brøndsted Sejersen, Nicholas Oakeshott, Gaspar Fajth, Taimur Khilji & Nicoleta Panta. 2014. Civil Registration, Human Rights and Social Protection in Asia and the Pacific. *Asia-Pacific Population Journal,* 29(1): 1–137.
Lucia Nistal Coelho. *Reservations to the Convention on the Rights of the Child: The Committee's Approach.* Thesis, University of Amsterdam.
Lyma Nguyen. 2017. *Report on Citizenship Law: Vietnam.* Retrieved from http://cadmus.eui.eu/bitstream/handle/1814/47966/GLOBALCIT_CR_2017_13.pdf?sequence=1 [Accessed 7 September 2018].
Maria Jose Recalde Vela. 2014. *How Far Has the Protection of the Right to Nationality under International Human Rights Law Progressed from 1923 until the Present Day?* Dissertation, Tilburg University.

Mark Manly & Santhosh Persaud. 2009. UNHCR and Responses to Statelessness. *Force Migration Review (FMR)*, 1(32).

Mark Manly. 2011. *Support for the Rabat Process on Migration and Development, Meeting of Experts on Civil Registry, Improving Civil Status Registration Systems and Combating Document Fraud*. Retrieved from http://www.processusderabat.net/web/uploads/activity/civil_registry/UNHCR%20Manly_EN.pdf [Accessed 8 November 2014].

Mark Manly. 2014. UNHCR's Mandate and Activities to Address Statelessness. In Alice Edwards & Laura van Wass (Eds.), *Nationality and Statelessness under International Law*. Cambridge: Cambridge University Press.

Marta Santos Pais. 2002. Birth Registration: Right from the Start. *UNICEF Innocenti Digest*, 9: 1–32.

Martin Stiller. 2012. Statelessness in International Law: A Historic Overview. *DAJV Newsletter*, 37.

Maruja M.B. Asis. 2004. Borders, Globalization and Irregular Migration in Southeast Asia. In Aris Arinata & Evi Nurvidya Ariffin (Eds.), *International Migration in Southeast Asia*. Pasir Panjang: Institute of Southeast Asian Studies.

Matthew Gibney. 2009. *Precarious Residents: Migration Control, Membership and the Rights of Non-Citizens* (Human Development Reports). United Nations Development Programme. Retrieved from http://hdr.undp.org/en/content/precarious-residents [Accessed 29 September 2015].

Matthew J. Lister. 2010. Citizenship in the Immigration Context. *Maryland Law Review*, 70: 175–233.

Maureen Lynch & Cook Thatcher. 2006. *Citizens of Nowhere: The Stateless Biharis of Bangladesh*. Washington DC: Refugees International.

Maureen Lynch & Melanie Teff. 2009. Childhood Statelessness. *Forced Migration Review*, 32: 31–33.

Maureen Lynch. 2008. *Futures Denied: Statelessness among Infants, Children and Youth*. Refugees International. Retrieved from http://www.refworld.org/cgi-bin/texis/vtx/rwmain?docid=48fef8632 [Accessed 20 January 2014].

Maureen Lynch. 2005. *Lives on Hold: The Human Cost of Statelessness*. Retrieved from http://www.refworld.org/docid/47a6eba00.html [Accessed 9 August 2013].

Meerah Dewi Raja Gopal. 2015. Does Illegitimacy Status of Children Matter? A Review on Malaysian Perspective. *International Journal of Applied Psychology*, 5(4): 109–114.

Mely Caballero-Anthony. 2018. A Hidden Scourge. *Finance and Development, IMF Quarterly*, 5(3). Retrieved from https://www.imf.org/external/pubs/ft/fandd/2018/09/pdf/fd0918.pdf [Accessed 19 January 2019].

Mekong Migration Network (MMN). *The Precarious Status of Migrants in Thailand: Reflections on the Exodus of Cambodian Migrants and Lessons Learnt*. Retrieved from http://www.cwcc.org.kh/wp-content/uploads/2015/07/FINAL-EDITED-REPORT-24-Nov.pdf [Accessed 29 September 2016].

Michael Caster. 2015, 26 August. The Truth About Myanmar's New Discriminatory Laws. *The Diplomat*. Retrieved from http://thediplomat.com/2015/08/the-truth-about-myanmars-new-discriminatory-laws/ [Accessed 19 January 2017].

Michael Freeman. 2007. *A Commentary on the United Nations Convention on the Rights of the Child, Article 3: The Best Interests of the Child*. Martinus Nijhoff Publishers.

Michael Hutt. 2003. *Unbecoming Citizens: Culture: Nationhood and the Flight of Refugees from Bhutan*. New York: Oxford University Press.

Michael Miller. 2004. *Birth Registration: Statelessness and Other Repercussions for Unregistered Children*. 3rd European Conference on Nationality. Organised by Palais del'Europe, Strasbourg, 11–12 October 2004.

Michael Wells-Greco. 2016. *The Status of Children from Inter-Country Surrogacy Arrangements: The Past, the Present, the Future*. Ph.D. Thesis, University of Maastricht.

Michele Tuccio. 2017. Determinants of Intra-ASEAN Migration. *Asian Development Review*, (2017) V. 34(1): 144–166.

Migration Policy Institute. 2005. *New Concepts in Regularisation: Earned Legislation.* Retrieved from http://www.migrationpolicy.org/newconcepts.php [Accessed 30 December 2015].

Migration Policy Institute. 2006. Citizenship in a Globalised World. Retrieved from http://www.migrationpolicy.org/article/citizenship-globalized-world [Accessed 30 December 2015].

Ministry of Foreign Affairs of the Kingdom of Thailand, *Press Release: Thailand announces additional measures to fight statelessness* (2017). Retrieved from http://www.mfa.go.th/main/en/news3/6886/74222-Thailand-announces-additional-measures-to-fight-st.html [Accessed 20 December 2018].

Minority Rights Group International. 2016. *World Directory of Minorities and Indigenous Peoples.* Retrieved from http://www.refworld.org/docid/49749d4832.html [Accessed 23 June 2016].

Murib Morpi. 22 February 2013. NRD Explains Law, Procedures on Birth Certificate, IC and Citizenship. *Borneo Post Online.* Retrieved from http://www.theborneopost.com/2013/02/22/nrd-explains-laws-procedures-on-birth-certificate-ic-and-citizenship/ [Accessed 7 July 2015].

Myers S. McDougal, Harold D. Lasswell & Chen Lung Chu. 1974. Nationality and Human Rights: The Protection of the Individual in External Arenas. In *Yale Law School Legal Scholarship Repository.* Retrieved from http://digitalcommons.law.yale.edu/cgi/viewcontent.cgi?article=3663&context=fss_papers [Accessed 2 November 2014].

Nantanee Jedsadachaiyut & Nadia Al-Jasem. 2016, 24 November. Overcoming Statelessness in Thailand One Case at a Time. Retrieved from http://www.unhcr.org/news/latest/2016/11/5836af624/overcoming-statelessness-thailand-case-time.html [Accessed 5 March 2017].

National Registration Department Malaysia. 2018. Home/Late Registration of Birth (Peninsular). Retrieved from http://www.jpn.gov.my/en/maklumat-kelahiran/pendaftaran-lewat-kelahiran-2/#1458289648764-bf711d6d-f9ed [Accessed 27 November 2018].

National Registration Department. 2018. *Home/ Late Registration of Birth (Peninsular).* Retrieved from http://www.jpn.gov.my/ [Accessed 10 July 2018].

Nay Pyi Taw. 2015, 24 August. Myanmar, Getting to the Goal of 100 Percent Birth Registration. Retrieved from http://www.unicef.org/myanmar/media_24526.html [Accessed 15 June 2016].

Nehemiah Robinson. 1955. *Convention relating to the Status of Stateless Persons: Its History and Interpretation.* Institute of Jewish Affairs.

Nicholas Oakeshott. 2013. An Analysis of Nationality Laws in South East Asia. Presentation Slides. Regional Statelessness Course: South East Asia Focus. Organised by UNHCR. 4–8 November 2013. Bangkok.

Nicholas Oakeshott & Napaumporn Bongkot. 2013. Statelessness in South East Asia. Presentation Slides. Regional Statelessness Course: South East Asia Focus. Organised by UNHCR, 4–8 November 2013. Bangkok.

Nicholas Oakeshott. 2016. Statelessness in the Asia Pacific: Introduction and Context. Presentation Slides. Workshop on Researching Statelessness and Citizenship in the Asia Pacific. Organised by UNHCR, Melbourne School of Government & Melbourne Law School. 27–29 January 2016. Melbourne.

Nicholas Oakeshott. 2017. The Search for Solutions to Statelessness in Southeast Asia: State Practice and Recent Developments. In L. van Waas and M.J. Khanna (Eds.), *Solving Statelessness.* Wolf Legal Publishers.

Nida M. Gelazis. 2004. The European Union and the Statelessness Problem in the Baltic States. *European Journal of Migration & Law,* 6: 225.

Nigel Cantwell. 1992. The Origins, Development and Significance of the United Nations Convention on the Rights of the Child. In S. Detrick (Ed.), *The United Nations Convention on the Rights of the Child,* p 19. Kluwer Academic Publishers.

Nyein Aye Tun, Role of Health Institutions in Vital Registration. Presentation Slides. Retrieved from https://shorturl.at/lrIZ7 [Accesssed 19 July 2019].

Official Portal of Ministry of Home Affairs Malaysia. 2010. *Citizenship.* Retrieved from http://www.moha.gov.my/index.php/en/?option=com_content&view=article&id=276:bahagian-kawalan-penapisan-filem-dan-penguatkuasaan&catid=63&lang=en [Accessed 30 December 2014].

Olivier W. Vonk. 2017. *Comparative Report: Citizenship in Asia.* Retrieved from http://cadmus.eui.eu/bitstream/handle/1814/50047/RSCAS_GLOBALCIT_Comp_2017_04.pdf?sequence=1&isAllowed=y [Accessed 10 April 2018].

Olivier W. Vonk. 2010. *Dual Nationality Private International Law and in the Municipal Laws of Four EU Member States.* PhD Thesis, European University Institute.

Online Innovative Creations. 2001. *The International Observatory on Statelessness: Thailand.* Retrieved from http://www.nationalityforall.org/thailand [Accessed 23 November 2014].

Online Innovative Creations. 2004. *The International Observatory on Statelessness: Malaysia.* Retrieved from http://www.nationalityforall.org/malaysia [Accessed 15 June 2013].

Open Society Justice Initiative. *Children's Right to a Nationality.* Retrieved from http://www2.ohchr.org/english/issues/women/docs/OtherEntities/OSJIChildrenNationalityFactsheet.pdf [Accessed 20 January 2014].

Paul Weis. 1956. *Nationality and Statelessness in International Law.* London: Stevens & Sons Limited.

Paul Weis. 1979. *Nationality and Statelessness in International Law.* Brill.

Paul Weis. 1979. *Nationality and Statelessness in International Law.* 2nd Ed. The Netherlands: Sijthoff & Noordhoff International.

Peter De Cruz. 1995. *Comparative Law in a Changing World.* London: Cavendish.

Peter J. Spiro. 2011. A New International Law of Citizenship. *American Journal of International Law,* 105(4): 694–746.

Peter Vink Maarten & G.R. de Groot. 2010. *Birthright Citizenship: Trends and Regulations in Europe, Comparative Report.* Retrieved from http://eudocitizenship.eu/docs/birthright_comparativepaper.pdf [Accessed 15 June 2014].

Philip Alston. 2001. The Historical Origins of the Concept of 'General Comments' in Human Rights Law. *The International Legal System in Quest of Equity and Universality/L'Ordre Juridique International, UN Système en Quête D'Equité et D'Universalité: Liber Amicorum Georges Abi-Saab.* Geneva: Graduate Institute of International Studies.

Philip L. Martin. 1991. Labor Migration in Asia. *The International Migration Review,* 25(1): 176–193.

Phuntip Kanchanachittra Saisoonthorn. 2006. Development of Concepts on Nationality and the Efforts to Reduce Statelessness in Thailand. *Refugee Survey Quarterly,* 25(3): 40–53.

Pia Oberoi & Eleanor Taylor-Nicholson. 2013. The Enemy at the Gates: International Borders, Migration and Human Rights. *Laws,* 2(3): 169–186.

Pinkaew Laungaramsri. 2015. Crafting Citizenship: Cards, Colors, and the Politics of Identification in Thailand. *Harvard-Yenching Institute Working Paper Series,* 1–31. Retrieved from https://www.harvard-yenching.org/wp-content/uploads/legacy_files/featurefiles/Pinkaew%20Laungaramsri_ReCrafting%20Citizenship.pdf [Access 10 January 2017].

Plan International. 2005. *Count Me In: The Global Campaign for Universal Birth Registration: Interim Campaign Report.*

Plan International. 2011. *Stateless Children Deprived of Their Basic Rights.* Retrieved from http://news.trust.org//item/20110824161100-1xdyc/ [Accessed 4 August 2014].

Proposed Amendments to the Naturalisation Provision of the Political Constitution of Costa Rica Inter-American Court on Human Rights, Advisory Opinion OC-4/84 of 19 January 1984, Series A No. 4.

Ruth Donner. 1994. *The Regulation of Nationality, 2nd Ed.* Leiden: Martinus Nijhoff Transnational Publishers.

Rabby Pramudatama. 2012, 18 February. Constitutional Court Affirms 'Illegitimate' Children's Rights. *Jakarta Post.* Retrieved from http://www.thejakartapost.com/news/2012/02/18/constitutional-court-affirms-illegitimate-children-s-rights.html [Accessed 22 June 2016].

Radha Govil & Alice Edwards. 2014. Women, Nationality and Statelessness: The Problem of Unequal Rights. In Alice Edwards & Laura van Waas. (Eds.), *Nationality and Statelessness under International Law.* Cambridge: Cambridge University Press.

Radha Govil. 2016. Statelessness and Key Concepts. Presentation Slides. Workshop on Researching Statelessness and Citizenship in Asia and the Pacific. Organised by UNHCR, Melbourne School of Government and Melbourne Law School, 27–29 January 2016, Melbourne.

Radha Govil. 2015, 21–24 April. Is the Concept of Legal Identity Relevant to UNHCR's Statelessness Mandate? *The Hague Colloquium on the Future of Legal Identity.*

Rainer Bauböck, Eva Ersbøll, Kees Groenendijk & Harald Waldrauch (Eds.), 2006. *Acquisition and Loss of Nationality. Policies and Trends in 15 European States. Summary and Recommendations:* Retrieved from http://www.ft.dk/samling/20051/almdel/ifu/bilag/81/261233.pdf [Accessed 25 April 2015].

Ramaa Prasad Dhokalia. 1970. *The Codification of Public International Law*, UK: Manchester University Press.

Rebecca M. M. Wallace, Ann Audsley, Nicole McCloy & Karen Wylie. 2012. *Mother to Child: How Discrimination Prevents Women Registering the Birth of Their Child (Report).* Plan & the UHI Centre for Rural Childhood.

Robert D. Sloane. 2009. Breaking the Genuine Link: The Contemporary International Legal Regulation of Nationality. *Harvard International Law Journal,* 50: 08–27.

Rodziana Mohamed Razali, Rohaida Nordin & Tamara Joan Duraisingam. 2015. Migration and Statelessness: Turning the Spotlight on Malaysia. *Pertanika Journal of Social Science and Humanities*, 23(S): 19–36.

Rodziana Mohamed Razali. 2017. Addressing Statelessness in Malaysia: New Hope and Remaining Challenges, *Statelessness Working Paper Series No. 2017/9*, Retrieved from http://www.institutesi.org/forum/workingpapers.php [Accessed 30 March 2018].

Samuel Cheung. 2012. Migration Control and the Solutions Impasse in South and Southeast Asia: Implications from the Rohingya Experience. *Journal of Refugee Studies,* 25(1): 50–70.

Sangita Jaghai. 2015. Statelessness and Transnational Migration: The Role of States as Duty-Bearers to Address Statelessness in the ASEAN Region under International Law. Thesis, University of Tilburg.

Sebastian Köhn. 2012. 'Soft Law' Entrepreneurship and the Right of the Child to a Nationality in an Era of Migration. *ASIL Annual Meeting Proceedings*, 67–69.

Shamsul Bari. 1992. Refugee Status Determination under the Comprehensive Plan of Action (CPA): A Personal Assessment. *International Journal of Refugee Law,* 4(4): 487–513.

Sharan B. Merriam. 1998. *Qualitative Research and Case Study Applications in Education. Revised and Expanded from Case Study Research in Education.* ERIC.

Sharon Detrick. 1999. *A Commentary on the United Nations Convention on the Rights of the Child.* The Hague/Boston/London: Martinus Nijhoff Publishers.

Sharon Detrick, Jakob Egbert Doek & Nigel Cantwell. 1992. *The United Nations Convention on the Rights of the Child: A Guide to the 'Travaux Préparatoires'*, Dordrecht / Boston / London: Martinus Nijhoff Publishers.

L. A. Sheridan, Harry E. Groves, K. C. Vohrah, T. N. Philip Koh & Peter S. W. Ling. 2004. *The Constitution of Malaysia* (5th Ed), Kuala Lumpur: MLJ.

Simon Heap & Claire Cody. 2009. The Universal Birth Registration Campaign. *Force Migration Review 32.*

Sophie Nonnenmacher & Ryszard Cholewinski. 2014. The Nexus between Statelessness and Migration. In Alice Edwards & Laura van Waas (Eds.), Nationality *and Statelessness under International Law,* p 247–263. Cambridge: Cambridge University Press.

Sriprapha Petcharamesree. 2013. The ASEAN Human Rights Architecture: Its Development and Challenges. *The Equal Rights Review,* 11:46–60.

Sriprapha Petcharamasree & Bongkot Napaumporn. 2020. Legal Identity of All Women and Children in ASEAN: A Regional Synthesis. ASEAN. https://asean.org/?static_post=legal-identity-women-children-asean-regional-synthesis [Accessed 5 December 2020].

Stacey Steel. 2004. Comments on OKUDA, Statelessness and the Nationality Act of Japan: Baby Andrew Becomes a Teenager and Other Changes? Retrieved from http://sydney.edu.au/law/anjel/documents/ZjapanR18_15_Steele.pdf [Accessed 12 January 2015].

Stacie Konsiki. 2009. State of Uncertainty: Citizenship, Statelessness and Discrimination in the Dominican Republic. *Boston College International & Comparative Law Review*, 32(2): 377–398.

Standing Committee of the Executive Committee of the High Commissioner's Programme. 2010, 9 February. *Birth Registration: A Topic Proposed for an Executive Committee Conclusion on International Protection.* Retrieved from http://www.refworld.org/docid/4b97a3242.html [Accessed 10 January 2016].

Stephen Castels & Alastair Davidson. 2000. *Citizenship and Migration: Globalization and the Politics of Belonging*, London: MacMillan Press.

Sukhumbhand Paribatra & Chai Anan. 1984. Factors behind Armed Separatism: Framework for Analysis. In Lim Joo-Jock & S. Vani (Eds.), *Armed Separatism in Southeast Asia*, Pasir Panjang: Institute of Southeast Asian Studies.

Sunil S. Amrith. 2011. *Migration and Diaspora in Modern Asia.* Cambridge University Press.

Susan Kneebone. 2010. The Governance of Labor Migration in Southeast Asia. *Global Governance: A Review of Multilateralism and International Organizations*, 16(3): 383–396.

Statista (The Statistics Portal). *Gross Domestic Product of the ASEAN Countries from 2008 to 2018 (in billion U.S dollars).* Retrieved from https://www.statista.com/statistics/796245/gdp-of-the-asean-countries/ [Accessed 20 October 2018].

Syed Abdul Razak Sayed Mahadi. 2014. *Indonesian Labour Migration to Sabah: Changes, Trends and Impacts.* PhD Thesis, University of Adelaide.

Tamara Joan Duraisingam. 2014. *International and Domestic Legal Analysis on the Protection of Stateless Persons Residing in Malaysia.* Ph.D. Thesis, Faculty of Law, National University of Malaysia.

Tali Yahalom Leinwand. 2014. Navigating Nationality: The Rights to Birth Registration and Nationality in Refugee Magnet States. *Columbia Journal of Transnational Law,* 53:114.

Tang Lay Lee. 2005. *Statelessness, Human Rights and Gender: Irregular Migrant Workers from Burma in Thailand.* Leiden: Martinus Nojhoff Publishers.

Teuku Afrizal & Diana Wong. 2001. The Irregular Labour Migration System from Indonesia to Peninsular Malaysia. *Akademika,* 58 (Januari): 99–108.

The Equal Rights Trust. 2010, July. *Unravelling Anomaly: Detention, Discrimination and the Protection Needs of Stateless Persons.* Retrieved from http://www.equalrightstrust.org/ertdocumentbank/chapter%202.pdf [Accessed 15 August 2015].

The Institute of Human Rights and Peace Studies (IHRP) 2014. *Equal Only in Name: The Human Rights of Stateless Rohingya in Malaysia.* Equal Rights Trust and Institute of Human Rights and Peace Studies: Mahidol University, Thailand.

The Women's Refugee Commission and Tilburg University Statelessness programme. 2013. *Briefing on Qatar, Iraq, Bahrain for Committee on the Elimination of Discrimination against Women (CEDAW), 57th Pre-Session Working Group.* Retrieved from http://tbinternet.ohchr.org/Treaties/CEDAW/Shared%20Documents/BHR/INT_CEDAW_NGO_BHR_14648_E.pdf [Accessed 12 March 2016].

Thomas Alexander Aleinikoff & Douglas Klusmeyer. 2011. *Citizenship Policies for an Age of Migration.* Carnegie Endowment for International Peace.

Thomas Alexander Aleinikoff & Vincent Chetail (Eds.), 2011. *Migration and International Legal Norms.* T.M.C. Asser Press. Vietnam Law and Legal Forum. 2015, 5 August. New Law on Civil Status. Retrieved from http://vietnamlawmagazine.vn/new-law-on-civil-status-4028.html [Accessed 6 October 2016].

Vivian Tan. 2014, 15 September. Stateless in the Philippines: Indonesian Descendants Feel Torn between Two Lands. Retrieved from www.unhcr.org/5416d3519.html [Accessed 10 August 2014].

William Samore. 1951. Statelessness as a Consequence of the Conflict of Nationality Laws. *American Journal of International Law,* 45: 476–477.

Wolfgang Benedek, Florence Benoit-Rohmer, Wolfram Karl, Matthias C. Kettemann & Manfren Nowak (Eds.), 2014. *European Yearbook on Human Rights.* Medieninhaber: NWV Verlag GmbH.

Women's Refugee Commission. 2013. *Our Motherland, Our Country: Gender Discrimination and Statelessness in the Middle East and North Africa*. Retrieved from https://www.womensrefugeecommission.org/images/zdocs/Our_Motherland,_Our_Country_final_for_ web.pdf [Accessed 20 February 2013].
F. Xavier Bagnoud. 2016. *The Impact of Persistent Exclusion: Rohingya Leaving Myanmar*. Centre for Health and Human Rights. Retrieved from https://cdn2.sph.harvard.edu/wp-content/uploads/sites/114/2017/12/ChildOnMove_Rohingya.pdf [Accessed 20 April 2017].
Yuyun Wahyuningrum. 2014, 12 December. The ASEAN Intergovernmental Commission on Human Rights: Origin, Evolution and the Way Forward (Discussion Paper). *Institute for Democracy and Electoral Assistance (IDEA).*
Yvonne Xin Wang. 2015. Contextualizing Universal Human Rights: An Integrated Human Rights Framework for ASEAN. *Duke Journal of Comparative & International Law,* 25:385–426
Ziba Vaghri, Adem Arkadas, Sami Kruse & Clyde Hertzman. 2011. CRC General Comment 7 Indicators Framework: A Tool for Monitoring the Implementation of Child Rights in Early Childhood. *Journal of Human Rights,* 10 (2): 178–188.

List of Treaties, Declarations, Principles and UN-Related Documents

Asian-African Legal Consultative Organization (AALCO), *Resolution on the Half-Day Special Meeting on Legal Identity and Statelessness.* 8 April 2006. RES/45/SP.1, Retrieved from https://www.refworld.org/docid/44eaddc54.html [accessed 5 August 2017].
African Charter on the Rights and Welfare of the Child (11 July 1990, in force 29 November 1999) Cab/Leg/24.9/49.
African Charter on the Rights and Welfare of the Child (Adopted 11 July 1990, in force 29 November 1999), Cab/Leg/24.9/49.
African Commission on Human and Peoples' Rights. 9–23 April 2013. Resolution 234 on the Right to Nationality. Banjul, the Gambia.
African Committee of Experts on the Rights and Welfare of the Child (ACERWC) (2014). General Comment on Article 6 of the ACRWC: The Right to a Name, Registration at Birth, and to Acquire a Nationality. Acerwc/Gc/02. Addis Ababa: African Union.
American Convention on Human Rights (Adopted 22 November 1969, in force 18 July 1978), OAS Treaty Series No. 36.
ASEAN. *About ASEAN: Overview.* Retrieved from http://asean.org/asean/about-asean/overview/ [Accessed 10 February 2014].
ASEAN. 2004. The Declaration on the Elimination of Violence against Women and Elimination of Violence against Children in ASEAN. Retrieved from http://aseanevaw.org/wp-content/uploads/2014/03/A4-declaration-eng.pdf [Accessed 12 August 2015].
ASEAN. 2007. ASEAN Declaration on the Protection for the Protection and Promotion of the Rights of Migrant Workers. Cebu City: Association of Southeast Asian Nations.
ASEAN. 2009. Terms of Reference of ASEAN Intergovernmental Commission on Human Rights. Retrieved from http://www.refworld.org/docid/4a6d87f22.html [Accessed 12 October 2015].
ASEAN. 2009. Terms of Reference of the ASEAN Intergovernmental Commission on Human Rights. 42nd Meeting of the ASEAN Foreign Ministers. Phuket: ASEAN.
ASEAN. 2012. ASEAN Human Rights Declaration. Association of Southeast Asian Nations. Retrieved from http://www.refworld.org/docid/50c9fea82.html [Accessed 9 September 2015].
ASEAN. 2012. Charter of the Association of Southeast Asian Nations. Retrieved from http://www.refworld.org/docid/4948c4842.html [Accessed 9 September 2015].
ASEAN. 2016. ASEAN Convention against Trafficking in Persons, Especially Women and Children. Retrieved from https://asean.org/wp-content/uploads/2012/05/APA-FINAL.pdf [Accessed 26 September 2018].

ASEAN. 2017. ASEAN Consensus on the Protection and Promotion of the Rights of Migrant Workers. Retrieved from https://asean.org/storage/2012/05/16-ASEAN-Declaration-on-the-Protection-and-Promotion-of-the-Rights-of-Mi....pdf [Accessed 26 September 2018].

Bern Convention of the International Commission of Civil Status to Reduce the Number of Cases of Statelessness, Bern (13 September 1973).

Committee on the Elimination of Racial Discrimination. 2005. General Recommendation 30: Discrimination against Non-Citizens. UN Doc. Cerd/C/Gc/30. Geneva: CERD.

Committee on the Rights of the Child (CRC). 13 July 2015. Consideration of Reports Submitted by States Parties under Article 44 of the Convention, Combined Second and Third Periodic Reports of States Parties Due in 2008: Brunei Darussalam, UN Doc. CRC/C/ Brn/2–3. Brunei: CRC.

Council of Europe: Committee of Ministers Recommendation CM/REC (2009) 13 of the Committee of Ministers to Member States on the Nationality of Children (9 December 2009) CM/REC (2009) 13.

Covenant on the Rights of the Child in Islam (Adopted June 2005), OIC/9-Igge/Hri/2004/Rep. Final.

Economic and Social Commission for Asia and the Pacific (UNESCAP). 2 June 2015. Resolution adopted by the Economic and Social Commission for Asia and the Pacific. Asian and Pacific Civil Registration and Vital Statistics, 2015–2024. UN Doc. E/Escap/ Res/71/14. New York: United Nations.

European Convention for the Protection of Human Rights and Fundamental Freedoms (Adopted 4 November 1950, in force 3 September 1953).

European Convention on Nationality, Strasbourg. 1997. Retrieved from http://conventions.coe.int/Treaty/EN/Treaties/Html/166.htm [Accessed 12 June 2014].

Human Rights Commission of Malaysia (SUHAKAM). Annual Report 2014. Retrieved from https://docs.google.com/file/d/0B6FQ7SONa3PRUG1nc25yRGV3TlU/preview [Accessed 15 July 2015].

Human Rights Committee. 1989. General Comment No. 17: Article 24 (Rights of the Child). Geneva: Office of the United Nations High Commissioner for Human Rights.

Human Rights Council. 2009. *13th Session, Agenda Item 3, Annual Report of the United Nations High Commissioner for Human Rights and Reports of the Office of the Commissioner and the Secretary General (a/Hrc/13/34)*. Retrieved from http://www.refworld.org/pdfid/4b83a9cb2.pdf [Accessed 20 January 2014].

Human Rights Council. 2014. *Report of the Working Group on the Universal Periodic Review, Addendum: Malaysia*, UN Doc.. A/ Hrc/25/10/Add.1.

League of Nations. 1930. Convention on Certain Questions relating to the Conflict of Nationality Laws. LNTS Vol. 1, No. 4137. The Hague: League of Nations.

League of Nations. 1930. Special Protocol Concerning Statelessness. C.27.M.16.1931.V. The Hague: League of Nations.

League of Nations. 1930. The Protocol relating to a Certain Case of Statelessness. 179 LNTS 115. The Hague: League of Nations.

League of Nations. 1930. The Protocol relating to Military Obligations in Certain Cases of Double Nationality. 178 LNTS 4117. The Hague: League of Nations.

Malaysian 13th Parliament. House of Representative, Third Term, First Meeting, No. 10, 24 March 2015.

Manley O. Hudson. 1952. *Nationality, Including Statelessness*. UN Doc. A/CN.4/50, Extract from the Yearbook of the International Law Commission. Vol. II: Retrieved from http://legal.un.org/ilc/documentation/english/a_Cn4_50.pdf [Accessed 1 April 2016].

Palermo Protocol to UN Convention against Transnational Organised Crime on the Smuggling of Migrants (Adopted 15 November 2000, in force 28 January 2004) 2241 UNTS 507.

Protocol to Prevent, Suppress and Punish Trafficking in Persons, Especially Women and Children (Adopted 15 November 2000, in force 25 December 2003), 2237 UNTS 319.

The Committee on the Elimination of Racial Discrimination. 2005. General Recommendation XXX on Discrimination against Non-Citizens. UN Doc. CERD/CG/C/30. Geneva: CERD Committee.

The Vienna Convention on Consular Relations 1963 (24 April 1962, in force 19 March 1967), 596 UNT 261.
UN Economic and Social Commission for Asia and the Pacific. 2019. *Get Every One in the Picture: Civil Registration and Vital Statistics in Asia and the Pacific.* Retrieved from https://www.getinthepicture.org/partners/unicef [Access 1 January 2019].
UN Economic and Social Council. 1949. *A Study of Statelessness.* UN Doc. E/1112; E/1112/Add.1. New York: United Nations.
UN Human Rights Committee. 7 April 1989. CCPR General Commnent No 17: Article 24 (Rights of the Child). UN Doc. Hri/Gen/1/Rev.6. Geneva: CCPR.
UN Human Rights Council. 17 June 2014. *Birth Registration and the Right of Everyone to Recognition Everywhere as a Person before the Law: Report of the Office of the United Nations High Commissioner for Human Rights,* UN Doc. A/HRC/27/22. Geneva: HRC.
UN Human Rights Council. 16 December 2015. *Impact of the Arbitrary Deprivation of Nationality on the Enjoyment of the Rights of Children Concerned and Existing Laws and Practices on Accessibility for Children to Acquire Nationality, inter alia, of the Country in Which They are Born, If They Otherwise Would be Stateless* (2015): UN Doc. A/HRC/31/29. Geneva: HRC.
UN Human Rights Council. 14 March 2017. *Report of the Special Rapporteur on the Situation of Human Rights in Myanmar* (2017): UN Doc. A/HRC/34/67. Geneva: HRC.
UN Human Rights Council. 14 March 2017, *Report of the Special Rapporteur on the Situation of Human Rights in Myanmar,* UN Doc. A/HRC/34/67.14. Geneva: HRC.
UN Human Rights Office of the High Commissioner. *Migration and Human Rights: Improving Human Rights-Based Governance of International Migration.* Retrieved from www.ohchr.org/Documents/Issues/Migration/MigrationHR_improvingHR_Report.pdf [Accessed 13 March 2016].
UNESCAP. Asia and Pacific Civil Registration and Vital Statistics Decade 2015–2014. Retrieved from http://www.unescap.org/sites/default/files/Asian_and_Pacific_Civil_Registration_and_Vital_Statistics_Decade2015-2024_Booklet.pdf [Accessed 9 May 2016].
UNESCAP. 2014. Regional Action Framework on Civil Registration and Vital Statistics in Asia and the Pacific. Retrieved from http://www.unescap.org/sites/default/files/Regional.Action.Framework.English.final_pdf [Accessed 12 March 2015].
UNESCO. 2008.*Citizenship Manual-Capacity Buildingon Birth Registration and Citizenship in Thailand: Citizenship Manual.* Retrieved from http://unesdoc.unesco.org/images/0016/001621/162153e.pdf [Accessed 20 August 2014].
UNGA Resolution A/RES/63/241 of 13 March 2009. United Nations.
UNGA Resolution A/RES/67/149 of 20 December 2012. United Nations.
UNGA Resolution A/RES/68/141 of 28 January 2014. United Nations.
UNGA Resolution GA/10022 of 11 October 2002. A World Fit for Children. United Nations. Retrieved from https://www.un.org/press/en/2002/ga10022.doc.htm [Accessed 4 Jun 2015].
UNGA Resolution 896 (IX) of 4 December 1954. Elimination or Reduction of Future Statelessness. United Nations.
UNGA Resolution 3274 (XXIV) of 10 December 1974. UNHCR's Role under Article 11 of the 1961 Convention on the Reduction of Statelessness. United Nations.
UNGA. 1959. Committee of the Whole, Summary Record of the Ninth Meeting, UN Doc. A/CONF.9/C.1/SR.9. Geneva: United Nations.
UNGA. 1959. Committee of the Whole, Summary of the Record of the Seventeenth Meeting, UN Doc. A/CONF.9/C.1/SR.17. Geneva: UNGA.
UNGA. 1959. Declaration of the Rights of the Child. General Assembly Resolution 1386 (XIV). UN Doc. A/Res/14/1386. New York: United Nations.
UNGA. 1959. United Nations Conference on the Elimination or Reduction of Future Statelessness, Summary Records, Sixth Plenary Meeting, UN Doc. A/CONF.9/C.1/SR.9. Geneva: United Nations.
UNGA. 1996. Office of the United Nations High Commissioner for Refugees. General Assemby Resolution. UN Doc. A/RES/50/152. New York: United Nations.

UNGA. 2007. Office of the United Nations High Commissioner for Refugees. UN Doc. A/RES/61/137. New York: United Nations.

UNGA. 2013. *Human Rights and Arbitrary Deprivation of Nationality*. UN Doc. A/HRC/25/28. New York: United Nations. Retrieved from http://www.refworld.org/pdfid/4b83a9cb2.pdf [Accessed 3 April 2015].

UNHCR & ASEAN Intergovernmental Commission on Human Rights. 2011. *Report of the Regional Workshop on Statelessness and the Rights of Women and Children*. Retrieved from http://www.refworld.org/docid/50f674c42.html [Accessed 20 January 2014].

UNHCR & Inter-Parliamentary Union (IPU). 2005. *Nationality and Statelessness. A Handbook for Parliamentarians*. Retrieved from http://www.ipu.org/pdf/publications/nationality_en.pdf [Accessed 24 June 2016].

UNHCR. *Stateless Action - Prevention*. Retrieved from http://www.unhcr.org/pages/49c3646c173.html [Accessed 18 July 2015].

UNHCR. *Stateless Actions - Identification*. Retrieved from http://www.unhcr.org/pages/49c3646c16d.html [Accessed 10 December 2013].

UNHCR. September 2013. *Submission by the United Nations High Commissioner for Refugees for the Office of the High Commissioner for Human Rights' Compilation Report-Universal Periodic Review: Brunei Darussalam*. Retrieved from www.refworld.org/pdfid/528346844.pdf [Accessed 10 January 2016].

UNHCR. 1950. Statute of the Office of the United Nations High Commissioner for Refugees. Retrieved from http://www.unhcr.ch/html/menu3/b/o_unhcr.htm [Accessed 12 May 2011].

UNHCR. 1984. Identity Documents for Refugees (Ec/Scp/33). Retrieved from http://www.unhcr.org/3ae68cce4.html [Accessed 1 April 2016].

UNHCR. 1995. Conclusion on Prevention and Reduction of Statelessness and Protection of Stateless No. 78 (XlVI). Geneva: UNHCR.

UNHCR. 1995. Prevention and Reduction of Statelessness and the Protection of Stateless Persons. Executive Committee, 46th Session. No 78(XLVI). Geneva: UNHCR.

UNCHR. 1996. Information and Accession Package: The 1954 Convention relating to the Status of Stateless Persons and the 1961 Convention on the Reduction of Statelessness. (Revised 1999). Geneva: United Nations.

UNHCR. 1997. *The State of the World's Refugees: A Humanitarian Agenda*. Retrieved from http://www.unhcr.org/3eb7ba7d4.html [Accessed 12 March 2015].

UNHCR. 2003. *The 1954 Convention Relating to the Status of Stateless Persons: Implementation within the European Union Member States and Recommendations for Harmonisation*. Retrieved from http://www.refworld.org/docid/415c3cfb4.html [Accessed 19 October 2013].

UNHCR. 2006. Conclusion on Identification, Prevention and Reduction and Protection of Stateless Persons of 2006 No. 106 (LVII). Document A/AC.96/1035. Geneva: UNHCR.

UNHCR. 2006. Conclusion on Identification, Prevention and Reduction of Statelessness and Protection of Stateless Persons. Executive Committee, 56th Session. No. 106 (LVII). Geneva: UNHCR.

UNHCR. 2009. Conclusion on Protracted Refugee Situations, No. 109. Retrieved from http://www.unhcr.org/excom/exconc/4b332bca9/conclusion-protracted-refugee-situations.html [Accessed 10 June 2016].

UNHCR. 2009. UNHCR's 2010–2011 Global Strategic Priorities. Retrieved from http://www.unhcr.org/4abb45419.html [Accessed 2 May 2014].

UNHCR. 2009. Addressing Situations of Statelessness. Retrieved from https://www.unhcr.org/4922d4370.pdf [Accessed 13 June 2017].

UNHCR. 2010. *Preventing and Reducing Statelessness: The 1961 Convention on the Reduction of Statelessness*. Retrieved from http://www.unhcr.it/wp-content/uploads/2016/01/preventing_and_reducing_statelessness.pdf [Accessed 10 July 2013].

UNHCR. 2010. Conclusions related to Statelessness. Retrieved from http://www.unhcr.org/refworld/docid/4c499c022.html [Accessed 9 March 2012].

UNHCR. 2010. *UNHCR's Action to Address Statelessness. A Strategy Note.* Retrieved from http://www.unhcr.org/protection/statelessness/4b960ae99/unhcr-action-address-statelessness-strategy-note.html [Retrieved from 20 January 2014].

UNHCR. 2010. *Expert Meeting - The Concept of Stateless Persons under International Law* (Prato Conclusions). Retrieved from http://www.refworld.org/docid/4ca1ae002.html [Accessed 22 October 2013].

UNHCR. 2010. *Statelessness Determination Procedures and the Status of Stateless Persons* (Geneva Conclusions). Retrieved from http://www.refworld.org/docid/4d9022762.html [Accessed 13 June 2014].

UNHCR. 2010. *Strengthening the International Legal Framework on Statelessness: Expert Meeting Series.* Retrieved from http://www.unhcr.org/4d78d5329.html [Accessed 7 July 2014].

UNHCR. 2011. *Interpreting the 1961 Statelessness Convention and Preventing Statelessness among Children: 'Dakar Conclusions'.* Retrieved http://www.refworld.org/docid/4e8423a72.html [Accessed 12 August 2014].

UNHCR. 2011. *Good Practices: Addressing Statelessness in South East Asia.* Retrieved from http://www.refworld.org/docid/4d6e0a792.html [Accessed 15 November 2014].

UNHCR. 2011. *Good Practices: Addressing Statelessness in South East Asia.* Retrieved from http://www.unhcr.org/refworld/docid/4d6e0a792.html [Accessed 25 March 2012].

UNHCR. 2011. Guidance Document on Measuring Stateless Populations. Retrieved from http://www.refworld.org/docid/4f6887672.html [Accessed 25 August 2014].

UNHCR. 2011. Guidance Note of the Secretary General. Retrieved from http://www.refworld.org/pdfid/4e11d5092.pdf [Accessed 12 April 2015].

UNHCR. 2011. *Regional Expert Roundtable on Good Practices for the Identification, Prevention and Reduction of Statelessness and the Protection of Stateless Persons in South EastAsia.* Retrieved from http://www.refworld.org/cgi-bin/texis/vtx/rwmain?docid=4d6e09932 [Accessed 10 July 2013].

UNHCR. 2011. *Report of the Regional Workshop on Good Practices in Birth Registration.* Retrieved from http://www.getinthepicture.org/docs/unhcr-birth-reg-rpt.pdf [Accessed 8 October 2014].

UNHCR. 2011. *Universal Periodic Review: The Philippines.* Retrieved from http://www.refworld.org/pdfid/4ee07aa22.pdf [Accessed 20 July 2016].

UNHCR. 2012. *A Framework for the Protection of Children.* Retrieved from www.unhcr.org/protection/children/50f6cf0b9/framework-protection-children.html [Accessed 8 December 2013].

UNHCR. 2012. Guidelines on Statelessness No.4 : Ensuring Every Child's Right to Acquire a Nationality through Article 1–4 of the 1961 Convention on the Reduction of Statelessness (Guidelines No 4). Retrieved from http://www.refworld.org/docid/50d460c72.html [Accessed 25 June 2016].

UNHCR. 2012. Guidelines on Statelessness No. 1: The Definition of 'Stateless Person' in Article 1(1) of the 1954 Convention Relating to the Status of Stateless Persons. (Guidelines No. 1). Retrieved from http://www.refworld.org/docid/4f4371b82.html [Accessed 6 January 2014].

UNHCR. 2012. UNHCR Lauds The Philippines for New Mechanism to Protect Refugees and Stateless People. Retrieved from http://www.unhcr.org/news/press/2012/11/5098ced59/unhcr-lauds-philippines-new-mechanism-protect-refugees-stateless-people. html [Accessed 10 June 2015].

UNHCR. 2012. *Self-Study Module on Statelessness.* Retrieved from https://www.refworld.org/docid/50b899602.html [Accessed 5 July 2017].

UNHCR. 2012. *The State of the World's Refugees: In Search of Solidarity.* Retrieved from http://www.refworld.org/docid/5100fec32.html [Accessed 12 December 2014].

UNHCR. 2012. *Under the Radar and under Protected: The Urgent Need to Address Stateless Children's Rights.* Retrieved from http://www.refworld.org/pdfid/514acd3e2.pdf [Accessed 15 June 2014].

UNHCR. 2013. Conclusion on Civil Registration No. 111 (LXIV). Geneva: UNHCR.

UNHCR. 2013. *Submission by the United Nations High Commissioner for Refugees For the Office of the High Commissioner for Human Rights' Compilation Report-Universal Periodic Review: Brunei Darussalam.*

UNHCR. 2013. Conclusion on Civil Registration No. 111 (LXIV). Doc. A/AC.96/1035. Geneva: UNHCR. Retrieved from http://www.refworld.org/docid/525f8ba64.html [Accessed 21 August 2015].
UNHCR. 2013. Child Protection Issue Brief - Birth Registration. Retrieved from http://www.refworld.org/pdfid/523fe9214.pdf [Accessed 20 March 2014].
UNHCR. 2013. *Submission by the United Nations High Commissioner for Refugees for the Office of the High Commissioner for Human Rights' Compilation Report - Universal Periodic Review: Malaysia.* Retrieved from http://www.refworld.org/docid/513d9a0e2.html [Accessed 30 June 2013].
UNHCR. 2013. *Submission by the United Nations High Commissioner for Refugees for the Office of the High Commissioner for Human Rights' Compilation Report - Universal Periodic Review: Socialist Republic of Vietnam.* Retrieved from http://www.refworld.org/pdfid/51c946514.pdf [Accessed 23 June 2016].
UNHCR. 2014. *#Ibelong Campaign to End Statelessness.* Retrieved from http://www.unhcr.org/ibelong-campaign-to-end-statelessness.html [Accessed 10 January 2015].
UNHCR.2014.*GlobalActionPlantoEndStatelessness:2014–2024.*Retrieved from http://www.unhcr.org/protection/statelessness/54621bf49/global-actionplan-end-statelessness-2014-2024.html [Accessed 4 June 2017].
UNHCR. 2014. *Ending Statelessness within 10 Years.* Retrieved from http://www.unhcr.org/546217229.pdf [Accessed 22 January 2016].
UNHCR. 2014. Fact Sheet: March 2014. UNHCR Philippines. Retrieved from http://unhcr.ph/_cms/wp-content/uploads/unhcr-philippines-factsheet-march-2014.pdf [Accessed 12 September 2015].
UNHCR. 2014. *Global Action Plan to End Statelessness.* Retrieved from http://www.refworld.org/docid/545b47d64.html [Accessed 20 January 2015].
UNHCR. 2014. *Handbook on Protection of Stateless Persons.* Retrieved from http://www.refworld.org/docid/53b676aa4.html [Accessed 13 April 2016].
UNHCR. 2014. *Nationality and Statelessness: Handbook for Parliamentarians No. 22.* Retrieved from http://www.refworld.org/docid/53d0a0974.html [Accessed 24 March 2016].
UNHCR. 2015. *UNHCR Refugee Resettlement Trends 2015.* Retrieved from http://www.unhcr.org/559e43ac9.pdf [Accessed 6 June 2015].
UNHCR. 2015. UNHCR Subregional Operations Profile - South- East Asia. Retrieved form http://www.unhcr.org/pages/49e4884c6.html [Accessed 15 June 2013].
UNHCR. 2015. *I Am Here, I Belong, the Urgent Need to End Childhood Statelessness.* Retrieved from http://www.unhcr.org/ibelong/wp-content/uploads/2015-10-StatelessReport_ENG16.pdf [Accessed 15 February 2016].
UNHCR. 2015. Malaysia Factsheet: August 2015. Retrieved from http://www.unhcr.org/cgi-bin/texis/vtx/home/opendocPDFViewer.html?docid=56167f6b6&query=malaysia [Accessed 7 June 2015].
UNHCR. 2015. *UNHCR Regional Operations Profile- Asia and the Pacific.* Retrieved from www.unhcr.org/pages/4a02d8ec6.html [Accessed 10 January 2015].
UNHCR. 2015. *Global Trends: Forced Displacement in 2015.* Retrieved from http://www.refworld.org/docid/57678f3d4.html [Accessed28 September 2016].
UNHCR. 2017. *Good Practices Paper: Ensuring that No Child is Born Stateless.* Retrieved from https://www.refworld.org/ pdfid/58cfab014.pdf [Accessed 5 January 2017].
UNHCR. 2016. Ending Statelessness. Retrieved from http://www.unhcr.org/pages/49c3646c15e.html. [Accessed 20 December 2016].
UNHCR. 2016. *Background Note on Gender Equality, Nationality Laws and Statelessness.* Retrieved from http://www.unhcr.org/4f5886306.pdf [Accessed 23 June 2016].
UNHCR. 2016. UN Conventions on Statelessness. Retrieved from http://www.unhcr.org/un-conventions-on-statelessness.html [Accessed 12 June 2016].
UNHCR. 2016. *Campaign Update.* Retrieved from http://www.refworld.org/docid/571e23fb7.html [Accessed 12 July 2016].

UNHCR. 2016. *Global Trend*. Retrieved from https://reliefweb.int/sites/reliefweb.int/files/resources/5943e8a34.pdf [Accessed 3 July 2017].

UNHCR. 2016. *The Campaign to End Statelessness: April 2016 Update*. Retrieved from http://www.unhcr.org/ibelong/wp-content/uploads/Campaign-Update-April-2016.pdf [Accessed 27 September 2018].

UNHCR. 2016. Overcoming Statelessness in Thailand One Caseat a Time. Retrieved from http://www.unhcr.org/news/latest/2016/11/5836af624/overcoming-statelessness-thailand-case-time.html [Accessed 5 March 2017].

UNHCR. 2017. *UNHCR Statistical Yearbook 2016*. Retrieved from https://www.unhcr.org/en-us/statistics/country/5a8ee0387/unhcr-statistical-yearbook-2016-16th-edition.html [Accessed 27 January 2017].

UNICEF. 2009. *Good Practices in Integrating Birth Registration into Health Systems (2000–2009) Case Studies: Bangladesh, Brazil, the Gambia and Delhi, India*. Retrieved from http://www.unicef.org/protection/Birth_registration_Working_Paper(2).pdf [Accessed 6 October 2016].

UNICEF. 2012. *State of the World's Children 2012: Children in an Urban World*. Retrieved from www.unicef.org/sowc2012/pdfs/ SOWC%202012-Main%20Report_EN_13Mar2012.pdf [Accessed 20 September 2014].

UNICEF. 2013. *A Passport to Protection: A Guide to Birth Registration Programming*. Retrieved from http://www.unicef.org/protection/files/UNICEF_Birth_Registration_Handbook.pdf [Accessed 20 June 2016].

UNICEF's Press Centre. 2013. One in Three Children Under Five Does Not Officially Exist. Retrieved from https://www.unicef.org/media/media_71508.html.

UNICEF. 2014. Monitoring the Situation of Women and Children. Retrieved from https://data.unicef.org/child-protection/birth-registration.html[Accessed 24 June 2016].

UNICEF. 2015. Myanmar, Getting to the Goal of 100 Per Cent Birth Registration. Retrieved from http://www.unicef.org/myanmar/media_24526.html [Accessed 15 June 2016].

UNICEF. 2015. *Unequal at Birth: Disparities in Birth Registration in EastAsia and the Pacific*. Retrieved from http://www.unicef.org/eapro/Unequal_at_Birth_UNICEF_EAP.pdf [Accessed 30 June 2016].

UNICEF. 2015. *Unequal at Birth: Disparities in Birth Registration in East Asia and the Pacific,* Retrieved from http://www.unicef.org/eapro/Unequal_at_Birth_UNICEF_EAP.pdf [Accessed 7 July 2017].

UNICEF. 2017. *Birth Registration,* Retrieved from http://data.unicef.org/topic/child-protection/birth-registration/ [Accessed 7 July 2019].

UNSD. 2015. *Civil Registration and Vital Statistics Knowledge Base*. Retrieved from http://unstats.un.org/unsd/demographic [Accessed 5 May 2016].

United Nations. Convention on the Elimination of All Forms of Discrimination against Women (Adopted 18 December 1979, in force 3 September 1981), 1249 UNTS 13.

United Nations. Convention on the Nationality of Married Women (Adopted 29 January 1957, in force 11 August 1958), 309 UNTS 65.

United Nations. Convention on the Reduction of Statelessness, New York (30 August 1961, in force 13 December 1975), 989 UNTS 175.

United Nations. Convention on the Rights of Persons with Disabilities (Adopted 13 December 2006, in force 13 May 2008), 2515 UNTS 3.

United Nations. Convention on the Rights of the Child (Adopted 20 November 1989, in force 2 September 1990), 1577 UNTS 13.

United Nations. International Convention on the Elimination of All Forms of Racial Discrimination (Adopted 21 December 1965, in force 4 January 1969), 660 UNTS 195.

United Nations. International Covenant on Civil and Political Rights (Adopted 16 December 1966, in force 23 March 1976), 999 UNTS 171.

United Nations. Convention on Consent to Marriage, Minimum Age for Marriage and Registration of Marriages (Adopted 7 November 1962, in force 9 December 1964), 521 UNTS 231.

United Nations. 1951. Convention relating to the Status of Refugees. 189 UNTS 150. Geneva: United Nations.

United Nations. Convention relating to the Status of Stateless Persons (Adopted 28 September 1954, in force 6 June 1960), 360 UNTS 117.

United Nations. 1948. Universal Declaration of Human Rights. UN Doc. A/810. New York: United Nations.

United Nations. 1949. A Study of Statelessness (6), UN Doc. E/1112; E1112/Add.1. New York: United Nations.

United Nations. 1951. Conference of Plenipotentiaries on the Status of Refugees and Stateless Persons: Summary Record of the Fifth Meeting. UN Doc. A/CONF.2/SR.5. New York: United Nations.

United Nations. 1952. Nationality, Including Statelessness. (UN Doc. A/CN.4/50). Geneva: United Nations.

United Nations. 1957. Convention on the Nationality of Married Women. 309 UNTS 65. New York: United Nations.

United Nations. 1961. Convention on the Reduction of Statelessness. 989 UNTS 175. New York: United Nations.

United Nations. 1965. Convention on the Elimination of all Forms of Racial Discrimination. 660 UNTS 195. New York: United Nations.

United Nations. 1966. International Covenant on Civil and Political Rights. 999 UNTS 171. New York: United Nations.

United Nations. 1979. Convention on the Elimination of All Forms of Discrimination against Women. 1249 UNTS 13. New York: United Nations.

United Nations. 1989. Convention on the Rights of the Child. 1577 UNTS 13. New York: United Nations.

United Nations. 1990. International Convention on the Protection of the Rights of All Migrant Workers and Members of Their Families. 2220 UNTS 3. New York: United Nations.

United Nations. 1998. *Handbook on Civil Registration and Vital Statistics System: Preparation of a Legal Framework.* Retrieved from http://www.uneca.org/sites/default/files/images/en-pages-from-handbook-on-civil-registration-and-vital-statistics-systems-preparation-of-a-legal-framework.pdf [Accessed 17 January 2016].

United Nations. 2002. Department of Economic and Social Affairs, Statistics Division (UNSD), *Handbook on Training in Civil Registration and Vital Statistic Systems, Series F No. 84.* Retrieved from http://unstats.un.org/unsd/publication/SeriesF/SeriesF_84E.pdf [Accessed 24 June 2016].

United Nations. 2006. Convention on the Rights of Persons with Disabilities. UNDoc.A/61/49. New York: United Nations.

United Nations. 2014. Department of Economic and Social Affairs, Statistics Division (UNSD), *Principles and Recommendations for a Vital Statistics System.* New York: UN Publications.

United Nations. 21 October 2015. *Transforming Our World: The 2030 Agenda for Sustainable Development*, General Assembly Resolution a/Res/70/1. UN Doc. 70/1. New York: United Nations.

United Nations Audio Visual Library of International Law. 2011. Convention on the Reduction of Statelessness. Retrieved from http://legal.un.org/avl/pdf/ha/crs/crs_ph_e.pdf [Accessed September 2014].

United Nations Economic & Social Affairs. 2006. *UN Economic and Social Affairs, Sustainable Development Knowledge Platform.* Retrieved from http://www.tandfonline.com/doi/abs/10.1080/13504620500526362#.V5w3e_196wU. [Accessed 16 June 2016].

List of General Comments

African Committee of Experts on the Rights and Welfare of the Child. 2014. General Comment No. 2 on Article 6 of the ACRWC. 23rd Ordinary Session. Addis Ababa: ACERWC.
Committee on the Rights of the Child. 1992. General Comment No. 20 (Article 7) (Replaces General Comment No. 7). 44th Session. Geneva: CRC.
Committee on the Rights of the Child. 2005. General Comment No. 6. 39th Session. Geneva: CRC.
Committee on the Rights of the Child. 2005. General Comment No. 7. 44th Session. Geneva: CRC.
Committee on the Rights of the Child. 2013. General Comments No. 14. 62nd Session. Geneva: CRC.
Committee on the Protection of the Rights of All Migrants Workers and Members of Their Families. 2017. Joint General Comment No. 4 of the Committee on the Protection of the Rights of All Migrant Workers and Members of Their Families and No. 23 (2017) of the Committee on the Rights of the Child on the General Principles regarding The Human Rights of Children in the Context of International Migration. Geneva: CMW.
Human Rights Committee. 1989. CCPR General Comment No. 17 (Article 24). 35th Session. Geneva: HRC.
Human Rights Committee. 1986. CCPR General Comment No. 15. 27th Session. Geneva: HRC.

List of Concluding Observations

Committee on the Rights of the Child. 2001. Concluding Observations: Democratic Republic of the Congo: CRC.
Committee on the Rights of the Child. 2003. Concluding Observations: Brunei: CRC.
Committee on the Rights of the Child. 2003. Concluding Observations: Czech: CRC.
Committee on the Rights of the Child. 2003. Concluding Observations: Indonesia: CRC.
Committee on the Rights of the Child. 2003. Concluding Observations: Kazakhstan: CRC.
Committee on the Rights of the Child. 2003. Concluding Observations: Romania: CRC.
Committee on the Rights of the Child. 2003. Concluding Observations: Zambia: CRC.
Committee on the Rights of the Child. 2004. Concluding Observations: India: CRC.
Committee on the Rights of the Child. 2004. Concluding Observations: Indonesia: CRC.
Committee on the Rights of the Child. 2004. Concluding Observations: Liberia: CRC.
Committee on the Rights of the Child. 2004. Concluding Observations: Myanmar: CRC.
Committee on the Rights of the Child. 2005. Concluding Observations: The Philippines: CRC.
Committee on the Rights of the Child. 2007. Concluding Observations: Malaysia: CRC.
Committee on the Rights of the Child. 2008. Concluding Observations: Bhutan: CRC
Committee on the Rights of the Child. 2010. Concluding Observations: Japan: CRC.
Committee on the Rights of the Child. 2011. Concluding Observations: Cambodia: CRC.
Committee on the Rights of the Child. 2011. Concluding Observations: Lao: CRC.
Committee on the Rights of the Child. 2012. Concluding Observations: China: CRC.
Committee on the Rights of the Child. 2012. Concluding Observations: Myanmar: CRC.
Committee on the Rights of the Child. 2012. Concluding Observations: Thailand: CRC.
Committee on the Rights of the Child. 2012. Concluding Observations: Viet Nam: CRC.
Committee on the Rights of the Child. 2013. Concluding Observations: China: CRC.
Committee on the Rights of the Child. 2013. Concluding Observations: The Philippines: CRC.
Committee on the Rights of the Child. 2014. Concluding Observations: Indonesia: CRC.
Committee on the Rights of the Child. 2015. Concluding Observations: Cambodia: CRC.
Committee on the Rights of the Child. 2015. Concluding Observations: Switzerland: CRC.

Human Rights Committee. 1997. Concluding Observations: Colombia: ICCPR.
Human Rights Committee. 2005. Concluding Observations: Slovenia: ICCPR.
Human Rights Committee. 2005. Concluding Observations: Syrian Arab Republic: ICCPR.
Human Rights Committee. 2011. Concluding Observations: Kuwait: ICCPR.

Index

R. M. Razali, *Safeguarding Against Statelessness at Birth*,
https://doi.org/10.1007/978-981-19-5371-2

MIX
Papier aus verantwortungsvollen Quellen
Paper from responsible sources
FSC® C105338

If you have any concerns about our products,
you can contact us on
ProductSafety@springernature.com

In case Publisher is established outside the EU,
the EU authorized representative is:
Springer Nature Customer Service Center GmbH
Europaplatz 3, 69115 Heidelberg, Germany

Printed by Libri Plureos GmbH
in Hamburg, Germany